The Millionaire Mind

G·K
Hall
&Co.

Also by Thomas J. Stanley, Ph.D.
in Large Print:

The Millionaire Next Door
  (with William D. Danko, Ph.D.)

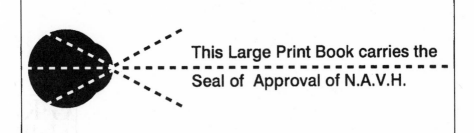

The Millionaire Mind

Thomas J. Stanley, Ph.D.

G.K. Hall & Co. • Thorndike, Maine

Published in 2000 by arrangement with
Andrews & McMeel, Universal Press Syndicate Company.

This publication is designed to provide accurate and authoritative information in regard to the subject matter covered. It is sold with the understanding that neither the author nor the publisher is engaged in rendering legal, investment, accounting, or other professional services. If legal advice or other expert assistance is required, the services of a competent professional person should be sought.

G.K. Hall Large Print Core Series.

The text of this Large Print edition is unabridged.
Other aspects of the book may vary from the original edition.

Set in 16 pt. Plantin by Al Chase.

Printed in the United States on permanent paper.

Library of Congress Cataloging-in-Publication Data

Stanley, Thomas J.
   The millionaire mind / Thomas J. Stanley.
     p.   cm.
   ISBN 0-7838-9125-3 (lg. print : hc : alk. paper)
1. Millionaires — Psychology 2. Capitalists and financiers — Psychology. 3. Rich people — Psychology. 4. Wealth — Psychological aspects. 5. Success in business — Psychological aspects. I. Title.
HG222.3 .S72 2000b
305.5′324—dc21   00-033494

For Janet, Sarah, Brad,
and a million visits from Mr. Flashlight

Contents

Tables

Acknowledgments

Most importantly I acknowledge my wife, Janet, for her guidance, patience, assistance, and unselfish support for this project. Without Janet, this book would never have been written.

I greatly appreciate the contributions of my children, Sarah and Brad, in their roles as research assistants for this project. Sarah did all of the computer analysis for the ad hoc survey. Brad participated in the coding and tabulating processes of this data.

A very special thank-you is in order to my editor, Christine Schillig. She is a total professional with a very keen eye for the critical concepts. Chris sets a very high standard for excellence in editing. I also appreciate the many contributions made by Tom Thornton, President of Andrews McMeel Publishing. His continuing interest in *The Millionaire Mind* throughout its development was a great source of encouragement.

It is with great pleasure that I acknowledge the significant contribution made by the Survey Research Center, Institute for Behavioral Research, University of Georgia in collecting and tabulating the geobased survey data for this book. Special praises are in order for Dr. James J. Bason, Director of the Survey Research Center, and for the fine efforts of his staff, specifically: Linda J. White, Kathleen J. Shinholsei Zelda R. McDowell, Mary Ann Mauney, and Cindy Burroughs.

A special thank-you is accorded to Beth Day for her assistance in conducting several of the interviews for the case studies.

I am indebted to Bill Marianes of Troutman Sanders for his extraordinary expertise in representing me.

Acknowledged also are the fine efforts of Ruth Tiller in word processing several versions of the manuscript, David Knapik for his excellent job of number crunching, and Art Gifford for his efforts in computing untold present values and sorting out the maze of economic opportunities.

I am deeply grateful to Dr. Molly S. Yelnats for her sage advice, encouragement, and support throughout this undertaking.

1

An Introduction to the Millionaire Mind

They live in lovely homes located in fine neighborhoods. Balance is their approach to life. They are financially independent, yet they enjoy life — they are not "all work, no play" type of people. Most became millionaires in one generation. Neither their lifestyle nor their wealth was generated from being highly leveraged financially. They are not credit junkies. How did they accomplish this? How did they balance their need to become wealthy and economically productive with their need to enjoy life? They have the millionaire mind.

Early in my career of studying wealthy people, I had a glimpse of this segment of the millionaire population. In 1983 I was asked to interview sixty millionaires from Oklahoma. What I learned from them was simple, yet the message had a lasting impact on me: You cannot enjoy life if you are addicted to consumption and the use of credit. These Oklahoma millionaires were just the opposite, as demonstrated by one focus group of ten. All ten were seasoned business owners, executives, or professionals. All were first-generation wealthy. Some were credit-dependent earlier in their careers, but they even-

13

tually saw the light. They went cold turkey, breaking the cycle of borrowing to consume, earning to consume, and borrowing more and more money. Others never became addicted to credit or the need to display their success.

All ten were multimillionaires. They lived in fine homes in well-established, older neighborhoods. They drove American-made motor vehicles. They enjoyed life. They were not workaholics. They spent a lot of time with their families and friends, borrowed little money, and became wealthy, in most cases, before they were forty-five years old. My interview with this group was scheduled to last about two hours, but it actually went on for nearly four hours. I only had to ask a few questions — the members enjoyed telling their own stories about becoming wealthy. If there were a Focus Group Hall of Fame, all ten of these millionaires would be inducted during the first round.

There were many important points made about how one can become an economic success, but one statement was riveting. It was made by Gene. He mentioned that those who are "credit-dependent" are in fact controlled by someone else, some institution.

Gene was in his late forties at the time. He listed his occupation as "owner of a salvage business." He purchased or "salvaged" real estate from various financial institutions. These institutions "have loans that are in default . . . six months or more."

Just a few weeks prior to the interview, Gene "salvaged" sixty-eight homes, a commercial shopping center, and five multifamily apartment complexes from a financial institution with which he'd had many previous dealings. Immediately after the deal was signed, the senior credit officer of the institution signaled to Gene and walked with him over to the large window in the officer's top-floor office. It was a tall building — they could see for miles and miles. There were thousands upon thousands of commercial buildings all around. Gene could even see some of the residential neighborhoods on the horizon.

As he looked out the window, the officer pointed to all the buildings, homes, offices, garages, shops, and so on, and said the words that made a lasting impression on Gene:

We [the lenders] own it all . . . all of it. The business out there? . . . You [borrowers] just run these businesses for us. You guys run them for us, the financial institutions.

How many people today in America run "their businesses," "their professional practices" but actually work for or are being controlled by lenders? How many live in luxury homes yet work hard to make payments to the ultimate owner of the mortgage? How many people take care of autos they lease from the real owner? Too many. But Gene is not among them, nor were any of the other members of his focus group. All possessed the millionaire mind. None had a private credit officer doling out cash. All lived in fine homes, but not one had a "jumbo mortgage."

The lesson I learned from Gene was repeated many times over by the millionaires surveyed for this book. They all have the millionaire mind, yet they believe it's possible to enjoy life and still become wealthy. They believe that financial independence and much economic success can be achieved without adopting a Spartan lifestyle. But there must be certain constraints, as discussed later in this book.

Some people are not controlled by credit institutions. For them it is just the opposite — they are controlled by greed. They are misers. They even shortchange their spouses and children. Money is their God. These people are not of the millionaire mind. Another millionaire who has the proper perspective said:

I taught my sons and daughters that money is not their God. You control it . . . not let it control you.

Most of the people profiled in this book became economic successes in one generation. They came from economic ground zero. Most inherited no money. They never received the proceeds of an estate or income from a trust account. How did they do it? Again, they are of the millionaire mind.

You may never be able to generate the sizable incomes that many of these millionaires have earned. You may not become a multimillionaire in a few short years. But you can still benefit from understanding how these people maintained an enjoyable lifestyle at the same time they were accumulating wealth. Only a few people, even those with high incomes, know how this can be accomplished. Those with the millionaire mind know how, and they are profiled in this book.

THE SEARCH

The research conducted for my earlier book, *The Millionaire Next Door*, and the results reported therein have expanded the knowledge about the characteristics of America's most affluent people. I decided to broaden the size and scope of my next study to include many more participants from a significantly wealthier population base. The new survey also focused on a different set of attributes and lifestyles, designed to project a deeper, more comprehensive look at the millionaire mind. The results of that study are presented in the following chapters.

It is a lot easier to profile the characteristics of people who have the millionaire mind than it is to find them. Why not survey all the households in America? Because only about 4.9 percent of the households in this country have a net worth of $1 million or more. Nor can you just survey all the people who live in expensive homes. Often these "big-home owners" are what I call Income Statement Affluent. They have big incomes, big homes, big debt, but little net worth. They are experts at preparing loan applications, most of which do not ask about one's real level of net worth.

In sharp contrast there are those whom I call Balance Sheet Affluent. These people are of the millionaire mind. They focus upon accumulating wealth. Their assets greatly exceed their credit liabilities. Often they have little or no outstanding credit balances.

If I surveyed people who live in fine homes nationwide, what would I find? Too many Income Statement Affluent respondents. Yet I always believed that certain types of neighborhoods attract the Balance Sheet variety and retain those with the millionaire mind, and these same neighborhoods might be unattractive to the Income Statement Affluent. My hypothesis was confirmed by the results of the survey conducted for this book.

In order to help develop a representative sample of people with millionaire minds, the Balance Sheet Affluent, I sought advice from my friend and associate Jon Robbin. He is the foremost authority on geodemography, the term used to describe the study of the characteristics of people within defined geographic areas. Often these areas are at the zip-code level, but for my survey I wanted to get down to an even smaller level — neighborhoods or block groups. Some of these neighborhoods had fewer than fifty households.

I told Jon about my problem, and he solved it in short order. Jon is a Harvard-trained mathematician and a brilliant researcher, and his geodemographic database is also extraordinary. He developed a sophisticated mathematical model that estimates the net worth characteristics for most block groups/neighborhoods in America.

Jon found that some neighborhoods have high concentrations of people who have substantial investment income and thus would have the millionaire mind-set. From his national database of 226,399 neighborhoods, Jon selected 2,487. His mathematical model predicted that these would contain high concentrations of people who were actually wealthy, as opposed to those who had big homes with big mortgages but low net worth. A national sample was generated by randomly selecting 5,063 households from those neighborhoods.[1] Each household selected was sent a questionnaire.

Of the 1,001 fully completed responses, 733 were from millionaires. Each had a net worth of $1 million or more. This national survey of 733 millionaires provided much of the empirical base for this book. Most of the respondents lived in old, well-established, upper-middle-class neigh-

[1]Details about the geodemographically based sample methodology are given in Appendix 1.

borhoods, in homes built in the 1950s or even in the 1940s or earlier. What? No homes with five Jacuzzis? What? No flashy new subdivisions or newly developed suburban estates? Could it be that those with the millionaire mind-set are not "trendy" when it comes to selecting homes and neighborhoods? It seems that's the case. Plus, most of the respondents had either small outstanding balances on their home mortgages or no mortgages at all.

The methodology of how each respondent was selected on a random basis was described earlier in an article (see Thomas J. Stanley and Murphy A. Sewall, "The Response of Affluent Consumers to Mall Surveys," *Journal of Advertising Research*, June–July 1986, pp. 55–58). The nine-page questionnaire completed by each respondent contained 277 questions. This project was the most comprehensive I have undertaken. The survey data were collected and tabulated by one of the premier survey organizations in America, the Survey Research Center, Institute for Behavioral Research, University of Georgia in Athens.[2] The center also did the univariate and multivariate computer analyses of the data.

Earlier, the questionnaire and survey methodology were pretested on an ad hoc sample of 638 millionaires. All had income statements and balance-sheet characteristics that would qualify

[2]Neither the Survey Research Center nor the University bears any responsibility for the analyses or interpretations presented here.

them for jumbo mortgages. This pretest survey was conducted by the author and his staff.

In addition, important case studies were developed from a series of personal interviews and focus groups. These cases are detailed throughout the book, and they provide an important piece of the puzzle. For it isn't easy to develop a full understanding of the millionaire mind. The results summarized in this book are intended to help people develop an understanding and appreciation of the meaning of a balanced lifestyle.

A DEMOGRAPHIC SKETCH

A demographic overview of the survey results follows below. Expanding and broadening the portrait of America's self-made millionaires provided in *The Millionaire Next Door*, here is a sketch, in their own "voices," of our most economically productive men and women.

A TRADITIONAL FAMILY

- I am a fifty-four-year-old male. I have been married to the same woman for twenty-eight years. One in four of us has been with the same spouse for thirty-eight or more years.
- On average, we have three children.
- Most of us, 92 percent, are married. And of those married, 95 percent have children.
- Only 2 percent of us have never been married. About 3 percent are widowed.

- We are financially well-off. On average, our households have a net worth of approximately $9.2 million. The typical or median level of net worth is $4.3 million. The average figure is skewed in an upward direction by those respondents who have very high levels of wealth.

- Our household's total annual realized income is $749,000. The median income figure is $436,000. Those of us who have incomes of $1 million or more (20 percent) skew the average upward.

- In spite of our wealth and income, the typical member of our group has never spent more than $41,000 for an automobile or $4,500 for an engagement ring. Neither our spouses nor we have ever spent more than $38 (including tip) for a haircut. Fully one in four of us has never spent more than $24 for a haircut; $340,000 for a home; $30,900 for a motor vehicle; or $1,500 for an engagement ring. Some of us, about 7 percent of those who are married, did not have to purchase an engagement ring. It was passed down from one of our relatives.

ABOUT INHERITED WEALTH

- We live in fine homes in quality neighborhoods, but only 2 percent of us inherited all or any part of our homes and property.

- Some of us have inherited a portion of our wealth. Nearly 8 percent inherited 50 percent or more of their net worth. In sharp contrast, 61 percent of us never received any inheritance, financial gifts, or income from an estate or trust.

SOME NAMES AND PLACES

- We can be found in more than two thousand well-established, older neighborhoods in towns and cities with such names as Shawnee Mission, Kansas 66208; New Canaan, Connecticut 06840; Richmond, Virginia 23224; Pittsburgh, Pennsylvania 15238; Fort Worth, Texas 75225; Kenilworth, Illinois 60043; Columbus, Ohio 43209; Atlanta, Georgia 30327; Summit, New Jersey 07901; Englewood, Colorado 80118; and Tulsa, Oklahoma 74137.

HOME STYLE

- Nearly all of us (97 percent) are homeowners.
- About twelve years ago we purchased our current home for an average price of $558,718. The median price was $435,000. We have enjoyed reasonably good appreciation on our home. On average, it is currently worth $1,381,729. The current median value is approximately $750,000. Thus, we have benefited financially and added to our net worth by the appreciation of our homes.
- In spite of the high value of our homes, we generally have small outstanding mortgage balances.
- Most of us (61 percent) live in homes that are currently valued at over $1 million. But only one in four (25 percent) paid $1 million or

more for our current homes.

- One in ten of us purchased a home in the three years that followed the stock market plunge of 1987. Many of us who did were searching for a foreclosure.
- We live in a home that was constructed forty years ago (median year). Fully one in four of us live in homes that were built before 1936. Only about 10 percent of us live in homes that were built in the past ten years.
- The majority (53 percent) of us have not moved in the past ten years. Only 23 percent of our group has moved two or more times during the same period.
- Only a minority (27 percent) of our group has ever had a home of any type built for them. We of the millionaire mind believe that it's better to purchase an existing home than to "get into the building business." It is much less time-consuming and probably costs less to purchase homes "out of existing inventory."
- Who among us are the least likely to have homes built for them? Attorneys! We have to wonder why they are so reluctant to build.

OUR VOCATIONS
- About one in three (32 percent) of us are business owners or entrepreneurs. Nearly one in five (16 percent) are senior corporate executives. One in ten (10 percent) of our group are attorneys. Nearly the same proportion (9 percent) are physicians. The other one-third of our

population is composed of retirees, corporate middle managers, accountants, sales professionals or new-business-development officers, engineers, architects, teachers, professors, and housewives.

- Business owners overall are the richest of our group, but senior executives are often among the ranks of multimillionaires. They account for 16 percent of the millionaires but for nearly 26 percent of the decamillionaires, those with net worths of $10 million or more.
- Nearly 50 percent of our wives do not work outside the home. Those who are employed are business owners or entrepreneurs (7 percent), sales professionals (5 percent), corporate middle managers (4 percent), attorneys (4 percent), teachers (3 percent), senior corporate executives (3 percent), and physicians (2 percent). About 16 percent of wives who were employed outside the home are currently retired.
- About two-thirds of us who are decamillionaires report that their wives do not work outside the home. About one-half of those wives who do work, work part-time.

EDUCATION
- We are well educated. Fully 90 percent of us are college graduates. More than one-half (52 percent) hold advanced degrees.

A Brief Look Inside
<u>the Millionaire Mind</u>

In addition to the demographic characteristics listed above, my survey provided the following glimpse into the millionaire mind. The chapters that follow expand this glimpse into a detailed portrait.

- We are financially independent, yet we tend to live a comfortable, not extravagant, lifestyle.
- Many of us "cluster" in certain upper-middle-class neighborhoods throughout America. We live in fine homes, but we have little or no debt. We tend to buy homes when many others are selling.
- Almost all of us are married and have children. In fact, most of us believe that having a family complements, not competes with the process of building wealth.
- We are self-made affluent.
- On average, we vacation overseas about once every two years.
- Few of us have Phi Beta Kappa keys or scored 1400 or higher on the SATs.
- Most of us love our chosen vocations, or, as one of our wealthier members stated, "It is not work; it is a labor of love."
- Few of us found it necessary to get out of bed at 3:00 or 4:00 A.M. each work day in order to accumulate wealth.
- Many of us play golf and/or tennis on a regular basis. In fact, there is a strong correlation be-

26

tween playing golf and level of net worth.

- We must admit that we are not into "do-it-yourself" tasks. Those among us who are tend to have significantly less wealth than the average for our group.
- We became rich without compromising our integrity. In fact, we credit our integrity with significantly contributing to our success. We are not workaholics, and we spend a lot of time socializing with friends and family. When we work, we work hard. We focus our energy to maximize the return on our efforts.
- We do spend time planning our investments and often consult with tax advisers. But many of us also have time to attend religious services and are active in raising funds for noble causes.
- We believe that it is more than just possible to balance one's financial goals with an enjoyable lifestyle. There is a positive correlation between the number of lifestyle activities that we take part in and our level of net worth.
- Often our lifestyle activities bring us into contact with people who eventually become clients, customers, patients, suppliers, or great friends.
- For many of our activities, we have found the old adage to be true: The best things in life are free, or at least reasonably priced. It doesn't cost much to attend your son or daughter's sporting event, visit a museum, or play bridge with good friends. It's much less than a trip to a casino.

SUCCESS FACTORS

In chapter 2, "Success Factors," millionaires speak their minds about the factors they rate as being very important in explaining their economic success. Their views may surprise some people. The factors they give credit to are at odds with many popularly held notions. Their views are especially different from the stereotypical profiles portrayed as reality by Hollywood: Good looks and a supermodel's figure were never mentioned by even one millionaire respondent. Not once.

Many well-intentioned parents, mentors, and teachers and even some of Wall Street's best gurus are out of sync with the opinions held by most millionaires. And what about all those advertisements for lotto and Publishers Clearing House sweepstakes? Millionaires have a different explanation for their successes.

What are the top five factors most often mentioned by millionaires as being very important in explaining their economic success? After you read them on the next page, take out a card or small piece of paper and write down these five elements of financial success. Keep the list with you in your wallet or purse and paste a copy on your television. Then the next time you see an advertisement for a lotto game, magazine sweepstakes, or casino, glance at the list. The ads tell you that you can hit it big with one of these gambles, but what does the list say? The foundation stones of financial success are:

- Integrity — being honest with all people
- Discipline — applying self control
- Social skills — getting along with people
- A supportive spouse
- Hard work — more than most people

Where does the element of luck rank? It's near the bottom of the list of thirty success factors, at number 27. But in this context, the millionaires were referring more to uncontrollable factors, such as the economy, that can and do impact one's net worth. Not one millionaire I interviewed had anything nice to say about gambling. A more detailed discussion of gambling habits or lack of them is given in chapter 9, "The Lifestyles of Millionaires: Real vs. Imagined."

Some may argue that many people, not just the millionaires in this country, have the five success elements mentioned above, but they are not millionaires today. These five are basic elements. What if you lack one or more of them? According to the large sample of millionaires studied, the odds will be against your becoming an economic success. But if you have these plus a few others, you may become wealthy in the future, if you are not already rich. Once again, allow the millionaires to speak for themselves.

- How did we become millionaires in one generation? Most of us saw an economic opportunity that others just ignored, and we had a willingness to take financial risk given the promise of good return. This is especially true for those of us who are self-employed. But we know there is a strong correlation between one's willingness to take financial risk and one's level of wealth. It is less about investing in the stock market and much more about investing in ourselves, our careers, our professional practices, our private businesses, and so forth.

- Most of us will say that we have strong leadership qualities. We have the ability to sell our ideas to our employees and suppliers, and our products to carefully targeted audiences.
- Why has the American economy been so generous in rewarding us? Because we provide a product or service that has strong demand but few suppliers to fulfill that demand. We do not follow the crowd. That applies both to what we sell and how we invest.

INTELLECTUALLY GIFTED?

Are millionaires intellectually gifted? Were they all Phi Beta Kappa graduates of top-rated colleges? It is a common belief that people who are intellectually gifted have high analytical intelligence. In turn, analytical intelligence is supposedly measured by standardized IQ "tests." Instead of using IQ scores I have substituted the more readily available SAT scores in my survey. There is a positive correlation between these two measures. Also, I have found that millionaires' self-assessment of their analytical intelligence, their SAT performance, and their college grades are related.

TABLE 1-1

THE ACADEMIC RECORD OF MILLIONAIRES: UNDERGRADUATE COLLEGE GRADE POINT AVERAGE* (GPA) AND SAT SCORE

OCCUPATIONAL CATEGORIES

Academic Measures	Business Owner/ Entrepreneur	Senior Corporate Executive	Attorney
Mean	32%	16%	10%
Grade Point Average (N=715)	2.76	2.93	3.04
SAT Score (N=444)	1235	1211	1262

	Physician	Other	All Millionaires
Mean	9%	33%	100%
Grade Point Average (N=715)	3.12	2.96	2.92
SAT Score (N=444)	1267	1090	1190

Do millionaires believe that they have superior intelligence? Even more basic, how important is intelligence in explaining variations in economic success? These and many related questions are

On a 4.00-point scale: A=4, B=3, etc.

detailed in both chapter 2, "Success Factors," and chapter 3, "School Days." As an introduction to these topics, consider the following facts about millionaires:

- Being well-educated does not mean that we all graduated with high honors from college. Our undergraduate grade point average (GPA) was 2.92 on a 4.00-point scale, as shown in Table 1-1.
- Our average SAT score of 1190 is significantly above the norm, but not considered high enough to gain admittance to so-called selective or competitive undergraduate colleges. Most of us did not attend such schools. Nor, when surveyed, did we indicate that graduating from a top-rated college was important in explaining our economic success.
- But even the 1190 SAT number may be a bit inflated. Nearly 90 percent of our cohort who were A students in college did recall and thus reported their SAT scores. Ironically, only about one-half of our group who were C students were able to recall their SAT scores. We know that SAT scores and GPAs are significantly correlated. What if the 1190 number were adjusted to reflect the expected SAT scores of those C students who could not recall their SAT number? It is estimated that nearly 100 points could be shaved off the 1190 average!
- Most of us have been told by some authority

figure or by the results of standardized test scores that we were not:

- Intellectually gifted
- Of law-school caliber
- Medical-school material
- Qualified to pursue an MBA degree
- Smart enough to succeed

- We often wonder how we as a group ever became so financially successful, given the fact that few of us were ever designated "intellectually gifted." Thus, we question the relationship between intellect, academic performance, and economic success. Are we successful in spite of our intellect, or because we always felt that we had to work harder to compensate for our deficiencies?

ASSIGNED READING

You can increase your understanding of the less than substantial relationship between intellect/analytical intelligence and various measures of success by reading Robert J. Sternberg's *Successful Intelligence* (New York: Simon & Schuster, 1996). Dr. Sternberg, a leading authority on human intelligence, has found that successful intelligence has three components, and analytical intelligence is just one. The others are creative intelligence and practical intelligence, or common sense. Could it be that most millionaires are economically successful because they are creative and have a lot of common sense? This and related questions are addressed throughout *The Millionaire Mind.*

<u>SCHOOL DAYS</u>

What school and college experiences influenced millionaires in becoming economically productive adults? The answer to this question is detailed in chapter 3, "School Days," but it's clear that millionaires learned much more in school than what was presented in textbooks. Most tell us they learned something about tenacity, getting along with people, self-discipline, and discernment. A good portion of the millionaire population is made up of people who worked hard in school but did not graduate with all As. Those millionaires whose SATs were not spectacular are given a special place in this book. I profile them under the heading of the 900 Club — only millionaires who scored under 1000 on the SAT were admitted. They say that:

- Some of us scored under 1000 on the SAT, yet we became millionaires. What school and college experiences influenced us in becoming economically productive adults? Fully 72 percent of our 900 Club members said it was:

Learning to fight for our goals because someone labeled us as having "average or less ability."

- The vast majority of us believe that we benefited from the educational experience. Most of us (93 percent) indicated that our school and college experience was:

Influential in determining that hard work was more important than genetic high intellect in achieving.

- Most of us also felt that school was important in enhancing our abilities to:

Properly allocate time and make accurate judgments about people.

The millionaire population contains many people who were not straight-A students, but they did learn a lot in school. It wasn't just the core courses that were key. Discipline 101 and Tenacity 102 were also important parts of the school experience.

OPPORTUNITY AND HOW TO FIND IT:
A PROFILE OF WARREN BIELKE

One self-described average student believes so strongly that people like him must find their own opportunities that he has created a scholarship to try to replicate his own experience. Warren Bielke has created a $1 million scholarship fund at his old high school in Minneapolis. Each year, ten students with average grades, good attendance, and a positive attitude receive about half the cost of their college education at a state school. He hopes they will work to earn the rest. And he wants them to live on campus, so they will have close contact with people from different backgrounds.

Why does Mr. Bielke put so much faith in those students who are often academically overlooked? "The smart kids, sometimes it's too easy for them," he says. "Sometimes they miss opportunities because they don't have to get involved and work so hard. The average kids get involved and come across more opportunities."

Mr. Bielke emphasizes the word "opportunities." He hopes a college education will expose these kids to more of them, and he thinks they're the type who will know how to take advantage of them.

"I think success really involves the situations you get yourself into and the people you meet," he says. "No one can be successful by themselves. It's the relationships that you develop with the people around you. Throughout my life, I've had people who helped me do better."

Mr. Bielke is vice president of investor relations for Advanced BioSurfaces in Minnetonka, Minnesota. The company is developing a polymer, currently in clinical trials outside the United States, that is injected into the knee joint to help people with osteoarthritis avoid total knee replacement. This is the seventh medical-device company for which Mr. Bielke has been involved in start-up and initial financing. How did an average student end up finding cutting-edge medical companies and taking them public, or selling them for millions of dollars to huge conglomerates?

When he attended Roosevelt High, his family didn't have a lot of money. He was raised by his mother, who worked twelve-hour days at a dry-cleaning store. He worked at a gas station at night. Watching his mother provided him with a foundation for discipline and hard work that made him stick it out through high school even though he didn't excel academically. "If you want to succeed, you have to be there," he says. "I was not a great student, and I didn't study much, but I went there every day."

A high school counselor was the first of those people who pointed him toward opportunity. The counselor convinced the senior to take an eleventh-hour SAT. The results? Not great, but good enough to get into a four-year state school.

"I had no intention of going to college," he says. "No Bielke had ever gone." But the counselor changed all that and the direction of Mr. Bielke's life. He also helped him get a job at Moorehead State University to help him pay his way through school. Mr. Bielke lived in a college dorm, and the students and professors with whom he came into contact there showed him another path through life.

"I wasn't a great student," he says. "I ended up with a C plus or B average. But without this counselor guiding me to go to college, I would have taken a full-time job at the gas station." The scholarships are Mr. Bielke's way of giving back to Roosevelt High School.

After college, he found a job in sales in the medical-device industry. He worked his way up, started his own company, and got involved in investments in medical start-up companies.

His advice to average students? "It sounds like a cliché, but it's the effort you put in: It's how hard you work," Bielke says. "Honesty is important, too. People will invest in you if they believe you are honest and hardworking. That's what happened to me.

"Somewhere I read, 'It's not really how smart you are, it's how you are smart.' I can't tell you how many Ph.D.'s I've had working for me. They are very, very smart people, very good at their specialties," he says. "But they're working for me.

"You've got to take advantage of the different opportunities that present themselves to you in life."

NOT AT THE TOP . . . WRONG

One of our most economically productive citizens recently passed away. In his biography, several key items about his college experience are important to mention. Consider the following quotes:

. . . *He did not finish at the top of his class. But*

38

not for lack of trying . . . Grades did not come easily. [And even one of his professors said] . . . I would not have expected him [Roberto Goizueta] to become chief executive of the Coca-Cola Company. (David Greising, *I'd Like the World to Buy a Coke.* [New York: John Wiley & Sons, Inc., 1997] pp. 14-15)

Could it be that Mr. Goizueta learned much more in college than he was given credit for on his grade transcript?

COURAGE AND WEALTH

What do most self-made millionaires have in common? They have courage. Do you have the courage to take financial risk, given the right return? If you do, then you have the mind-set that most millionaires possess. But having the courage to take financial risk doesn't mean that millionaires are gamblers. Few gamble at all. In fact, the higher a millionaire's net worth, the less likely he is to ever gamble. Yet there is a positive correlation between taking financial risk and net worth.

Obviously, gambling and financial risk taking are not the same type of behavior. The most basic form of financial risk taking relates to choice of occupation, or vocation. A disproportionately high percentage of millionaires, multimillionaires, and decamillionaires are self-employed business owners and entrepreneurs or self-employed professionals.

What is so risky about being self-employed? You are on your own and there is no employer backing you up. If you fail to deliver what the market demands, you may be out of business tomorrow. Worse, you may lose every dollar you have in assets.

Those who have the millionaire mind look at being self-employed in a much different way than the "scenario of failure" given above. They are of the mind-set that it is risky *not* to be self-employed. Being self-employed means that you are in control of your own destiny. Profits that are made are yours. And there is no real ceiling on how much you can make. The millionaires said:

- We think of success, not of failure. We take risk but we study the probable outcomes. And we do everything we can to enhance the odds of generating returns.
- How do we eliminate or reduce fear and worry and bolster our courage? We practice believing in ourselves and hard work.
- How do we bolster our belief in ourselves? We focus on key issues; we prepare and plan to succeed; and we are well organized to deal with big issues.
- Some of us have conditioned our minds to offset fears and certain limitations through the mental toughness we developed playing competitive sports. There are a good number among us who have compensated for deficien-

cies by having what we call the athlete's heart. This term refers to both physical and mental tenacity and courage.

- Nearly four in ten (37 percent) of us reduce the fears and worries associated with making critical decisions about financial resources in another way — we call upon our strong religious faith. In fact, those among us who have strong religious faith have a higher propensity to take financial risk than others.

VOCATION VOCATION VOCATION

According to *Webster's* dictionary, the term *ace* denotes one who excels at something. It is also a title given to combat pilots who have at least five in-air victories. World War II produced more fighter-pilot aces than any other conflict, with 1,285 pilots earning the title during this period ("The Last Ace," *Wall Street Journal*, January 29, 1999, p. W11). How did they accomplish this feat? Most did it the traditional way, in dogfights. Many were eventually shot down themselves. But at least two did it quite differently. Their unique method and rationale for its use have significance for people who want to become economically productive. Like the two aces, the majority of millionaires surveyed became economic successes because they learned to focus their energies and other resources in ways that maximized their output. But what drove them to this focused approach?

Both of the pilots who "did it differently" were

more than aces (see Raymond F. Toliver and Trevor J. Constable, *The Blond Knight of Germany* [Blue Ridge Summit, PA: Aero Books, 1970]). One, Major Erich Hartmann, is known in military literature as the Ace of Aces. He had 352 confirmed in-air victories. The other pilot who had the same unique strategy was Sergeant "Paule" Rossmann, Hartmann's mentor. He himself had more than 80 victories.

It was Rossmann who invented the approach that ultimately led to Hartmann's extraordinary success. Early in his career, Rossmann suffered an injury to his arm that never healed, and he was unable to dogfight. In a typical dogfight, victory goes to those with superior physical strength. Rossmann knew he could never survive this kind of battle, so he developed a compensating technique. Substituting a much more calculating method for the macho dogfighting strategy, he carefully planned each and every attack. He spent much more time analyzing various targets of opportunity than actually firing bullets at his quarry. He attacked only when he was in the best possible position to win. Then he would focus all his resources at the ideal target — the one that would give him the maximum return on his investment. Hartmann credits Rossmann's approach, the "see and decide prior to firing" method, with his own success. It also explains how Hartmann survived 1,425 combat missions, yet he was never even wounded.

What does all this have to do with becoming

an economic success in America? Most millionaires understand that they have certain limitations, and they developed an understanding of their strengths and limitations before they even finished school. Like Rossmann, they realized that they had some type of "injured arm," some type of limitation. So they developed their own unique strategy for becoming economically productive.

Most millionaires, for example, are not intellectually gifted in an analytical sense. They did not receive all As in school, nor were they in the 1400-and-above SAT club. That's why they decided not to compete in macho dogfight environments where superior analytical intelligence is a requirement to succeed.

These same people usually did not score high enough on the standardized tests that are requirements for law school, medical school, or graduate school. Many millionaires did not have a high enough grade point average to be hired by major corporations. But they still wanted to become economically successful, so many chose to be self-employed. They hired themselves when other employers would not.

Many millionaires who designated themselves as "other than intellectually gifted" are, in fact, gifted in other ways. They have an abundance of common sense, and they have what some call creativity. How else can we explain their ability to discover economic opportunities that most so-called geniuses were unable to see?

After studying millionaires for more than twenty years, I have concluded that if you make one major decision correctly, you can become economically productive. If you are creative enough to select the ideal vocation, you can win, win big-time. The really brilliant millionaires are those who selected a vocation that they love — one that has few competitors but generates high profits.

Selecting a vocation is like building a home. If you build in a less than ideal location, if your ground is sand or swampland, nothing else matters. You can spend millions on what is above ground, but it won't matter — your home is unstable. You will be in a constant dogfight with shifting sand, water, and swamp. It is a battle you cannot win. But if your foundation is on bedrock, your home will easily withstand wind and rain. You are insulated from the dogfight with the elements.

What if you select the bedrock foundation of the ideal vocation? You love the products that you produce. You have affection for your customers and suppliers. In addition, you know more about your niche market than anyone else. And your customers don't care if you were a C student in college. To them you are the one who is enlightened.

So perhaps you should feel sorry for those superior students, the intellectually gifted. Often, those who are told they are gifted feel economically invincible. Too often they assume that superior intellect will translate into superior income and levels of wealth. But those who believe this are in for a rude wake-up call. Too many select vocations are filled with competitors, all of whom also have high analytical intellect. They may be one of hundreds of thousands of MBAs who graduated in the past twenty years. They were hired by major corporations because they did A-grade work, at fine business schools. Perhaps they went directly from those schools into the dogfight. Unknowingly, they entered a sector of our economy where there are very few top dogs and CEOs. Just ask a sample of middle-aged MBAs how many dogfights they've been in in the past twenty years. How many were shot down or had their jobs eliminated?

Sure, they were all bright. But they forgot one thing: choice of vocation. Where you will fight is much more important in winning than what you do once the dogfight begins. Even some of the best and brightest MBA students I have ever taught lost most of their dogfights.

Why not select a vocation and target where you can more easily emerge as the winner? It is easier to love what you do for a living when you win most of the time, if not all the time. What do most millionaires tell me they learned in their salad years? They learned to:

Think differently from the crowd.

Much of this book has been designed around

that central theme: It pays to be different. The millionaires say:

- How did we become wealthy in one generation? It has a lot to do with our selection of the right vocation. Thus, the laws of economics and psychology are in our favor. Otherwise, we'd be swimming against the tide.
- We believe that a minority of people in the general population can honestly say their current vocation allows them full use of their abilities and aptitudes. But we are different. We are of the millionaire mind. We were wise in selecting the ideal vocation given our abilities, aptitudes, and strong interest in becoming financially independent.
- Was our ideal vocation suggested by an employment agent or headhunter? Only 3 percent of us did it that way. Nor did we discover it at a job fair.
- Many of us are intuitive as well as creative. How else could we select such wonderful economic opportunities?

CHOICE OF SPOUSE

It's a popular notion — if you want to become wealthy, just marry a millionaire. Or you can marry the son or daughter of a millionaire couple. Eventually, your spouse will inherit a pot of gold, and, you assume, your husband or wife will share this wealth with you. Or perhaps it's much simpler and more productive not to marry

46

at all. That way you won't have to share your economic resources with a spouse and children.

The data strongly indicate that neither of these hypotheses is true. Yes, choice of spouse is important in accounting for variations in wealth, but most millionaires did not select their spouse because of his or her wealth characteristics. Nor were they even initially attracted to their husbands or wives because their parents "had money." In fact, the wealth factor was not even rated by our millionaires as an important quality of a spouse that contributed to a successful marriage.

Yet there is a substantial correlation between the number of years a couple is married and the wealth they accumulate. And a large majority (92 percent) of millionaires are married. Only 2 percent have never been married, and about 2 percent are currently divorced or separated. The rest are widowed. Are there certain economies of scale associated with being married, as opposed to being single? The data clearly show that the answer is yes.

Does this mean that the two-career couple is the prototypical millionaire household? Not at all. In fact, the higher a couple's net worth, the more likely it is that the wife does not work outside the home. Contrast this with married couple households that produce high income but are not in the millionaire league — nearly -70 percent of the wives in those households work outside the home. They are employed as teachers, sales professionals, middle-level corporate executives, and attorneys. Only about one wife in three in the decamillionaire households works outside the home. The millionaires tell us:

- The typical couple in our millionaire group has been married for twenty-eight years. Most of us (eight out of ten) believe that "having a supportive spouse" was either very important or important in accounting for our economic success.
- What qualities initially interested us in our spouses? What qualities of our spouses are the most important contributors to our successful marriages? It is much more than physical attractiveness. These qualities are complements to building wealth, and they are part of the millionaire mind.

These and many other questions are detailed in chapter 6, "Choice of Spouse."

A PROFILE OF PAULETTE RAKESTRAW,
CEO AND OWNER, AMS CORPORATION

As a twenty-one-year-old divorced mother of a toddler, Paulette Rakestraw was building a direct-mail business out of her apartment. She certainly was not looking for a spouse when she met her current husband, Von. His caring demeanor and the way he treated her daughter were among the qualities that drew her to him.

Today, says the founder of AMS Corporation, he is very family oriented and likes to spend all his free time with their three children. "We just clicked," she says. "He's real laid-back, very go-with-the-flow — just a good companion."

Even during the years the two worked together building her business, they got along great. "We were together twenty-four hours a day — we lived together, worked together — but we never fought," she says.

Rakestraw started her fulfillment and mailing-service business in 1988, after the company she worked for had repeated bad experiences with mailing services. "This is ridiculous," she recalls thinking. "We're paying a lot of money for this, and it's not rocket science." So she started hiring friends and family to do projects for the company she worked for. Soon other companies were asking her to coordinate mailing projects. "I was just determined there was a need for this, and I was going to pursue it," she says.

Paulette's and Von's different personalities complement one another. She is a risk taker, he is not. She is inclined toward action, while he encourages thinking about things and taking their time.

"Sometimes he has to rein me in and I have to push him along," Rakestraw says. "It's a good partnership all around: We kind of suit each other and bring each other back to earth."

Another difference: He thinks about the money and is a big saver, while she focuses on

49

building the company. "My whole drive has always been I like doing this and I want to provide quality service," she says. "He always thought, 'Gosh, you can make a lot of money doing this,' while my focus through the growth of the company has been service."

In the company's infancy, they lived and worked in an apartment with a monthly rent of $325. When she wanted to commit to an $800-a-month Yellow Pages ad, he told her she was crazy.

"I did it anyway," she says. "I told him months later when the ad came out, and he was glad because it really made our phones ring."

Today the company has many Fortune 500 companies as clients. Instead of an "apartment business," the company is in a fifty-thousand-square-foot office complex. Specifically, what qualities initially attracted Paulette to her husband? She judged him to be sincere, down-to-earth, polite, affectionate, even tempered, open-minded, accepting, wise, encouraging, cheerful, and compassionate. And for more than ten years of marriage her initial judgment has proven to be correct.

THE ECONOMICALLY PRODUCTIVE HOUSEHOLD

Go right ahead — spend a week or a month with these people, the people with the millionaire mind. You will probably conclude that their shopping behavior is a contradiction. First, ask them about their income and net worth. Then ask them about the shopping actions they take to reduce the cost of operating their households. As they stated earlier:

- On average, our household's total annual realized income is $749,000.
- We have an average household net worth of $9.2 million.

Given these average income and net worth figures, these households are in the top fraction of 1 percent of the income and wealth distribution in our country. Would you assume that such people don't concern themselves with reducing the cost and enhancing the productivity of their household? So much for assumptions based on wealth and income statistics. In fact, the millionaires say:

- The majority of us (70 percent) regularly have our shoes resoled and repaired.
- Nearly one-half of us (48 percent) regularly have our furniture reupholstered or refinished instead of buying new.
- About seven in ten (71 percent) develop a shopping list before grocery shopping.
- Nearly one-half of us buy household supplies in bulk at warehouse stores like Sam's or Costco.

What seems like a contradiction to you isn't

one to those with the millionaire mind. The millionaire mind is sensitive to the variations in time and money associated with shopping and making purchasing decisions.

- Ultimately, we find that having shoes resoled is much less costly than buying new. The same applies to refinishing furniture.
- We firmly believe that time is money. It takes much less time to resole or refinish than shop for new.
- Most of us have a shopping list before we even enter a supermarket. Not only do we save money and avoid impulse buying, but we also find that our in-store shopping time is greatly reduced if we have a list for minimizing in-store minutes. We prefer to spend the time saved working or with our families or friends, rather than randomly walking and impulsively buying in a supermarket.

If you want to run a productive household, start thinking like millionaires. Adopt their mind-set. Thirteen productive actions taken by millionaires, and their rationale for these activities, are discussed in chapter 7, "The Economically Productive Household."

THE HOME

Millionaires have told me they were criticized about their choice of home. Why would anyone pay more than $500,000 twelve years ago for a home that was thirty, forty, even fifty years old? Why would they pay so much for a home that typically had only four bedrooms? Many millionaires have three children — where do they put their overnight guests?

Given the scenarios above you might wonder if the millionaire mind comes up a bit short in the real estate section of the brain, but that's not the case. Overall, their homes have appreciated significantly over the past dozen years or so. And these homes tend to be very well constructed — many are brick or stone, some have slate roofs, most have hardwood floors.

Yet there is no doubt about it — these are not modern homes. Why do so many people with the millionaire mind select older homes over newer ones? It has something to do with the quality of neighborhoods where these homes are located. These are homogeneous neighborhoods in terms of the socioeconomic characteristics of the residents. Nine in ten of the residents are college graduates. Most are very successful people. But as a group these highly productive business owners, corporate executives, attorneys, physicians, and other winners are conservative or traditional in the homes they select. Modern, newer homes are likely to be much larger, with five, six, even eight bedrooms. And don't forget the twenty-foot vaulted ceilings, four Jacuzzis, and saunas that are all part of the package.

How could any millionaire pass up these new homes for something that is so old? Homes are not like automobiles, and millionaires are not like most other people. New does not necessarily translate into "better," "improved," "far superior to last year's model." We are a culture that has been trained to be "new sensitive," believing that new is always preferable to old. But those with the millionaire mind are not like most people.

There is a distinct downside risk in buying a $1 million home in a brand-new subdivision filled with $1 million homes. Who is to say that the homes are really worth the asking price? Where is the history, the price-trend data? None exists. What types of people tend to purchase expensive homes in those brand-new neighborhoods? They are not bad people, but they tend to be Income Statement Affluent. Again, that is "Big Income, Small Net Worth." They tend to be enamoured with "new" and with the many gadgets that are part of the sales strategy associated with "new." Who currently lives in the older neighborhoods where the value of a home is $1.4 million? They are different kinds of people. They tend to be Balance Sheet Affluent, with high net worth and little use of consumer credit. This doesn't mean that every single buyer of a new home is Income Statement Affluent. But the numbers are telling — people who accumulate wealth tend to live and buy homes in well-established neighborhoods, and only a minority of millionaires ever have any type of home — primary, secondary, or vacation — built for them. Many of the reasons for this reluctance to build are detailed in chapter 8, "The Home." According to the millionaires themselves:

- In order to get a good deal on the homes we purchase, we never pay the initial asking price for any home and are willing to walk away from any deal at any time.
- Most of us have mortgages, but 40 percent have no mortgage at all. Less than 5 percent of us have an outstanding mortgage balance of $1 million or more. Only about one in three (34 percent) of us have a mortgage balance outstanding of $300,000 or more.
- What is the median outstanding mortgage balance for those in our millionaire group? It is just under $100,000, or about 7 percent of the current market value of our homes. We are not, as some people refer to them, credit types.
- Part of our mind-set is to purchase homes that appreciate in value. In turn, part of this appreciation is a function of the high-quality public schools in our area. Sending three children to public schools (grades K through 12) saved us hundreds of thousands of dollars over the costs associated with private-school expenses.
- Most people, even those who do not earn anywhere near the incomes we generate, can still benefit from our orientation toward the home.

What activities are millionaires involved in? Remember that, overall, these people are at the top of the income and net worth scales in our nation. They live in homes valued at $1.4 million, located in fine neighborhoods. Their neighbors and friends are successful business owners, senior corporate executives, and top attorneys and physicians. Most are college graduates. In terms of social class, most of our millionaires are part of the upper-middle strata. The lifestyle activities they engage in are likely to be quite different than what most people imagine.

- We don't do the same things that jet-setters and beautiful people do. In fact, some swingers might say our overall activities and interests are mostly from Dullsville. In spite of our economic position, only 3 percent of us took an ocean cruise around the world last year. Only 4 percent skied in the Alps. Yet 20 percent of us did vacation in Paris last year. Of course, some of us who vacationed overseas had their trips partially subsidized by "business purposes."

- What have we done with our non-working time in the past twelve months? Most of us (85 percent) consulted with a tax expert; 81 percent visited a museum; 68 percent engaged in community/civic activities.

- Most of us do little or no "do-it-yourself" activities. Only about one in five (19 percent) mowed his or her lawn in the past year. Nor are we likely to be found painting our homes or doing plumbing repairs. The millionaire mind tells us to work hard at our main vocation and enjoy the rest of our free time doing what is enjoyable.

- Our thirty-day diary of activities is equally telling. Some may conclude that we are "cheap dates" because most of our activities are not costly. Whether you are rich or not, the best things in life are free or close to it. Entertaining friends, studying investments, and watching our children play sports are not expensive activities, yet these are the things that most of us love to do.
- Our lifestyles are congruent with strengthening relationships with friends and family, and many of our activities are not substitutes for wealth building but complements to it.

These and related topics are discussed in detail in chapter 9, "The Lifestyles of Millionaires: Real vs. Imagined."

2

Success Factors

Are you confused? America is supposed to be the land of opportunity, but after years of searching and studying opportunities, you're overwhelmed. Everyone you've consulted has a unique formula for becoming an economic success in America, and you've spoken to many, many people. When you ask these people if you can see their balance sheets, the evidence of their net worth, most say that they will be rich tomorrow and their current economic status is totally irrelevant. But it is very relevant to you — you are a seeker of truth. Just what are the factors that underlie financial success in America?

Each week you stop by the quickie mart and buy gasoline. You pay with cash. As a result, you often get stuck in line with people waiting to buy lotto tickets. So you ask the question of questions: Is lotto the way to become rich, economically successful in America? They all tell you the same thing — wealth is all about luck, and lotto is the most direct way to Millionairesville. Yet none of these people appear to be millionaires. Many even have holes in their shoes.

Then you stop by your local bank. Again you ask about the road to wealth. The teller says it's all about CDs. While you are in line, a man standing behind you introduces himself. Johnny Brown is an insurance agent. He whispers in your ear: Whole life and annuities. He says he can provide you with the key to economic success. "Just stop by my office today," he tells you. You decline his offer. Instead, you stop by the local high school because it's your child's parent-teacher day. While you are there, five teachers all say the same thing: Economic success is a direct mathematical function of one's grades in school. But many of these less successful people were once A students. Are they exceptions to the rule? How is it possible that some A students are not economically successful? You are now more confused than ever.

So you go home to relax. The TV is on and your children are channel surfing. On one of the cable channels a fellow says you can be rich if you listen to his audiotapes. The tapes are specially priced at $399 plus shipping.

On the next channel, a woman is selling her "professional matchmaking services." She claims the way to Millionairesville is through marriage. Too bad, you are already married.

Just then your phone rings. It's a cold-calling stockbroker. He wants to send you his card and other information. While you have him on the phone, you ask him the question of questions about economic success. He tells you that he is the way to wealth in America. He is the only person in America who can sell you shares in a company that just discovered a cure for AIDS. So you ask him to send you a copy of his financial statement. For some reason he hangs up on you.

And on and on it goes.

- The fellow on the radio this morning says you get rich with soybean futures.
- The lady who owns the local jewelry store tells you the key is owning investment-grade gems.
- The local antiques dealer says: "You just can't believe how many people have become rich in the antiques business."
- Members of your son's rock band tell you: "It's all about rock and roll."
- Most of the kids on the high school basketball team tell you that wealth in America is a sure thing if you are an athlete.
- On a special Saturday last fall, the kids lining up to take the SAT told you: "It's the SAT numbers. Score big and you go to a great college and then get big bucks later in life."
- Mr. Aladdin, down at the lighting store, promises something different. If you buy his special brand of lamp, a genie will appear and make you richer than you can imagine.

It is very confusing, all this information about the keys to becoming economically successful. How did millionaires become rich in America? The best way to answer this question is to ask them.

WHAT FACTORS EXPLAIN
YOUR ECONOMIC SUCCESS?

The 733 millionaires who responded to my survey were asked to rate thirty success factors. The list is not an exhaustive one — it was distilled from more than one hundred success factors mentioned by millionaires who participated in a series of preliminary personal and focus-group interviews I conducted. However, the thirty success factors selected were among those most often mentioned and represented many redundant factors. Table 2-1 presents the results.

Most millionaires place importance on pathways to success that are far different from those cited earlier. Becoming wealthy is the product of elements that are more fundamental than soybeans, life insurance, or the lotto. It's even more basic than grade point average, SAT scores, or graduating at the top of one's class, as the list demonstrates.

The following sections discuss these real success factors in detail. I have grouped them into response clusters as follows:

SOCIAL SKILLS
• Getting along with people
• Having strong leadership qualities
• Having an ability to sell my ideas, products, etc.
• Having good mentors

ORIENTATION TOWARD CRITICS
• Ignoring the criticism of detractors

- Having a competitive spirit or personality
- Having the urge to be well respected
- Having extraordinary energy
- Being physically fit

INTEGRITY AND MORAL VALUES
- Being honest with all people
- Having a supportive spouse
- Having strong religious faith

CREATIVE INTELLIGENCE
- Seeing opportunities others do not see
- Finding a profitable niche
- Specializing
- Loving my career or business

INVESTING: THE STOCK MARKET OR ONE'S OWN BUSINESS
- Investing in the equities of public corporations
- Having excellent investment advisers
- Making wise investments
- Investing in my own business
- Being my own boss
- Willing to take financial risk given the right return
- Living below my means

LUCK VS. DISCIPLINE
- Being lucky
- Being well disciplined
- Being very well organized
- Working harder than most people

TABLE 2-1

MILLIONAIRES' SUCCESS FACTORS
(N=733)

	Percentage of Millionaires Indicating Factor Very Important (Important)	Rank[1]
Being honest with all people	57 (33)	1[2]
Being well disciplined	57 (38)	1[2]
Getting along with people	56 (38)	3
Having a supportive spouse	49 (32)	4
Working harder than most people	47 (41)	5
Loving my career/business	46 (40)	6
Having strong leadership qualities	41 (43)	7
Having a very competitive spirit/personality	38 (43)	8
Being very well organized	36 (49)	9
Having an ability to sell my ideas/products	35 (47)	10[2]
Making wise investments	35 (41)	10[2]
Seeing opportunities others do not see	32 (40)	12
Being my own boss	29 (36)	13[2]
Willing to take financial risk given the right return	29 (45)	13[2]
Having good mentors	27 (46)	15[2]

TABLE 2-1 (continued)

	Percentage of Millionaires Indicating Factor Very Important (Important)	Rank[1]
Having an urge to be well respected	27 (42)	15[2]
Investing in my own business	26 (28)	17
Finding a profitable niche	23 (46)	18[2]
Having extraordinary energy	23 (48)	18[2]
Being physically fit	21 (44)	20
Having a high IQ/superior intellect	20 (47)	21
Specializing	17 (36)	22
Attending a top-rated college	15 (33)	23
Ignoring the criticism of detractors	14 (37)	24[2]
Living below my means	14 (29)	24[2]
Having strong religious faith	13 (20)	26
Being lucky	12 (35)	27[2]
Investing in the equities of public corporations	12 (30)	27[2]
Having excellent investment advisers	11 (28)	29
Graduating near/at top of my class	11 (22)	30

[1]Rank was computed according to the percentage of millionaires who indicated that the success component was very important in explaining their economic success.

[2]Tied for this position with another factor.

INTELLECTUAL ORIENTATION
- Having a high IQ/superior intellect
- Attending a top-rated college
- Graduating near/at the top of my class

The Intellectual Orientation is of particular interest. I have compared it to the Social Skills cluster, and to the clusters concerned with Orientation Toward Critics, Integrity, and Creative Intelligence. Although many people would predict that Intellectual Orientation (high IQ and such) would outrank the factors in each of these clusters, the data prove exactly the opposite.

THE DAWNING IN BIRMINGHAM: HIGH INTELLECT VS. SOCIAL SKILLS

I arrived in Birmingham, Alabama, just before dawn on a foggy winter Monday. My seminar was scheduled to begin at 8:30 A.M., but I arrived nearly an hour early and had the opportunity to chat with some of the two hundred executives in attendance during the preseminar continental breakfast.

A senior sales executive — I'll call him Hugh — told me that he had played for Coach Paul "Bear" Bryant at Alabama. During our conversation I learned a great deal about the factors that accounted for this executive's success in business. I wasn't surprised by some of the things Hugh told me. He mentioned that there were several other executives in the room who had played football for "the Bear," and I recalled meeting others all over America who played football for Coach Bryant.

There was something particularly compelling about Paul "Bear" Bryant's extraordinary achievements. His teams won many football championships, and were often number one. Even before I met Hugh that foggy winter morning, I recognized that productivity was Coach Bryant's hallmark. He established a superlative record without being number one in spending or by recruiting talent from fifty states.

I wanted to ask why Coach Bryant was so successful, but thought it might take hours for this former football player to respond. So I asked Hugh a different question: "What was the first thing Coach Bryant said to you and the other scholarship athletes after you arrived on campus?"

Surprisingly, Coach Bryant asked the group:

Have you called your folks yet to thank them?

According to Hugh, after hearing those words the players looked confused — most had their mouths open. They looked at one another with disbelief. Apparently not one of them had anticipated this question.

These freshman athletes had been on campus less than twenty-four hours, but they already had their first lesson in team productivity. I understand that no one in the room that day acknowledged having called home with words of thanks. What was the essence of this lesson?

Hugh said that Coach Bryant followed up his initial question with a second statement:

No one ever got to this level without the help of others.
Call your folks. Thank them.

In other words, the coach had news for these gifted freshmen. Extraordinary natural athletic talent does not fully account for success in football. Without their folks' nurturing, protecting, and sacrificing for them, they would not have had the opportunity to play football at Alabama.

Hugh told me that he never forgot this initial experience. It served him and his teammates well during four very successful years playing football. He also gives much credit to this and related lessons from the coach for his success and achievements in business.

It's rare that anyone becomes successful without the assistance of others. A group of individuals, no matter how gifted, is not a team at all. How many running backs became All-Americans without their linemen opening up opportunities? Zero. Becoming wealthy in America is very similar. I have never met one affluent person who takes complete credit for his economic success. Most will I give credit to their spouse, key employees, mentors, and others. No man or woman is an island, whether the context is sports, business, or building wealth — nobody gets to the highest peaks without the help of others.

It may be relatively easy to perform well when certain conditions are present. You may be on a very talented team playing much weaker opponents, or your business and net worth may be skyrocketing under favorable economic conditions. But what if the opponent is very strong or market conditions are unfavorable to your business? Then you won't even have a chance to win if you don't seek and nurture important human resources. Without such support, you will probably be overwhelmed. Fear and worry will set in; fear is the mother of panic, and panic is the precursor of bad decisions and ultimate failure. As demonstrated in my survey, throughout life most successful people go out of their way to attract, motivate, appreciate, and nurture key advisers, suppliers, and employees.

SUPERIOR SOCIAL SKILLS
VS. SUPERIOR INTELLECT

Note how valuable the coach's message was in view of the results of this survey of a large number of economically productive adults, millionaires. How do they account for their enormous productivity — is it a matter of being born with superior intellect? Not at all.

Nearly all of the millionaires surveyed, 94 percent, rated "getting along with people" as either very important (56 percent) or important (38

68

percent) in accounting for their economic success (See Table 2-2). Based on the percentage of respondents who rated it as "very important," this factor ranked third in overall importance relative to the other twenty-nine success factors studied.

So whether it be in sports or business, one's ability to get along is critical. Yet far too many of us believe that success is predetermined, a direct result of genetics, and that successful people just have higher IQs than those who are "less successful." So what if you receive all As in school and near-perfect SATs? So what if your IQ is in the ozone layer of the intelligence scale? Will these factors assure you of a place among the ranks of America's millionaires? It's doubtful, if you don't get along with people. This is not just my view. The large sample of millionaires surveyed were asked about the importance of intellect in explaining their economic success. As Table 2-2 shows, only one in five (20 percent) felt that "having a high IQ or superior intellect" was very important. Superior intellect ranked twenty-first on the list. Two other measures of intellect were found to be highly correlated with this factor. Only about one in ten (11 percent) indicated that "graduating near the top of my class" and only about one in seven (15 percent) felt that "attending a top-rated college" were very important elements in explaining their economic success.

Some millionaires do feel that their IQ was a

TABLE 2-2

MILLIONAIRES' SUCCESS FACTORS: SUPERIOR
(N=733)

PERCENTAGE OF MILLIONAIRES INDICATING OCCUPATIONAL CATEGORIES

	Business Owner/ Entrepreneur 32%	Senior Corporate Executive 16%
INTELLECTUAL ORIENTATION		
Having a High IQ/ Superior Intellect	16(45)	18(49)
Attending a Top-Rated College	12(31)	12(31)
Graduating near/ at Top of My Class	5(16)	8(22)
SOCIAL SKILLS		
Getting Along with People	61(35)	59(37)
Having Strong Leadership Qualities	45(43)	43(39)
Having an Ability to Sell My Ideas, Products, Etc.	45(47)	41(50)
Having Good Mentors	28(43)	29(51)

[1]Rank was computed according to the percentage of millionaires who indicated that the success component was very important in explaining their economic success.

INTELLECT VS. SOCIAL SKILLS

FACTOR VERY IMPORTANT (IMPORTANT) BY

Attorney	Physician	Other	All	
10%	9%	33%	100%	Rank[1]
34(49)	24(50)	20(47)	20(47)	21
18(50)	23(31)	16(30)	15(33)	23
26(34)	20(29)	8(24)	11(22)	30
43(47)	47(47)	56(38)	56(38)	3
29(51)	37(43)	35(43)	41(43)	7
16(46)	17(46)	35(45)	35(47)	10[2]
18(56)	30(52)	26(43)	27(46)	15[2]

[2]Tied for this position with another factor.

factor in their successful achievements, although most others feel just the opposite. This can be accounted for in part by considering the occupational groups that tend to rate their IQ as an important factor: millionaire attorneys are first in line, followed by physicians. The rationale is obvious because, as a general rule, one must score high on standardized tests to be admitted to either law school or medical school, and these board scores are high correlates of IQ. If the millionaire attorneys and physicians are netted out of the national sample (these two groups combined account for nearly one in five millionaires), the importance of "intellect" declines significantly.

There is another interesting result of removing the data from attorneys and physicians from the sample — the importance of "getting along with people" and other social skill factors is even more pronounced. Note that 61 percent of the millionaires in the business owner or entrepreneur category and 59 percent of the senior corporate executives feel that "getting along with people" is very important. A significantly smaller percentage of attorneys (43 percent) and physicians (47 percent) rated this factor as being very important.

This isn't surprising when you consider that a successful executive or business owner is more often part of a team than most attorneys or physicians. But in all vocational categories, social skills overall are rated higher by more respondents than are the intellectual factors.

Note the four components of the social skills domain listed in Table 2-2. All four of these are highly significant correlates — in other words, respondents who rated "getting along with people" as being important also tended to similarly rate "having strong leadership qualities . . . having an ability to sell my ideas, products, etc.," and "having good mentors."

GOOD SALESMEN HAVE AN EDGE

Reflect for a moment and visualize a great coach telling his audience, "You can't get to the next level without the help and cooperation of others." Getting along today is the foundation of becoming a strong leader tomorrow, and leaders, not followers, tend to become economically successful. But to become a leader, you must also have the ability to sell your ideas, your game plan, your dream, your product, or your services.

It's no wonder that coaches like Paul Bryant produced so many successful executives by teaching social skills. This is especially true in the field of sales and marketing. Sales professionals cannot achieve or excel, nor will they ever be promoted, without generating revenue. So selling is a lot like football — you win in both environments if you score more points than the competition.

The greatest salesman I ever met is William "Billy" Featherstone Gilmore Jr. Mr. Gilmore is a direct descendent of Colonel W. S. Featherstone, a Civil War hero who served with the Army of Northern Virginia. Bill's father was a decorated bomber pilot with the Eighth Air Force who flew fifty missions over Europe during World War II. Certainly his son Billy inherited some of his father's courage, for it takes a lot of courage to sell and be compensated strictly on performance.

I have done many studies on the characteristics of top sales professionals, and found they rated very high in courage and outstanding social skills. Billy excels in both dimensions. Some years ago he was in one of my classes at the University of Georgia. The midterm exam he handed in after hours contained just one paragraph. At first I put an F on the top of his paper, and then I thought, "Not good enough for a paper this bad." I raised it exponentially — F to the third power — and I wrote, "Dear Featherstone, this is the worst paper I've ever read in my life. Drop the course." And I told him that in front of ninety-nine of his colleagues.

I've had over ten thousand students in my teaching career, but only one had the audacity, the boldness, and the courage to come to my house unannounced and ask for a change of grade: William Featherstone Gilmore Jr. We sat, had a glass of wine, and he told me, "You forgot one thing in your class. If you have courage, you can win. You don't have to be the fastest, the smartest. You have to have tenacity."

Since then, I've often seen Billy Gilmore sell. It's still hard to believe that a fellow with a 2.01 GPA in college can be so very smart about people. Actually, his 2.01 GPA was very predictable. Billy was told by his dad that he needed a college degree to get a job. But what really mattered was his ability to sell. Billy went to college on a full-time basis, but he also worked full-time selling real estate. He polished his social skills by attending every formal, semiformal, and informal party and all football games. Yes, Billy is productive. Anything over a 2.01 GPA would have cut into his selling time or social-enhancement skills, so he just didn't bother to do better!

For more than twenty years Billy Gilmore and I have been friends, and we occasionally work together. Recently, the senior vice president and national sales manager of a major public corporation asked me to provide a seminar to one hundred of his top professionals in Dallas on a Saturday morning. Since role-playing and situation analyses were part of my seminar program, I telephoned Billy, who sells ladies' sportswear, including blue jeans, to firms like J. C. Penney, which is headquartered in Dallas. I suggested that he stay over through Saturday and help me do some role-playing during the seminar. Billy immediately agreed.

Tommy, it's a deal. . . . Give me the name of your contact (national sales manager). I'll get all the details from him. . . . I'll meet you Saturday morning.

Billy did much more than call my contact for details. He telephoned the national sales manager's secretary and got the particulars about the seminar's location and time schedule. Then he asked the secretary a series of interesting questions.

BILLY: Does Mr. Herman's wife wear blue jeans?

SECRETARY: I believe so.

BILLY: Do you have any idea what size jean Mrs. Herman wears?

SECRETARY: just like me — a tight ten or really a twelve.

On the morning of the seminar, I walked into the ballroom about thirty minutes early. The national sales manager saw me, and in an instant he zipped across the room and said, "My God, Tom, my wife loves the blue jeans. She can't thank you enough. She feels a lot better about me giving up my Saturday when there are blue jeans involved. They fit her perfectly."

While Mr. Herman praised me, I wondered what the heck he was talking about. Just then I looked over at Billy. He had a very large smile on his face, and in an instant it hit me. Billy, via his special "Featherstone Fit" jeans, had struck again. Once again, he'd demonstrated how to "get along with people." It was Billy who started Mr. Herman out in such a great mood. With a start like that, I wasn't surprised that the entire seminar was a major success. After he'd determined Mrs. Herman's jean size, he had his senior seamstress construct a dozen pairs of specially made jeans. But high quality was only part of his plan — inside each pair was a label that indicated "size 8."

Even today I'm not sure. When Mr. Herman calls and asks me to give another seminar, I ask myself, Is it my seminar or Billy's blue jeans that precipitated the call? Billy never even told Mr. Herman that it was he who sent the jeans. He put a note in the box saying, "From Tom Stanley." I got the credit, all the goodwill. Eventually, Mr. Herman's company purchased many of my seminars, books, tapes, and other materials.

What was the source of Billy Gilmore's empathy for the needs of people? I asked him the same question, and he told me his mother always told him that:

Me, me, me is dull, dull, dull.

In other words, always focus on the needs and interests of others. His dad was a sales professional and he played a role, too. When Billy was just a young boy, his dad often took him on sales calls selling school buses to county school districts. Before each call, his dad explained why it was important to understand the interests and backgrounds of each person who made school bus purchasing decisions. His dad was a top sales professional and a great mentor, and he, too, believed and practiced the fundamental rule of selling:

Me, me, me is dull, dull, dull.

LEADERSHIP QUALITIES

CONCERNED PARENT: We are very concerned about our son. With his grades, top colleges are out of the picture.

HEADMASTER: Don't worry about Richard. He'll do well in life. People like him and respect him. They follow him. Richard is a natural leader.

The headmaster was accurate in his assessment of Richard. Recently he wrote on the questionnaire he completed for me: Poor student in high school and college. But he also indicated that he was rapidly approaching decamillionaire status. He is a leader and a very successful business owner and has great enthusiasm for his vocation. He demonstrates a lot of appreciation and empathy for the needs of all his employees, who are paid significantly above the norm. In turn, Richard is well liked by his employees. As a token of their appreciation, they all chipped in and gave Richard and his wife the gift of a European vacation.

Yet Richard's life might have turned out

differently. What if he'd had a different set of parents and an insensitive headmaster at the prep school he attended? What if they'd told Richard:

With these grades, you'll never amount to a hill of beans. With your academic record, you'll be lucky to get a job washing dishes or sweeping floors.

Instead, Richard's parents never said such things. They never gave up on him, nor did his mentor, the headmaster. In school, Richard was a leader in sports and social activities. He was never made to feel inferior because of his lack of academic achievements.

Richard is like many very successful people. He got a lot more out of the school environment than was ever noted on his report cards and transcripts. Let's take another case study demonstrating this point about leadership vs. school grades.

A LEADER OF LEADERS

You recently completed undergraduate school, and now you are contemplating pursuing a graduate degree. Before you are admitted, you must take the Graduate Record Exam (GRE). Several weeks after you take the exam, your scores arrive in the mail. You quickly open the envelope and look them over. They are not that easy to interpret, so you look at the legend.

There are several parts to the GRE. Two major components are the verbal aptitude score and the quantitative score; other parts include tests in physics, chemistry, biology, social studies, and fine arts.

How do you rank? You discover that your verbal aptitude score is in the third quarter, or below average range. Naturally you are disappointed, so you look at your other scores. Your quantitative score places you in the bottom 10 percent, and you are in the bottom quarter for tests in physics, chemistry, biology, social studies, and the fine arts.

If these were your scores, would you still think about going to graduate school? What if you showed these scores to a team of guidance counselors or career advisers? They might advise you that you aren't graduate school material. Some might even be bold enough to tell you that you should lower your sights, which is a nice way of saying: You will never amount to much.

How many counselors would be likely to say to you:

Young man, you have extraordinary leadership qualities, great vision. Someday you will change the social conscience of America. You will have more to do with social and political changes in America than anyone since FDR.

I wager that you'll say zero, because most advisers judge our futures on the basis of standardized test scores. It's unfortunate that test scores, which take only one day to complete, fulfill their speculations about the next thirty or forty years of your career. If you believe them, you will spend the rest of your life thinking and acting like someone with low aptitude.

Can you imagine if Dr. Martin Luther King Jr. had spent his life thinking and acting this way? The GRE scores described above were those of Martin Luther King Jr. (Ethan Bronner, "Colleges Look for Answers to Racial Gaps in Testing," *New York Times*, November 8, 1997, p. A8), but he never allowed naysayers to stand in his way. He understood the true meaning of achievement.

There must be a balance. Certainly, we all want our children to excel in school, but at the same time we must encourage them to do more, to take leadership roles in school. Encourage them to participate in extracurricular and team-oriented activities. If we do this, we can expect to have a greater number of leaders. We will even have a growing population of leaders with both social and analytical skills.

IGNORE OR BE INSPIRED BY CRITICS

What do millionaires tell me about the relationship between their success and how they deal with critics? The majority either ignore their critics or use criticism as an inspiration to succeed. Most millionaires define a critic as someone who makes negative judgments and predictions about other people. Unlike mentors, who focus on how others can improve themselves, critics are not interested in helping their targets improve. In fact, they seem to enjoy watching people fail. It's as if they get satisfaction from watching their predictions come true.

Critics are those who have told many a millionaire:

- You will never succeed.
- You lack the intellect to become an attorney.
- That's the dumbest idea for a new business I have ever heard.
- There is no place for women in the medical profession.
- There is just no hope for you ever succeeding.
- You are not graduate school material.
- Given your combined SATs of 900, you'll never succeed in college.

Those who accepted such negative reviews withdrew early from the economic battlefield, while others discounted the criticism. Many millionaires actually viewed such comments as merely being theories, and they enjoy disproving theories. The really vicious, negative critics have a common trait — their only talent is voicing negative predictions. Often they are jealous of people with real talent, people with the will to succeed. But I find that most professional critics are lacking in this same quality — they can't stand other people criticizing their views. So what do they do to ensure that they won't be criticized? They play offense. They aggressively and offensively criticize those who are or will be successful. It's one way they enhance their own status, like playing judge, jury, even God.

Most self-made millionaire business owners can tell you a lot about critics. They've had their loan applications turned down repeatedly, and in their minds, loan officers are critics. They tell applicants that "your business will never make it," yet they don't offer suggestions on how to improve the business. But what great power it is to lend other people money!

Consider what one self-made multimillionaire from Oklahoma once told me during a focus-group interview:

> *It was Friday morning. I had to make payroll for my employees by 4:00 P.M. that day. . . . I went to the bank that I have borrowed millions from for years. They put me in a room with yet another new loan officer. This thirty-something guy proceeded to tell me that my business was under review. . . . Had to get some updates. . . . All these years, I never missed a repay. Then he took over an hour telling me about his latest ski trips to Vail, Aspen, and Steamboat. . . . He went on and on. While I'm there worried that I can't pay hundreds of people.*

Yes, he made payroll that afternoon, "just barely." But needless to say, he is no longer a client of the "Bank of Abuse."

The "Bank of Abuse" also lost another member from that same focus group, a successful business owner who had never defaulted on a loan in his career. All of a sudden, the bank telephoned and called in all of his outstanding loans because the day before, a local newspaper had printed a notice that this millionaire entrepreneur was divorcing his wife!

There are countless examples of critics who try to destroy the dreams of ambitious men and women. But critics are a necessary part of our social system in America — they screen out those who lack the courage and resolve to take criticisms and triumph in spite of them.

Successful entrepreneurs tend to have extraordinary drive and resolve. A recently published article reported on the source of their motivation (see Adrienne Sanders, "Success Secrets of the Successful," *Forbes*, November 2, 1998, pp. 22, 24). Bill Bartmann, founder and chairman of Commercial Financial Services, indicated in the article that his sister-in-law was a major motivating element because she was a critic of sorts. Her negative evaluation of him gave Mr. Bartmann strong motivation to prove that she was wrong. He is quoted as saying, "She [the sister-in-law] didn't like me . . . I wasn't good enough [for her sister]. It . . . absolutely infuriated me" (Sanders, p. 22).

It seems that "Mr. Bartmann was a high school dropout, but, motivated by criticism from his sister-in-law, he received a GED and then went on to college. In college he motivated himself to study by placing a five-by-seven-inch index card with the name of his sister-in-law on it on the wall. Whenever his head moved away from studying his lessons, he saw the name of his arch critic and was instantly motivated to get back to his books.

In the same article Debra Streicker-Fine, president of Interactive Media, revealed her source of motivation. Her small-town neighbors thought that being a female entrepreneur was degrading. In turn, she was motivated by her strong desire to reject their evaluation of her and her vocation (Sanders, p. 24).

The lesson of the millionaire mind is that you should be careful of whom you listen to, and be sensitive to the motives of so-called advisers. If you're ambitious and hardworking and your career is accelerating on an upward trend, you may be a threat to some people. Unfortunately, many of these same people are the very ones our young people rely on for career advice.

So the majority of millionaires ignore their critics, and in addition, they never allow negative evaluations or forecasts to weaken their resolve. Ignoring the criticism of detractors is a significant correlate of economic success and career achievements (see Table 2-3).

Keep one fact in mind. The successful population, regardless of intellect, is more heavily criticized than the unsuccessful. In fact, I believe

TABLE 2-3

MILLIONAIRES' SUCCESS FACTORS: SUPERIOR (N=733)

PERCENTAGE OF MILLIONAIRES INDICATING BY OCCUPATIONAL

	Business Owner/ Entrepreneur 32%	Senior Corporate Executive 16%
INTELLECTUAL ORIENTATION		
Having a High IQ/ Superior Intellect	16(45)	18(49)
ORIENTATION TOWARD CRITICS		
Ignoring the Criticism of My Detractors	20(40)	9(39)
Having a Very Competitive Spirit/Personality	37(49)	46(40)
Having an Urge to Be Well Respected	23(44)	28(42)
Having Extraordinary Energy	24(50)	22(45)
Being Physically Fit	24(44)	19(48)

[1]Rank was computed according to the percentage of millionaires who indicated that the success component was

INTELLECT VS. ORIENTATION TOWARD CRITICS

FACTOR VERY IMPORTANT (IMPORTANT) CATEGORIES

Attorney 10%	Physician 9%	Other 33%	All 100%	Rank[1]
34(49)	24(50)	20(47)	20(47)	21
11(28)	11(47)	13(34)	14(37)	24[2]
40(33)	37(44)	34(42)	38(43)	8
21(47)	38(39)	31(38)	27(42)	15[2]
16(43)	26(58)	24(45)	23(48)	18[2]
16(36)	18(49)	23(44)	21(44)	20

very important in explaining their economic success.
[2]Tied for this position with another factor.

that criticism is a necessary form of hazing, the tempering of steel, the boot camp for candidates wanting to succeed. Ask the typical millionaire today and he will probably have many boot camp experiences to relate.

Successful people are different; they don't follow the crowd, and those who don't follow the crowd are often criticized for being different. The most productive professor I ever took a class from once told me just before I graduated:

If you don't publish you may not get tenure at a good school. But you will have a lot of friends. Publish a lot and you will not be real popular among your colleagues.

Often success comes at the price of not being one of the gang, the good old boys. In fact, three out of four millionaires (76 percent) report that learning to think differently from the crowd while they were in their formative years was an important influence in becoming productive adults in later life. Being different comes with rewards like economic success, and punishments like criticisms and exclusions from social groups.

A millionaire in one of my first interviews told me something about rejection:

Never take rejection personally.

Another gave me great advice.

When you are criticized, wait two weeks before you get angry . . . [or] upset. After two weeks, if you still wish to get angry, wait another two weeks. What if at the end of these two weeks you still want to get angry? Write the critic a long letter. Spell out why you're interested in becoming angry. After all this time and the process of purging your concerns via letter writing, you may be cured of destructive anger. Chances are, you will not even feel the need to send the letter.

PHYSICALLY CONDITIONED TO WIN:
A CORRELATE OF DISPROVING CRITICS

According to the survey, the majority of millionaires exercise regularly, although being physically fit ranks at number 20 on the list of success factors (see Table 2-1). Decamillionaires, those with net worth of $10 million or more, have the highest incidence of regular exercise. About two-thirds exercise regularly. Many of the others play golf or tennis, but not always on a regular basis.

The more economically successful you become, the more critics you will attract. Keeping in excellent physical condition can be an important tool in dealing with detractors because it helps to hone one's competitive spirit. Many millionaires, especially decamillionaires, are extremely competitive — and even welcome criticism. It gives them stronger motivation to prove that their critics were wrong in their assessments. Also, physical conditioning is one of the main sources of the extraordinary energy that most multimillionaires possess. I've found very few self-made millionaires who are lethargic or even noticeably overweight. Exhaustion and lethargy are friends of critics. So if you want to be able to ignore criticism or, even better, thrive on it, never allow yourself to get fat and lazy. Being physically fit is a significant underlying correlate of several other domains of success. Those who credit their willingness to take financial risk (see chapter 4) are significantly more likely to be physically fit than risk avoiders.

Physical fitness can also be a strong correlate of one's overall contentment, even affection for one's vocation. It's much easier to work hard if you love what you are doing, and the ability to work hard is, in turn, related to one's physical conditioning.

Wealth does not have much meaning if you don't know how to enjoy your job, people, and diversions. And you can't get much out of your economic achievements if you die before your time, as did Mr. Powell, a multimillionaire. The executor of his estate recently returned a questionnaire that I'd addressed to Mr. Powell, with a note saying, "Dr. Stanley — in spite of his wealth, Mr. Powell died recently."

INTEGRITY AND MORAL VALUES

I personally examine every questionnaire that is completed by respondents, because some of the most important information comes in the form of handwritten comments and suggestions that are not part of the "fill in the blanks" components of my surveys. These comments are written in margins, under other objective choices, and often in unexpected places.

One character wrote his own added explanations all over the questionnaire. When asked to estimate what others thought of him, he wrote: Fair and honest. He also wrote short notes next to each question about the experiences that influenced him. It indicated that his parents and one other major factor explained his economic success — three years in the U.S. Marines!

What do factors such as being fair and honest and spending time in the Marine Corps have to do with becoming an economic success? The millionaire population contains a disproportionately high concentration of people who tell me that integrity is a critical factor in explaining their success. "Being honest with all people" was rated as a very important or important success factor by the large majority of millionaires.

Another respondent indicated that he managed commercial real estate. When I read this and some of his related comments, I said to myself: I bet that this respondent, No. 0103, circled "very important" when he was asked about the relative importance of one particular success factor. I was correct in my speculation. What factor was so very important in explaining his success as a manager of commercial real estate?

TABLE 2-4

MILLIONAIRES'
SUPERIOR INTELLECT VS.
(N=733)

PERCENTAGE OF MILLIONAIRES INDICATING OCCUPATIONAL

	Business Owner/ Entrepreneur 32%	Senior Corporate Executive 16%
INTELLECTUAL ORIENTATION		
Having a High IQ/ Superior Intellect	16(45)	18(49)
INTEGRITY		
Being Honest with All People	62(30)	61(32)
Having a Supportive Spouse	55(30)	48(38)
Having Strong Religious Faith	15(22)	12(27)

SUCCESS FACTORS:
INTEGRITY/COMPLETENESS

FACTOR VERY IMPORTANT (IMPORTANT) BY CATEGORIES

Attorney	Physician	Other	All	
10%	9%	33%	100%	Rank[1]
34(49)	24(50)	20(47)	20(47)	21
46(41)	55(36)	55(33)	57(33)	1[2]
32 (39)	54(33)	47(30)	49(32)	4
11(20)	17(21)	13(15)	13(20)	26

[1]Rank was computed according to the percentage of millionaires who indicated that the success component was very important in explaining their economic success.
[2]Tied for this position with another factor.

Being honest with all people.

This factor is so vital because integrity is a critical element of success when one manages other people's property or money. Respondent No. 0103 is not alone. This measure of integrity, "being honest with all people," was tied for first in regard to the percentage of millionaires who rated it as a very important reason for their economic success (see Table 2-4).

Unfortunately, today's headlines and news stories are full of reports about people in high places who lack integrity. Even President Bill Clinton suggested that his deceptive acts be placed in a "box score" context, implying that his overall batting average as president was good to terrific. Most economically successful people don't believe that integrity, or lack of it, can be averaged into one's overall grade point average. Let's see, that's an A for the economy, B for foreign policy, B for domestic tranquility, B for enhancing social mandates, but an F for integrity. In college terms, that's enough to get by with a 2.6 GPA.

But integrity is a different part of life's curriculum. It is a pass/fail course. If you lack integrity, most millionaires will tell you that you will not and should not graduate to economic success. What if a young up-and-coming business owner or physician just starting a practice deceives his customers or patients? What if a business owner misrepresents the products he offers? They fail

Integrity 101, and they will never succeed or graduate without having integrity.

Dr. Robert, age forty-five, is a case study in integrity. He had a thriving medical practice, but, unfortunately, this internist had a difficult time keeping his hands off his female assistants. He had numerous adulterous affairs with several members of his staff. Eventually, his wife discovered her husband's transgressions, and in short order, she divorced him.

Even before the divorce decree was finalized, Dr. Robert's wife joined a local support group for women in transition from being married to being divorced. Mrs. Robert detailed to the group members the adulterous behavior of her husband, with numerous case examples. Several fellow members were patients of Dr. Robert's, but they are no longer his patients today. Neither are the countless numbers of patients who heard about Dr. Robert's deceit through the grapevine. At this time, Dr. Robert is also in transition. He is in the process of moving his office to another market area.

FIFTEEN SQUARED

Integrity is defined in *Webster's* as "firm adherence to a code of especially moral values; incorruptibility." People with integrity know the difference between right and wrong, between the truth and fabrication. The survey shows that most economically productive people value integrity highly and credit it for their success.

Jon Barry is the owner of a successful real estate management firm and a man of great integrity. He built the business from ground zero. Most of his clients are owners of shopping centers, and Jon's firm is responsible for managing these properties. The firm does everything from collecting rent to hiring contractors when repairs or renovations are required.

To make such repairs, Jon hires contractors who provide the best products and services for the most competitive prices. It sounds easy, but it's not always a simple process. Jon goes out of his way to ensure that his clients receive the best deal for their dollars. Jon documents his fiduciary responsibility at every step in the process of selecting and directing contractors.

Integrity and the reputation that goes along with it are extremely important elements that underlie his success. Jon told me that his father, a rather famous and successful manager of talent in the entertainment business, taught him much about integrity. He often told his son:

Never lie. Never tell one lie. If you tell one lie, you will have to eventually tell fifteen more to cover up the first lie.

According to Jon's dad, one lie requires a cover of 15 more. In turn, each of these 15 requires 15 more, or 225 lies. Furthermore, each of the 225 lies next requires fifteen more. Now we are at 225 times 15, or 3,375 lies. Again,

3,375 times 15 equals 50,625. And so on. It is a much more productive use of one's time, energy, and intelligence to always tell the truth, to be honest with all people.

EGGS, PLEASE, JUMBO AND SMART

Today, through the miracle of medical science, many infertile couples who want to have children are being helped. That's why the market for both egg and sperm donors is growing at an increasing rate. Most couples, whether they are fertile or not, have a strong need to have children, and many don't care if their first- or second-born child is a boy or girl, has blue eyes or brown, "so long as it's healthy."

But there are some couples who want more than "so long as it's healthy." They have a strong need to produce a child who has certain characteristics — particularly high intelligence. Consider the advertisement that was recently placed in several college newspapers (see Gina Kolata, "$50,000 Offered to Tall, Smart Egg Donor," *New York Times*, March 3, 1999, p. A10) with the following headline: "Egg Donor Needed: Large Financial Incentive."

According to a report published in the *New York Times*, the advertisement was placed in the newspapers of some of this country's most prestigious colleges. The term "large financial incentive" was a bit of an understatement. The infertile couple was offering $50,000 to an egg donor, but the donor must have certain characteristics. She must be intelligent and athletic. The advertisement stated that the donor must have a 1400 SAT score (or higher) and be least five foot ten, a proxy measure of athletic ability.

The assumption is that an egg from a tall person with a 1400-plus SAT score will produce a child who has high analytical intellect and will also be tall. Keep in mind that the infertile couple in this case is:

Highly educated . . . and want a child who can be highly educated as well. They are tall, so they want a child who is tall. . . . (Kolata, p. A10)

I read this information several times, and each time I couldn't help but feel that I was reading about some fellow who breeds hunting hounds.

I have to assume that the infertile couple probably had good intentions in their quest for a match. They are apparently high on the analytical-intelligence scale, so what's wrong with trying to find a donor who also possesses high analytical intelligence? And both are tall and athletic, so naturally they want to enhance the probability. But life can play many tricks on people. Just because Mom and Dad are high up on the intellect scale doesn't mean their offspring, Thad and Buffy, will also be intelligent, and it's possible that Thad and Buffy will have some undesirable traits. I recently read an Associated Press story with the headline "National Merit Scholar." Near this subheading was a picture of the recipient, a tall, attractive young woman. Was she intelligent? Yes. Otherwise, how could she even be considered a candidate for a National Merit Scholarship? The article also stated that she was a college student in need of funds "so she could concentrate on her art" (Martha Mendoza, "College Student Held in Robberies," *Atlanta Journal Constitution*, January 28, 1999, p. A10).

I suspect that the infertile couple would not purchase the eggs from this young scholar. She was not featured in news stories because of her performance on the SAT.

> *Emma . . . , 18, a National Merit Scholar, is accused of pointing a . . . handgun . . . while robbing a hair salon.* (Mendoza, p. A10)

Intellect and integrity are not the same constructs, so if you had a choice, what would you do? You are a married couple in need of an egg — would you take smart eggs from a donor who commits armed robberies? Or would you insist on eggs from a donor with high integrity? Personally, I would tone down the IQ requirements if I could enhance the probability of producing a child who is honest, well adjusted, and personable. The experiences of the self-made millionaires surveyed support that decision if you want your child to achieve economic success. Being a genius is no guarantee that one will become financially independent.

BIRDS OF A FEATHER

If you ever judge the quality of a person by the quality of his neighborhood, you're not alone. Some neighborhoods have much higher concentrations of college graduates than others, and some have much higher crime rates than others.

As a general rule, in America, birds of a socioeconomic feather do flock together. This is the basis of much of my sampling of affluent households. I oversample those neighborhoods in America with the highest concentrations of millionaires, which is the most efficient method of focusing on the millionaire population.

In a nationwide sample, without selecting neighborhoods, one would expect that only one in twenty respondents would be in the millionaire category. But in this book, the sample was taken from neighborhoods that contained upwards of 80 percent millionaires. These affluent respondents are typically well educated and they hold positions that pay high salaries. Some would even say that, on average, they are smarter or more intelligent than people who live in other areas. Of course, as discussed throughout this book, "smart" has many definitions.

If you define smart as having an above-average IQ or SAT score, then people who live in affluent neighborhoods generally are "smarter" than those living in, say, lower-middle-class areas. But it would be wrong to conclude that all the smart people live in affluent neighborhoods, just as it would be wrong to conclude that all those who live in blue-collar neighborhoods have lower levels of intellect. There are several significant relationships between neighborhood type and the characteristics of the people who reside there, as demonstrated in the following case example.

I received a letter from a stranger, asking for my assistance. Where do you think this fellow lives?

Dear Dr. Stanley:

I have read your most recent works. I have an extremely high mathematical aptitude. I hold advanced degrees in advanced math . . . from ——— University.

So far, you know this fellow can read. It's not a certainty, but you might play the odds and guess that he lives in a neighborhood with a higher than average concentration of middle-class, college-educated people.

Then you note that this fellow is a math genius, and he holds advanced degrees from a prestigious university. He probably lives among other people with high IQs, SATs, GPAs, incomes, and net worths.

Could it be that he lives in one of those same neighborhoods as my respondents, and that he is a millionaire with a prototypical home valued at $1.4 million? Your assessment changes a bit after you read more of his letter.

> *I'm currently in transition. Eventually I want to pursue a different career path.*
>
> *You are well versed in the study of wealthy families. Thus I have a request of you. I'm intensely interested in becoming a math tutor for the children of the wealthy. Can you supply me with the names and mailing addresses of millionaires in the following areas: —— ?*

Perhaps he's not a millionaire. Full-time math tutors usually don't become wealthy. Now you picture him as perhaps a very bright fellow with limited ambition who, at the very least, may live in a nice lower-middle-class neighborhood. If that was your guess you'll win no prize on this quiz show. Consider the rest of his story.

> *I'm currently in prison. . . . I am scheduled for release next September.*

Well, you did get part of the correct answer — the fellow lives in a neighborhood with a high concentration of people with similar characteristics. But most are not millionaires, nor are they mathematically inclined. They are all 100 percent convicted felons.

This convict was extraordinarily arrogant. He thought that because he was brilliant in math, I would overlook the fact that he was judged by a jury to lack integrity. Imagine you are a wealthy person with children who need math tutoring. One day you get a letter postmarked: *Jailbird University*. It contains the "please hire me" note, with the "applicant's" résumé attached. Under employment objectives you read:

To get out of prison and tutor rich kids . . . for dollar compensation plus free room and board in a mansion setting.

There is a simple message here. There are people like this convict who are gifted intellectually, but that doesn't mean they also have high integrity. The halo that surrounds smart people often blinds us. We automatically think they are better in all of life's key dimensions. In fact, some smart people are not people of high integrity.

YOUR SPOUSE

Lincoln said, referring to politicians, you can't fool all the people all the time, but in the business world it's difficult for those who lack integrity to fool even some of their customers some of the time. Quoting Mark 3:25, Lincoln also said that a house divided cannot stand, and that can also refer directly to a relationship with a spouse. Note that one of the success factors strongly correlated with integrity is:

Having a supportive spouse.

Nearly one-half (49 percent) of the millionaire

respondents indicated that this element was very important in accounting for their economic success. Most of the respondents believe that

Integrity begins at home.

You cannot expect your spouse to be supportive if you lie and cheat. Your spouse and your children have many, many opportunities to observe your behavior. It's not enough to say you are honest or merely attend religious services each week. You have to be a role model of integrity for your spouse, your children, and all others. If you are, your spouse will probably support you through good times and bad, during thin years and plump years.

A more detailed discussion of the role that spouses play in the affluent family is presented in chapter 4, "The Relationship Between Courage and Wealth." Also included in chapter 4 is a profile of millionaires who have strong religious faith. For many millionaires religious faith is also closely related to integrity, as shown in Table 2-4. In addition, the millionaire's choice of spouse is detailed in chapter 6. It is important to note that "having a supportive spouse" is a strong correlate of most of the major factors that underlie economic success in the millionaire population.

CREATIVE INTELLIGENCE

What if you are not an analytical genius? Your

school counselors often reminded you that you're just average or somewhat above. Your SAT results indicated that you aren't likely to be accepted at a competitive college, and your B-level grades are in sync with your SAT scores. You are not intellectually gifted, but you have another gift.

You are smart enough to know that it would be a bad idea to try to compete in the same vocational area with the whiz kids from your school, so you rule out becoming an attorney or physician. Then you search for a business opportunity that would provide significant profits and few competitors. You discover the ideal business opportunity — ultimately you just had an intuitive feeling about the type of intellect you possess. You have a lot of creative intelligence.

People with creative intelligence who apply themselves are among the very most economically successful people in America. So what if they aren't high on the analytical-intelligence scale? They are not normally encouraged to enter a rigorous graduate school program or competitive professional school, but they often are big winners in the economic arena. How is it possible?

Millionaires who have high creative intelligence often make one very important career decision correctly: They select a vocation that provides them with enormous profits, and very often this same vocation is one they love. Remember, if you love what you are doing, your productivity will be high and your specific form of creative genius will emerge. Professor Robert J. Sternberg, one of America's leading authorities on human intelligence, notes that creative people tend to love their chosen vocations, and this is one of the main reasons they succeed in life. Creative intelligence is a major component of Sternberg's definition of successful intelligence (see Robert J. Sternberg, *Successful Intelligence* [New York: Simon & Schuster, 1996], pp. 251-52).

Even analytically intelligent people often select vocations that are filled with competitors and discover that they don't love their careers. Even if they are geniuses, it's hard to win a competitive economic battle if your heart and emotions are not completely dedicated to victory. Consider what Mo Siegel, the founder and chair of Celestial Seasonings, recently told a reporter about being successful.

> *Unless you've got a near-perfect IQ . . . passion about your product really helps. . . . I want everybody in the company to be passionate.* (Josephine Lee, "You Are What You Sell," *Forbes*, February 22, 1999, p. 22)

In the results given in Table 2-5, nearly one-half (46 percent) of the millionaires indicate that "loving my career or business" is a very important factor that explains their economic success. Another 40 percent rated this factor important.

Combined, 86 percent of millionaires believe that the love of their vocation is significant in accounting for their millionaire status. In contrast, "having a high IQ/superior intellect" was rated as very important by only one in five, or 20 percent, of these affluent respondents. "Seeing opportunities that others do not see" was also rated as being more important by more millionaires than "having a high IQ/superior intellect." Note that "business owner" is the largest occupational segment, and more than four in five believe that "seeing opportunities others did not see" and "finding a profitable niche" were very important or important success factors.

Seeing opportunities and finding a profitable niche both contribute to loving one's career, because generally it is the millionaire himself who saw the opportunity, or personally found the niche that excited him. His choice of career was not imposed on him by parents or significant others. In fact, there is a highly significant correlation between level of net worth and the importance rating of "finding a profitable niche."

Creative people know what to do when one door is locked. They try another way to succeed. They seem to know their strengths as well as their shortcomings. If they lack funds, they will probably select another vocation. Consider the example of Hazel Bishop. She couldn't go to medical school for economic reasons, so she took a job as a chemist and worked for a top dermatol-

TABLE 2-5

MILLIONAIRES' SUCCESS FACTORS: SUPERIOR (N=733)

PERCENTAGE OF MILLIONAIRES INDICATING OCCUPATIONAL

	Business Owner/ Entrepreneur 32%	Senior Corporate Executive 16%
INTELLECTUAL ORIENTATION		
Having a High IQ/ Superior Intellect	16(45)	18(49)
CREATIVE INTELLIGENCE		
Seeing Opportunities Others Do Not See	42(43)	34(40)
Finding a Profitable Niche	35(54)	21(38)
Specializing	16(42)	9(21)
Loving My Career/Business	51(37)	45(41)

INTELLECT VS. CREATIVE INTELLIGENCE

FACTOR VERY IMPORTANT (IMPORTANT) BY CATEGORIES

Attorney	Physician	Other	All	
10%	9%	33%	100%	Rank[1]
34(49)	24(50)	20(47)	20(47)	21
19(35)	28(31)	25(40)	32(40)	12
14(43)	16(49)	17(42)	23(46)	18[2]
20(37)	43(30)	12(37)	17(36)	22
29(48)	56(38)	43(41)	46(40)	6

[1]Rank was computed according to the percentage of millionaires who indicated that the success component was very important in explaining their economic success.
[2]Tied for this position with another factor.

ogist who studied cosmetic-related allergies.

From this and related experiences, she invented the first kissproof lipstick in her kitchen. Eventually her brand captured 25 percent of the market. Her creativity overcame her economic adversity, and it's more than likely that she never would have become as economically successful as a dermatologist. There were many highly skilled dermatologists, but there was only one inventor of kissproof lipstick — "that stays on you . . . not on him" (Mary Tannen, "Hazel Bishop . . . Innovator Who Made Lipstick Kissproof," *New York Times*, December 10, 1998, p. C24).

My databases are filled with responses from millionaires who started businesses that are very, very unique. Creative people come up with unique business ideas, and often these creative types are not loved by their teachers and professors. They are some of the same radicals who might have written in the margins of objective tests "more than one answer possible," and then given a logical explanation. Many of these case studies are discussed in some detail in chapter 5, "Vocation Vocation Vocation."

Our economy is filled with successful entrepreneurs who were encouraged early in their lives to think differently. Creativity was nurtured. So when our young people are criticized for being outperformed on standardized tests by their counterparts in other countries, I recite the following quote:

When the education minister of Singapore came here [the United States] . . . people [asked him]: "What are you looking here for? Your kids . . . score on top of all international [standardized achievement tests]. . . . He said . . . "all that our kids can do is take tests." (Ethan Bronner, "Freedom in Math Class May Outweigh Tests," *New York Times*, March 2, 1999, pp. A1, A4)

Apparently, the education minister of Singapore understands something that our own educators do not. Creativity, the discovery and exploitation of unique opportunities, has a lot to do with our economic position in the world today. As a society, we need to nurture even more creativity in our young people.

It's unfortunate that many educators focus only on the part of the brain that houses analytical intellect. What if they continue to tell kids who are not analytically inclined that creativity doesn't count in our economy? We are in big trouble. Tell even the most creative student over and over again, "Your test scores are inferior, therefore you're inferior," and the result is yet one more economic dropout. Instead, tell a youngster there are many ways to win. Tell him that creativity and even common sense, social skills, and integrity count in the economic arena. If we convey that message, we will have many more people becoming productive citizens.

Testing has its place in society, but there should be more testing of the interests that young people have inside of them. Tell them this: If you want to be successful, select a vocation you love. It's amazing how well people do in life when their vocation is one that stimulates dedication and positive emotions.

Unfortunately, most people who find a vocation they love were never directed to it by testing or through the academic environment. It's especially important to note that only 14 percent of the millionaires studied indicated "finding the ideal vocation with standardized aptitude test results." Even fewer (6 percent) found it through suggestions from their college placement office.

AN ATHLETE'S HEART

Are desire, careful selection, and a strong affection for a vocation enough to compensate for lack of high analytical intellect? Some years ago one of my undergraduate advisees wanted to go to graduate school and earn an MBA. He'd spent his first two years in college generating a lot of Cs, and then later as a junior and senior he started doing B work. He took the GMAT (Graduate Management Aptitude Test), which was a requirement for admission to the school he was applying to. From the look on his face the morning he consulted me, I could tell he was unhappy with his performance.

The graduate school of business he was interested in was not an academic powerhouse, with a GMAT of 450 as the lower minimum for acceptance. But my advisee's score was "somewhere in the 300s." He thought that a personal interview with some key people at the business school would offset his low score on the GMAT, but he was told, "You are not graduate school material."

What do you tell a young student who has just had his dream of attending graduate school shattered? I told him there were many MBA programs. At the time, some night and part-time programs were really interested in building their student bases, and some did not even require the GMAT.

My young advisee soon recovered from the hurt of being told that he wasn't "graduate school material," and I was not surprised. This fellow was a gifted athlete, and he had demonstrated a great deal of discipline and determination in sports. He applied those same qualities to finding a school that would accept him, and he succeeded.

While in the program, he studied day and night. Early in his graduate studies, one of his professors became his mentor. The professor was impressed with his study habits and creativity — so much so that he hired him as his research assistant. He proved to be a very valuable resource for the professor, and he did well in his course work.

The professor, who had a fine reputation as a researcher and had published many papers, encouraged his assistant to pursue a Ph.D. in business. The professor wrote to several of his many contacts in a variety of Ph.D. programs, endorsing his research assistant's application for admission to their programs. He made it clear that the applicant "would never score big on the GMAT. But he would work hard and be a major asset to anyone for whom he did research."

The student was eventually accepted to a quality Ph.D. program and worked closely with a distinguished professor. During this time he began writing articles, and to this day he is still publishing papers in top journals. Note that the editorial-review boards of these journals never ask for an author's GMAT scores. They don't care that this fellow was twenty-five before he received his undergraduate degree. They look for "breakthroughs, new ideas, unique findings."

I've followed this remarkable young man's achievements over the years. How is it that today he holds a distinguished chair as a research professor? What happened to so many of the other Ph.D. candidates who were in graduate school at the same time that he was a student? Most are professors today. Most scored big, on the GMAT and GRE. But very, very few have achieved what this former advisee has accomplished.

I am particularly interested in the rejection he received in his early college years. He was told by his first-choice college that he was not of graduate school caliber. Yet there were several years when this fellow outpublished every single one of the faculty members at that college.

THE ACID TEST IN THE TESTING SOCIETY

What is the relationship between intelligence, as measured by the so-called intelligence and related tests, and success in life? In a landmark article published more than a quarter century ago, Professor David C. McClelland of Harvard challenged the validity of standardized intelligence tests and related aptitude tests (see David C. McClelland, "Testing for Competence Rather Than for 'Intelligence,' " *American Psychologist*, January 1973, pp. 1-4).

Validity has many definitions, but the acid test of a measure is how well it predicts certain a priori defined behavior. According to McClelland, traditional measures of intelligence do not account for a substantial portion of the variation in achievement and success in life. However, he maintains that intelligence tests and their close relatives, aptitude tests, are highly correlated with grades in school and college. The reason is that these tests are loaded with certain types of questions, problems to be solved, analogies to be made, and readings to be comprehended — the same kind of topics, assignments, and questions given in course assignments and exams.

So here is the logic, or lack of it, that fans of intelligence and aptitude tests propose to us. The tests predict performance in school, and performance in school predicts success in life. Sorry, fans of intelligence testing. Most people involved in research on this subject will agree that results on intelligence tests and grades earned in school are significantly correlated. My own surveys of the affluent confirm this. But do the tests predict anything other than performance in an academic environment?

So what about grades? How valid are they as predictors? Researchers have in fact had great difficulty demonstrating that grades in school are related to any other behaviors of importance — other than doing well on aptitude tests. (McClelland, p. 1)

But the popular myth continues. It just seems so logical. The A students are supposed to succeed big-time. The B students are predicted by definition to do "above average" in life. And those who receive Cs, Ds, and Fs are predicted to do not as well as their classmates who are on the honor roll and dean's list.

What a perfect world it would be if one could predict the variations in success from grades on transcripts. If this were the case, you could say with great certainty to your son or daughter who just graduated with a straight-A average, "Buffy, Skippy, you will do well for your entire lifetimes, the next fifty-five years." But what about your other son or daughter, who just barely made the minimum grades to graduate? You'll have to tell your child, "You will have fifty-five years of just barely making it."

Life is a marathon. How well you do in this

race involves much more than grade point averages, and upsets often occur. Standardized testing cannot be substituted for actually running the race. Otherwise, our government could just redistribute our nation's wealth each year — give it all to those with high IQs. If they're going to end up with it all anyway, why not just speed up the process?

Well, how about giving our youth a chance. Let them play life's game. Don't tell them just before it starts:

The game's over. You lose. You can never win. You won't succeed with those grades, those SATs.

The general public and many psychologists and college officers simply have been unable to believe or accept the fact that high test scores predict only performance in school and don't predict success in other behaviors and outcomes (see McClelland, p. 2). Why is our society so concerned with testing intelligence? We place great emphasis on achievement, and we want to know even beforehand who will achieve tomorrow in the real world of work. We want to give awards to achievers even before they achieve. We are the a priori, the presumptive society.

In spite of this, some students never allow such academically oriented predictions to influence them. A disproportionately large percentage of multimillionaires fit into this category. Those who did well in school and on so-called intelligence tests never assumed for a moment that success was predetermined. What about those multimillionaires who were not A students and who didn't generate high numbers on achievement tests? They never allowed the academic "odds makers" to dictate their performance in life. They recognized that creativity, hard work, discipline, and certain social skills, including leadership, were more significant than grades and aptitude-test results. These are the people who confound their teachers and other fans of aptitude and intelligence testing.

It seems so self-evident to educators that those who do well in their classes must go on to do better in life that they systematically have disregarded evidence to the contrary that has been accumulating for some time. (McClelland, p. 2)

This is not to discount the importance of an education in explaining economic success. According to McClelland, a college degree is a credential that opens doors to higher-paying positions. However, he found that students with lower grade point averages in college eventually did as well economically in life as the top students. The results of my research on millionaires are highly congruent with Professor McClelland's. Grades received in college do not explain a statistically significant portion of the variation in wealth or income, nor do SAT results.

The only noticeable exception were those respondents who attended medical school or law school. They were required to have superior grades in college and high scores on aptitude tests to be admitted to these professional schools. However, most are not in the decamillionaire category today. Usually, they have net worth levels in the $1 million to $5 million range. So who are the decamillionaires in America? They are successful entrepreneurs. Most of these people were not A students, and most were not predicted to become major economic successes based on their test scores.

Another problem related to scoring high on SATs and other standardized tests is that sometimes people allow their performance to dictate their choice of study, and ultimately their choice of vocation. For example, take Dr. R.A., the math whiz. She scored very high on the math portion of the SAT — so well that top technical universities expressed great interest in her. She was offered several scholarships if only she would major in computer science, engineering, or mathematics.

But Dr. R.A. has more than high SATs and analytical intelligence. She also has a lot of creativity and common sense, and she is a people person. She is very gregarious and has many friends. So what if she scored a 5 (top score) on the calculus advanced placement test — should math and engineering be her only choices? Dr. R.A. wants to be around people and study them. Numbers bore her unless they relate to human behavior. So Dr. R.A. majored in psychology. Her main interest is in psychological measurement — she loves the program she recently completed and loves her career.

If Dr. R.A. had listened to the guidance counselor who told her she should major in math, science, or engineering, Dr. R.A. would have been unhappy in those programs. The counselor just looked at her math scores, and didn't give any weight to other factors.

My data clearly show a strong negative correlation between job satisfaction and those "strong" mandates about career choice that come from parents and counselors because of test scores. Follow Dr. R.A.'s lead. Have the strength and the resolve to fight for what you want and need. Do not allow others to tell you what is supposed to make you happy.

If you have a high level of intelligence as predicted by IQ test scores, you have great capacity or potential. But if it's not used in ways that fulfill you psychologically, it's not likely that you will become a total success. Total success usually requires that you enjoy your vocation. Professor Sternberg says it best:

. . . Nevertheless, between 75 percent and 96 percent of the variance in real world criteria such as job performance cannot be accounted for by indi-

vidual differences in intelligence test scores. (Robert J. Sternberg, et al., "Testing Common Sense," *American Psychologist*, November 1995, p. 923)

As for economic success, the logic is simple. If you perform well in your chosen vocation, you are likely to earn more than others, especially if you are self-employed. If you earn more, you have a great chance of accumulating wealth. This is especially true if you have the common sense to save and invest more than you spend.

INVESTING: PUBLIC OR PRIVATE

There is a lot of talk about the stock market successes that many investors have enjoyed lately. Is it the stock market that produces most of the first-generation millionaires in America? If you read the business and investing periodicals lately, you'd probably answer yes. But I have a different view about the creation of wealth, based on the data I've collected from millionaires for more than twenty-five years.

Examine the data presented in Table 2-6. Only about one in eight millionaires (12 percent) indicated that "investing in the equities of public corporations" was a very important factor in explaining their economic success. Three in ten (30 percent) rated this factor as important. Does this mean that most millionaires do not invest in stocks? Not at all — they just tend to be more realistic about the stock market than many other investors. They seem to view it as one of many places to invest their money. A significantly higher percentage of millionaires (35 percent) rated "making wise investments" as a very important factor in explaining their economic success, as opposed to the 12 percent who gave the same rating to "investing in the equities of public corporations."

Millionaires make wise investments. But not all wise investments are listed on the stock exchanges.

Most millionaires will tell you that investing in the stock market is not the only game in town. A significantly larger percentage rate as very important: "investing in my own business" (26 percent); "being my own boss" (29 percent); and "willing to take financial risk given the right return" (29 percent). As expected, most business owners and entrepreneurs are especially sensitive to the importance of investing in their own businesses. Eighty-seven percent of these millionaires rated "investing in my own business" as either very important (50 percent) or important (37 percent). In sharp contrast, only 12 percent of these business owners rate "investing in the equities of public corporations" as very important; 28 percent rated it as important.

Why so much "love" for investing in one's own business, and so little credit given to the stock market? The typical respondent in this survey had an annual realized income in excess of $600,000. Almost all of this income derives from their main vocation as business owners, corporate executives, attorneys, physicians, and so forth. I often quote a multimillionaire I interviewed years ago who summed it all up by saying:

My source (of wealth) . . . my business . . . any [economically] successful man doesn't gamble. . . . I don't gamble. . . . I . . . worked too —— hard for what we got. Once you do that, you're not about to throw it away.

This fellow does not invest in high-risk offerings, and he is realistic about the risks involved in investing in other people's corporations. Most millionaires do invest in quality stocks, but they don't intend to make a fortune by doing so. They don't believe that ups in the stock market, after netting out fees and taxes and downturns, can outpace the returns they get from their own business, or as being a partner in a productive law firm or medical practice. Note that a component of the "one's own business" domain is "living below my means." The self-designated wise investors, risk takers, and those who invest in their own businesses have this in common: they are significantly more likely to "live below their means."

Although frugality and "living below one's means" is not a top factor in explaining eco-

TABLE 2-6

MILLIONAIRES' SUCCESS FACTORS:
vs. "ONE'S
(N=733)

PERCENTAGE OF MILLIONAIRES INDICATING (IMPORTANT) BY

	Business Owner/ Entrepreneur 32%	Senior Corporate Executive 16%
STOCK MARKET INVESTING		
Investing in the Equities of Public Corporations	12(28)	10(36)
Having Excellent Investment Advisers	13(29)	8(32)
"ONE'S OWN BUSINESS"		
Making Wise Investments	41(42)	27(41)
Investing in My Own Business	50(37)	12(20)
Being My Own Boss	45(40)	12(31)
Willing to Take Financial Risk Given the Right Return	42(49)	27(43)
Living Below My Means	14(30)	9(23)

STOCK MARKET INVESTING
OWN BUSINESS"

FACTOR VERY IMPORTANT
OCCUPATIONAL CATEGORIES

Attorney 10%	Physician 9%	Other 33%	All 100%	Rank[1]
11(32)	13(26)	14(30)	12(30)	27[2]
6(22)	20(33)	11(27)	11(28)	29
23(43)	33(48)	35(39)	35(41)	10[2]
15(21)	24(38)	14(23)	26(28)	17
19(40)	46(39)	21(34)	29(36)	13[2]

[1]Rank was computed according to the percentage of millionaires who indicated that the success component was very important in explaining their economic success.
[2]Tied for this position with another factor.

nomic success for the entire population in my survey, the most ardent investors, the financial risk takers, are relatively more frugal than other millionaires surveyed. They know they can invest more if they are frugal and spend less on consumer items.

PREDICTIONS AND SEEDS: PUBLIC VS. PRIVATE

Today's self-made millionaires are street-smart about money and sensing economic opportunities. If they felt that market predictions could be accurately and consistently made over time, many would go out and sell their businesses, cash in their shares in law practices, and put it all in the stock market. This doesn't happen because most millionaires understand what the stock market is and what it is not — it is not something that an individual investor can control or influence. But most millionaires have a lot of control and influence over their own private businesses, their medical practices, and their law firms, and most have a well-diversified set of assets. Rarely do they place all their eggs in one basket.

The stock market is one of many depositories where millionaires invest some of their dollars. But where did these dollars originate? Stock market zealots will answer that the money was earned in the market and reinvested there. If you look at the thousands of advertisements sponsored by investment companies and mutual funds, you certainly get this impression. Rarely, if ever, do they discuss the fundamental source of the wealth. They talk about the excellent return that investors in stocks and stock mutual funds have received over the years, but they rarely tell where the wealth came from.

What do they exclude? A simple point: You cannot invest in the stock market if you don't earn enough money from your primary vocation to pay for more than your food, clothing, and shelter. Almost all millionaires will tell you that the seed of their wealth is their vocation. Very few are professional stock pitchers — they made their money doing other things. But what about people who have more than a few million dollars? Do decamillionaires give more credit to their investments in equities of public corporations than those with lower levels of wealth? Not really. In fact, one in three decamillionaires indicated that "investing in equities of public corporations" was not an important factor in explaining their economic success. Only about one in five millionaires in the $2 million to $5 million range felt the same way. On average, decamillionaires have more of their wealth invested in private or closely held stocks than they do in stocks that are traded publicly. The reverse is true for millionaires with net worths less than $10 million (see Table 2-7).

In a similar vein, decamillionaires are less likely to credit investment advisers as a source of their economic success. Note that the term *investment advisers* in this context refers to those

TABLE 2-7

THE INVESTMENTS OF MILLIONAIRES: PUBLICLY TRADED STOCK VS. OTHER FINANCIAL ASSETS[1]

	Net Worth Category ($ Millions)		
	$1 to under $2	$5 to under $10	$10 and over
Net Worth (Average)	$1.471	$6.809	$27.917

SELECTED FINANCIAL ASSETS[2] AS A PERCENT OF NET WORTH:

Publicly traded stock	16.8	23.6	26.4
Private/closely held stock	8.5	15.8	28.3
Bonds/tax exempt	8.8	12.4	12.4
Cash/equivalents	7.5	4.1	2.3
Loans/receivable	3.2	3.8	3.1
Equity in noncorp. business	2.7	3.8	6.1
Partnerships	1.1	3.1	4.1
Commercial/investment/income-producing real estate	18.1	15.1	11.0
Total	66.7	82.3	93.7
Total Less Publicly Traded Stock	49.9	58.7	67.3
Publicly Traded Stock as % of Financial Assets Listed	25.2	28.7	28.2

[1]Source: Estimates from MRI database and IRS data 1995.
[2]Assets excluded were: equity in personal residence(s); corporate bonds; foreign bonds; net value of life insurance; savings bonds; equity in motor vehicles, collectibles, and personal property.

who sell and provide advice related to publicly traded stock. This is especially true for self-made millionaires. What about those who inherited their wealth? Millionaires who received at least 10 percent of their wealth from inheritance or gifts have a different view.

About one-half of the "inherited wealth" group credited investments in public corporations and investment advisers in accounting for their economic success. But would they have been able to invest if they had no money from inheritance? On the other hand, self-made millionaires are particularly fond of private investments. They know that not all the great executives manage large public corporations — there are many extraordinarily gifted managers within the segment called private business. Attorneys are often offered equity positions in private corporations as partial or full compensation for representing these organizations. Or the principals of a small accounting firm are invited by a client to form a limited partnership.

YOUR OWN BUSINESS

If you were able to earn several million dollars a year in your own private business, what would you do with your time and energy? Like most millionaires, you would probably focus your resources where they would generate the greatest return — your own business. But then how would you feel about the stock market, investing in the equities of public corporations?

Assume that you are a successful attorney earning several million dollars per year. Your job is very demanding, with sixty- to eighty-hour work weeks being very common. But you cannot inventory your services — each case and each client are different. So even if you earned $3 million last year, unless you work harder next year, you will not earn more.

If you cannot inventory your services, you take another approach — you invest your earnings. Some dollars are allocated to stocks, and you hope the current value of your earnings invested this way will at least keep pace with inflation. If you can earn a decent return, that's even better. If your stock portfolio has been cranking out 30 percent gains in the past few years, you might even think about quitting your job as a highly successful attorney and becoming a full-time investment specialist.

There are many reasons why you'll never, ever take this course of action. In your mind, being a full-time investor is not a real business. A real business has clients or customers. Sitting in a room by yourself working at a computer screen will never generate hundreds of loyal clients. It may never make you a more marketable entity in the labor market. And you are well aware that some of the biggest public corporations make the biggest strategic mistakes. You know, because you participated in some successful lawsuits that took countless millions from these mistake makers. If you ever made mistakes like that, you'd be bankrupt. You know that your own business is much more productive than most large corporations. Your firm's sales, as well as its revenue per employee, are just two measures of superior productivity. Besides, you realize that the high returns in recent stock market history are an artifact of an inflated growth market. So you decline the market offer to close your law practice and become a day trader.

Never try to do another man's job.

You control your own destiny when you are a business owner or senior executive or even a self-employed physician or attorney. A multimillionaire summed it up as follows:

> *We feel power and control. We know what we're gonna do. We make decisions. . . . It's a sense of power. You become king within reason.*
>
> *I have a small corporation. . . . I go into the bathroom and we hold a [board of directors] meeting [while shaving].*
>
> *Those that don't agree with me can resign . . . simple . . . very democratic.*

THE ACID TEST FOR INVESTMENT GURUS

Look at it this way. Only 11 percent of the millionaires indicated that "having excellent investment advisers" was a very important factor that accounted for their financial success. In sharp contrast, 35 percent of the millionaires believe that "making wise investments" was a very important factor. That is more than three times as many than those who gave credit to advisers. Why so little credit to "stock advisers"? Although the majority of millionaires have an account with at least one full-service brokerage firm, most make their own investment decisions.

Millionaires ignore or at least "discount" many of the suggestions generated by stockbrokers. In interviews they tell me that stockbrokers are experts at selling, and if they spend most of their time selling, that leaves little time left to study investment opportunities. As one respondent told me, "If the stockbrokers could predict the future, they would never keep on being stockbrokers. They can't [predict]. They make money selling."

But more than just the opinions of millionaires are important here. The acid test is this: Given the same levels of income within the same age group, who accumulates more wealth? Would you guess "stockbrokers"? After all, they are touted to be investment experts.

In a recent survey of affluent people throughout America, 121 stockbrokers completed questionnaires. These respondents reported having annual incomes from the low six figures to well over $1 million. How do they compare with business owners and entrepreneurs, senior corporate executives, attorneys, and physicians who had similar incomes? In my comparison, both income and age were taken into account when making these comparisons.

The older participants are expected to have accumulated more wealth — on average, age is a significant correlate of wealth. Income is also a significant correlate of net worth. For this particular data set, the equation that was used to determine the expected net worth for each respondent is as follows: Expected net worth = age X .112 X income. In other words, Mr. Edison, a business owner who is 50 years of age and has a total annual, realized household income of $340,000 is expected to have a net worth of $1,904,000. Mr. Smythe, who is 45 years of age with an income of $155,000, is expected to be worth $781,200.

What if Mr. Edison actually has a net worth of at least twice the expected value? Then he would be in what I call the Balance Sheet Affluent (BA) category. If, on the other hand, Mr. Smythe had a net worth of one-half the expected value or less, he would be categorized as Income Statement Affluent (IA). This means that Mr. Smythe has a low level of real wealth given his age and income.

The results in Table 2-8 tell an interesting story. Nearly four in five business owners (77.7 percent) had actual net worths that exceeded the expected levels. Only one in three stockbrokers (34.4 percent) had net worths that exceeded expected levels. This means that for every one stockbroker who exceeded the norm, there were 2.3 business owners who exceeded it.

TABLE 2-8

STOCKBROKERS VS. OTHER
OCCUPATIONAL GROUPS:

Economic Performance Measure	Stockbroker (N=121)	Business Owner (N=244)
% Above Expected Net Worth	34.4	77.7
% in Balance Sheet Affluent Category (Wealth Accumulators)	13.6	46.3
% in Income Statement Affluent Category ("Big incomes, Low Net Worths")	27.0	7.0
Ratio: Balance Sheet Affluent (%) to Income Statement Affluent	0.5	6.6

HIGH-INCOME-PRODUCING
WHO HAS MORE WEALTH?

Senior Corporate Executive (N=120)	Attorney (N=93)	Physician (N=78)	Expected Values: All High-Income Producers
80.0	59.1	56.4	50.0
43.3	29.0	21.8	25.0
10.8	22.6	12.8	25.0
4.0	1.3	1.7	1.0

It's even more telling to compare these two high-income-producing groups in terms of the Balance Sheet Affluent (BA) criterion. BAs are those in the top quarter of wealth builders. That is, they are the best at building net worth compared to their income and age groups. In my survey, respondents who had net worths at least twice the expected level are designated Balance Sheet Affluent (BA).

Nearly one-half the business owners (46.3 percent) were Balance Sheet Affluent, while only 13.6 percent of the stockbrokers were in this category. In sharp contrast, 27 percent of the stockbrokers were found to be in the Income Statement category, but only about 7 percent of the business owners were designated as Income Statement Affluent.

Finally, consider the ratio of BAs to IAs for the two groups. For every business owner in the IA group (bottom quarter of net worth) there are 6.6 in the BA group (top quarter). In contrast, for every 2 stockbrokers in the IA group there is only 1 in the BA group.

Could it be that many of those who aggressively sell stocks and related investments don't follow their own recommendations? If they did, one might expect to find more stockbrokers in the BA group. But stockbrokers made up a disproportionately high percentage of those who have big incomes yet relatively small levels of wealth. There are some outstanding stockbrokers who are Balance Sheet Affluent types. They are not only wise about investing, they are also wise about how they spend their hard-earned money.

A CASE STUDY OF A BA VS. AN IA

To illustrate my points, consider the following two cases. Both of these respondents are excellent examples of their respective orientations. One I will call Mr. Ward, the BA. The other is a high-income-producing stockbroker, Mr. Rogers.

Mr. Ward is a business owner with a net worth in the mid-eight-figure range. He owns and manages a very successful recycling business. He lives in a home valued at well over $1 million. He purchased it more than twenty years ago for a bit over $200,000, and there is no outstanding mortgage.

How does Mr. Ward account for his economic success? Factors that he rates as being very important include: "Investing in my own business," "willing to take financial risk given the right return," and "finding a profitable niche." Mr. Ward rates as not important: "investing in the equities of public corporations" and "having excellent investment advisers." Mr. Ward thinks that investing in public corporations is a way to inventory his profits from recycling, but he doesn't view the stock market as the seed of his economic success. He has about 30 percent of his wealth invested in publicly traded stock, and his stock holdings have appreciated, but he feels that the core of his wealth is his private corporation. The stock market is just a place to put profits from that core investment.

Mr. Ward doesn't take advice from stockbrokers, not even Mr. Rogers, who purchased a $2 million home near him three years ago. Unlike Mr. Ward, he has an outstanding mortgage balance in excess of $1 million, and there are other differences. Mr. Ward has a net worth that is five times the expected level given his age and income characteristics, while Mr. Rogers has a net worth that is only 34 percent of what is expected, given his age and income parameters. Yet Mr. Rogers has convinced himself that he is wealthy. In his mind, one factor stands out from all the rest as being very important.

Having the ability to sell my ideas, products, and the like.

At the same time, Mr. Rogers discounts the importance of what he sells in accounting for his economic success. He claims to sell advice as well as stocks. But guess what factors he did not rate as important in explaining his economic success:

1. Investing in the equities of public corporations.
2. Having excellent financial advisers.

Could it be that Mr. Rogers believes wealth is a function of selling more than investing? That appears to be the case.

Whom would you like to provide you with investment advice and products? You'd be better off searching for an investment adviser who is a solid member of the BA crowd. They tend to practice what they preach. I don't deal with financial advisers, physicians, attorneys, or any other professional who is income-statement oriented, and I've had to fire a few of them over the years. Their objective is to maximize their income, often to pay for a high-consumption, highly leveraged lifestyle. They normally have substantial debts, and I personally believe that many cannot provide superior service when bankruptcy is a potential threat.

Precious treasure remains in a wise man's dwelling; but a foolish man devours it.
— Proverbs 21:20

DISCIPLINE OR LUCK?

Webster's defines *discipline* as "training that corrects, molds, or perfects the mental faculties or moral character." In turn, one who possesses discipline is marked by perfection of mental faculties and moral character. The moral character relates to integrity, for part of being disciplined means perfecting behaviors in productive and moral ways.

Most millionaires are well disciplined. They set their own high goals and then go on to reach these standards. More often than not, they don't have others telling them what must be done. In fact, one of the hallmarks of discipline is one's ability to become economically successful without being given a road map. Millionaires make their own road maps, and no one tells them what time to wake up or go to work.

Once at work they determine their own priorities, work schedule, and tasks. The discipline to manage their own lives well makes them different from so many others who could never survive if they didn't have someone telling them when, how, what, why, and where to do things.

Millionaires, by definition, are accumulators of wealth. Not so for most people in America — they spend all or most of their income. As a result, nearly three in ten American households have a negative net worth. Most millionaires started at economic ground zero, and fully 60 percent never received a single dollar of inheritance. Only about one in ten inherited more than 10 percent of their wealth. Most millionaires did it the traditional way — on their own.

Their success was usually due to discipline and had little to do with luck or happenstance. Note the results given in Table 2-9. Only 12 percent of the millionaires surveyed indicated that "being lucky" was a very important factor in explaining their economic success. Contrast this with the percentage of millionaires who attribute their success to "being well disciplined" (57 percent rated it very important) and "working harder than most people" (47 percent cited this factor as very important). Countless millionaires have told me they are lucky to live and work in America. And it's lucky that there is enough rain for millionaire farmers to grow millions of dollars worth of crops. Yes, luck does play some role, but most economic success derives from proactive behavior.

One of my closest friends once told me that I was lucky to have a book on the *New York Times* best-seller list. "It's all genetics," he said. I told him that he needed to analyze the relationship between making the 1.5 million symbols (letters of the alphabet) required to write the book with my Papermate medium-point blue pen and being lucky. Or as countless self-made millionaires have told me:

The harder I work, the luckier I become.

A detailed discussion of the role of luck in becoming wealthy is given in chapter 4, "The Relationship Between Courage and Wealth." A disciplined person sets his or her sights on a lofty target, then figures out productive ways to reach the target. Disciplined people are not easily sidetracked — they could live in a warehouse filled with top-brand alcoholic beverages and not indulge themselves. They could live in a French bakery and not gain weight. Or they could encounter hundreds of economic opportunities and then select the one or two that are best suited to their strengths and the market's needs.

It's particularly interesting to note how most

TABLE 2-9

MILLIONAIRES' SUCCESS FACTORS:
OF
(N=733)

PERCENTAGE OF MILLIONAIRES INDICATING
BY OCCUPATIONAL

	Business Owner/ Entrepreneur 32%	Senior Corporate Executive 16%
HAPPENSTANCE		
Being Lucky	17(35)	12(43)
THE ELEMENTS OF DISCIPLINE		
Being Well Disciplined	54(39)	57(37)
Being Very Well Organized	36(48)	32(48)
Working Harder Than Most People	49(40)	42(46)

HAPPENSTANCE VS. THE ELEMENTS DISCIPLINE

FACTOR VERY IMPORTANT (IMPORTANT) CATEGORIES

Attorney 10%	Physician 9%	Other 33%	All 100%	Rank[1]
7(34)	4(35)	11(32)	12(35)	27[2]
63(35)	73(24)	54(42)	57(38)	1[2]
42(42)	50(40)	32(54)	36(49)	9
49(39)	61(35)	44(43)	47(41)	5

[1]Rank was computed according to the percentage of millionaires who indicated that the success component was very important in explaining their economic success.
[2]Tied for this position with another factor.

of the millionaire physicians feel about luck. Only 4 percent felt it was very important in accounting for their economic success, yet 73 percent indicated that discipline was very important. Most of these people had a desire to become physicians before they even entered high school — they had the goal and never lost sight of it. Besides, what does luck have to do with graduating from medical school? What does luck have to do with successfully running a medical practice? Very little, according to these physicians.

It is hard to overemphasize the importance of discipline in accounting for variations in economic success. But let me say that if you lack discipline, the chances of your ever accumulating wealth are very, very small. Yes, you can win the lotto. But in most cases, you have a better chance of contracting leprosy!

At a dinner party in Sugar Bush, Vermont, my friend John introduced me to the head radiologist at a major hospital. Later he told me something interesting about the radiologist — he was once a high school dropout! When I wondered how a high school dropout had become a radiologist, John said, "He got disciplined by his experience in the army. He was just seventeen when he . . . spent a night in a bomb crater at the Battle of the Bulge."

All night long this fellow thought the very next shell fired would kill him, and all night long he cursed himself for dropping out of high school.

He figured that if he'd been better disciplined, he wouldn't be in this near-death situation. That night he made a promise to himself. "If I get out of here alive, I'll become a doctor some day."

The difference in this fellow before and after the night he spent with death all around him was the same except for one factor — he now was committed to becoming disciplined. And he became one of the most disciplined individuals who ever completed medical studies.

A person with self-discipline possesses an internal compass, a control and navigational system. Self-discipline means that you make course changes or corrections only when they will be productive in reaching your goals.

Kenneth Tuchman, founder of TeleTech, defined his own form of discipline in a recent interview.

> *I'm a finisher in a society of starters. . . . I have this vision that is constantly evolving in my head.* (Adrienne Sanders, "Success Secrets of the Successful," *Forbes*, November 2, 1998, p. 24)

Even if you are lucky, there are no guarantees. At the age of thirty you hit the lotto for $5 million, but — will you still be a millionaire by the time you're sixty-five? It takes more than luck just to keep even.

I have asked many people who have been fortunate enough to inherit millions of dollars.

Those who have enhanced these fortunes will tell you: "It ain't luck." At the very least they hired highly qualified trust or asset managers to help them, but they also did a lot of work in allocating their investable dollars.

What is discipline? To one multimillionaire from Nevada it's all about understanding that "leasing a Mercedes doesn't make you rich. [The target is to] . . . keep thinking net worth!!!" Discipline also means standing by your spouse through thick and thin. It means counting your blessings each day, for having that great spouse and related gifts. It's paying homage to your spouse every day, just like a decamillionaire construction contractor from Georgia does by saying, "[My wife is] . . . tolerant, rational, self-reliant, even-tempered. . . . I am thankful."

It is also finding a source for becoming disciplined when you know you are lacking. I once asked a multimillionaire from Nashville about the sources of his productivity and his strong work ethic. He wrote the word *military* seven times.

To become wealthy one must be disciplined in thought and deed, disciplined enough to search for great economic opportunities.

3

School Days

How would you define the geniuses who have worked for you? They know more and more about less and less.
— John Parks, millionaire and C student

If you ask the average American what it takes to become a millionaire, he'd probably cite a number of predictable factors: inheritance, luck, stock market investments, and so on. Topping his list would be a high IQ, high SAT scores and grade point average in school, along with attendance at a top college or university. It may be difficult to dislodge this cherished myth from our thinking, but my survey of self-made millionaires disproves it, as you will read in this chapter. The statistics demonstrate that a minority of millionaires whom I surveyed achieved high test scores or grades or went to top schools. These factors were probably useful to a small percentage of the millionaires, but most attained their high levels of economic productivity without those "assets."

Somehow, the publishing industry discovered that I was writing another book. Its trade journal, *Publishers Weekly*, reported that:

Stanley . . . is working on his next book, The Millionaire Mind. *. . . He hasn't yet signed a publishing contract for it. . . .* (Daisy Maryles, "No Shotgun Approach for This Millionaire," *Publishers Weekly,* September 1, 1997)

This article generated considerable interest. But one caller, a senior editor at a major publishing house, did more than express interest in *The Millionaire Mind.* He asked if I could give him a short verbal summary of the work, and I did. He was particularly interested in the following:

Most of the millionaires I have interviewed do not have a superiority complex. On the contrary, they are more likely to have one or more components of inferiority in their self-image. When I ask the typical self-made millionaire to tell his life's story, he says:

"I was a C student in college."

"My college boards (SAT scores) were nothing spectacular."

"I am only *worth $10 million."*

"I received a D in psychology."

"My story is not something you would be interested in reporting."

148

"I have a learning (reading) disability."
"I flunked out of Wake Forest."
"I was held back in the sixth grade."
"I only have a high school equivalency diploma."
"Not one law school accepted me."

What do these self-deprecating millionaires have in common? During their formative years, some authority figure such as a teacher, parent, guidance counselor, employer, or aptitude-testing organization told them: *You are not intellectually gifted.*

The editor expressed considerable interest in the work and suggested that I read a book which has been very insightful to my research. In the preface to his book *Successful Intelligence*, Robert J. Sternberg, again, one of the most respected authorities on human intelligence, states:

I'm a full professor with an endowed chair at Yale. I've won many awards, published over six hundred articles and books, and been awarded about $10 million in research grants and contracts. I am a Fellow of the American Academy of Arts and Sciences and am listed in Who's Who in America. *. . . . Odd then, that my greatest luck in life may well have been a failure. I bombed IQ tests when I was a kid. Why was that so lucky? Because I learned in elementary school that if I was going to succeed, it wasn't going to be because of my IQ. And . . . just as low scores on tests of inert intelligence don't pre-*

149

clude success, neither do high scores guarantee it.
(Robert J. Sternberg, *Successful Intelligence*
[New York: Simon & Schuster, 1996], p. 12)

What does Professor Sternberg have in common with most of the millionaires I have studied? They were degraded by someone or something during their formative years and school days. Both responded by outworking and eventually outperforming the so-called intellectually gifted. Sternberg also demonstrated considerable ingenuity by developing measures of various types of intelligence. Professor Sternberg dedicates his book to his fourth-grade teacher. Apparently, Mrs. Alexa did not pay much attention to IQ scores. As his mentor, she demanded that he become an A student, and he has been ever since. Professor Sternberg earned a BA degree, summa cum laude, from Yale and a Ph.D. from Stanford.

In the middle of writing this chapter, I took time out with my daughter, Sarah, to hear him speak at the University of Georgia. The program began at 3:30 P.M. on a lovely spring Friday. Normally, few students or graduate students attend lectures late on Friday afternoons. But this one was different — there was standing room only. No one was disappointed in Professor Sternberg's program. He is not only a fine writer, he is an excellent speaker. He points out that most successful people have great affection for their own selected vocation, as he does. But

150

he is obviously creative as well, because he has published more than six hundred articles. Professor Sternberg has enough unique ideas for ten Ph.D.'s to be granted tenure at most colleges.

Walking back to the car after the lecture, my daughter and I had a conversation. My advice to Sarah is echoed by the millionaires who responded to my survey:

> Read Sternberg's Successful Intelligence. *Use it as a template for achieving your goals. Remember what he says. If you love your job and the topics you will write about, you're very likely to succeed. But you must work hard and use your creative and analytical intellect. Do you know how he has published more than six hundred publications? He* wrote *six hundred articles. Think a lot about your choice of topics, work hard, do much research, write often. If you do, you will succeed.*
>
> *No matter how gifted you are analytically, you will not become successful unless you publish. And to publish, you must work hard at writing about creative and innovative ideas.*

People who give advice to young people about careers should all be required to read Sternberg's work. Success has many parents, and no single dimension or component fully explains it — not by a long shot. Young people can succeed if they capitalize on their strengths, and Sternberg has many great ideas about how people can enhance their probabilities of succeeding. His own story is a perfect demonstration of one of the important insights revealed about the millionaire mind in my survey: Most of the millionaires were not considered to be "intellectually gifted," as determined by standard test measurements or school grades.

THE SMARTEST KID IN THE DUMB ROW

When Mr. James X. Patrick was in the third grade, a memorable thing happened to him. His teacher, Sister Eileen, a.k.a. "The Punisher," divided the class of thirty students into three groups.

Members of the first group were placed in rows one and two. Sister Eileen designated these students as the "smart kids." The second group filled up seats in rows three and four. This group contained the "average kids." Rows five and six were reserved for children the Sister referred to as "slow" or "dumb."

How did Sister Eileen assign students to these groups? According to Mr. Patrick, she used the following criteria: penmanship, spelling, and turning in completed homework assignments on time. Are these the proper criteria to judge one's intellect? Not according to Mr. Patrick! He says: "If her criteria were correct, I must have been the smartest kid in the dumb row!"

Perhaps he is correct. Today, he has a Ph.D. degree (with distinction) from a top university. He is a multimillionaire who owns and operates three businesses. He claims that he still cannot spell and that no one but his secretary "on a good day" can read his handwriting. He is, however, diligent about getting his homework assignments completed on schedule!

According to Mr. Patrick, teachers in elementary school are insensitive to the criterion called creativity. He asks: "Can you imagine Sister Eileen's reaction when I suggested adding a new letter on to the alphabet?" Mr. Patrick is creative, and has founded several innovative businesses during his career. He asks: "What if all the potential inventors in America were preselected in the third grade by people like Sister Eileen?"

All those smart kids in row one with great spelling skills and fine handwriting would be expected to create tomorrow's great innovations and inventions. Thank goodness that formal preselections of this type are rare. But Mr. Patrick wonders about what happened to all his fellow members in the dumb row.

Did these people believe that they were dumb? Did they give up early on any idea of achieving success in our economy? Mr. Patrick thinks that many do give up. He feels that his case story is the exceptional one.

All my life people have told me you can't . . . you don't have the aptitude. The odds are stacked heavily against you succeeding in your own enterprise. Believe Sister Eileen. If I did I'd be col-

lecting tolls out there on the bridge . . . or driving a
truck and paying tolls.

Mr. Patrick never believed Sister Eileen's evaluation of him. In fact, even as a young boy, he questioned her authority. He always asked himself while sitting in class:

How can penmanship and spelling be so important, and the quality of ideas in a paper be totally unimportant? Then in the sixth grade I remember book reports . . . all they were, really, were summaries of other people's ideas. But Sister Eileen and her clan just loved to assign book reports. These people were probably incapable of judging or dealing with original thought.

Mr. Patrick is not alone; most self-made millionaires who are successful business owners had their own experiences with the Sister Eileens of America.

Questioning the norm, the status quo, and authority are hallmarks of the thinking of self-made millionaires and those destined to become affluent. Skills in writing (without original ideas), spelling, or penmanship are not likely to make one rich. But people with these skills are given seats in the smart row.

Mr. Patrick was and still is criticized and downgraded today. But even as a youngster, he learned to question people who sat in judgment of him. In reality he became immunized to what

154

fellow "dummies" took to heart. Others in the dumb row were defeated by Sister Eileen's judgment of their intellect, but not Mr. Patrick. He was inoculated. Sister Eileen's judgments were like small doses of antibodies.

When he had a bad evaluation at school, he would go home and build a model airplane or make a new design with his Erector set. His parents responded to his finished products by telling him: "You are mechanically inclined . . . are very creative."

And later, in high school and college, it was Mr. Patrick, the D or C student in English and foreign languages, who received As and Bs in his major. He always felt that the A English students had few really novel ideas. Also, in his estimation they lacked any aptitude in math and science. He constantly told himself that these people would be humbled someday by the harsh realities of the world outside the classroom. In the real world, who succeeds? People who have built up immunity to pain. For Mr. Patrick, his immunization started with Sister Eileen's dumb-row designation.

What about Mr. Patrick's classmates who were always placed in the smart row? How do they handle a negative employee review or having their jobs eliminated? They've never before had to deal with authority figures who place them in the "dumb" row. Who is better able to deflect criticisms of their innovative ideas, behavior, and thinking? Mr. Patrick and his type — the ones who have a track record of telling critics to "jump in the lake" and who are motivated by people who downgrade their innovative thinking.

I have to wonder how many thousands of Mr. Patricks were inspired by a recent newspaper article on this topic, and I would be especially interested in learning how many underlined a key paragraph.

Children who are better at mathematics, design or music than reading and writing may tune out early lessons . . . children whose good verbal skills earn them diplomas from prestigious schools sometimes turn into adults who speak beautifully but have nothing to say. . . . (Cynthia Crossen, "Mind Field: Think You're Smart? Then Just Try to Sell a New Kind of IQ Test," *Wall Street Journal,* June 5, 1997, p. 12A)

What about those who didn't accept Sister Eileen's intellectual segmentation model — why did they refuse to accept the label of inferiority? Some found an enlightened mentor. Others had parents who encouraged them, motivated them to succeed. Many millionaires have plain old-fashioned tenacity. They think of the Sister Eileens of the world merely as inferior opponents. Mr. Patrick was tickled that he proved his opponent wrong — for several years after he became a multimillionaire he carried in his wallet a short version of his financial statement.

On top were the words: Smartest kid in the dumb row.

WHAT REALLY COUNTS:
TENACITY AND LEADERSHIP ABILITY

If our traditional measurements of an individual's potential for success, high test scores and grade point average in school, are not reliable predictors of who has the millionaire mind, what are the factors that count? Millionaires possess two essential attributes: tenacity and leadership ability.

SPEAKING OF TENACITY

Dave Longaberger recently passed away. His long career as a successful business owner could not have been predicted by some of his grade school teachers. It seems that Mr. Longaberger was held back three times in elementary school. He was twenty-one before he finally graduated from high school. His poor performance in school was partially due to the fact that he had epilepsy and a significant stuttering problem (see Robert McG. Thomas Jr., "David Longaberger, Basket Maker, Dies at 64," *New York Times*, March 22, 1999, p. A18).

It doesn't seem possible that a fellow who was left back three times in school could eventually become a multimillionaire. How many of the seven thousand people he employed were left back even once in grade school? How many would want to work for a guy who didn't graduate from high school until he was twenty-one? But, realistically, I doubt that anyone of the seven thousand cared about class rank. They wanted to work for a man on whom they could depend. Who cares if the fellow paying your salary was not numero uno in school?

What qualities and experiences do millionaires who were academic underachievers have in common? Most often they started working early in their lives. While their self-esteem may have been tarnished at school, it was often enhanced by working part-time. Mr. Longaberger got his first job at the age of six working at a store as a stock clerk. But he and most of his fellow self-made millionaires developed and then:

Demonstrated a certain tenacity.

One has to be tenacious to overcome stuttering, epilepsy, and being held back repeatedly. He also had parents who motivated and inspired him to overcome his shortcomings. Enlightened parents tell all their children, "You can achieve if you work hard." Hard work is a better predictor of success than grade school experiences. How many of Mr. Longaberger's customers, who last year purchased more than $700 million of his product, were influenced by his performance in grade school?

I'LL NEVER BUY A CHRYSLER PRODUCT

Why is it? You say that you just cannot even think of purchasing a motor vehicle made by Chrysler. And you have every justification for your attitude. Perhaps we have little faith in a corporation that allowed an academic under-achiever to become its leader. Yes, Robert A. Lutz, former president and vice chairman of Chrysler Corporation, was twenty-two years of age when he finally graduated from high school. Seven years later he graduated from college with a bachelor's degree (Robert A. Lutz, *Guts* [New York: John Wiley & Sons, 1998], pp. 4, 13). So forget about it! You don't care that Chrysler makes great products — you only buy cars from companies headed by Phi Beta Kappa members.

Many of our millionaires, like Mr. Lutz, are not beaten down by this early lack of academic achievement. Like most, his strength had something to do with his relationship with one or both of his parents. I'll bet he had a kind and supportive father — perhaps that's why he dedicated his fine book to his dad. Are you like Mr. Lutz's dad? Or would you give up encouraging, mentoring, and supporting your son or daughter if he or she were still in high school at the age of twenty-one? I hope not.

Like most millionaires, Mr. Lutz had some great mentors. And the U.S. Marines taught him something about discipline, leadership, and integrity. He later went on and received an MBA. When he was president at Chrysler, many of his subordinates probably had outstanding records in high school and were accepted to many colleges. But these same honor graduates were now working for Mr. Lutz.

It's difficult to predict success using academic measures. In the best tradition of the American economy, Mr. Lutz was made president because he was best at that position. He rose over others because he was a leader of people. No matter that those people were considered intellectually gifted or not, they were inspired by a leader. A leader knows how to maximize the productivity of people and other resources, and Lutz proved this ability time and time again.

Obviously, Mr. Lutz never believed that his underachievements in high school were precursors of his entire future, or he would never have had the *guts* to run Chrysler. Nor would he have had the *guts* to tell his readers that he finally graduated from high school at twenty-two.

In any other society Mr. Lutz might have sealed his fate with his academic performance in high school. But what is considered to be an irreversible trait in China, Japan, England, India, and other countries is reversible in America. We are a nation of "comeback kids." Some just take a bit longer to finish the course that will enhance their economic productivity.

Early failures, dismal classroom performances, disastrous academic records, and dreadful SATs will defeat those who allow these academic measurements to dishearten their souls. But if one keeps working toward lofty goals, one can and will succeed in America. Luck has nothing to do with it. You are only lucky that you live in America, especially if you plan on being a comeback kid.

ALL AS ALL LEADERS?

If we just decide to follow the cultural stereotype, we would automatically assign all senior leadership roles to those who:

- Were straight-A students in grades pre-K through 12
- Were straight-A students in college
- Scored a perfect 1600 on the SAT.

All the rest of us could just go to work for these leaders. But being perfect in school does not translate into becoming a high-performance leader, because analytical intelligence is not a strong correlate of leadership ability. In a well-documented review of extensive research on this relationship, Fred Fiedler and Thomas Link concluded:

> *Cognitive ability tests have been notoriously poor predictors of leadership performance. . . .*
>
> *Relations between intelligence and leadership and managerial performance . . . accounting for less than 10 percent of the variance. . . .*
>
> *Even these low correlations are likely to be overestimates of the true relationship. . . . Leader intelli-*

gence under certain conditions correlates negatively with performance. (Fred E. Fiedler and Thomas G. Link, "Leader Intelligence, Interpersonal Stress and Task Performance," in R. J. Steinberg and R. K. Wagner, eds., *Mind in Contest: Interactionist Perspectives on Human Intelligence* [New York: Cambridge University Press, 1994], p. 152)

Unfortunately, counselors rarely tell students that 90 percent of the variation in leadership performance is *not* explained by standardized intelligence measures. How many kids gave up on themselves early in the game of life because they did poorly in school or ranked low on the SAT totem pole? Perhaps they should be told, "You still have a chance. You may have to work harder, but you may also have the ability to lead other people." It is the hope that they can succeed that motivates people to do so. Take away hope and what's left is one more economic dropout or a marginally productive person.

If you have both leadership qualities and tenacity you may eventually outpace all the whiz kids in your class. That is exactly what many millionaire respondents have actually accomplished.

WHAT MILLIONAIRES REALLY LEARNED IN SCHOOL AND COLLEGE

Many parents with children in high school contact me about academic issues. They may be very dedicated to their kids, but they often worry themselves and the children to the point of panic.

One woman was considering legal action against a school because her child was not selected for the so-called TAG program, that is, Talented and Gifted. She felt strongly that her son was both talented and gifted. Only about one in five students qualified for TAG, and admission was based, in part, on standardized test scores. Other factors included grades received in core courses taken in middle school.

Mom was having bad visions. She worried about the stigma of being a member of OTTAG, Other Than Talented and Gifted. Let's see, in a sophomore class of 433 students, 20 percent are in TAG and 80 percent, or approximately 346 students, are OTTAGs. Just because this woman's youngster was labeled an OTTAG doesn't mean that he won't grow into a highly productive adult. I worry that if we label an impressionable youngster this way, he may never live up to his potential. He may believe that he has no talents or gifts, and he may assume that only the gifted will succeed in life.

Labels often have a way of activating behaviors that are congruent with the designations. In this case, Mom strongly believed that her son's future rested upon a label, but that would only be true if she believed it so. And if she believes that her son will grow up to be a failure, he may pick up the message and act accordingly.

But life is not one short race — it is a marathon of marathons. Labels come and go. If you believe that you can succeed in life in spite of degrading labels that predict your failure, you are likely to win most of the marathon. This is the common experience among millionaires. The large majority report that at some point or points in their lives they were labeled inferior, average, or mediocre, but they did not allow critics to forecast their future achievements, and they overcame their label of so-called inferiority. This is the message I gave to Mom.

I also told her something else. The process of overcoming labels like OTTAG makes the recipients stronger. It is like adding titanium to steel — it makes steel many times stronger than it is alone. Only a minority of America's top business leaders, attorneys, and physicians report they were never once labeled as being inferior or even worse. Not everyone can become the valedictorian of his or her class. All the others still have many years and countless opportunities for achievement. Mothers and fathers who consistently tell their children they can succeed are likely to produce offspring who are productive adults.

So this woman is better off changing her beliefs. She can save the money she earmarked for legal fees and use it to hire a tutor for her son. Tell him that he can and will achieve if he works at it. It is unconscionable to write off the future of a sixteen-year-old student because of a label.

I asked millionaires about their high school and college experiences. Did all of them graduate in the top 1 percent of their college classes? Hardly. About 2 percent of the millionaires surveyed indicated being in the top 1 percent. It isn't usually the very top graduates who become economically successful, but it isn't those who graduate at ground zero either.

Millionaires also report that they were not A students in college. In fact, only about three in ten reported receiving a greater percentage of As than either Bs, Cs, Ds, or Fs. About 90 percent graduated from college. Overall, their GPA was 2.9 — good but not outstanding.

Almost all of the millionaires stated that their school and college experiences somehow influenced them in becoming productive adults in later life (see Table 3-1). But some experiences were more important than others, much more important than grades and labels. For the large majority, "developing a strong work ethic" was an influence. Nearly all of the millionaires rated this experience as influencing them to become economically productive adults.

When millionaires evaluated the work-ethic issue, they were not just referring to studying and attending classes. Many had part-time jobs while attending school, and many also spent considerable time learning how to make accurate judgments about people. This learning process was enhanced through the many social interactions and activities they participated in on and off campus.

Some might consider such socializing to be unproductive in an academic setting, but it seems to be a key factor that separates those who become skilled at judging other people and those who can not. There is a rather clear negative correlation between high grades earned in college and the millionaire's self-reported high ability to make accurate judgments about people. So it may be true that all work makes John a dull boy, and it also has something to do with John's inability to read other people accurately.

The most economically successful people discussed in this book do many things well. Others may be analytical geniuses, but they come up short on people skills, or vice versa. If you aim to achieve wealth, it's best to learn multiple skills and qualities. Work hard, socialize, enjoy people.

Consider the school and college experiences listed in Table 3-1 that many millionaires believe were important foundation stones of their successes. It is more than studying a specific course in school or college, or high grades, rank, and SATs. The really big influences have generic labels such as: strong work ethic, effective time or resource allocation, judgment, tenacity, and empathy.

TABLE 3-1

ENHANCING SELF-DISCIPLINE AND DISCERNMENT: SCHOOL AND COLLEGE EXPERIENCES THAT INFLUENCED MILLIONAIRES IN BECOMING ECONOMICALLY PRODUCTIVE ADULTS

Result of School or College Experience	% Millionaires Influenced[1] (Not) by Experience (N=733)
SELF-DISCIPLINE	
Developing a strong work ethic	94(2)
Learning how to properly allocate time	91(1)
Working at part-time jobs while in school	55(21)
Receiving an academic scholarship to college	20(60)
DISCERNMENT	
Learning how to make accurate judgments about people	88(3)
Developing an appreciation for your interests/abilities	86(3)
Learning to think differently from the crowd	76(6)

[1]"Influenced" means that respondent indicated that experience had either a high or moderate degree of influence. Excluded were those responses in the "low degree of influence" category.

167

SURMOUNTING OBSTACLES
AND FORGING ARMOR

Did our millionaires attain this status in spite of some obstacle or perceived handicap, or because they had the experience of compensating for their deficiencies? I have discovered that most self-made millionaires were confronted with one or more significant obstacles in their life. Without overcoming these potentially devastating roadblocks, they would not have become economically productive. It was the struggle, the hard journey, that gave them the foundation for becoming successful.

It's unfortunate that most nonmillionaires accept the negative evaluations given them by authority figures. Most people who "bomb" the third-grade IQ test, the SAT, and other measurements accept their fate. They capitulate even before they reach voting age. To them, inferior grades and other low scores automatically translate into a lifetime of low economic productivity. Our self-made millionaires choose another path — they discredit the authority figures who attempt to degrade them, often repeatedly during their lifetime. They had the insight, courage, and audacity to challenge the assessments made by teachers, professors, amateur critics, and the Educational Testing Service.

Self-made millionaires seem to have an interesting immune system. I'm not talking about their ability to fight off infectious diseases — I'm referring to their mental strength. They have an acquired ability to deflect even the harshest evaluations by some of the nastiest critics. This mental armor plate was initially forged during their salad days. Over time, their inoculation system grows in strength. Why? Because even in their later years, these millionaires constantly counter negative evaluations by various critics and authority figures.

Even steel cannot be hardened unless it's hammered, and it's no different with people. Self-made millionaires report that degrading evaluations and comments by certain authority figures played a role in their ultimate success in life. Hammering built the antibodies they needed to deflect criticisms and temper their resolve.

FORGING RESOLVE

How did people who are successful today acquire their armor plate during their formative years? Preliminary evidence suggests that one's ability to overcome downgrading comes from several sources. Most first-generation millionaires are the products of loving, caring, and well-adjusted parents who were rarely in divorce court. Most marriages lasted the full term. Contrary to what the popular press believes, most self-made millionaires did not grow up in a pressure-cooker home environment. Thus, the children who became economically successful adults were never told by their parents:

- With these grades (in high school), you will never amount to anything.
- If you don't get high grades in school, you will turn out to be a loser.
- With SAT scores like these, your only shot is to go to a community junior college.

Parents of economically successful people are much more positive. The parents' support and constructive suggestions provided a foundation for their children's armor plate, and these parents never built psychological barriers to future success in their children's minds. Their fathers did not abuse them, and their parents did not constantly pressure them to excel, excel, excel through negative cues. When today's self-made millionaire brought home a bad report card many years ago, their parents typically said:

- You can do better.
- Figure out a plan to get you back on track.
- I'll work some problems with you.
- I know of a great tutor who will help you master these topics.
- I always had problems with this topic, but you just have to work through it.
- It took a mathematical genius a lifetime to invent calculus. So don't be discouraged if you are not on top of it overnight.

And then the long lecture:

So what if your classmate Brian has all As and will be the valedictorian. He studies day and night. He has zero friends and no extracurricular activities. I'll hire you, Todd, not Brian. You're a good B student, president of your class, and a varsity athlete. You're well-rounded; that's why you will succeed. I'll bet Brian will be working for someone like you one day! Don't let your class rank dictate what you can do with the next fifty years of your life. If your teachers and guidance counselors were that great at predicting the future, they would all be millionaire stock pickers on Wall Street or top-ranked bookmakers in Las Vegas.

What did Todd gain from this message from an authority figure? Armor plate! Todd has learned how to deflect and protect himself from those who will attempt to degrade his future level of productivity. Who is more likely to become an economic success in the future? Is your guess Brian, the straight-A student who was voted the "most intellectually gifted"? Not according to my studies of self-made millionaires. Brian has never developed the armor plate needed to succeed in the world of commerce.

In the commercial world, one can work day and night for years and still go bankrupt the next year. In the commercial world, you can write the most brilliant business plan as part of a loan application and still be turned down for a commercial loan. Yes, turned down by a dozen bank officers at a dozen banks. Bank lending officers, as one millionaire defined them, are a convention of Dr. Nos!

Who would be more likely to deflect the negative evaluations of twelve lending officers and have the audacity to keep asking until the loan was approved? I will bet on the Todds of America. In the process of interviewing thousands of self-made millionaires, I have found that their pet ideas have all been turned down at one time or another. Many have been turned down dozens of times. They just move on to the next lending establishment. They have been conditioned from childhood to discount the critics who say that their plan for the future won't work. For them, it's merely a matter of time and some effort to find an enlightened lender.

When I ask self-made millionaires whether they have recently attended a high school reunion and what their most notable impressions were, the answer is usually: The smartest kids, the stars from my high school class, don't seem to be doing so well today!

Most millionaires will tell you they feel a bit uncomfortable at these reunions because of the incongruities. In the vast majority of cases, the students designated "Most Likely to Succeed," the intellectually gifted, the ones the teachers bet on to be most successful are no longer in the front of the pack. Who is in the lead? Not the Brians but the Todds.

SENIOR SUPERLATIVES? THINK AGAIN

Webster's defines *superlative* as being "supreme . . . surpassing all others." High school faculty and students are often asked to vote in the academic beauty pageant called "Senior Superlatives." Who is the most likely to succeed? Who is the most talented? Who is the most intellectually gifted? In more than twenty years of studying millionaires, I have found that few were ever designated "most likely to succeed," "most talented," or other superlatives during their school years.

In my research, I have asked self-made millionaires to respond to questions about "senior superlatives." They were asked:

During your high school years, how do you think your teachers in general judged or evaluated you?

Very few of the respondents indicated that their teachers would be "very likely" to judge them as being "most likely to succeed" (see Table 3-2). Nor were they likely to be evaluated as "most intellectually gifted" or having the "highest level of intelligence." Even more interesting is the fact that they consistently report that their teachers never even considered them for such designations. In other words, they were not perceived as being near the top in any of a variety of superlative designations.

It seems that school-related evaluations are poor predictors of future economic success.

173

TABLE 3-2

MILLIONAIRE, HOW DO YOU THINK YOUR HIGH SCHOOL TEACHERS JUDGED OR EVALUATED YOU?

Evaluation a.k.a. "Superlatives"	% Millionaires Indicating Judgment Very Likely (N=733)
Most Dependable	28
Most Likely to Succeed	20
Most Conscientious	17
Most Industrious	16
Most Logical	15
Hardest Worker	14
Highest Level of Intelligence	12
Most Ambitious	12
Most Intellectually Gifted	11
Highest Grade Point Average	10
Most Popular	9

Could it be possible that lack of early recognition motivates some to excel economically? Is it in spite of, or because of, receiving no "senior superlative" awards that some students achieve economic success? How is it possible that they outperform their classmates designated as "most likely to succeed"?

According to my respondents, there are two problems associated with using "senior superlatives" as predictors of future productivity. First, teachers are not very good at making predictions of future economic productivity because they are not economically productive themselves. Thus, these wealthy respondents discounted the evaluations they received from teachers. Second, teachers often use the wrong criteria to make these predictions. Students who excel scholastically and are given related awards receive no guarantees that they will excel later in life.

Interestingly, three school and college-related experiences often motivated the millionaires to succeed financially. These factors come under the general heading of tenacity (see Table 3-3). Most importantly, millionaires developed a clear understanding about productivity. While they were still in their formative years, they discovered that:

Hard work is more important than genetic high intellect in achieving success.

Compare the percentage of millionaires who

TABLE 3-3

FORGING TENACITY: SCHOOL AND COLLEGE EXPERIENCES THAT INFLUENCED MILLIONAIRES IN BECOMING ECONOMICALLY PRODUCTIVE ADULTS

Result of School and College Experience Tenacity	% Millionaires Influenced[1] (Not) by Experience (N=733)
Determining that hard work was more important than genetic high intellect in achieving	76(8)
Never allowing poor grades to destroy your goals to achieve	52(23)
Learning to fight for your goals because someone labeled you as having "average or less" ability	45(29)

[1]"Influenced" means respondent indicated that experience had either a high or moderate degree of influence. Excluded were those responses in the "low degree of influence" category.

reported that school experience influenced them in this regard, versus those who reported "not influenced." Most millionaires believe that economic success comes from hard work and not from having genetic high intellect. They also feel they can win the economic race even against people who are "smarter."

Most millionaires never allowed poor grades to destroy their goal to succeed.

Even millionaires who graduated high in their high school and college classes received poor grades from time to time. But as people who are determined to succeed, they viewed all reversals as temporary. Tenacity is part of the millionaire's character.

Most learn early to fight and compete for important goals.

Many millionaires, even honor students, have often been labeled by some authority figure or some standardized test result as being "average" or "inferior." But as the results of this research point out, such evaluations make some people all the more tenacious. Some millionaires thrive upon such judgments, as they have made very clear to me. Where did they get their resolve? It was a direct result of their earlier experiences in deflecting negative judgments.

Why do so many undistinguished students

become business owners, and why do many become millionaires? The answers relate to how they respond to being designated as not intellectually gifted, not receiving "senior superlatives," not being accepted to law school, and not being courted by an army of corporate recruiters. There is a segment of the millionaire population that was judged as not being college material, and some of this group never attended college. Others flunked out.

These "intellectually undistinguished" disproved their "graders" by becoming part of the next generation of millionaires, more often than not by owning and operating a successful business. Thus, they were not trying to directly compete with the super seniors and those who were accepted to medical school and law school. Ownership of a business is the base upon which most people become independently wealthy.

The alternative theory holds that some self-made millionaires did believe what their teachers told them. If you are not intellectually gifted or your academic record is mediocre, you can survive in a competitive world by working very hard for yourself and building wealth. Wealth can offset your so-called inferior intellect and provide protection from a hostile environment. While it is often difficult for millionaires to state, "I am inferior," they report such feelings in other ways, by constantly referring to their poor grades in college or to the fact that they are not worthy of being interviewed for this or other books.

178

THE CASE OF MR. WARREN

What if your academic performance in college was "horrible"?

That was what one multimillionaire recently called his short stay in college. At best he was a D student. This experience so traumatized him that even today he says, "I'm unemployable." In the long run, he discovered that only one person would hire him after he was fired from his first great job. He hired himself and started his own business. At that time he had great fear of failure, but he became a successful entrepreneur anyway.

He believed his teachers' evaluations of him — he was not intellectually gifted. Today he's glad he was never a member of the intellectually gifted clan and that he never made As in college. He's content not to have an MBA from a top school. This fellow will tell you that he would have never, ever worked so hard to build his fortune or take entrepreneurial risks if he were gifted and well educated. He contends that he would have accepted a "cushy" corporate position, and he would never have achieved or been motivated to succeed. Why did he eventually succeed? The following case study details the experiences of this remarkable character.

I have often said that some adversity is essential in bringing out the best in people. Some call it character. Mr. Warren not only has a lot of character, but he also is a character. He recently sold his $30 million carpet business and "sort of" retired. He now "invests his own money" for a living.

Take a snapshot of Mr. Warren today. He is very wealthy and quite confident. He lives in a fine home, dresses well, although casually, and enjoys life. But he still has what many self-made millionaires possess — i.e., "fire in the belly." Or, in other words, he has considerable interest in enhancing his wealth.

He still works hard and is very committed to managing and planning his investments. But why would someone who is in the top one-half of one percent of the wealth holders in America still be so interested in building more? Mr. Warren is only in his early fifties; he is in excellent health and is easily bored, so full retirement is not for him. He has enormous energy and an obsession for living.

His health, energy, and love of life are not the most significant factors underlying his motivation to continue building wealth. His experiences as a child and as a young man made an indelible imprint on his psyche. His success is, in fact, a direct result of encountering and then overcoming both academic and financial adversity. Also, his early experiences and suffering had much to do with the selection of his primary vocation, which was critical to his goal of financial success. In his own words:

I was terribly poor as a child. We had wealth and then we lost it. All through high school and my adolescence there was tremendous stress and strain on the finances in my family. I was a terrible student.

Consider the trauma that young Mr. Warren experienced. These events would have destroyed the spirit of many youngsters, but he never allowed adversity to defeat him. In fact, he maintains that the tough journey molded him into a success. Part of the reason Mr. Warren did poorly in school was directly attributable to the financial problems he and his parents had to deal with each day.

It took me longer [more than four years] to get out of high school. Most of the time I was doing things to hustle. . . . I hustled to make money. . . . I dropped out of college . . . to make money.

Mr. Warren made enough money to fund his first two years of college, but then the unexpected happened and he had to quit college. At the age of twenty, when he was just starting his junior year, Mr. Warren got married.

I came home . . . got married and had a baby right away.

So again, a reversal. Mr. Warren was now a college dropout with a family — a young man with a lot of responsibility but little in the way of financial resources. In spite of his circumstances, he was undaunted. He realized that his part-time job as a night clerk at a hotel would never support his growing family, so he searched for other opportunities. Instinctively and almost unconsciously, he looked for a job that would let him utilize his natural gifts better. Although it was not yet fully apparent, Mr. Warren was born to sell. He is what I have often referred to as an ESP, an extraordinary sales professional. He sold a variety of products door-to-door while he was in high school and college, and so while he was losing confidence in himself as a student, Mr. Warren was gaining some pride through his income-producing activities.

A certain event on Mr. Warren's wedding day had a lot to do with him later becoming a multi-millionaire. On that day, his choice of the industry that made him a success was established.

Coming back from the wedding, I wasn't employed [fulltime]. I felt like kind of a duffer . . . a night clerk in a hotel. . . . I passed by a brand-new Macy's. . . . I went in and applied for a job. . . . They took me and gave me a salesclerk's job.

Mr. Warren was assigned to the home furnishings department, and he thrived in this area. He did so well selling furnishings that he was promoted and placed in the executive training program. His success encouraged him to seek a position that paid more than retailing. With his résumé, which now mentioned his executive experience:

I decided to go to New York and booked up with an employment agency and they got me all these interviews. I lied about being a college graduate. . . . I was offered jobs as a sales trainee.

Mr. Warren worked for several months as a sales trainee for a large international corporation, but he had to leave the job on his "own volition" because a variety of aggressive creditors were harassing him at work. Collection agencies were not only hitting on Mr. Warren, they were in contact with his employer regarding the garnishment of salary and commissions.

I didn't have any money when it was really rough. . . . But then I was able to get an interview with a large conglomerate.

How did Mr. Warren get hired by a company that preferred to hire only college graduates?

I talked my way into the front office . . . they hired me and things began to straighten out for us.

"Straighten out" is an understatement. Mr. Warren's career exploded. At the age of twenty he was just a sales trainee. Within four short years, Mr. Warren occupied one of the top spots in marketing and sales in the entire home furnishings industry.

By a fluke . . . I became involved in consumer products . . . from beds to carpet cushions, mattresses.

Was it a fluke? Not really — Mr. Warren loved the home furnishings industry and its products. Once he was installed there, no one asked about his academic background. He was particularly interested in the floor-covering business, and this affection led him into the carpet-cushion segment of the industry.

Before I knew it, when I was twenty-five years old, I actually became the prodigy of the carpet-cushion industry in New York . . . probably the best job in the carpet industry at the time. Sometimes I think about it . . . it was unbelievable.

At the age of twenty-five, Mr. Warren was earning several hundreds of thousands of dollars annually, and he was in the top one-tenth of one percent of all income-earning households in America! But that's not all.

It was a terrific job. . . . Big office in New York . . . unlimited expenses . . . slush funds . . . millions of dollars at my disposal to do whatever [marketing and public relations] I chose. I traveled all over . . . first-class. I had a suite on Fifty-ninth at

Park Avenue. I was it. Diamond Jim. The barbers . . . the tailors came to my office.

Why would any corporation pay a twenty-five-year-old college dropout hundreds of thousands of dollars annually, and give him the discretion to dole out millions of dollars for marketing and related activities? The answer is quite simple: Mr. Warren performed extraordinarily well. He was responsible for major multimillion-dollar accounts. He made lots of money for his employer, and he was justly rewarded. But all during this time, Mr. Warren thought he was dreaming. How could a college dropout with a D average be successful? It was unreal, unbelievable.

Mr. Warren was so productive at selling carpet cushion because even at the age of twenty-five, he had a great deal of sales experience. In high school he'd sold everything from cutlery to carpets, and he did it the hard way — on his own and paid by commission only. He was paid only when he performed. He was a tenacious door-to-door cold caller. Later, he discovered and appreciated the fact that selling millions and millions of dollars of carpet cushion is much easier than selling knives and forks door-to-door.

Mr. Warren possessed many of the essential traits common among ESPs — he was personable, tenacious, and persuasive. But most people with these traits never reach Mr. Warren's level of economic productivity. There is yet another element in the equation, one that you will be exposed to throughout this book:

Millionaires love their careers.

Mr. Warren is like most millionaires in this regard. He was able to perform at an extraordinarily high level because of his love for his business. The task of selling to major accounts also allowed him to fully utilize his abilities, and as long as no one looked at his academic credentials, he could keep his job. Remember that Mr. Warren was surrounded by other executives at the corporate headquarters. In his mind, these people had excellent academic records. At times, Mr. Warren even felt like an impostor. How else could he explain his lofty position in corporate America?

Mr. Warren's love for his job kept him producing at a very high level. Such patterns are well documented by the results of my national survey of millionaires. In fact, there is a direct positive correlation between the love of one's vocation and level of net worth. You are much more likely to become wealthy in the future if you enjoy your vocation. The effect of positive energy and emotion that can be directed into one's career cannot be understated.

How could someone fall in love with carpet cushion? In Mr. Warren's case, it was not just carpet cushion that turned him on.

I liked the carpet business. What I liked most . . .

was the freedom of being on the road and the people I was associated with. . . . It was about the loosest industry I could ever have conceived of. They had great trade shows. The carpet business was really a fun business to be in.

I was selling carpet cushion and the job really was more than selling. . . . [It was] entertaining and public relations.

Call it what you like — selling, public relations, or entertaining — Mr. Warren was the major force in cutting deals with the biggest industrial buyers of carpet cushion. In this role he was happy and riding high in the so-called economic saddle. Accordingly, he spent much of his income, saving little for a rainy day.

Mr. Warren, the young high-income producer, thought of himself as invincible. He was the top sales executive in the industry, and his company relied on him to generate an increasing number of multimillion-dollar deals. He sold day and night, weekdays and weekends, so he had no time to worry about saving and investing a portion of his large salary. He was the ultimate consumer, spending liberally on products and services that don't retain their value. He enjoyed spending big dollars on custom suits and, of course, luxury home furnishings.

One morning, Mr. Warren was summoned to the office of his CEO. Without any warning, he was told that the company had been sold. Even worse, the corporation that acquired it had zero interest in retaining Mr. Warren as its head of sales. Yes, in an instant his dream job vanished. The loss of his job conjured up many ghosts that he had repressed — all those dreaded memories of his early experiences in a household under severe economic strain returned. Equally frightening, Mr. Warren recalled all those Ds and Fs on his college transcript. Who would hire him with such a horrible record?

Reversals can have positive influences, and Mr. Warren's trauma paved the way for him to become a multimillionaire by owning his own business.

> I didn't opt for self-employment. I was forced into it. The company I worked for . . . they were sold . . . and I was fired! . . . [I] lost the job because I was the highest-paid man in the company. . . . Where am I going to get a job? I wasn't hirable because I was making so much darn money. . . . [And I was] not a college graduate.

Shortly after he received the bad news, Mr. Warren was told to return the company car he had recently received. So he walked out to the car and just sat in it, reflecting on his misfortune.

> I just sat there bawling my eyes out. . . . It was horrible.

Not long after, Mr. Warren received a call from the CEO and owner of a carpet-manufacturing company who'd heard the news about his dismissal. The CEO knew of his extraordinary ability to sell carpet cushion, and although he wasn't in a position to hire him, he did propose an alternative solution. He suggested that Mr. Warren establish a sales agency, and Mr. Warren took his advice.

It was not an easy transition. It required a great deal of hard work and living on a Spartan household budget. It also meant that Mr. Warren had to give up living and working in New York City. It was a major change to move from cosmopolitan New York City to Carpet Country USA, in Dalton, Georgia, but he did it.

So I went to Dalton [Georgia]. . . . This guy down there really gave me a break . . . put me in business. He supported me with inventory and price and everything else that anybody could ever need to be successful. [He] knew I could sell carpet.

In his mind, Mr. Warren had no choice but to start his own business because he thought it was the only way he could earn as much as he once had in his dream job as a corporate executive. He believed that no corporation in America would be able to compensate him at such a high level.

It took me about seven years to get back on my feet from the great job I had. I saw the opportunity.

Mr. Warren's modesty is one of the reasons that he is such a likable fellow. He typically understates both his aptitude and his achievements, and repeatedly reflects on his shortcomings as a marginal high school student, college dropout, fired executive, and struggling entrepreneur. He underplays his achievements, and even today he constantly wonders how he ever became a financial success. Deep down inside he feels that college dropouts are not supposed to succeed in the American economy.

. . . Started from scratch and I built the business. It doesn't sound like much but from 0 to 30 million dollars. In the carpet industry that's a pretty big thing.

Today, Mr. Warren still works hard, but at a different kind of work. He spends many hours managing and planning his investments. He will never again take his financial success for granted. He never forgot for a single moment what it was like to have a lot of cash as a young executive and then lose all of it.

According to Mr. Warren, the seven years that it took to rebuild his financial position were in his words, "absolute torture. . . . It was horrible." This experience is still today a strong motivator. He has a "terrible fear" of having to go through it all again.

I swear if I ever lost it all and I didn't see any

chance to live with any comfort at all, if it was just back to that drudgery, I'd rather die. It's fear of real poverty. I never want to be that poor again.

There is no doubt that self-confidence and positive thinking play a role in explaining success, but then how can we explain Mr. Warren's achievements? In general, he has a lack of confidence and he is more negative in his thinking than positive. He is motivated by fear — he fears returning to the position of poverty he and his family once experienced.

He did have confidence, however, that he could always outsell all his competition. This confidence, coupled with his need to avoid poverty, thrust him into the entrepreneurial environment. He believed that "I was not hirable . . . couldn't get a job." So in his mind, self-employment was his last hope.

He believed that no major corporation would give him a second look because he was a college dropout. He believed that only the "beautiful people" are hired for "big bucks" by major corporations. Mr. Warren never thought of himself as being a member of the "beautiful people" club. If he did, he probably wouldn't be a multimillionaire today. Consider Mr. Warren's own thoughts about the "what ifs" in his life.

I think about this all the time. . . . I dwell on these things. A company . . . they hire these kids right out of college and they get the cream of the crop [beautiful people]. My friend, the principal [CEO and owner of a major carpet company], he would hire the top students from his alma mater. And you'd see these guys and they looked like they never sweated and were tall and handsome. All these guys that got these great jobs. . . . I used to say, boy, if I only looked that way and had the [academic] credentials . . . how much easier my life would have been.

If Mr. Warren could turn the clock back, he would have the opportunity to get all As in high school and college and earn an MBA from a top university. Then he would be hired as a junior executive like the rest of the beautiful people. Then he would exude confidence and be much more positive about his economic prospects. But does Mr. Warren really want to turn the clock back? Does he really miss not being beautiful? No, he does not. His thinking about this closely parallels the results gleaned from my surveys.

Most people who become wealthy in one generation had no choice — they *had* to be financially independent. Many realized that being an employee smothers the fire in one's gut. Mr. Warren's goal was to become a financially independent person by building wealth. His net worth was his main defense against poverty. His entrepreneurial endeavor produced this wealth, along with seven years of living a frugal, barebones lifestyle.

He maintains that he would never have felt compelled to become a millionaire if he had the credentials and confidence to be a corporate executive.

If I had the credentials [to be an executive] I would have accepted mediocrity. . . . I didn't plan on getting into the carpet business. . . . Frankly, had I been able to get a decent job, I would have never gone into business for myself. . . . I was forced into self-employment.

According to Mr. Warren, the "beautiful people" have their own form of capital. Their education, résumé, and transcripts with all As are their wealth. It is their way of surviving and protecting their lifestyles. But without an outstanding résumé, Mr. Warren felt that he had to substitute. His fortress is his financial success. He built wealth because he bet "the farm" on his business venture, and if he'd had other options, he would never have worked so hard and become really wealthy.

The data from my surveys support Mr. Warren's assertions. People like Mr. Warren have learned that there is no such thing as a permanent job working for others. In college he learned that he was not intellectually gifted. Thus, the only way he could succeed was to outwork the "beautiful people." This, coupled with his willingness to take entrepreneurial risk, made him a wealthy man.

What did Mr. Warren discover eventually about America? We are a society that gives two, three, four, even ten chances to people who wish to achieve, and success will not be withheld from those who use their early failures as a foundation for success.

THE PARENT TRAP

Many parents believe that their children will have a difficult time becoming productive adults without first having "outstanding academic credentials." As we have seen throughout this chapter, that assumption simply isn't true. In fact, most self-made millionaires report that they were not A students in either high school or college. Most never scored extraordinarily high on the SAT, nor did their teachers ever think of them as becoming successful in the future. Most, more than 80 percent, never attended a so-called top undergraduate program. Every parent should understand those facts before relentlessly pushing their children to achieve in school in traditional ways.

But there is yet another game being played here. Some parents define success differently than others, and they want their children to become more than productive adults. They want them to become members of the high-status occupational groups — medical doctors, lawyers, scientists. High grades are part of the entrance requirements for medical school, law school, and Ph.D. programs. Interestingly, these so-called high-status occupations produce only a minority of the millionaire population. Of course, money isn't everything, and these are noble occupational goals. But many parents who want their children to attend medical school are focusing on prestige, income, and wealth. I can assure you that earning a high income does not ensure financial independence. Not all those in high-status occupations even earn high incomes, because many feel a compulsion to spend heavily on status products.

For other parents, it's very important to be able to tell their friends, relatives, and neighbors that Becky is going to Tufts, Earl to Vassar, and Joel to Columbia. I call this academic status. Parents feel that their own status is enhanced by taking credit for producing a son or daughter bound for "Prestige U." It's difficult to account for variations in economic productivity, but of this I am sure: Academic performance in high school and college does not explain the wide variations in wealth in America.

Parents often look back over their own lives and generate a series of "what ifs."

What if I had gone to Prestige U — I'd really be successful today.

Certainly they realize that their own history can't be changed, but parents still have a chance — their children can do it right. These parents are, deep down inside, living vicariously through their children. They deflect questions about their own academic credentials by over-whelming friends and associates with stories of their children's academic triumphs and college-entrance victories. Little do they know that they may be trapping their children into mediocre futures by pushing these achievements unnecessarily.

Given the following standards, most of the millionaires today would not be admitted to my state's university.

The freshman class at the University of Georgia. . . . Average SAT score for those accepted was 1220, while the [high school] GPA was 3.7. (Rebecca McCarthy, "99 Freshmen: UGA Will Take 4,200 in Class," *Atlanta Journal-Constitution*, April 6, 1999, p. 1E)

For the high net worth/high income population, income typically peaks between the ages of 44 and 54, while net worth peaks later, normally between ages 55 and 64. I find no substantial statistical correlation between the economic-productivity factors (net worth and income) and SATs, class rank in college, and grade performance in college (see Table 3-4). For example, note the correlation coefficient (.05) between net worth and SAT scores for those in the 44 to 54 age cohort. What portion of the variation in net worth is explained by SAT scores? Just

TABLE 3-4

CORRELATION COEFFICIENTS: SAT SCORE, CLASS RANK, AND GRADE POINT AVERAGE[1] VS. NET WORTH AND INCOME

Economic Productivity Measures:	Age: 45-54 (N=252)		Age: 55-64 (N=205)	
	SAT[2]	Significant Correlation[3]	SAT	Significant Correlation
Net Worth[4]	.05	No	.02	No
Total Annual Realized Income[5]	.07	No	.06	No
	Rank		Rank	
Net Worth	.01	No	.04	No
Total Annual Realized Income	.17	Yes	.01	No
	GPA		GPA	
Net Worth	.01	No	.04	No
Total Annual Realized Income	.11	No	.02	No

[1] Refers to undergraduate/college grade point average on a 4 point scale: A=4, B=3, and so forth.

[2] Refers to combined scores.

[3] Probability at less than 0.01 level. Thirty correlations were generated (2 economic productivity measures) X (3 academic performance measures) X (5 age groups). One of the 30 correlations (income vs. rank for age 45–54) was statistically significant.

[4] Net worth refers to the household's assets less all liabilities.

[5] Total annual realized income refers to the household's income.

square .05 to compute the answer. It is a small percentage, less than 1 percent. That leaves a great deal which can be explained by other factors.

If not income or net worth, what do SAT scores explain? In this study they account for 11 percent of the variation in grade point averages, and vice versa. But in the real world, economic productivity is not defined by GPA. Overall the only statistically significant correlation found was between income and rank within the 45–54 age group. But here again rank accounts for a small portion of the variation in income (.17 square), less than 3 percent.

THE 900 CLUB

In my office I have created an exclusive club called the 900 Club — only those millionaires who scored below 1000 on their SATs are admitted. I arbitrarily used scores under 1000 to define less than spectacular performance. This is not to suggest that a disproportionate share of the millionaire population has SAT scores under 1000. Actually, a minority of millionaires fall into this category. But the point is that it's possible to become an economic success with scores that are mediocre or worse.

What if we tell people with low SAT scores that they can succeed? Perhaps then more would become economically successful one day. The same applies to our grading system. Generating mediocre grades when you are sixteen or seventeen does not preclude you from achieving later in life, but too many adults believe otherwise.

One of the first members of the 900 Club was a man I'll call Mr. Refuse. He struggled with his course work in school, but he eventually graduated from college. Why the "Refuse" handle? First, he refused to accept his less than stellar performance in high school, on the SAT, or in college as an indicator of his future productivity. Second, while he was in school, he majored in academic subjects and "minored in scrap, trash, garbage, and refuse." Later he added a course called "recycling." Like many members of the 900 Club, Mr. Refuse was greatly influenced by his experience with part-time and summer jobs in the trash and recycling businesses. Later he turned his experiences with scrap into a multi-million-dollar business of his own. The earlier a youngster starts developing interest and experience with his or her vocation, the more likely he or she is to become a productive adult.

CONTRASTING 900 VS. 1400

What if your son or daughter took the SAT three times, and each time he or she scored below the national average? You realize that your child may not be admitted to many of the better colleges and universities, but there are many that would gladly admit your son or daughter. This is especially true if your child has good study habits and determination. Also, if your child does well at his or her second- or third-choice college for a year or two, then he or she could transfer, to perhaps even his or her first choice.

Attending and completing college are significant factors in explaining economic success. Be more concerned with your child's finishing school than worrying about rejection notices. Rejection notices will not hurt your child's chances unless you allow them to damage his or her spirit. The key to motivating John and Sally has a lot to do with convincing them they have the potential to succeed. If they believe that results on standardized tests like the SAT are perfect predictors of future achievement, then it's likely they won't be motivated to compete anymore if their scores are low. Their future is now programmed. Below-average scores are taken very seriously by parents and their children, and low scores can be totally devastating. But not to everyone. What are some of the key differences between those millionaires who are members of the 900 Club and those who scored 1400 or higher on their SATs? In order to answer this question, I analyzed the survey responses from two subsamples of millionaires. The responses from one hundred members of the 900 Club were contrasted with one hundred millionaires who scored 1400 or higher on their SATs.

Only 3 percent of the millionaires in the 900 Club indicated that having a high IQ or superior intellect was a very important factor in ex-

TABLE 3-5

FACTORS EXPLAINING ECONOMIC SUCCESS: MILLIONAIRES WITH SAT SCORES UNDER 1000 VS. 1400 OR HIGHER

PERCENTAGE INDICATING SUCCESS FACTOR VERY IMPORTANT

	SAT Score:	
Success Factor	Under 1000 (N=100)	1400 or Higher (N=100)
Having a high IQ/ superior intellect	3	50
Being honest with all people	65	50
Having a supportive spouse	57	46
Loving my career/business	51	39
Getting along with people	63	49
Seeing business opportunities others did not see	42	29
Specializing	26	17
Being very well organized	42	30
Ignoring the criticism of my detractors	34	25
Having good mentors	31	26
Being well disciplined	61	56
Finding a profitable market niche	38	27

plaining their success (see Table 3-5). Again, results from standardized IQ measures and SATs are related. Also note that not one of the 900 Club members believed that his or her high school teachers were very likely to judge them as having the "highest level of intellect" or being the "most intellectually gifted" (see Table 3-6).

In sharp contrast, 50 percent of those respondents who had SAT scores of 1400 or higher believed that having a high IQ or superior intellect was a very important factor in explaining their economic success. How did they think their high school teachers judged them? Much differently than those in the 900 Club. More than four in ten (42 percent) indicated that their teachers very likely judged them as having the highest level of intelligence; 41 percent, "most intellectually gifted"; 32 percent, "most likely to succeed"; and so forth.

What can be said of the members of the 900 Club? Most, if not all, realized in their formative years that they were not at the very high end of the analytical-intellect scale, yet they still wanted to become economically successful. During their school days, a majority (72 percent) of the 900 Club members learned to fight for such goals even though they were labeled as having just average or less ability (see Table 3-7). They also discovered that there are other significant factors in the wealth equation. Most (93 percent) discovered that hard work was more important than genetic high intelli-

TABLE 3-6

HOW THEIR HIGH SCHOOL TEACHERS LIKELY JUDGED THEM: MILLIONAIRES WITH SAT SCORES UNDER 1000 VS. 1400 OR HIGHER

PERCENTAGE INDICATING SUCCESS FACTOR VERY IMPORTANT

"Superlatives"	SAT Score:	
	Under 1000 (N=100)	1400 or Higher (N=100)
Highest level of intelligence	0	42
Most intellectually gifted	0	41
Most likely to succeed	3	32
Highest grade point average	2	28
Most logical	8	31
Most dependable	28	30
Most popular	27	23
Most conscientious	13	19
Hardest worker	12	20
Most industrious	16	18

TABLE 3-7

SCHOOL AND COLLEGE EXPERIENCES THAT INFLUENCED MILLIONAIRES IN BECOMING ECONOMICALLY PRODUCTIVE ADULTS: THOSE WITH SAT SCORES UNDER 1000 VS. 1400 OR HIGHER

PERCENTAGE MILLIONAIRES INFLUENCED[1] BY EXPERIENCE

| | SAT Score: | |
Experience	Under 1000 (N=100)	1400 or Higher (N=100)
Learning to fight for your goals because some labeled you as having "average" or less ability	72	21
Determining that hard work was more important than genetic high intellect in achieving	93	60
Never allowing poor grades to destroy your goals to achieve	66	34
Being exceptionally creative	62	51
Working at part-time jobs while in school	58	47
Receiving encouragement from teachers	64	60

[1]Influenced means respondent indicated that experience had either a high or moderate degree of influence.

gence in achieving success.

Look once again at the twelve contrasts between 900 Club members and those with 1400 or higher SATs given in Table 3-5. As indicated, those with high SATs place more weight on intellect in explaining their economic success. But the 900 Club members give more weight to the other eleven success factors.

Who are those who emphasize high intellect as a key success factor? Attorneys and physicians are well represented among those in the 1400 SAT group. Also included are senior corporate officers who hold advanced degrees, MBAs or Ph.D.'s from top-rated schools, and business owners who are engaged in scientific and technical areas. Overall, those who say that superior intellect equates with success are referring to analytical intellect, which is supposedly measured by the standardized IQ batteries that are in turn related to scores on SATs, GREs, and other such tests.

In contrast, how do members of the 900 Club explain their successes? Obviously, from the results given in Table 3-5, it is not a function of having superior analytical intellect.

BEING HONEST

Note that nearly two-thirds of the 900 Club members believe that "being honest" was a very important factor in explaining their success, a significantly greater number than for the other group. This is not to suggest that people with superior intellect are dishonest — almost all successful people place considerable emphasis on integrity. But many of the 900 Club members are business owners who are involved each and every day with the selling activity. Every day, integrity is always on the line. In contrast, many of those with superior analytical intellect are involved in professions that focus on science, research and development, designing a legal defense to support a client's claim, or developing a strategy to extend the life of a cancer patient.

In contrast, integrity is a really key issue at the point where money changes hands. If one lacks integrity at this juncture, in the long run he will never become or remain a successful person. There are a lot of definitions of integrity, but I particularly enjoyed reading Robert A. Lutz's views about its importance. Lutz believes that integrity is absolutely essential if one hopes to become an executive, and he has no tolerance for dishonesty. When offered a $10 million bribe he declined the offer and made certain that the firm never, ever did business with that fellow again (Robert A. Lutz, *Guts* [New York: John Wiley & Sons, Inc., 1998], pp. 183–86). People with common sense or practical intelligence place great importance on integrity in everything they do. If Mr. Lutz had graduated from high school at age fifteen instead of twenty-two, or had he been an analytical whiz kid who lacked integrity, he would never have succeeded in becoming a senior executive.

Many members of the 900 Club give high credit for their success to their "supportive spouse." Having a supportive spouse is not an accident or random occurrence. Even before they marry, 900 Club members tend to be more sensitive to certain differences among potential spouses than those with much higher SAT scores. Many 900 Club members may have realized even before marrying that they needed a supportive spouse — maybe they recognized that two heads are better than one. If a 900 Club member perceives a deficiency in his analytical aptitude but at the same time envisions having a successful career or operating a highly productive business, he may feel that he needs a self-disciplined, frugal, even-tempered, secure, and accepting spouse. Also, many would probably be attracted to a spouse who clearly had the ability to be economically productive. About four in ten 900 club members were attracted to their spouses because of this productivity dimension.

Given a choice beyond love and physical attractiveness, I prefer to marry a woman who can manage a business.

I have heard many successful business owners make similar statements.

Does this mean that 900 Club members are more likely to have long-term successful marriages? I find no statistical evidence to support this speculation. Both the 900 Club members as well as the "superior intellect" group in the millionaire population tend to have long-term marriages.

But the economic productivity of a married couple is another issue. There are often significant economies of scale when a married couple works together as a team to produce income. Economies even exist when one spouse becomes an informal confidant or provides psychological support. A detailed discussion of choice of spouse is given in chapter 6.

Members of the 900 Club have another rather well-demonstrated propensity — they tend to use a much greater number of advisers, mentors, and significant others, including husband or wife, as counselors and support units. More often than not, they use more than their own head to enhance the probability of succeeding in life. What about those in the superior-intellect group, those with SATs in the 1400 or higher category? It's just the opposite. In fact, the higher one's reported SAT score, the more likely he is to use only himself as an adviser.

Do you realize the value of hiring advisers who may be superior to you in regard to some area of your success equation? If so, you may see the value of hiring superior talent. If you don't get along with people, especially people who can give you advice, you have a problem. You may be "too smart." You may not be willing to admit that you need help. Or you may be so convinced of your intellectual superiority that you perceive no need for advice from intellectual inferiors.

OTHER FACTORS

So what if you're labeled as "about average," "below average," or even a bit "above" according to standardized test results but you're determined to become an economic success. You know intuitively that you can succeed. Perhaps your determination is aided by someone who told you that you had what it takes to excel. Maybe your mentor or a teacher said, "What you have is special. We have not yet figured out how to measure this quality in our students."

That's what happened to Sharon. An enlightened middle school counselor told her she possessed a special quality of creativity. Sharon scored above average on standardized achievements tests, but her real strength was in the creative domain. Today she is one of the top graphic designers in this country, and her parents have finally forgiven her for not going to medical school. Sharon has twice won the designer-of-the-year award.

Give some teachers and school counselors credit for enhancing the population of the 900 Club. Nearly two-thirds, 64 percent, of its members indicated that "receiving encouragement from teachers" (see Table 3-7) influenced them in becoming an economically productive adult. Often it only takes one teacher, counselor, or coach to influence a youngster in this positive way. Coaches often play a major role in this regard. A significant portion, 63 percent, of 900 Club members report having played competitive sports. Perhaps this experience had something to do with their ability to deal with criticisms of detractors and "win games" they were predicted to lose.

Working part-time while in school was also an experience that most 900 Club members (58 percent) say molded them in a positive way. Read the profiles of America's most productive people. It's rare to find one who doesn't mention part-time job experiences. If nothing else, these experiences led them to realize that they didn't want a career as a desk clerk at a motel or a server in a restaurant.

Mr. Nielson sold his 20 percent stake for $100 million. He worked as a ranch hand, truck driver . . . rigger . . . janitor . . . before investing in the oil business. (Barnaby J. Feder, "Glenn E. Nielson, 95, Builder of Oil and Asphalt Business," *New York Times*, November 5, 1998, p. C27)

One of the reasons Mr. Nielson succeeded in life was that he saw a business opportunity that most others overlooked and found a profitable geographic niche to exploit. It's hard for a person to recognize opportunities if he stays in one place and remains in one job — most self-made millionaires have had a rather wide experience with various part-time and temporary jobs.

DEFINE "GENIUS"

John Parks is a multimillionaire today, but when he graduated from college thirty-five years ago he'd never envisioned that he would ever become a major economic success. Mr. Parks was a C student throughout his college career. He majored in engineering, and on graduating he was hired by a large engineering consulting firm.

Mr. Parks was quickly recognized by his superiors as having strong leadership qualities. Before long, he was given command of a major division of the firm. Later, he left his executive position in order to establish his own materials-testing firm.

Recently, the firm Mr. Parks started was purchased by a Fortune Fifty corporation, and today John is "slightly retired but active in two businesses . . . and still consulting." Throughout his career, John has hired hundreds of people from various backgrounds. Some were scientists or engineers, others were accountants and administrators.

John's experiences with hiring and managing people, as well as in building wealth, made him an ideal respondent to my survey. Just how is it that a fellow with a C average became a multimillionaire? Why were John's classmates with straight A averages working for him instead of the other way around? John actually asked these questions before I had a chance to ask them myself. In John's mind, there is something of a negative correlation between performance in school and economic success. He referred to his own personal experiences in his answer:

I was an average student, but I went to engineering school. I went primarily because my mother told me I should. They needed a professional in the family and I really don't think I was that well suited, but the one thing that I know — my mantra has always been that nobody's going to outwork me. Nobody's going to try harder than I try. If I do my best, and I never really worried about accumulating wealth or I don't feel like I had any fear, but I feel like if I do my best, I'm very satisfied with that. But I've had to struggle, to work very hard to do things. I ended up being in management. I have had to hire some of these geniuses. They are not in management because they weren't people oriented.

I think their intellect . . . the way intellect is measured is a little bit faulty. Geniuses, they don't have a feel for the work environment or how to say the right thing and you combine that with not working hard. So particularly in the engineering field, I'm sure . . . a lot of people [geniuses] just don't get it. They are very strong in that sort of narrow area.

The geniuses who have worked for me know more and more about less and less! *A lot of the intellectuals get drawn into careers in research,*

212

academia . . . things that tend not to be manage-rial or entrepreneurial. . . . They're not practical for the most part.

What is John's message? If you're told you are marginal or even below average in intellect but you want to succeed, you'll have to work very hard. You will also have to get along with people, work harder than others, and go out of your way to develop empathy for the needs of others. If you do, you may be selected to lead. Many of the intellectually gifted never felt the need to exert themselves at those skills. It is indeed ironic that the gift of high intellect can be an occupational handicap.

Most millionaires never put themselves in a position where they have to compete directly with those who are intellectually gifted. They know it's foolish and typically unprofitable to match IQ against IQ. So instead they hire the intellectually gifted. They hire lots of them. Then they let the geniuses compete among themselves.

NO EXCUSES PLEASE
Readers — your grades in school can no longer be used as an excuse for not becoming economically successful in America!

DR. STANLEY: How much income did you generate on your best day?
EXTRAORDINARY SALES PROFESSIONAL (ESP): In one day I sold about $8 million. Earned a $240,000 commission. That's net.

DR. STANLEY: What was your grade point average in college?

ESP: C.

DR. STANLEY: How many As did you receive in college?

ESP: At least one or two. I certainly would have had a lot of As if I had been paid a commission for each A I earned. I work for money, not As.

Note: Parents, be careful what you tell your children about the future. Far too often parents with good intentions unknowingly condemn their own children to a life of low economic productivity by telling them ten thousand times:

You will never amount to anything if you don't do well in school.

Some of these children who have mediocre academic records are compelled to fulfill their parents' prophecy, in spite of their potential to become millionaires. They are sentenced to a life of low economic productivity. Their minds have been conditioned to respond negatively to cues concerning wealth-building opportunities. Thus, they act in ways that assure mediocrity or never amounting to anything.

4

The Relationship Between Courage and Wealth

Never take counsel of your fears.
— General Stonewall Jackson

It's easy to understand why courage is part of the profile of our self-made millionaires, particularly the courage to take financial risk. Overcoming life's obstacles and making it to the top income levels would clearly require brave actions at some point, as well as the ability to conquer fears. How, then, did our millionaires acquire this courage? Is it only a genetic trait inherited from ancestors and parents, as most of us think? Surprisingly, the millionaires say no. Virtually all feel that their courage was nurtured and consciously developed all throughout their careers, and in this chapter we'll learn about the various techniques that helped them confront and take financial risks.

THE COURAGE TO TAKE RISKS
What role does courage play in the process of becoming a millionaire in one generation? Almost all self-made millionaires have it because accumulating wealth required that they take risks, including financial risk. And that takes

courage. One of the major characteristics of these millionaires is that they usually own and manage their own businesses. It takes courage to be self-employed. It takes courage to invest in one's own business. Most people associate high risk with these activities, and risk is the companion of fear and danger.

Another part of their pattern is that, independent of the capital they have invested in their own businesses, they also own shares of publicly traded corporations. There are certain risks associated with being an equity investor — one must have some courage to invest without guarantees. It takes courage not to panic every time the stock market corrects itself. Those with little courage are too often the last to invest in an up market and the first out during a short correction.

The millionaires who are senior corporate executives also have courage. If they didn't, they would never have been promoted to senior positions. They had to take some risks to succeed. What if the new product line they introduced failed to break even? Conversely, what would happen if the line broke all sales records?

As one's income approaches the higher levels, it's more likely that he or she is a self-employed business owner or professional, a senior corporate executive, a sales professional (paid strictly on commission), or a sales agent. But none of these vocations guarantee a sure-fire level of income, so many people are unwilling to take the economic risk often associated with them. For many, the downside is filled with danger. They seek the safety and security of working on a set salary.

Why do those who are likely to become part of the next generation of millionaires take risk today? In their minds, economic risk taking is a requirement for becoming financially independent. They believe the benefits of becoming financially independent greatly outweigh the risks often associated with accumulating wealth. But many people in America forgo owning their own businesses, being self-employed, investing in the stock market, or even working on an incentive basis because of fear, a very strong emotion. The fear of economic failure is not easy to overcome — that's why so few people are self-employed today. They suffer through the what ifs. What if I am self-employed but have no sales? What if my business and capital go down the drain? What if I can't support my family? What if my friends, in-laws, and neighbors find out that my business failed?

The risk of failure is always present, but millionaires learn how to deal with economic risk and ultimately keep control of their fears. Paraphrasing and combining the thoughts of several self-made millionaires, this is how they respond to the idea of safety and security in working for someone other than themselves:

[Working for others] may actually put you at

*greater risk. . . . Having a single source of income
. . . not being given the opportunity to learn how
to make thousands of decisions . . . decisions you
would have mastered if you were self-employed.*

  *[Working for others] . . . you never build your
own customer base. . . . You are not doing things
that are in your own best [economic] interest for
you to become successful in terms of becoming
wealthy. . . . You are merely doing what is in the
best interest of an employer.*

Do you want to become wealthy in one generation? If so, you'll have to develop the courage to offset your fear of economic failure. You'll have to nurture that courage throughout your adult career. It's easy to say what must be done, but it's very difficult for the average person to develop courage spontaneously. That's why the material in this chapter is so important.

The reason that so few people are financially independent today is that they place many negative roadblocks in their heads. Becoming wealthy is, in fact, a mind game. And millionaires often talk to themselves about the benefits of becoming financially independent. They constantly tell themselves that it is very difficult to achieve that without taking some risks.

Before you can become a millionaire, you must learn to think like one. You must learn how to motivate yourself constantly to counter fear with courage. Making critical decisions about your career, business, investments, and other re-

218

sources conjures up fear, fear that is part of the process of becoming a financial success. This is especially true of those who are self-employed or have a substantial part of their wealth invested in areas that have no guaranteed return.

Can people learn how to control their fears and develop courage? Can they be taught not to panic when sudden crises are encountered? If so, where will this enlightenment come from? The millionaire respondents to my national survey reported on the actions, tactics, and techniques they use to bolster their courage. I have identified more than one hundred techniques that millionaires use in the game called "mind over fear." Of these, I selected the twenty-four most often repeated during my focus groups and personal interviews with millionaires, as detailed in Table 4-1. Note that most of these actions and thought processes can be grouped under the headings displayed in Table 4-2. The most important of these activities are discussed in this chapter.

MR. BENJAMIN VS. MR. TRUCK

Mr. Benjamin paid all of his children's tuition. His daughter and sons all attended private elementary and high schools and prestigious private colleges, medical colleges, and graduate schools. Mr. Benjamin paid for all of it — room, board, tuition, books, and related expenses. Who is this man who demonstrated the ability to fund these enormous tuition bills — a highly

TABLE 4-1

ACTIONS AND THOUGHT PROCESSES USED BY MILLIONAIRES TO ELIMINATE/REDUCE FEARS AND WORRIES
(N=733)

	MILLIONAIRES WHO USED ACTIONS/PROCESSES	
	%	Rank
Hard Work	94	1[1]
Believing in Myself	94	1[1]
Preparation	93	3
Focusing on Key Issues	91	4
Being -Decisive	89	5
Planning	87	6
Being Well Organized to Deal with Big Issues	83	7
Taking Immediate Action to Solve Problems	80	8
Countering Negative Thoughts with Positive Ones	72	9
Outworking, Outthinking, Outtoughing the Competition	71	10
Visualizing Success	68	11
Never Allowing Fears to Control My Mind	66	12
Defeating Fear by Attacking It	65	13[1]
Sharing Concerns with Spouse	65	13[1]
Counting My Blessings	64	15

Table 4-1 (Continued)

MILLIONAIRES WHO USED ACTIONS/PROCESSES

	%	Rank
Exercising Regularly	60	16
Seeking Advice from Outstanding People	59	17
Consulting Skilled Advisers/ CPA/Attorney	56	18
Never Dwelling on Past Mistakes	55	19
Sharing Concerns with a Trusted Friend	50	20[1]
Using Mental Toughness Developed in Sports	50	20[1]
Reading About People Who Had Courage	40	22
Having Strong Religious Faith	37	23
Praying	32	24

[1]Tied for this position.

paid physician or perhaps CEO of a major public corporation?

Before he retired, Mr. Benjamin was a school-bus driver, a school-bus driver who generated enough income to send his children to private colleges, medical school, and graduate school. He was frugal, but being frugal is not enough to pay six-figure tuition bills.

When they were very young, Mr. Benjamin realized that his children were extremely bright. He realized that each would greatly benefit from a top-quality education, so he constantly worried about funding that education with his low-paying job. Consequently, Mr. Benjamin began a "self-improvement" reading program. The central topic of it was investing.

Being a bus driver had one side benefit. It gave Mr. Benjamin several hours of free time each day. His fellow drivers often used this time for snoozing, reading newspapers and magazines, drinking coffee, or chatting. Mr. Benjamin used his downtime more wisely. He read about various types of investments. Early in his self-study program, he discovered the truth about the long-run returns generated by corporate bonds, pass-book savings accounts, treasury bills, municipal bonds, CDs, stocks, precious metals, and real estate.

Mr. Benjamin concluded that after adjusting for inflation and taxes, only stocks paid a real return on one's investment dollars. But his mother had always told him never to invest in

TABLE 4-2

ACTIONS AND THOUGHT PROCESSES USED BY MILLIONAIRES TO ELIMINATE/REDUCE FEARS AND WORRIES GROUPED BY DOMAINS

ELBOW GREASE
- Hard Work

PLANNING
- Planning
- Being Well Organized to Deal with Big Issues
- Preparation
- Focusing on Key Issues

DECISIVENESS
- Being Decisive
- Taking Immediate Action to Solve Problems
- Outworking, Outthinking, Outtoughing the Competition

THE POWER OF POSITIVE THINKING
- Visualizing Success
- Defeating Fear by Attacking It
- Countering Negative Thoughts with Positive Ones
- Reading About People Who Had Courage

MIND CONTROL
- Never Dwelling on Past Mistakes
- Never Allowing Fears to Control My Mind

MENTOREE
- Seeking Advice from Outstanding People
- Consulting Skilled Advisers/CPA/Attorney
- Sharing Concerns with a Trusted Friend
- Sharing Concerns with Spouse

Table 4-2 (Continued)

ATHLETE'S HEART
- Exercising Regularly
- Using Mental Toughness Developed in Sports

RELIGION
- Praying
- Having Strong Religious Faith
- Counting My Blessings

the stock market. She was around during the stock market crash in 1929. But the 1929 downturn was included in Mr. Benjamin's calculations, and he knew that in spite of the crash, in the long run stocks outperformed all other investment alternatives.

Mr. Benjamin eventually became a serious investor in the stock market. Every extra dollar he and his wife could muster was earmarked for stocks, but not just any stocks. Mr. Benjamin spent much of his free time studying specific corporations and their stock offerings. Over the years, he became an expert in his chosen avocation.

The result of Mr. Benjamin's self-improvement reading and investing program was that when he recently retired, the former bus driver had a net worth in excess of $3 million. Remember, that is $3 million *after* sending his children to the finest, most expensive schools in America.

What is the point? Mr. Benjamin became financially independent because he had courage. It takes courage to invest in the stock market. The market guarantees nothing. It goes up and it goes down! Often, people get in the market late and get out early and they lose a lot of money. Mr. Benjamin was always a long-term investor. He never let fear outweigh the knowledge he obtained from his reading program. When Mr. Benjamin bought a stock, he rarely sold it within ten years of his initial investment. In good times and bad times, he held on to his picks. He frequently had some fears and concerns, but dealing with fear in a positive manner is a foundation stone of becoming wealthy in America.

It takes courage to invest in public corporations as well as in one's own business enterprise, but often it takes even more courage to hold on to one's investments when the public mood is full of fear and panic. Without courage Mr. Benjamin's children would not be doctors today.

Contrast Mr. Benjamin's profile in courage with a fellow I refer to as Mr. Truck. Mr. Truck was working for UPS the day after the stock market recently "corrected." His route was the financial district of a large city.

DR. STANLEY: Mr. Truck, what effect has the sudden drop in the stock market had upon your own investing habits?

MR. TRUCK: None.

DR. STANLEY: Aren't you concerned that the market will drop even further?

MR. TRUCK: No. I don't own any stock. If I did, I could never sleep at night.

DR. STANLEY: You mean you don't even own any shares of UPS?

MR. TRUCK: No. I don't want to worry.

I was dumbfounded by Mr. Truck's response. At the time UPS was one of the most profitable private billion-dollar business in this country, and he can purchase shares in the company because he is an employee. Over the past twenty years, the stock has significantly outpaced the Dow.

Could it be that Mr. Truck's fear of stocks has clouded his reasoning? Could it be that Mr. Benjamin sleeps more soundly than Mr. Truck because he has found a way to fund his children's tuition and become financially independent? It seems very likely that Mr. Truck is fooling himself into thinking he can become financially independent without taking some investment risk.

There is hope for Mr. Truck only if he educates himself as Mr. Benjamin did. Mr. Benjamin's courage overwhelmed his fears of risking his investment dollars. His courage to do so is a direct product of educating himself and taking control of his own financial destiny.

WHY SO FEW?

Webster's defines *courage* as "mental or moral strength to venture, persevere, and withstand danger, fear, or difficulty." For most people, even the idea of being a self-employed business owner conjures up considerable fear because they perceive the situation as being dangerous. The danger of being a self-employed business owner is the financial risk associated with such a venture.

One of the reasons that only a small percentage of Americans are millionaires is that only 18 percent of households are headed by a self-employed business owner or professional. Why are there so few business owners in America, the center of the free-enterprise economy? I have asked hundreds of intelligent, well-educated, hardworking middle-management employees:

Why don't you go out on your own and start a business? Why don't you seek work where you are paid according to your productivity?

Most of the respondents admit to asking themselves the same question. Why do they remain salaried employees? A major reason has to do with their definition of courage, meaning the absence of fear. Most believe they lack courage because they must perceive no fear, sense no danger from taking the substantial financial risk associated with being self-employed. They are wrong. I have never found one successful self-employed business owner who is completely without fear. How do I, a successful, self-employed business owner, define courage?

Just like all the other successful business respondents whom I have interviewed:

Courage is taking positive moral actions that conjure up fear.

So the true meaning of "entrepreneurial material" is that in spite of fear, there is the courage to "go it alone." Successful entrepreneurs deal with and overcome their fears.

Another misconception about courage is that, like wealth, it's usually inherited. Both assumptions are incorrect. I have found that courage may reveal itself early in a career, but many respondents have told me they were able to develop, nurture, and enhance their courage when they were in their forties and even fifties.

I have spent a considerable amount of time profiling people who have demonstrated courage, and this knowledge is very useful when I play the role of guidance counselor. People often consult me when they are contemplating the change from being an employee to being self-employed. I give them a book to read — I've probably given away several cases of the same book to those who aspire to be self-employed. Of all the courageous people I have studied, one stands out from the rest. He was Erich Hartmann, the World War II fighter pilot and holder of the world record of 352 air victories.

I tell my advisees to read this book because they all seem to think that people who are courageous are without fear, but Hartmann's book presents a more realistic understanding of courage, as in the following paragraph:

> *I was afraid . . . of the big unknown factors. Clouds and sun were hate and love. . . .* (Raymond F. Toliver and Trevor J. Constable, *The Blond Knight of Germany* [Blue Ridge Summit, PA: TAB Books, Inc., 1970], p. 175)

Yes, even the Ace of Aces was afraid, but he acted courageously nevertheless. Fear and courage are related. Courage does not exist in the absence of fear of some danger. If more people understood this fact, there would be more courageous business owners and, ultimately, more millionaires.

WHERE IS THE REAL RISK?

Countless numbers of my MBA students once thought that they avoided taking much risk. Many never even considered being self-employed business owners — it was just too risky. Accepting positions with major corporations was the way to all but eliminate the risk of being unemployed someday. And why spend countless hours studying investment opportunities? "The company" will always take care of its middle-level executives. For many of my former students, their creed was simply to earn, spend, and let "the company" take care of them for life.

That was the ideal, low-risk method. But they misjudged the odds, and at one time or another most have had their middle-level positions eliminated.

For example, just before Christmas one year I was talking to one of my contacts at a large public corporation. He was quite candid about the corporation's internal changes and said, "We plan to eliminate fourteen hundred middle-manager positions right after the first of the year." Later, I kept seeing the fourteen hundred unlucky families in my mind, all celebrating the holidays. Happy New Year! Little did any of them know what was in store for at least one of their main breadwinners.

Several of my former students were among the unlucky fourteen hundred. It seems ironic that these were some of my best students. Others who barely made it through the program were not offered positions with top corporations, and so many of these marginal students eventually became self-employed business owners. They thought of themselves as economic risk takers, but were they? Perhaps my students among the fourteen hundred actually took more risk — most had a single source of income and a single career track.

My more marginal students have the millionaire's mind — they confronted their fears and took risks. They bolstered their decision to become self-employed business owners by constantly reminding themselves of one simple reality. Ultimately, the big risk with the long odds, the real vulnerability, is allowing others to control one's career. Why did fourteen hundred bright, well-educated, hardworking managers abruptly lose their single source of income overnight? Because a few senior executives thought it was a good idea.

WAS IT LUCK?

Self-made millionaires will certainly tell you that wealth accumulation is all about taking financial risk, working hard, being disciplined, and keeping focused. However, about one in eight millionaires believe that luck was very important in explaining their economic success. There is a very interesting relationship between high net worth and what respondents perceived to be luck.

Only about 9 percent of high-income-producing nonmillionaires, and about 9 percent of the millionaires with $1 to $2 million net worth believe that luck accounts for economic success. But among decamillionaires, those with a net worth of $10 million, more than one in five (22 percent) believe that luck was *very important* in accounting for their economic success! Four in ten of these decamillionaires felt that luck was *important.*

If luck is the key to becoming wealthy, we should all take up gambling. But the luck that these millionaires are referring to is not the luck of casino patrons and lotto fans. Millionaires are

not the gambling industry's best customers —
only one millionaire in four has set foot in a gambling casino in the past twelve months, and some
of this patronage can be accounted for because
they were attending trade shows or professional
meetings in or near a casino hotel.

Almost by definition, wealth builders believe
that a different type of luck plays some role in accounting for high economic returns. Those who
are most adamant about the role of luck feel that:

"The harder you work the luckier you become!"

That statement was written on a questionnaire
completed by a respondent who was worth more
than $25 million. To him and his fellow million-
aires, luck relates to uncontrollable factors like
weather, competition, the tightening of credit,
changes in consumer income, recessions, and so
on.

It's worthwhile to contrast the views of self-
employed decamillionaires with those of high-
income-producing attorneys and physicians.
Most professionals in these categories discount
luck in explaining their success. They believe it
was part of a proven track record. They studied
hard, received high grades in college, and were
accepted to law or medical school. Then they
worked hard, picked the right specialty, and invested wisely, so they became wealthy. It's
almost pro forma.

But what about business owners and entrepreneurs? Their success was not nearly as predictable when they started their businesses. Many will say that unexpected things happened in their pursuit of wealth. But these unanticipated events had a positive impact on their balance sheets. Some believe that intuition had a part in the decisions they made, but at the highest levels of wealth, these people believe that luck is an important correlate of becoming very wealthy in America. Luck and risk taking go hand in hand.

RISK TAKING, NOT GAMBLING

Ask 1,001 high-income-producing respondents one simple question:

How important is your willingness to take financial risk, given the right return, in explaining your financial success?

Those who answer "very important" are significantly more likely to have net worths in the multimillions of dollars (see Table 4-3). More than four in ten (41 percent) of the decamillionaires gave "very important" as their answer. Only about two in ten (21 percent) of those in the $1 to $2 million net worth category gave the same answer. How about those high-income respondents who were not millionaires? Only 18 percent attributed their economic success to the financial risk-taking factor.

There is a clear and very significant correla-

TABLE 4-3

TAKING FINANCIAL RISK VS. PLAYING THE LOTTERY: CORRELATES OF WEALTH?

Risk and the Lottery	Net Worth Category Percentage (in $ Millions) (N=1001)				
	Under $1M	$1– Under $2M	$2M – Under $5M	$5M – Under $10M	$10M or More
"Willingness to take financial risk" rated as very important in explaining economic success	18	21	28	39	41
Played the lottery in the past thirty days	38	36	27	21	14
Played the lottery in the past twelve months	47	48	35	27	20

tion between willingness to take financial risk and net worth. The risk versus reward theory so often touted in the financial press is, once again, validated. Those who attribute their economic success to financial risk taking are not foolish about how their money is invested, and most consider gambling to be a foolish alternative for their financial resources. In the lottery, for example, winning is a matter of chance, and most wealthy people or those who will likely become wealthy never play the lottery. Most never gamble — the risk takers are not likely to be gamblers.

The millionaires I've interviewed understand probability theory. In essence, they "know the odds" and the expected payouts. The expected payouts are so very, very small that "it's better to burn a few dollars with a match each week than lay money down for the lotto!" They know that in most gambling situations, especially the lottery, players have no control over the winning numbers that are selected, they do not know the odds or expected payouts, and the expected payout is less than the price of the lotto ticket. There is nothing one player can do to increase his chances of winning significantly except by buying more lotto tickets.

Other less affluent people tell me that it's only one, two, or ten dollars a week, and look at the prize! But what is your expected payout? A one-dollar lotto ticket with a $1 million payout may be one in several million purchased, so your odds of winning are one in several million. Say it is your one ticket against 4,500,000 others. Your chance of winning is 1 in 4.5 million, while your payout is only $1 million. Even that $1 million is what I call funny money, because as the winner, you'll have two choices. Your million dollars may be in annual payouts of $100,000 for ten years, so in today's current dollars, it's not close to one million. Or you can take a lump sum, which is considerably less than $1 million. In essence, the real expected payout of one dollar invested in a lotto ticket is a fraction of that dollar. Often it is less than fifty cents. In terms of risk and reward, most lotto games are a consumer rip-off.

As shown in Table 4-3, there is a very significant negative correlation between playing the lotto and one's level of wealth. Decamillionaires are the least likely of all net worth categories to have played the lottery within the past thirty days, and nonmillionaires had the highest percentage of lotto players for the same period of thirty days. For every decamillionaire who played lotto in the past thirty days, there were nearly three nonmillionaire players, a ratio of 2.7 to 1. Note that these nonmillionaires are high-income producers, earning $100,000 or more annually. Could it be that if they allocated more of their income to genuine investments, they might be in the millionaire category?

People counter with, "It's only a few bucks a week." It is more than money; it is also time. Assume it takes ten minutes to purchase a lotto ticket; that figure includes waiting in line and a few minutes for travel time. Assume you make one purchase per week. That translates into 520 minutes per year allocated to an activity that has a near-zero probability of winning a big pot of gold.

In turn, 520 minutes translates into 8.7 hours

per year. The typical millionaire earns the equivalent of approximately $300 per hour. Prorated times 8.7 hours, you can understand his reluctance to stop by the neighborhood convenience shop each week. Those 8.7 hours are allocated to more productive tasks like working, learning a new skill, or socializing with family and friends. Computed in working time, the millionaire's cost is $300 times 8.7 hours, or $2,600 per year. Over twenty years, it amounts to $52,000. If this money was fully invested in Home Depot stock during this same period, it would have translated into multiple millions of dollars.

Decamillionaires on average earn the equivalent of nearly $1,000 per hour of work. Their cost in lost work opportunity to play the lotto each week would be $8,700 per year, or $174,000 in twenty years. Imagine if this sum was invested as in the example above, the sum could be an estimated $1 million or more.

Self-made millionaires know that the time and money allocated to playing the lottery can be spent on more productive activities. Too many people spend too much of their adult lives playing this game of little chance. Does such long-term loyalty make you a better, more intelligent player? Does it make you a better father or manager?

THE RIGHT ADVICE:
A KEY TO REDUCING RISK
One of the strong similarities among the mem-

bers of the millionaire population is their strength in selecting advisers. This asset includes knowing when they need to consult key advisers, who they are, and how to select them. There is a strong positive correlation between finding good advisers and wealth accumulation, because having good advice reduces the risk involved in financial, career, and even personal decisions.

DR. HEART: BIG BRAIN, NO BUCKS

His call came just two days after my article was published in *Medical Economics* (July 1992). Allow me to paraphrase an excerpt from our conversation.

DR. HEART: I'm wondering when I will be able to retire. How much will I need? I'm sixty-three . . . earned about $200,000 last year.

DR. STANLEY: Well, as the equation in the article stated, one-tenth of your age, that's sixty-three, times your annual income of $200,000 equals your expected net worth, or about $1.26 million. But if you are in the top quarter, you need at least twice that number, or about $2.52 million as a threshold.

DR. HEART: I don't have nearly $2.5 million. So when will I be able to retire?

DR. STANLEY: That's really up to you.

DR. HEART: Well, I had a situation recently. I

changed investment managers. For many years I had a well-known asset-management firm in Philadelphia manage my pension. They had discretion but mostly invested in stocks of quality companies.

DR. STANLEY: I'm familiar with that firm. It's well respected. It's been around forever. . . . It's conservative in its philosophy.

DR. HEART: Well, that's one of the reasons I switched fund managers — lackluster performance.

DR. STANLEY: How is your pension performing today?

DR. HEART: That's one of the reasons for my call. I have a problem. I lost everything — I mean *everything*. Over $1.5 million.

DR. STANLEY: How did that happen?

DR. HEART: It's a long story.

DR. STANLEY: I've got all afternoon.

DR. HEART: About two years ago I was invited to a seminar. The speaker was touring the country. It said he was a famous asset manager. He had all kinds of performance numbers and charts. The investments he managed did ten times better than mine. I was very impressed with what he had to say. It seemed that he had a track record of making people wealthy.

DR. STANLEY: What types of investments did he plug?

DR. HEART: Private partnerships, investments in private companies, some real estate, some energy, high technology.

DR. STANLEY: What did your CPA or your attorney advise you about these investments?

DR. HEART: I never asked for their opinions.

DR. STANLEY: How did you get from $1.5 million before the seminar to ground zero after the seminar?

DR. HEART: I believed what he said. I was impressed with his numbers and disappointed in the performance of my own plan. So I switched managers. The new manager lost every dime!

What was I supposed to tell this unfortunate fellow? His question was, "When will I be able to retire?" The answer is perhaps never.

DR. HEART: Do you by chance know someone who can do a better job managing my plan in the future?

DR. STANLEY: I don't have a list of top investment advisers — not in your area, not even in my own. But I will tell you what many economically successful people do regarding investment advisers. You have an accountant and an attorney?

DR. HEART: Yes, but do they know about investing?

DR. STANLEY: The next time you ever even

think about making changes, ask both your accountant and your lawyer for their views. If they don't feel capable of making such judgments, ask them to refer you to some others in their professions.

I also suggested that he find a professional investment adviser who would be part of his investment advisory committee. The other members should include an enlightened accountant and a top attorney. Both his accountant and attorney should be able to judge the variations in quality among an ever-growing population of stockbrokers, asset managers, financial planners, and the like. Accountants often know which of their clients make money investing, and they can ask these clients who their investment adviser is.

MILLIONAIRES HAVE GOOD ADVISERS

Imagine that Dr. Heart had had an advisory committee intact several years before he called me. If the committee members had accompanied him to that seminar given by "Mr. Famous," the so-called asset manager, perhaps Dr. Heart would be able to retire in comfort today. If he had only retained that "old conservative asset-management firm," his pension would be worth more than $3 million today.

Even simpler, Dr. Heart could have screened invitations from investment gurus himself. If you find yourself in the same situation, telephone the guru's office and ask the following question:

What percentage of your invitations were sent to attorneys? In Dr. Heart's case, the percentage was likely zero because dishonest marketers of investments and related services have great fear of the legal profession. A multimillionaire once related this to me. "They won't rip off attorneys because attorneys can sue for free." Call the sponsor and ask if you can bring your attorney. His response will give you a clue to his intentions. On the other hand, an investment expert who has high integrity and novel ideas might actually encourage attorneys to attend his presentations, and lawyers are quite often members of multiple informal investment committees for wealthy clients.

Most millionaires do not have one investment adviser — they have at least three. More often than not, their CPA and trusted attorney are part of the team, and these advisers help select and screen stockbrokers, financial planners, and insurance agents. There is a built-in system of checks and balances. Stockbrokers feel compelled to give outstanding service to clients who interface with enlightened CPAs and attorneys. Poor service or bad recommendations are more likely to be noticed if multiple influential parties are involved. Also, enlightened professionals often have other clients with ventures that need capital, and some of these may have extraordinary potential for growth. But you will never discover this unless you patronize the best professionals. Most libraries have a directory of law firms and lawyers — the *Martindale-Hubble Law Directory* gives a bio of each attorney.

In the long run, it is very beneficial to have a trusted CPA and attorney work with you throughout your adult life. Do-it-yourself patronage decisions concerning financial advisers, à la Dr. Heart, are rare among the self-made-millionaire population.

THE DO-IT-YOURSELF DOWNFALL

Why do people like Dr. Heart "work without a net"? Why are they do-it-yourselfers when it comes to investing their life savings? The more data I collect about this issue the clearer it all becomes. Dr. Heart was and still is a scholar. He was a scholar in college and medical school, and his writing and reading habits indicate that he is still a scholar today. In a nutshell, he has a high level of analytical intellect. The data about such people indicate that only a minority use skilled advisers like CPAs and attorneys when making investment and related patronage decisions. As noted before, we use SAT scores as a measurement of analytical intellect. Only about 40 percent of millionaires with SAT scores of 1400 and over use advisers. Yet more than 60 percent of those in the 1000 to 1200 range regularly consult with skilled advisers.

What's the connection here — why do some people with very high levels of analytical intellect become do-it-yourself investors? Having high analytical intellect does not necessarily guarantee a high level of practical intelligence, and part of practical intelligence relates to one's ability to make accurate judgments about people. In this regard, I suspect that Dr. Heart's practical intelligence is not very high, and he's not alone. He and his group greatly enhanced and nurtured their analytical skills in college and medical school but neglected another component of intelligence. Physicians are the least likely of all high-income occupational groups to report that as part of their overall educational experience they:

Learned how to make accurate judgments about people.

There are several other theories that might explain the irony of:

Big brain, no bucks.

One was summarized succinctly by a respondent in one of my focus group interviews.

Money is boring.

Yes, some highly intelligent people feel that way. They are more challenged, more excited about doing heart surgery or solving high-order math problems than "counting every dime." Given the choice, they'd rather be in the running for a Nobel Prize than become a decamillionaire.

Taking time and energy away from such pursuits in order to work with advisers is just not their cup of tea.

But there is another more compelling theory. The analytical-test results of people like Dr. Heart indicate that he's close to genius level. So perhaps he doesn't need any advisers. Perhaps he thinks he's smarter than any adviser. So why spend time and money dealing with these people? When it comes to investing, some people do think they are, financially speaking, immortal. Being very, very intelligent may have some drawbacks. Most high-income people with average to above average intellect realize they aren't brilliant, but the majority have great common or practical intelligence. They know their strengths and weaknesses and act accordingly. They never make major investment decisions without first seeking advice from skilled professionals.

So here is yet another set of rules taught by self-made millionaires:

- Never be too proud to seek advice from skilled investment advisers, especially CPAs and tax attorneys.
- Be more sensitive to the long-term benefits of having high-grade CPAs and attorneys as your advisers than to the short-term benefits of doing it yourself.
- If you're not good at judging talent, hire advisers who are.

How do you make critical decisions concerning allocation of your financial resources? What type of decision process do you go through when making major changes in your business or career? If you are like the majority of millionaires, you do not make such changes without first consulting your key advisers. In the following pages we'll learn more about who millionaires rely on to give them the best advice.

One of the most frequent questions that I am asked concerns sources of advice. People write and call, and the questions are similar: "Who is the best source for investment advice — stockbrokers, financial planners, insurance agents, or marketers of mutual funds?" I can often tell that the caller is not a millionaire when he asks that question, because I've learned that these professionals are not the key investment advisers for most millionaires. In fact, there is a direct positive correlation between one's net worth and the use of certified public accountants, attorneys, or tax consultants as investment advisers.

Take a representative sample of all high-income earners in America, and look at each category of high income, i.e., $100,000 to $199,999, $200,000 to $299,999, and so forth. In each category ask the members of the sample a simple question:

Who do you use for investment and related financial advice?

Within each income group, respondents who have higher levels of wealth are likely to indicate that CPAs and attorneys provide them with investment advice. In fact, they are three to five times more likely to consult with CPAs and attorneys regarding investments than with stockbrokers. Note that I am referring to advice and counsel — not executing stock trades. Also, most millionaires generally don't limit themselves to stocks, bonds, and related investments — they invest heavily in private businesses and real estate.

So when people contact me regarding investment and financial advisers, I tell them what millionaires tell me. More than two-thirds of the self-made millionaires in America rely on the advice of CPAs and attorneys. Of course, not all professionals in these two categories offer investment advice, so it does take some searching to find the ideal set of advisers.

There is a major difference between using the basic services offered by any professional and taking his investment advice. For example, you may employ a CPA to complete your tax returns, a stockbroker to execute your trades, and an attorney to help you draft a will. These are basic, boilerplate offerings. But a growing number of highly skilled CPAs and attorneys do much more than boilerplate. They provide customized investment advice on areas not just involving securities of public corporations. These professionals can be very valuable advisers concerning the tax implications of many other alternatives, from private investments to industrial real estate.

Most millionaires gained their economic status in part from investing in things other than stocks and bonds, but many of these unconventional categories have their own set of risks and opportunities. It often takes intelligent, well-seasoned CPAs and attorneys to sort these things out for the millionaire.

What about conventional investment categories like publicly traded stocks? Even here many millionaires view the worlds of advice and execution of trades as being far apart. Take the results of a regional study I conducted of 185 multimillionaires. Each respondent had a minimum net worth of $5 million, and each was asked four questions:

1. Who has provided you with investment advice in the past twelve months?
2. How productive or useful was this advice in helping you attain your investment goals?
3. Who has provided you with any other financial service(s) in the past twelve months?
4. What level of quality did you receive from each of these service providers?

Most of the multimillionaires used CPAs (71 percent) and attorneys (67 percent) as investment advisers during the twelve-month period prior to being surveyed (see Table 4-4). Three in

248

TABLE 4-4

THE PATRONAGE HABITS OF MULTIMILLIONAIRES: INVESTMENT ADVISERS AND OTHER SERVICE PROVIDERS
(N=185)

Category of In-vestment Adviser	Investment Advice		Other Financial Services	
	Rec'd (%age)	Rated as Very Productive (%age)	Provided (%age)	Rated as Excellent or Good Quality (%age)
Certified Public Accountant	71	75	85	87
Attorney	67	78	81	84
Tax Specialist/Consultant	46	82	48	88
Close Friend	38	61	23	72
Business Associate/Colleague	35	69	28	75
Life Insurance Agent	29	32	35	66
Real Estate Agent	25	28	35	69
Commercial Lending Executive	22	60	52	70
Stockbroker	21	62	72	64
Trust Company	18	55	55	50
Relative/Spouse	16	64	11	60
Financial Planner	15	70	15	65
Investment/Asset Manager	14	56	16	65

four (75 percent) rated the investment advice received from CPAs as being very useful in helping them achieve their investment goals, while nearly four in five (78 percent) rated the investment advice received from attorneys in the same manner. Nearly one-half (46 percent) received advice from a tax specialist. Of these, 82 percent indicated the advice was very productive.

Interestingly, only 21 percent received investment advice from a stockbroker, but most of these multimillionaires, 62 percent, rated the advice as being very productive. A much greater number than those receiving advice rely on stockbrokers for other services. Nearly three-fourths (72 percent) rely on stockbrokers to make stock and related transactions. Most multimillionaires also read and rely upon the research reports prepared by stockbrokerage firms.

One multimillionaire respondent, whom I'll refer to as "Alvin," was particularly vocal about how he employs stockbrokers and attorneys, and there were many who echoed his views. Asked how he would advise someone looking for an investment consultant among the ranks of stockbrokers, he replied:

Hmm . . . I couldn't recommend one. I wouldn't recommend one. I use a stockbroker for the purpose of executing orders. That's it.

I don't want 'em to give me any information. I don't want 'em to tell me what day it is or what time it is. . . .

I want a broker who doesn't give me advice, doesn't give me recommendations, just gives me the service that I want to have. . . . I'm happier when it's done that way.

The only service Alvin needs from his brokers is executing trades and supplying him with research reports written by investment analysts and other experts. That's why so many Alvins I have interviewed are now using the Internet for investment information as well as for trading.

How did Alvin find stockbrokers who act according to his mandate?

You don't find a stockbroker who handles it that way. Ya train a broker to handle things like that for you.

Alvin reads a lot of research reports before making any changes in his investment portfolio, but he often asks his attorney as well as his CPA for their input.

In general, Alvin believes in hiring the top attorneys from the top law firms in his geographical area. He finds that this is the fastest and most economically productive way to hire talent. He tends to hire law firms that are "the largest," "the best," and the most influential, because he believes that the bigger the better, and the best law firms hire the best people. The biggest and best firms are filled with skilled specialists, and Alvin relies on specialists who know a lot about tax-advantaged investments. Can hiring a top law firm be prohibitively expensive? Not according to Alvin.

> *I've dealt for many years with individual lawyers [one-man firms] or some small law firms. And by and large they tend to charge me the going rate, hundreds an hour, even if they're reading a law book.*
>
> *Whereas I go to [the biggest firm] and they have specialists in every field, and if I want to know about . . . the offshore deals, they got a guy down there who knows all about offshore deals.*
>
> *I call him [the senior partner at a top law firm] and I say, "Charlie, I wanna talk to somebody about offshore." [He says], "We got a guy." So I went down, spent a couple of hours with him.*

So for less than $1,000 Alvin received three hours of sound investment advice, and for him, the benefit received from that fee was well worth it.

Also as a result, Alvin has fully adopted Rule 20. The tax attorney/offshore expert always tells Alvin the same thing:

> *Alvin, invest if you want to (offshore). If you really want to . . . we'll eventually get you out of jail [even] if it takes* twenty years!

HUMOR THE COLD CALLER
It was one of many calls I received at the uni-

versity that day. But this one was unique.

> CALLER: *USA Today* quotes you. . . . gives the size of the millionaire market in each state. Even the number living outside the country. I just want your list of the names and addresses of America's millionaires.
>
> DR. STANLEY: I don't have a list. Those numbers are estimates. The figures are generated by a statistical model. You don't think I'm going to count every millionaire one by one, do you?
>
> CALLER: I want to buy your list. Can I get it on labels?
>
> DR. STANLEY: I don't have a list. As I told you, I'm not in the list business.

The fellow who called was a cold-calling salesperson who targets millionaires. He markets tax shelters, "tax-advantaged concepts." He called me eight times. During the first seven conversations I told him the same story, i.e., I'm not in the list business. During one of these conversations I suggested that he take a different approach.

> DR. STANLEY: Most wealthy people rely upon the judgments of their accountants and attorneys when evaluating the type of investments you offer. Why not contact CPAs and tax attorneys? If they like your ideas, they may endorse your products.

CALLER: CPAs . . . CPAs! They are deal busters. None of 'em want to take any risks. They won't let their clients do anything out of the ordinary. No guts. Their clients are paying too much tax, and they do nothing. . . . They are deal busters, that's all.

DR. STANLEY: Well, most CPAs are well versed in the tax codes. Some CPAs even have law degrees and specialize in tax issues. The last thing they want is for their clients to get audited.

CALLER: As far as I'm concerned, if you're *not* audited every year, your accountant is not doing his job! You got to be willing to take risks. There are still a lot of gray areas.

As you can imagine, this guy and his offering would frighten even seasoned investors. I know he scared me, even though he never attempted to sell me a tax shelter. After his seventh call I decided that I must take a more aggressive posture. During the eighth call — placed to my home on a Saturday morning — the following conversation transpired.

CALLER: Have you made up your mind? Do you want to become a wealthy man? I want your list and I'll pay big numbers.

DR. STANLEY: Okay, okay, you win. Let's start with a test list. Then you can see if it fits your needs. You're based in New York. So how about New York's millionaires?

CALLER: I knew it. I knew you had the list. Can we start with New York City?

DR. STANLEY: Even better, how about Manhattan?

CALLER: How many millionaires live in the borough of Manhattan?

DR. STANLEY: About thirty-three thousand.

CALLER: How much?

DR. STANLEY: How about ten cents a name, including street addresses and phone numbers?

CALLER: It's a deal. I need it soon.

DR. STANLEY: I can send it overnight. Just give me your air-express billing number. I'll include an invoice for $3,300. That's thirty-three thousand names at ten cents each.

CALLER: It's a done deal . . . like white on rice!

On the Monday following this conversation, I prepared an invoice for $3,300 and placed it in an overnight package. But also included was something else. I enclosed a two-year-old Manhattan telephone directory (the white pages). The package was received by "Mr. Caller" the next morning. And as expected, he immediately telephoned my office. He was unhappy.

DR. STANLEY: Hello, this is Tom Stanley.

CALLER: This is not a list of @#$%! millionaires. What the !$%#@ are you? This is a @#$%! telephone book. I'm not paying you #@!$#!

DR. STANLEY: Actually, it is indeed a list of millionaires. About one in every seventy people listed are millionaires. The list I sent you is much like yourself. Both you and the list are unrefined.

To date, the caller has yet to send me a check for $3,300. He never even returned my telephone directory. In fact, he has never contacted me since he complained about the unrefined list!

Changing the Odds

What are the odds that the business venture you're considering will bear fruit? Are you the type of person who will take financial risk given the right return? Perhaps you think you lack the courage "to venture," or you believe the odds are too long. Before you question your courage, consider this fact: Most millionaires who take risk do many things to increase the odds of winning, some of which are described in this section.

THEIR OWN BUSINESS

Most decamillionaires attribute their wealth to owning and investing in their own, rather than in other people's, businesses, which include the ones listed on the various stock exchanges. The millionaires state that they can control their own

TABLE 4-5

CRITICAL SUCCESS FACTORS ACCORDING TO SELF-DESIGNATED FINANCIAL RISK TAKERS VS. NON-RISK TAKERS
(N=1001)

Percentage of Respondents

1. Investing in my own business	52(7)
2. Making wise investments	56(12)
3. Seeing business opportunities others did not see	52(10)
4. Finding a profitable market niche	42(10)

businesses, but they can't control or dictate policy to public corporations, let alone determine prices in the stock market. Most will also tell you they believe they are better able to operate a particular type of business than anyone else. The "particular type" is the key element here. Successful risk takers are market nichers — they do things that others do not do, or, at the very least, they do things in a market area where there are few competitors.

It's interesting to contrast those who are self-designated risk takers with those who attribute their success to other elements. As shown in Table 4-5, risk takers are significantly more likely to rate certain other factors as critical in explaining their economic success.

For most financial risk takers, the really long odds are involved in investing in other people's businesses. Their philosophy is that the best people to work for are me, myself, and I. Otherwise, they are at the mercy of someone who may not be sensitive to their needs and financial goals.

Business owners are the most frequent of all high-income groups to give credit for their success to their willingness to take financial risk. Senior corporate executives are in second place, followed by physicians and, finally, attorneys. The majority of these risk-taking professionals are self-employed.

THE RIGHT NICHE

In the twenty-five years I have studied millionaires, I have discovered that they do a lot to reduce the risk associated with being self-employed. In all the years that I have studied the wealthy, I have rarely found a multimillionaire who tells me:

> *I just thought it would be a good idea to be self employed. . . . I just thought that I would like to become an excavation contractor or a wholesaler of fish oil or a sandblasting contractor.*

Almost all the self-made multimillionaires whom I have interviewed had some experience, some leverage in the vocational area they selected. Many studied the profitability of various types of businesses before making a decision. Financial risk takers are nearly twice as likely to have studied the profitability of different businesses before they took the entrepreneurial plunge than non–risk takers. And they were very likely to have an understanding of the growth and income potentials of different ventures. In essence, risk takers succeed in part because they do a lot of homework before investing. They also seem to have some intuition about the category of business that they would enjoy. Most often it is at least a two-step process. Risk takers first select an industry for which they have some affinity. It's more than money; it's a feeling of belonging. They often begin their careers as employees, and then have some intuition about their affinity for that industry.

As a second step, risk takers develop a business concept. Affinity, knowledge of the industry, training, experience, and just plain old contacts with potential customers and suppliers are the influential factors. What is the real risk of starting one's own business under these circumstances? It's much less than most people imagine. Moving from being an employee to a self-employed supplier within the same or related industry is much less of a stretch than mastering a vocation and industry that are new to you. It's much easier to succeed if you like the business, industry, and people who are part of your enterprise.

Financial risk takers are nearly twice as likely to attribute their financial success

to "love of their career or business" than are risk avoiders.

THAT SIXTH SENSE: OPPORTUNITY

Financial risk takers often have a special sensitivity, and they "see business opportunities that others do not see." Time after time when I interview a group of self-made millionaires, a pattern emerges. The respondents with the highest levels of wealth give credit to their ability to recognize opportunities that other people do not appreciate.

The so-called risk takers know how to reduce the odds of failure and enhance the probability of succeeding by investing in business categories that others avoid or don't appreciate. Competitors stay away because there is a perceptual barrier — they just don't see the light. A detailed discussion of how millionaires select business opportunities is given in chapter 5, "Vocation Vocation Vocation."

Countless numbers of successful people can and do see what others can never perceive. Along these lines, consider the note that I recently received from the son of a man who had a great eye for economic opportunities. It was such a keen sense that it countered his bad experiences as a child.

My father died last year. I'm sure he would have been glad to fill out your survey [questionnaire]. He never went past the sixth grade. His father and teachers hit him constantly. He went from hell to hell.

He . . . built —— Corporation (picture of headquarters enclosed). He helped many in my family build businesses from [shops in garages] into factories.

He saw opportunities people walked past every day.

R.J.R.
President

Even if you see great opportunities, it takes courage to capitalize on them. It took courage for a fellow who dropped out of school in the sixth grade to even think that he could build several multimillion-dollar businesses. The actions of his father and teachers were not ego-enhancing, confidence-building experiences, but his vision of opportunities overcame the negative actions of authority figures. In some cases, the instinct for recognizing business opportunities is so strong that it outweighs criticism and other impediments. Such instincts can enhance one's courage and resolve.

What if you are the one with the great idea that others don't appreciate — how can you persuade them to follow your lead? Most economically successful people have some ability to "sell their ideas" to others. It is a hallmark of successful business owners and senior corporate executives, but they also know how to identify people who will most likely be persuaded to follow their lead — people of courage.

One of the finest examples of the balance between courage and vision was the strategy Ray Kroc initially employed in selling McDonald's franchises. It was based on finding people with courage. Believe it or not, Mr. Kroc once found it difficult to sell what is today the trophy of franchises. But he had vision. He saw what few others could even before he started selling franchises.

Mr. Kroc instructed his secretary to send in all cold-calling sales professionals. Who were these people so intent on selling him everything from life insurance to Bibles? Mr. Kroc knew that cold callers are people with courage and guts. He assumed that if they had enough courage to sell via cold calls, they certainly had the guts to purchase and operate a McDonald's franchise, and he was correct. An excellent discussion of this "selling the sales professional" is detailed in John Love's outstanding book *McDonald's: Behind the Arches* (Toronto: Bantam Books, 1986). The book is required reading for those who wish to understand the meaning of vision.

FEAR REDUCTION 101: POSITIVE THINKING

The most economically successful people in this country have the courage to take economic risk, and often their courage is tested over and over again. What if you mortgaged all your possessions in order to start a business, or gave up your position as partner in a successful law firm to go out on your own, or, as a senior corporate executive, completely changed the firm's product offerings? How do millionaires deal with fears and worries conjured up by these decisions?

As shown in Table 4-1, "believing in myself" is one of the most important techniques they use. These words are similar to the first three words contained in a famous book, the one that holds the all-time record for consecutive weeks on the *New York Times* bestseller list, *The Power of Positive Thinking*, by Norman Vincent Peale. It is still in print, although it was originally published in 1952.

I recently received a centennial edition of the book, commemorating the birth of Norman Vincent Peale on May 31, 1898. His work is still very much alive: *The Power of Positive Thinking* has sold more than 20 million copies and has influenced many people. Countless sermons, lectures, seminars, motivational speeches, and even therapy sessions have included the principles espoused by Dr. Peale.

Dr. Peale often cited principles from the Bible, and many of his special principles have been adopted by a large number of the millionaires in America. His work has a religious orientation, so it is particularly appealing to millionaires who indicate having a strong religious faith. Yet many others, perhaps unknowingly, have adopted at least some of Dr. Peale's principles, whether they have strong religious orientation or not.

Dr. Peale's advice is echoed by other successful professionals and writers. For thirteen years I was on the marketing department faculty at Georgia State University with Dave Schwartz. Dave wrote the best-selling book *The Magic of Thinking Big.* More than 3.5 million copies of the book have been sold, along with over 9 million copies of the audiotape. His book outlines the importance of thinking big thoughts in order to accomplish big deeds (see David J. Schwartz, *The Magic of Thinking Big* [New York: Fireside, 1965]).

When I asked Dave about his own successes, he told me that he always kept positive thoughts in his mind. He always thought of succeeding and never of failing.

You know, Tom, you can think positive or negative. You can only think one thought at a time. . . . It is up to the individual. . . . Do you want to be positive or negative? . . . If I were any more positive, I would be worried about my mental health.

Dave exuded optimism. If he had fears or worries, he overwhelmed them with positive thoughts. Dave had much in common with other successful people — like them, he knew how to deal with fear and related negative thoughts. As suggested in *The Magic of Thinking Big* (p. 28), he encouraged people who wanted to succeed to:

- Think success, never think failure.
- Develop a strong belief in yourself.
- Think big.

Many of Dave's guidelines about thinking big, positive thoughts are followed by millionaires, who are proficient at controlling their thought processes. They think and correspondingly act in ways that precipitate success. They cast out even the notion that they are inferior. Dave Schwartz cited the words of Publilius Syrus as a last thought in *The Magic of Thinking Big* (p. 186):

A wise man will be the master of his mind; a fool will be its slave.

If you think you can't succeed, you probably won't. Do you feel inferior to others? Does taking even the slightest financial risk conjure up a debilitating fear inside you? For too many people today the answer to both questions is yes. Fear and worry are first cousins to feeling inferior.

Some millionaires developed their own methods of self-motivation and positive thinking; others followed role models. A mentor doesn't always tell you how to think and act — just being positive and acting in ways that stimulate positive thought can have a profound influence on one's audience.

Regardless of the source, most risk-taking millionaires think positively, employing a variety of processes that stimulate optimism. Those who are able to do so overcome the fears and worries that deter them from acting in ways that build wealth.

FAITH IN WORMS AND YOURSELF

Almost all the millionaires surveyed indicate that a major key to their success and their ability to overcome fear and worry is a direct function of:

Believing in myself.

They don't always have perfect, complete self-confidence, especially when confronted with major changes or challenges in their life, but they do have the know-how and the skills to regain their self-confidence.

Tom Mann is often credited with inventing one of the most widely used lures for fishing. Billions of this type of lure have been sold — the rubber worm. Mr. Mann is more than an inventor. He is a world-class fishing pro, and he has scientifically studied fish and the productivity of fishermen, lures, and techniques. I had the pleasure of hearing him discuss the really big element in the fishing equation, but he was not touting his own invention. Mr. Mann says that the best lure for catching fish is the one the fisherman has the greatest confidence in. If you have great confidence in your lure, you'll fish with confidence. You will succeed if you believe. Even the fish know who has confidence.

What Mr. Mann told his audience hit me like a bolt. I love to fish, and I have many lures. I've been fishing since age seven, but I don't think I ever caught a fish with a lure that I didn't completely trust to catch fish. I cannot recall one exception to Mr. Mann's statement.

So it is with success in life. If you lack self-confidence, you'll find it difficult to become successful, because it's extremely hard to be motivated if you don't believe in yourself. You can't really believe in what you're doing, and, in turn, you are communicating your lack of belief to others. How can you convince the best people to work for you if they see self-doubt in your eyes? How can you sell anything, from medical care to ball bearings? You can't, if your target clients sense that you don't believe in yourself and what you are trying to sell.

My national surveys of millionaires have taught me that if you believe you can succeed, the probabilities are greatly enhanced that you will reach or even exceed your goals. The millionaires often indicated that "believing in myself" is a proactive tactic or thought process that works when they deploy it. They utilize this process when fear and worry are conjured up by the need to make critical decisions about their career, business, or other economic resources.

What is the source of this "believing in myself"? Some say that certain people are just born with confidence. I have a different view. Confidence is and can be instilled in people by their family upbringing, or nurtured and developed on their own. Most millionaires have this ability to enhance their self-confidence, their belief in themselves.

Some people assume that the successful have permanent and unwavering belief in themselves. Not so. I have never interviewed one millionaire who did not have some fears and worries. However, when they encounter fears, they are able to overcome these feelings. Successful people know how to defeat fear and worry, and one of the first ways they do this is by calling on their inner self-confidence and belief in their own abilities.

The attributes that most often produce economic success were detailed in chapter 2, "Success Factors." These are general, even generic assets like discipline, getting along with people, loving one's career, investing wisely, having leadership skills, working hard, taking financial risk, having integrity, and finding a profitable niche that are essential if you want to have some chance of attaining millionaire status. If your goals are higher, if you aren't satisfied with just becoming a millionaire and want to become a decamillionaire or even more, you'll need more than generic success factors to go that extra mile.

You will need to constantly enhance your protective covering, your armor plate. In essence, you will need a greater degree of courage at each and every increasing stage of economic success. Few people outside the inherited-wealth category ever become decamillionaires without encountering increasing economic risks. With increasing risk, you need increasing levels of courage, and there is no courage without fear, economic or otherwise.

For millionaires, like everyone else, fear and worry are never defeated permanently. The really big issue is that these economically productive people are able to constantly build up their self-confidence and belief in themselves. Then it's possible to imagine one economic success following the next. And accordingly, as continued successes pile up, self-confidence is being constantly upgraded.

ACTIONS THAT REDUCE FEAR: RISK TAKERS VS. RISK AVOIDERS

How do financial risk takers reduce the fears and worries often associated with taking financial risk? How do they differ from risk avoiders? To answer this question, I analyzed the responses from the entire sample of 1,001 respondents, of which 733 were millionaires. The balance were high-income-producing people who were not millionaires. These high-income, lower net worth respondents are the most risk averse — in general terms, they are spenders, not investors. They believe that having a high income earns them the title of "economically successful." Also these people are more likely to state that it is their superior IQ and intellect that accounts for their economic success, rather than financial risk taking and the courage that accompanies it.

Overall, there is an inverse relationship between taking financial risk and various measures of analytical intelligence such as SAT scores.

While others talk about their superior intellect, the typical financial risk taker has significant amounts of practical and creative intellect. What Professor Sternberg has discovered about many successful people is confirmed by my survey: What risk takers lack on the analytical side, they compensate for by hiring high-grade advisers, by studying and analyzing a great deal of financial literature, and by recognizing opportunities that others ignore. These skills are the product of creative intellect. It also helps to have a practical mind-set, common sense.

Financial risk takers, in contrast with risk avoiders, are significantly more likely to engage in actions or thought processes that reduce fear and worry. They have a system of bolstering their belief in themselves, enhancing their courage, and ultimately increasing the odds of selecting investments that bear fruit, as previously discussed. Several other techniques are described below.

SHARING CONCERNS WITH SPOUSE (71 PERCENT RISK TAKERS VS. 59 PERCENT RISK AVOIDERS)

There is strong evidence that risk takers are especially careful in selecting their husbands and wives. Statistically, they are significantly more sensitive to certain qualities when selecting their mates: compassion, wisdom, acceptance, self-discipline, security, even temper, virtue, reliability, and down-to-earth temperament. The risk takers are significantly more likely than risk avoiders to indicate that successful marriage is a function of having a mate who is respectful, patient, cheerful, and unselfish.

These qualities are especially important in marriages where financial risk taking is part of the couple's economic livelihood. They may encounter ups and downs in cash flow and return on their business investments. Often, a commitment in the couple's investments will take priority over an upgrade of a home, automobile, or vacation. This is especially true during the early years of marriage. Not all people are cut out to be the spouse of an economic risk taker. People who are likely to become economically successful deliberately select spouses who have qualities that are complements of wealth building, as detailed in chapter 6, "Choice of Spouse."

EXERCISING REGULARLY
(64 PERCENT VS. 53 PERCENT)
AND USING MENTAL TOUGHNESS DEVELOPED
IN SPORTS (55 PERCENT VS. 43 PERCENT)

He was an athlete in high school and college, but he didn't always keep himself in tip-top physical condition. About five years after Dr. John Peterson opened his first dental office, he decided that it was time for a change. He wanted to enhance his physical condition, so he hired a personal trainer.

Dr. Peterson has been in excellent condition ever since he started this exercise program, and he maintains that there is a direct correlation between exercising and his ability to deal with significant financial risk. As a self-designated financial risk taker, he constantly invests large sums of money in state-of-the-art equipment and facilities, but he rarely worries that he can recoup all the millions he has invested or generate enough revenue to pay for his equipment. He is a well-trained, highly skilled professional, but his ability to conquer fear is more than training and skill. Dr. Peterson works out in a gym each and every morning, in a program like the one designed for young Marine recruits in boot camp. It's strenuous, to say the least.

The result is much more than physical conditioning — Dr. Peterson believes it is the key to his mental strength. He feels it is much easier to maintain his positive mental attitude and personality as a result. Dr. Peterson believes that

fear and panic are the products of an uncondi-
tioned body, mind, and spirit. What if Dr. Peterson felt frightened each time he contemplated
investing large amounts of money in his operation? Then he would never have invested at all,
and he wouldn't be the manager of one of the
most productive business operations in Nassau
County, New York.

Some people suggest that a positive mental
attitude and the courage to offset fears are just part
of one's genetic structure. Not according to Dr.
Peterson. I asked him if he thought it was possible
to maintain a healthy, positive attitude and keep
his composure in stressful situations without physical conditioning. "Impossible," he replied. "I
don't care who your parents are. Fatigue brings
out the worst in people who are confronted with
job-related stress and financial risk. Why do you
think the best military outfits . . . [and] top athletic
teams are in the best physical condition? If I didn't
exercise at least one hour each morning, I would
have to retire or do something else with my ten-
hour days. If you panic, you will make mistakes.
And if you make mistakes in this business, you
won't be in business very long."

DEFEATING FEAR BY ATTACKING IT
(74 PERCENT VS. 51 PERCENT)
AND VISUALIZING SUCCESS
(76 PERCENT VS. 57 PERCENT)

Risk takers are what I call "pen and pad"
people. They list all the pluses of a venture on

one side of the page and the negatives on the other. First, they examine the list of negative factors, then they deploy the positive features as destroyers of fear, killers of the negatives. Even financial risk takers will venture into activities only where the positive features greatly outweigh the negatives. In order to do this balancing act of pros and cons, the risk taker must be able to visualize success — all the benefits of the venture. Millionaire risk takers often must be leaders of both human and capital resources, and in that role they must be able to offset the fears of their followers by teaching them to visualize success. They are innovators, teachers, sales professionals, and motivators, but first they are self-motivators, with great vision.

LOVE AND FAMILY

Some people keep working toward their goals in the face of long odds — they even excel under adverse conditions. Most economically successful people were conditioned early in life by their parents to withstand the fears and worries so often associated with adversity and taking major risks. Their parents provided them with a loving, warm, stable, and positive environment. This kind of upbringing used to be more common, even pro forma, in America. But today it is not so common. More than one-half of America's marriages eventually end in divorce. Single-parent households abound. Recorded spousal- and child-abuse figures reach new levels each year. These facts don't bode well for the future of America.

Simply stated, stable people come from stable, warm, caring, and loving families, and those who are unstable tend to be the product of unstable, dysfunctional, and high-stress family environments. Love and warmth are often scarce commodities in such homes. Even in traditional family settings, if certain freedoms are not allowed, it's likely that the children will not become uniquely successful.

Does this mean that every person who comes from a stable background where innovative behavior is nurtured will become a self-made multimillionaire? Certainly not. But it's just more difficult to become an economic success if one comes from a background of instability, because financial success requires one to overcome many strains and stresses. It requires some risk taking and the ability to conquer fears and worries. Part of the process of becoming an economic success is the ability to get along with and inspire people, to lead, to be a role model. Often, success is the product of having a supportive spouse and stable marriage. The self-made affluent are focused and committed to succeeding, and these goals apply to both their vocation and their marriage.

Without the conditioning to be stable, it's an uphill climb to become an economic success. Conversely, the unstable tend to be unfocused and temperamental, and they have difficulty getting along with people, including their spouses and their children. They also tend to lack the determination and resolve to deal with recurring economic threats, risks, fears, and worries. There are numerous case examples of people who overcame their unstable histories, and they should be praised for their achievements. This is especially true given the handicap of an unstable home life. But these people are the exception.

You might never know or even appreciate the importance of your family background until you are placed in a high-risk or threatening situation. Countless numbers of millionaires at some time have had to bet everything they owned to start a business or professional practice. What if they failed? Who was there to pull them out of Chapter 11? They took considerable risks, which is part of becoming affluent in America.

Time and time again, the millionaires bolster their courage with thoughts like these:

What if I lost everything, every dollar? I would still have what's most important, my husband/wife and my children. They would never abandon me.

In my interviews, these statements are as common among millionaires as their desire to succeed.

As you read this book, case study after case study describes millionaires who selected ideal vocations, operated innovative businesses, and made wise investments. But beneath all these elements are some that are more fundamental. Stable upbringing, the love of parents, a loyal and supportive spouse, and, in certain cases, strong religious faith are not often touted. These elements rarely get the headlines in the press when successful people are profiled, but few people make it without them. For almost all millionaires, their self-confidence originates at home; their parents instilled it in them.

A SOURCE OF COURAGE: RELIGIOUS FAITH

Many economically successful people credit their strong religious faith as a source of their ability to eliminate or at least reduce the fears and worries associated with placing financial and related resources on the line. Nearly four in ten (37 percent) of these millionaires report that "having strong religious faith" was a key thought process in this regard, and accounted for their "believing in myself" philosophy. As religious faith grows, so does their self-confidence. In turn, with enhanced self-confidence the religious millionaire is able to deal with new and bigger challenges and risks. What about the other six in ten? They also have growing self-confidence and an ever-strengthening belief in themselves, and some of the techniques and strategies they use to enhance their courage include careful planning, focusing on key issues, and being well organized. But the religiously oriented are much more likely to employ prayer and their overall strong religious faith and values in dealing with the fears and worries that are part of their ever escalating success path.

The survey indicates that 75 percent of religious millionaires (RMs) pray when confronted with fear and worry. Only 8 percent of the other millionaires (OMs) employ prayer in a similar fashion. That is a ratio of more than nine to one.

AN INTERVIEW WITH S. TRUETT CATHY,
CHAIRMAN, CHICK-FIL-A
How does your faith help you overcome fears and worries or make decisions?
I see no conflict between good Biblical principles and good business practices: We honor God in our successes and not our failures.

God created us all to be successful.

God's on our side to want us to be successful. Personally I'm a Southern Baptist and I . . . received Christ as my personal savior at the age of twelve. I've always been committed to my family and to my church. I teach thirteen-year-olds in Sunday school.

I feel God's presence in my business: Our corporate goal is to glorify God by being a faithful steward and having a positive influence on all the people with whom we come into contact.

I think every decision should be weighed out in prayer and meditation and seeking God's will for the personal instance. Through circumstances that have come about I feel God was concerned about the decisions I make and the opportunities that are presented to me. I believe God sometimes tests our faith. Sometimes God has a better plan for us than what we have ourselves. If everything went normally all the time, [we wouldn't have the opportunity to grow]. It's when those obstacles are put in our place [that we learn and grow].

Can you give some examples of this overcoming of obstacles?

I've had two fires in my restaurants: one burned to the ground. I've had surgery and didn't know if I was gong to live or die. [These things] made me realize what is important. . . .

How does your faith influence your personal investment style?

I think it would be wise to evaluate a company based on its principals, ownership. If you've got some questionable individuals setting up a company. . . . These [Christian] values are very important to successful companies. I have very little invested other than in my business [Chick-fil-A] and some real estate.

What influence does your faith have on your productivity?

I'm not a lazy person. My time needs to be [spent] being productive in what I do. People like to follow a person that's excited about work. I try not to be a workaholic, try to keep my values in proper order. We have eleven foster homes, where we have one hundred and ten children. We provide vacation homes for them and a two-week camp experience on the campus of Berry College. [This is] one of the things that gives me joy outside of what the business brings to me.

[Chick-fil-A promotes Christian principles through its] scholarship program for employees, its observance of Sunday by being closed, and kids' meal prizes, which often focus on morals, character.

You have to have faith in yourself and in the Lord and faith in life:

A tremendous amount of want-to.
That's the difference between success and failure.

SUCCESS FACTORS AND RELIGIOUS FAITH
For RMs, "having strong religious faith" is a key to reducing fears and worries. They are thirty-five times more likely to maintain that:

Having a strong religious faith is a very important factor in explaining their economic success.

There are several other success-related factors that are closely linked with religious faith. These include, in rank order:

1. Being honest with all people
2. Having a supportive spouse
3. Getting along with people
4. Loving my career/business
5. Being physically fit
6. Having strong leadership qualities
7. Making wise investments
8. Seeing business opportunities others did not see
9. Being willing to take financial risk given the right return
10. Having good mentors
11. Investing in my own business
12. Living below my means
13. Having excellent investment advisers

RMs don't seem to pray to God in petition for more, but they do seek guidance from God. Many told me that their faith in God gives them confidence. If you are absolutely sure that your vocation, for example, is best suited for you, it's much easier to succeed. You have no doubt. Your belief in God translates into your belief in yourself and how you make a living. For many RMs their senior adviser or mentor is God. They have a history of studying religious literature, and their study provides insights about dealing with fear, worry, and concerns.

For Ken Melrose, chairman and CEO of Toro Company, faith is a source of courage and a moral compass in making the tough decisions he's faced in turning around the company. Ken says he came by his job of running Toro "kind of accidentally." In 1981, the company for which he had worked for eleven years was in disarray and on the brink of financial disaster. When the board appointed him president (with no CEO), he knew he would have to make painful decisions that affected hundreds of people's lives.

"Terminating people, restructuring, closing plants . . . things so foreign to my nature and so hard for me that it took faith in partnering with God," Melrose remembers. "A lot of people were going to have to lose their jobs.

"I remember searching for how I was going to run this company, make the decisions that would turn the company around and still value people in a caring way," he says. "In those days I felt totally lost."

So he turned to God for strength and direction. In addition to daily prayer, he hung a sign right above his computer that says:

God meant you to be here, now.

"It was very vivid and a real source of strength," Melrose recounts. "Each morning I asked God to help me get through this day because I need to be led, I can't do it myself. I trusted God to lead the company out of the hole and guide me in making decisions."

He asked two management teams to come up with a list of positions necessary for the company's survival. After working out priorities, 735 of about 1,300 salaried positions made the list. In one of the buildings vacated by the layoffs, Toro set up a work center to help the terminated employees find jobs — with phones, administrative support, counselors, and other services. Melrose is proud to say many of those employees came back to Toro after the company regained its health.

It took about two years for the company to come out of the hole and prove it would survive. He has since harnessed Christian principles to transform Toro's rigid top-down culture into a participative, caring work environment.

In articulating the values the company wanted as its foundation, he developed leadership principles from the Gospels that affect everything from the company's long-term vision to its ideals of communicating with employees on a day-to-day basis.

Building an environment where employees have the trust to take risks is vital to a company that is steeped in a history of product innovation. "We give positive and negative feedback in a caring way — not in a caretaking way — like Jesus did for the Apostles."

Melrose sums up his partnership with God: "God has given all of us the gift of a potential to contribute." Helping people contribute that potential "is the leader's role and privilege."

THE REAL INVENTOR

The Sunday school class was filled to capacity with middle-aged men and women attendees. In terms of income, wealth, and education, this group was at the very high end of the scales. But as in most groups of wealthy people, not all were well educated. In fact, the attendee who had the largest amount of economic wealth had never spent one day in a college classroom — an extraordinary man named Henry.

Henry was not only very wealthy, he was also the most respected member of the church. He had strong leadership skills and was an important adviser to the church and its ministers. He also contributed many, many dollars to the church building fund.

Henry's parents were sharecroppers. They had little money to give their sons and daughters, but they did give Henry and his siblings a more important gift. Henry has used this gift well. Ask him how he is able to deal with the risks associated with being a very successful business owner, how he is able to reduce, even eliminate, the fears that crop up when his financial resources are at risk. Ask him how he deals with feeling inferior to people who have superior levels of formal education. Henry will tell you it is all about:

Having strong religious faith.

Strong religious faith has done more for Henry than help him deal with fears and worries. He has a high degree of mechanical aptitude, and he invented many of the products that he manufactures. Where did Henry get the idea for his most successful product? He had a vision one night. Henry takes little credit for the innovation — he claims that God appeared to him and revealed the innovation in a vision. It was God's invention.

Henry is not alone. His personal relationship with and strong faith in God are shared by many other millionaires in America who overcame significant poverty and academic disadvantages.

Be strong and of a good courage; be not afraid, neither be thou dismayed: for the lord thy God is with thee whithersoever thou goest.
— Joshua 1:9

5

Vocation Vocation Vocation

My father was an entrepreneur, without formal education . . . born in Lithuania . . . started two successful businesses . . . by age twenty-two . . . ice cream and salami . . . one for the summer and one for the winter. . . . And then started a textile mill.

— B.N.R.

Why did Mel become a decamillionaire? There are many reasons, but one stands out from all the rest. Like many of the other affluent Americans I have interviewed, he chose the ideal vocation at the right time and in the right place.[1]

Mel was drafted into the army and spent two years there. He always considered himself to be a "big-city boy," but when he was stationed in the rural South, he made the most of his experience there. While his army buddies complained about army food and the rural environment, Mel spent much of his spare time looking for economic opportunities in real estate. Just before he finished his service, he found a real estate opportunity

[1] The types of businesses owned and managed by the respondents to this survey are given in Appendices 2 and 3.

near where he was stationed.

> . . . *There was a piece of property . . . being sold on a foreclosure by the local sheriff . . . [who] wanted $7,000 for it.*

No one saw the opportunity that twenty-four-year-old Mel recognized. Who would want to buy an old building in a small town in the Deep South?

> *Even my dad, who was a very astute businessman, said, "Mel, don't buy that property." I bought it anyway.*

Mel's dad and most of his associates were dyed-in-the-wool "Yankees . . . city people." They all had a prejudice against the South in general, and investing in Dixie specifically. Mel looked at the objective reality of the opportunities in what is now called the Sun Belt, and had an intuitive feeling that the area where he made his first investment had growth potential. He saw the town as a future intercept point between key areas in the North and South. He also recognized that the area surrounding his investment was just beginning to show industrial growth.

> *My building . . . was near a big plant . . . twenty thousand employees. I leased the building . . . at $100 per month. Today I'm getting $3,000 per month.*

After Mel leased his building, he started playing his own version of Monopoly.

. . . In the next five years I went around to the other people who owned the other land there . . . gave them anywhere from $7,500 to $10,000 for their properties.

Eventually, Mel ended up owning three city blocks, by using OPM (Other People's Money).

[Today] I have $175,000 in it all . . . it was all bank money. . . . [I] built fifty stores in the first fifteen years. They all paid off and I've got an income of $750,000 a year from that.

To accomplish all of this, Mel borrowed all the money. To begin, he borrowed $7,500 from a bank and purchased his first commercial property. His dad cosigned the loan after Mel described his research on the growth potential in his targeted area and because he was impressed that his son demonstrated considerable financial savvy. Mel then leased his $7,500 building, before he bought it. The value of the two-year lease was more than enough to repay the principle and interest, so his cash flow was impressive from day one.

Soon Mel quietly but methodically began acquiring commercial lots and buildings. Each time he acquired another winner he used OPM. He dealt with more than a dozen lenders, and he never actually used a dollar of his own money.

Today, the decamillionaire can't help but wonder what happened to his army buddies who complained about being stationed in "the awful South." Who's not just "whistling Dixie"?

Not only did Mel have an eye for opportunity, he also had his dad as a mentor. Mel's dad told his son many stories of people who made fortunes from small-dollar investments in real estate. The key was to sniff out the best opportunities — those that others ignored. He followed his dad's advice, and his two years in the army eventually translated into a sizable fortune.

Mel is now approaching the age when many people retire, but he has no such plans. He is still looking for opportunities, although he owns much more than the three blocks in Dixie. Mel is especially fond of commercial real estate. He only buys property that is suitable for retail — stores and other types of commercial organizations. He never deals with the ultimate consumer, and so he doesn't own apartments: "Just too much hassle." Mel has always believed that commercial businesspeople are more serious about their obligations. He also holds to another belief that has served him well over the years.

As far back as I can remember, I have believed . . . the Lord gave us land. . . . When it's gone there will be no more!

Mel defines his vocation as "landlord of a three-block monopoly."

Millionaires tell me that there were several important factors in their "discovery" of a vocation, and it's rare to find a single reason that was responsible. The data in Table 5-1 indicate that some of these discovery factors are more important than others. Overall, nearly four in ten millionaires (39 percent) indicated that they discovered their vocation through intuition, and intuition was most frequently mentioned as important by all four occupational groups. These four groups account for the largest share (67 percent) of the millionaire population.

According to *Webster's, intuition* is "the immediate knowing or learning of something without the conscious use of reasoning; quick and ready insight." Note that nearly one-half (46 percent) of the business owners and entrepreneurs say they discovered their specific vocation through intuition. Most millionaires who are business owners will tell you over and over again:

My financial success is a direct result of selecting a specific type or category of business.

The business owner category is the largest group in the millionaire population, but most business owners in America are not millionaires, nor will they ever become millionaires within their lifetimes. Obviously, owning a business is no absolute guarantee of becoming wealthy, but business owners can greatly improve their odds of achieving success by careful selection.

ONE MAN'S JUNK AND TREASURE

Mr. Richard is an excellent case example of smart vocation selection. How did a young man who grew up in an upper-middle-class environment, attended prep school, and spent his first eighteen years in a fine neighborhood in metropolitan New York end up owning and operating a junkyard in the Deep South? I asked him these questions.

Mr. Richard earns more than $700,000 annually and can be classified as a wealth accumulator, one of the Balance Sheet Affluent group. He has more than twelve dollars in net worth for every dollar he generates in realized annual income. Each weekday morning he wakes up at 5:35 A.M. with a smile on his face and can't wait to get to work.

DR. STANLEY: What motivates you? What gets you excited every morning?

MR. RICHARD: It's not financial worries . . . I must want to get to the job. . . . It's very important to me to meet my goals for my business.

I don't have financial problems. It's different for the guy that's got the expensive home and does not have anything in the bank. . . . He has financial worries.

Still, I want to get to the damn yard. I want

291

TABLE 5-1

HOW MILLIONAIRES
IMPORTANT "DISCOVERY"
(N=733)

PERCENTAGE OF MILLIONAIRES RATING
OCCUPATIONAL

Discovery Factor	All Millionaires 100%	Business Owner/ Entrepreneur 32%
INTELLIGENCE GATHERING		
Idea Through Intuition	39	46
Studied Profitability of Business	30	39
Read About in "Trend" or Trade Periodical	14	16
VOCATION "BY ACCIDENT"		
Stumbled Across a Great Opportunity	29	31
Discovered After Trial and Error	27	30
Disliked or Lost Previous Job	12	15
Opportunity Former Employer Overlooked	7	9
OPI: "OTHER PEOPLE'S IDEAS"		
Suggested by Employment Agent	3	2
Discovered at Opportunity or Franchise Fair	2	2

SELECT A VOCATION: FACTORS

FACTOR AS IMPORTANT BY CATEGORIES

Senior Corporate Executive 16%	Attorney 10%	Physician 9%
37	30	31
33	15	23
15	2	8
33	13	12
29	13	8
10	5	4
4	3	2
6	1	0
1	3	0

TABLE 5-2

HOW MILLIONAIRES SELECT A VOCATION: IMPORTANT CHOICE FACTORS
(N=733)

PERCENTAGE OF MILLIONAIRES RATING FACTOR AS IMPORTANT BY OCCUPATIONAL CATEGORIES

Discovery Factor	All Millionaires 100%	Business Owner/ Entrepreneur 32%
AFFECTION FOR VOCATION		
Allowed Full Use of My Abilities/Aptitudes	81	83
Gave Me High Self-Esteem	62	52
In Love With Career/Product	55	55
Fulfilled Lifelong Dream	30	33
NEED FOR INDEPENDENCE		
Chance to Be Financially Independent	66	79
Provided Great Profit/ Income Potential	58	71
Needed to Be My Own Boss	49	73
ACADEMIC INFLUENCES		
Directly Related to Courses Studied in College	44	36
Suggested by Mentors	29	19
Suggested by Aptitude Test Results	14	8
CHOICE BY LEGACY		
Suggested by Parent(s)	20	20
Was Part of Family's Business	13	24
THE CO-OP METHOD		
Related to Part-time Employment	13	15
Suggested via College Placement Office	6	3

TABLE 5-2 (Continued)

HOW MILLIONAIRES SELECT A VOCATION: IMPORTANT CHOICE FACTORS
(N=733)

PERCENTAGE OF MILLIONAIRES RATING FACTOR AS IMPORTANT BY OCCUPATIONAL CATEGORIES

Senior Corporate Executive 16%	Attorney 10%	Physician 9%
77	87	83
63	65	83
55	38	72
19	43	63
53	52	85
55	46	42
22	34	77
44	53	56
34	39	33
17	30	23
11	30	38
8	11	6
10	13	4
9	6	6

to do this and I want to do that. Every day I've got this drive to do something . . . just got to get it done.

What's behind this urge to work long hours, to wake up early each morning? Mr. Richard's motivation is the same for most economically successful people — the more wealth they have, the more likely they are to say:

My success is a direct result of loving my career or business.

Among the success factors cited in chapter 2, love of career was rated as being very important by 46 percent and important by 40 percent of the millionaires in explaining their success. Time and time again people like Mr. Richard tell me that:

If you love, absolutely love what you are doing, chances are excellent that you will succeed.

Oftentimes passion for a career is not love at first sight. In Table 5-2, only 55 percent of the millionaires stated that they initially selected their career because of love for their chosen vocation, but as stated in chapter 2, "Success Factors," in time this figure jumps to over 80 percent in terms of ultimately explaining their economic success. Not all millionaires instantly recognized that the vocation they chose would provide them with substantial profits, but about two-thirds (66 percent) indicated that they initially selected their vocation because it gave them the chance to be financially independent. Fifty-eight percent indicated that an important choice factor was the "great profit or income potential" provided by their vocation.

Business owners and entrepreneurs like Mr. Richard are especially sensitive to profit and income issues. They look for business opportunities that will ultimately make them rich and financially independent. They are less likely than the millionaire population in general to suggest that their vocations give them high self-esteem. Yet a majority of business owners (52 percent) cited the high self-esteem factor in their choice. In sharp contrast, 83 percent of the millionaire physicians selected their vocation, in part, because it enhanced their self-esteem.

Although about two out of three millionaires will tell you that "the chance to be financially independent" was an important vocation selection factor, few retire after becoming wealthy. Mr. Richard is now a very wealthy man who still loves his career. Even though he has enough for himself and his family to live comfortably for the next twenty or more years, he still gets up before dawn and goes to work every day. He still wants to make his business more and more productive.

Mr. Richard achieved his financial goals years ago, but he still loves his business. That's why few people like Mr. Richard want to cash in their chips, sell the business early, and retire. And it is more than love of the job. The large majority, 81 percent of the millionaires, selected a vocation because:

My job/career allows me full use of my abilities and aptitudes.

Most people cannot honestly say this. Too often they accept the job that's offered. It's just a job, not a labor of love.

Most millionaires selected an ideal occupation — were they just lucky to find a job they love, one that gives them high self-esteem? Some luck is involved, but in order to find the ideal career, you first have to understand yourself. What are your strengths and weaknesses, likes and dislikes? If you can't answer these questions, it will be nearly impossible to hook up with a vocation that you will love and that will enhance your self-esteem.

This process doesn't happen in a vacuum — the millionaires didn't just wake up one day and say: I want to manufacture ball bearings. Like Mr. Richard, most millionaires have had other, often unrewarding or unpleasant job experiences before they found the ideal vocation.

> DR. STANLEY: I'm wondering again about your background. What was it that motivated you to start a business in used truck parts?

MR. RICHARD: I faltered for about eight years before I found it. . . . I just worked for other people. I never got paid anything, so I went into business for myself.

DR. STANLEY: I understand that. But why not just any business? Why used truck parts?

MR. RICHARD: I'm completely different . . . really different. . . . Find a very profitable market niche. Otherwise, you can beat your brains out if everybody else is doing the same thing. . . . That competitiveness will make it so you can't make a profit.

Too many people do just the opposite of what Mr. Richard did in selecting a vocation — he targeted one specific, very well-defined audience. And he made certain years ago that he was the only real alternative in competing for customers. Mr. Richard is an expert on niche marketing and specialization, and he recognizes other superior niche marketers when he encounters them. Consider his discussion of "Dr. Jaw."

MR. RICHARD: . . . But a friend of mine did it differently. . . . The friend, . . . a dentist, took care of teeth in cases where a jaw was damaged. . . . This was his original specialty. [Then] he went back to medical school to become a medical doctor so that he could set the jaw as a medical doctor and turn around and set the teeth as a dentist.

DR. STANLEY: How is his business today?

MR. RICHARD: He has zeroed in on the most specialized field that you could possibly get into. . . . He's making a killing . . . because of his specialization.

Dr. Jaw has something in common with most of the self-employed millionaires whom I've interviewed, and it's especially true of business owners who became wealthy in one generation. They specialize — they are "nichers," and they have little competition.

Dr. Jaw first had some experience with a particular market segment and a related professional service, dentistry. But he was very sensitive to an extraordinary market opportunity, and he recognized that he would be much more productive if he offered patients a total package of services. So the good idea to offer one-stop jaw and teeth repair did not just drop out of the clear blue sky.

Most millionaires had some experience in the field they ultimately selected. It is a dentist who eventually realizes that two degrees, a DDS and an MD, are much more productive than the sum of their parts. Dr. Jaw was in the right place to understand fully the total needs of patients with jaw problems.

Mr. Richard was also involved in part of the industry that he eventually capitalized on in a very profitable manner, and he also had a strong affinity for his service offering. He always liked trucks and the people in that industry. Both of these men enjoyed conceptualizing and operating a particular type of business. Today, one is the master of used truck parts and the other is the master of the law within a specific geographic region. These gentlemen really don't have a single close competitor in their area.

In his late twenties, Mr. Richard had worked for a large manufacturer and distributor of trucks for five years. He was a college graduate with a so-so grade point average, and he wasn't making enough money to do much more than keep up with living expenses. He and his wife were rather frugal, and they always wanted to be financially independent. But Mr. Richard recognized that he would never become wealthy in his current employment position, so he was restless. He wasn't sure what to do with himself, and then a series of interesting situations took place at work.

I was working for White Motor Company [as assistant manager]. My boss asked me to sell this wrecked truck to a junk dealer. . . . Sold it for $500. . . . About two weeks later he asked me to go back to the junk dealer. We needed a used engine for another truck.

They [the junk dealer] pulled the engine out of the same truck that we sold them two weeks ago. And the guy invoices me out $500, plus we had to exchange another engine that needed to be replaced.

The light bulb turned on inside Mr. Richard's head. He reasoned that many of the other parts on the truck also had value. In fact, that truck, which sold for $500 in total, was worth five to ten times or more when sold as parts. At this moment in his life, Mr. Richard had what people call intuition. He immediately recognized the extraordinary business opportunity within the vocation he refers to as junk.

Mr. Richard has much in common with other millionaires, especially those who are business owners. Nearly one-half (46 percent) indicated that intuition was an important "discovery" factor (see Table 5-1). Thirty-nine percent of the millionaire business owners also "studied the profitability of their business" or vocation prior to making a selection decision. Mr. Richard also indicated, as did 31 percent of his fellow business owners, that he "stumbled across a great opportunity." Because of his affinity for trucks and the people who worked distributing them, Mr. Richard's decision was not just a random, stumbling event — he found a refined niche in a generic industry that he loved.

I'm looking at this invoice. And I said to myself, "This guy's got the transmission, the rear end, the tires, the doors, the radiator, and he's even getting our old engine [exchange] for $500."

We just . . . two weeks ago sold him the entire truck for $500. [Now] he's selling us just our motor back for $500. Now who's really making *the money — our company or the junk man? I said to myself, "This guy is making a killing."*

And Mr. Richard has been making a killing out of used truck parts ever since this revelation. Within two weeks of discovering the profit potential of used truck parts, Mr. Richard was in business for himself. He purchased his first wrecked truck for yet another $500, and he eventually sold the disassembled components for seven times his original investment.

In the case of Mr. Richard and his fellow self-made millionaires, I refer to vocation as a choice process. There are thousands and thousands of businesses in America. In fact, several years ago I identified more than twenty-two thousand distinct categories of business. Thus, there are more than twenty-two thousand vocations within the domain of self-employed business owners. Through his own intuition, Mr. Richard just added one more to the growing list of twenty-two thousand. Also, there are dozens of geographic markets in America. Several dozens of areas times twenty-two thousand vocations means that there are several hundred thousand geo-defined businesses. Many millionaires have told me that their financial success is a direct function of owning a specialized business in a geo-area that contains little or no competition.

Mr. Richard is in a highly specialized business. He is not just a run-of-the-mill distributor of parts — his specific business buys wrecked eighteen-wheel tractor trailers. He and his crew disassemble these wrecks and sell the parts. It is a simple business, and it is also an extremely profitable operation. Many people imagine a junkyard of used truck parts and they envision only junk. But that junk is wealth to Mr. Richard. Today, he has a net worth approaching eight figures, and his net personal income last year was in excess of $700,000. His head mechanics earned over $130,000 last year for disassembling trucks. That $130,000 has a ring to it — it's close to the average net income earned by a medical doctor in America.

Many people, even some of this country's intellectually gifted, lack Mr. Richard's intuition. They often find themselves in fields where the competition is fierce. Consider the fact that 80 percent of the associate professors at Harvard — among the most intellectually gifted people in this country — are denied tenure. These professors accept positions at other universities, and many eventually became tenured. So it is not only choice of vocation, it's also the level of competition within a chosen geographic or other environment that influences whether a career choice succeeds.

The way I look at the American job market is very different from the views of guidance counselors and college placement personnel. They are well intentioned, but they don't fully realize the enormous benefits of being self-employed in the ideal industry, or even being a senior executive in an ideal industrial sector.

The day after interviewing Mr. Richard, I stopped by Kinko's to have some of my work photocopied. The fellow behind the counter looked at my chapter heading and expressed interest in reading the material. He also said that my material might be beneficial to his profession, and I found out that he was a practicing attorney. He is in a very competitive profession in my hometown, so he needs to supplement his income by working part-time at Kinko's. Even though he is self-employed as the owner of his own law practice, he can barely keep his head above the waves.

There are more than seventy pages of attorneys listed in our city's Yellow Pages. How many pages are devoted to companies that sell used truck parts? Mr. Richard's business is listed under the heading "Truck Equipment and Parts," a category that takes up about one page. All the others listed sell new equipment and parts or used equipment and parts for small trucks. Only Mr. Richard sells truck parts exclusively for large tractor trailers. He literally has a monopoly within this geographic region. As for the prototypical smart fellow I met in Kinko's — he's intelligent; he passed the bar exam; he went to an accredited law school. So what? He's just one of thousands of attorneys listed with seventy-four pages of other very smart competitors.

It is akin to building a home. If the foundation is of poor quality, then no matter how much money and effort you put into the rest of your home, it will never be anything but a heartache. Even worse, you will begin to hate your home. Select the wrong vocation and you may also grow to dislike it. People like Mr. Richard are so productive because work is a joy to them.

Why is it that only a minority of our population absolutely love their work? Why do so many of us overlook economic opportunities? One reason has to do with social status. Did your parents ever tell you that you should go to college and select a vocation that provides high occupational status? Maybe they didn't tell you that explicitly, but they may have communicated it in other ways. My folks always told me that a suitable job for a college graduate had something to do with wearing a suit and tie to work each day. Well, not all millionaires wear suits. Mr. Richard wears a navy blue cotton work shirt and matching pants, and so do all his employees.

Parents can paint their sons and daughters into corners. So let's see, if my Johnny cannot become a professional, a physician, an attorney, or a CPA, then he should accept a position with a major, prestigious corporation. A teaching position or civil service career might be acceptable. Titles, affiliations, and dress codes are important career-selection criteria, along with liberal fringe benefits. Many people in this country were socialized to pursue such status-oriented careers. Few would even consider a vocation like Mr. Richard's.

My mother would say, "Anyone can own a junkyard. Why did you go to college — not to own junk!"

Another factor is that some members of the middle class may not be comfortable owning and operating a blue-collar business. If that's the case, they'll never be eligible to become Mr. Richard's type of millionaire. He came from an upper-middle-class background, but he's at ease interacting with his crew of good old boys and girls each and every day.

I surround myself with a lot of competent and capable people. It makes your life a lot easier. If you've got mediocre people, life can be miserable.

Mr. Richard hires quality people and doesn't care about their class background. But the "intense need for social status" blinds people to many significant economic opportunities. They may never realize Mr. Richard's level of wealth or his affection for his business and its employees. It's sad but true: Snobs do not make great entrepreneurs.

It is often the simple solutions to problems that are the basis for a successful business. People often overlook the everyday problems that can define an innovative business like Mr. Richard's.

> DR. STANLEY: Why do you think that you started a used-truck-parts business and ten thousand other people did not?
> MR. RICHARD: The hard-to-sees . . . it's not been done before. The bigger the rewards are. . . . There is not one on every corner. . . . People will seek you out. Now people can see what I'm doing. It's no big secret. But even now nobody wants to do it.

Mr. Richard is talking about "template career selection." Certain high-status occupations have an established process of training, and our top students are channeled into these vocations. Physicians, attorneys, and CPAs follow a set procedure. But people like Mr. Richard define their own channel. They create unique and highly profitable businesses, and they have little competition.

VOCATION BY ACCIDENT

Self-made millionaire Jim R. never graduated from college, and he will tell you that several factors were significant in helping him become financially independent. Most important, Jim selected an ideal type of business in which to invest his resources, one with a rather unique description. Jim owns, operates, or manages several exclusive "executive" clubs and country clubs.

Jim is well suited to his vocation. He has great affection for his business, but his choice didn't crystallize overnight. He had several reversals in his life, and it was a rather long, involved search for a vocation that would:

• Allow full use of his abilities and aptitudes
• Provide an excellent chance to be financially independent
• Give him high self-esteem.

Like many self-made millionaires, Jim enjoyed a lot of different experiences as a young man, and his choice of specific vocation comes under the general heading "vocation 'by accident' " (see Table 5-1). He has what many other successful people possess — what I call the hunter's nose, or intuition. He can smell opportunity, and he can distinguish the truly great ones from the fakes. This was not always the case with Jim — some bitter experiences tempered his perception and made his successful ventures all the sweeter.

Jim is one of many millionaires in America today who don't have a college diploma. He started at the University of Florida but "flunked out" and joined the army. Eventually he earned a commission. He told me that his experience as an army officer provided the key skills of discipline, organization, and leadership that served him well later in life. The army was Jim's executive training program. After fulfilling his military commitment, Jim left the army and soon re-entered college.

Jim had a preference for living in a house as opposed to an apartment, but most of the houses offered for rent were too big for his needs. Still, he was determined to live in a house, so he rented one with excess space, thereby providing the seed for most of his future endeavors. He rented out the excess space to fellow students and managed the house. None of his tenants had any interest in collecting rent, acquiring furniture, writing checks to utility companies, mowing the lawn, or any of the other tasks associated with being a manager and building superintendent.

Jim enjoyed his role as the manager of the house, and he discovered that money could be made in real estate. This is where his intuition came into play — he had a feeling that managing real estate could make him a wealthy man. Before long, Jim leased twenty-four homes and small apartment houses near campus. He had little difficulty subleasing space, and at one time he had over five thousand students as customers.

TO SERVE OR BE SERVED?

With the profits from his management company, Jim started a real estate development company because he thought that developing was the natural next step up the economic and status ladder. He also felt that he'd make more money developing than managing, and developing appealed to his creative side. According to Jim, there is more prestige — a developer is in charge. All the contractors and subcontractors, as well as a variety of suppliers, are ultimately accountable to the developer. But Jim learned that all that glitters is not gold. More often than not, it is the institutions that lend developers money who are really in control. Jim and many others have what I call the manufacturer's mentality. People with this affliction strongly believe that the lion's share of the profits go to the creators, manufacturers, and developers. In reality, it is often the people who serve the developers and manufacturers who generate a higher return on what they have invested in their businesses. Real estate management, not development, is one of the most profitable businesses in America. This is the case no matter how one measures profitability.

Those who serve are typically the winners in the economic race. It's what I call the rock-and-roll dilemma. Your son wants to become a recording artist. He tells you that "The Stones" are making hundreds of millions. Or your daughter wants to be an author, and she quotes from *Publishers Weekly* that John Hancock Jr. just signed a $2 million deal with a major publisher. It sounds wonderful, but the odds are long that anyone will ever make a dollar of profit singing, writing, developing, or manufacturing. And those who beat the odds will have to share the revenue big-time.

The agents are the ones who gain the largest rate of return on their so-called investments. Consider this example. It may take an author 3,000 hours to research and write a book that eventually becomes a best-seller. His literary agent normally earns 15 percent of his royalties. That doesn't sound like a lot, but it is a great deal if you figure it by hours invested. The author invests his life, his career, his 3,000 hours. The agent may invest as little as 100 hours marketing the manuscript. The publisher sells 1,000,000 copies, and the author gets 15 percent of the $20 retail price, or $3 million. The agent earns $450,000, or 15 percent of $3 million. This leaves $2,550,000 for the author.

Now normalize these numbers. The author earned $2,550,000 divided by 3,000 hours, or $850 per hour. The agent's hourly wage, however, is $450,000 divided by 100 hours invested, or $4,500 per hour! If the agent had allocated 3,000 hours, the expected return would be $13.5 million, or more than five times what the author received for his 3,000 hours of work. And the agent doesn't have to go on tour or do book signings.

Who is better off financially? Do you want to be a manager, investment banker, attorney, agent, server, marketer of talent, or manager of real estate? Or do you want to be the developer, manufacturer, or creator of books?

I will tell you what I tell my children — the smart people place their bets on the servers.

They have questioned this response, so I shared the figures given above with them. But I also told them there are more than 300,000 books published each year, and two out of three never make it to the bookstores. Of those 100,000 that do get distributed, few ever sell 1,000,000 copies or more. My own estimates are that about one-tenth of 1 percent get close to the 1,000,000 mark! There are thousands of authors who have spent thousands upon thousands of hours researching and writing books and never sold more than 10,000 copies. None of them earned more than $10,000. And several of these authors were brilliant in their respective fields.

Given these facts, why do so many people want to be authors, developers, or even manufacturers? Certainly, there are some issues of status involved, but in reality, most people don't know the odds of making even a single dollar of profit in such endeavors. Even worse, they don't initially appreciate the extraordinary amount of dollars at risk and the other resources required.

If Jim R. had the profitability data beforehand, he wouldn't have made the transition from real estate manager to highly leveraged developer. He was overwhelmed by the euphoria of "beginner's luck" because he did well as a manager. He had some early success with his development company, but economic euphoria can easily cloud one's vision. This is especially true when success is encountered at a young age, and Jim, before he was twenty-eight, had developed units

in five states. All the while he had not encountered a single setback to his business. Economic
euphoria had a lot to do with Jim's business decisions and lifestyle at the time.

> *. . . At the tender age of twenty-eight I was the
> largest personal bankruptcy in Florida history.
> But it was a great ride. I had a villa in Acapulco.
> I had a Learjet . . . [personal] apartments in
> twelve cities and a different girlfriend in every
> city.*

Jim lost it all. His real estate development
business was highly leveraged, and so was his
lifestyle. When interest rates climbed suddenly,
his young empire collapsed. Overnight he literally went from the penthouse back to his mom
and dad's house. His grandmother even chipped
in by giving Jim the keys to her old Studebaker.

But he wasn't down for long. Shortly after his
reversal, he accepted a position with a large commercial real estate management company, and
there, he says,

> *[I] learned a lot of good lessons coupled with what
> I had learned during my business failure.*

Jim then spent two years as regional executive
for the management firm, and there he learned a
lot about real estate finance. Once again, he
went out on his own and founded his own management firm. In addition, he purchased proper-

ties for investment purposes. In spite of his previous setback, Jim also developed a variety of condominiums and apartments.

After several very productive and profitable years, Jim sensed that the real estate market was about to tumble. He liquidated all his holdings just ahead of the crash and focused on his property management business. One of Jim's major clients was a large commercial bank for which he managed several investment properties.

Often the bank found it necessary to foreclose on a real estate development it had financed, and they hired Jim as a consultant. He provided them with advice concerning the liquidation of assets. In some cases, Jim realized that the developments would ultimately be winners if completed on a timely basis. One that the bank ended up owning was a large upscale residential subdivision with its own country club. The club included a fine eighteen-hole golf course, multiple tennis courts, swimming pools, and a large, well-appointed clubhouse. The bank faced a dilemma. Should it just sell or liquidate each remaining builder lot (there were hundreds), the partially completed homes, and the country club, or would it be better to take over the project and complete the development?

Jim's advice was to the point: The only way the bank could avoid losing millions and millions of dollars was to complete the development. But the bank was not in the construction business, so it wanted Jim to manage the construction and completion of the project. Since Jim did have experience managing construction projects, he accepted the bank's proposition.

Managing construction resources was second nature to Jim, but there was a related problem. Imagine that you are a prospective home buyer in that subdivision. Would you purchase a home in a country club setting without the country club being fully operational? Probably not — the club had to be open and operating if buyers were going to pay decent prices for homes in the development.

The bank's problem became a major economic opportunity for Jim, and for that reason he considers himself "one of the most fortunate men" today. He had an outstanding track record for managing various projects, so once again the bank turned to him to solve "the club" problem. He managed it for them. Jim had never done anything quite like that before, and he told me he had never tended bar or played golf. But he looked at the experience as a great opportunity to learn while being paid to do it.

I just had to learn. I used their nickels for two years and really learned the [club] business. The actual club business was a result of taking over [the completion] of the subdivision . . . to finish up the houses, the streets, the sewers, the water.

Two years after Jim took over the club and completion of the development, it was a success.

Nearly all the homes were completed and sold, and the club was up and running smoothly. But the bank still worried about the club. If they sold it, the new owners might not operate it at the high level committed to the members, and the bank's reputation would be damaged. The bank again called on its number one problem solver, Jim. He was presented with an extraordinary opportunity — the bank gave him a sweetheart deal on the purchase price and a great deal on a loan package to finance the purchase.

Jim soon realized that owning and managing clubs was far better than being in the real estate development business. He discovered that no matter how good he was as a developer, the market dictated his success or failure. In his mind, property management is a better business. It provides a steady stream of income, and it allows Jim full use of his abilities and aptitudes. His extraordinary leadership and organizational skills match up perfectly with the requirements necessary to manage exclusive clubs effectively, so his accidental vocation has become his career of choice for more than twenty years.

EARLY EXPERIENCES

Today, when Jim wonders how this all happened, he realizes that it began with his grandmother. When he was still a young boy, she taught him the value of discipline, hard work, and being self-employed. She also tutored him in the art of recognizing and capitalizing on economic opportunities.

His rapid ascent to millionaire status before age twenty-eight and his subsequent bankruptcy tempered him. His hard work, especially with one major bank, was rewarded. His success was not "dumb luck." Jim believes that if you seek out opportunity and work hard, you will be amazed at how much luck will come your way.

One of Jim's sons recently graduated from college. He expressed an interest in working in his dad's management business. How did Jim respond to his son's proposition?

I required him to go somewhere else for three or four years before he comes into the business.

Where will his son receive the leadership training to manage two hundred employees and several businesses? According to Jim, the answer is the U.S. Marine Corps' officers' candidate program. After spending three years in the Marines, "he will be mature . . . become a leader."

Jim is a strong believer in the benefits of military training. It's essential that his son learn to lead and manage people, and Jim also believes that his own military experience enhanced his ability to seize the initiative and to get along with people. Certainly, these qualities are a major reason why Jim is successful today, but they had their origin long before Jim joined the U.S. Army.

Jim's grandmother was his mentor. She was a

dyed-in-the-wool entrepreneur and farmer. Even before he was six years old, she encouraged him to "make his own way," and she trained him to recognize economic opportunities when they presented themselves.

She first introduced Jim to the world of free enterprise with an offer. Jim would be given one-half interest in a cow and the revenue from its milk if he milked the cow every morning. Jim did so well in this task that his grandmother gave him a bonus — he was granted ownership in the calves that the cow produced.

Most people don't have Jim's eye for opportunity, but they probably didn't have a grandmother like his. She even encouraged Jim to appreciate the economic opportunities associated with cow manure.

I started bagging the cow manure from the barn. I sold it to people who used it to grow tomatoes.

Jim's folks were good providers of basic food, clothing, and shelter, but even when he was a small boy, they told him that if he wanted anything other than "my basic needs, I had to earn it." He did have more than basic needs, so he was motivated to earn extra cash. But it was his grandmother who taught him the benefits of owning, managing, and caring for his income-producing assets.

There were life lessons there. My grandmother

said, "Take care of this cow . . . this calf and they will give you milk."

She often lectured Jim about the creed of the financially independent business owner.

. . . If you can't figure out how to make money for yourself, you're going to be working for the other fellow all your life.

A career of working for someone else is a cardinal sin for Jim. He believes that one must always be sensitive to the benefits of leveraging relationships and economic opportunities. He learned how to do that while still in high school. During his freshman year, Jim persuaded a local veterinarian, whose services his family had used for many years, to hire him.

Jim worked for the veterinarian during all his high school years. He worked every afternoon on school days, every weekend, and full-time during the summer. When he was first employed there, Jim came up with an idea to leverage his position by raising golden retrievers. This side-line was rather profitable. Jim was able to purchase dog food at wholesale prices because of his relationship with his employer. Many of the veterinary fees normally associated with raising dogs were either waived or provided at a significant discount. And Jim was readily able to sell his golden retriever puppies through the communications network that his employer enjoyed.

When Jim entered college, he had to give up this "great" job and his sideline as a breeder. He thought that college would teach him how to make a living, but he didn't realize that he already knew how to support himself, thanks to his grandmother's life lessons.

A VOCATION STUDIED IN COLLEGE

Joe Smith's case analysis highlights another successful millionaire's choice of vocation, but one that's a bit different from other business owners. As shown in Table 5-2, only 36 percent of the business owners indicated that an important factor underlying their choice of vocation was directly related to courses studied in college.

Mr. Smith is in the hardware business — he owns and manages a small chain of extremely productive hardware stores. What can one learn about the hardware business in college? It all depends on the orientation of the student. If you knew, while you were still in college, exactly what you wanted to do for the rest of your working life, you would have a goal, a road map. You'd know why you were there, and what you want to do when you complete college. Thus, you would probably take college seriously and select a major that would be useful in your career. You could look at every concept in each course with one major issue in mind, "How can I use this knowledge given my chosen vocation?"

In each course that Joe Smith took from his third year of college on, he became a collector of wisdom and ideas. It's unusual for most students to have such clear goals about their chosen vocation, and thus their actions are not goal oriented. The "collector's mentality" is very important in explaining economic productivity.

While Joe was in college, several changes in his life molded him into a collector. He began collecting courses in the business school that could help him make a retail hardware operation more productive. In each course, he'd ask himself,

What concepts in this course can I leverage in helping make my operation more productive?

But during Joe's first two years in college, he was not a collector — he wasn't even sure why he was attending college. Nor did he make the connection between what he learned in college and how it might be applied to his vocation someday.

Joe's dad started his career as a counter clerk at a hardware store and later opened a small hardware store of his own. Joe was never much involved with his dad's business, and his father believed that a college degree would be the key to his son's success. He assumed that once his son had a degree he would automatically be qualified to run the hardware business. His dad often told him:

Joe, I want you to go to college . . . to learn how to run this business so we can be a big success with it.

At first, Joe was a marginal student. He really didn't have much interest in school, and he never connected his schoolwork with hardware.

So I went to the university . . . [for] two years . . . A preliminary two years, I guess you'd call it. Never learned anything about the hardware business.

Then, in the summer between Joe's sophomore and junior years his father died. Joe was now in charge of his family's business, and he still wanted to fulfill his dad's wish for a college graduate in the family.

So I went to the state college [part-time]. . . . I continued there . . . four years . . . part-time student . . . and running the hardware business, too.

Sink or swim, it was now all in Joe Smith's hands. A twenty-year-old was responsible for running a business and supporting his family. Fear and adversity can be great motivators, and that was the case with Joe. While he sat in every class, he always asked himself the same question:

. . . [I] kept asking myself what I'm going to learn that's going to help me in this business. . . . I did learn . . . and did graduate.

Joe was transformed into a collector of wisdom while attending night school. At that time, he began to realize the importance of his accounting class and related business courses. Even his English courses now seemed important. After all, he had to write many letters and reports as part of his job description. Joe became a straight-A student and graduated in the top 5 percent of his class. He did a lot more than merely take over his dad's operation — he transformed it into one of the most profitable retail operations in this country.

LEARNING TO PLAY DEFENSE AND OFFENSE

I have never interviewed one successful business owner who is not cost sensitive. It matters little if it's a retail hardware operation, a legal practice, or a junkyard. Defense, that is, paying very close attention to expenses, is the foundation of productivity. A business that does not control costs is out of control.

What did young Joe Smith know about costs and expenses? Very little to start, but Joe began collecting information about "playing great defense" from his accounting books and class lectures. Then he applied this knowledge every day in running the hardware operation.

MR. SMITH: I figured out that if I was going to be a success at that business, I had to buckle down and learn every little in and out of that business. So every little expense and every little cost and every little thing I kept my finger on.

DR. STANLEY: Joe, where did you find the

time to operate a business, go to night school, study, and then keep track of all those expenses?

MR. SMITH: I do a lot of that before work. I get up early in the morning and come in before work [prior to the store opening].

While Joe became a master of controlling expenses, he also began collecting something else. Most successful business owners realize that customers are collected one by one. Joe developed a strong customer base by locating and relocating stores at ideal intercept points. His stores were also located adjacent to areas where large concentrations of ideal hardware customers lived or worked.

It isn't enough just to be physically closer to customers — you must have empathy for their needs. You must take the time and energy to study their needs, and then make certain that you stock your stores with offerings that reflect these needs.

Joe Smith woke up each day at 5:00 A.M. and arrived at his office before 6:00 A.M. Then he would study the cost data. He studied the sales and profitability numbers for each item sold. Just before the flagship store opened, he'd position himself in the front.

During the day I would post myself up front. I would be sure that everybody was waited on . . . that they got what they needed. . . . I figured that if anyone came to the business, they had a need. If I had to send them someplace else, we weren't supplying the people's needs. That is our philosophy.

Major home-improvement warehouses are opening up more and more stores in Joe's region, but his business keeps improving. Even in the hardware business it's possible to win by specializing, by developing a market or competitive niche.

DR. STANLEY: Can you give us some specifics about how you compete?

MR. SMITH: . . . Lots of little things . . . innumerable small amounts of things.

You find your niche . . . find out what works for you . . . and do it.

. . . Our business is not like any other hardware business. We sell things no one else sells. We found there was a demand for that.

If there is demand for certain items and only you offer them, you have a niche. Joe realized that many customers were always popping up, searching for particular items that no one else in the market area carried. He capitalized on that need, and in so doing he collected customers by responding to their unique needs.

For example, we stock stainless steel pipe fittings. You would not find them in any other hardware store. . . . But there is demand so we'll stock a wide variety. . . . It brings in trade. And we have O-ring cabinets. So what I'm saying is if you're open enough to observe, you will find a niche . . . and it will work.

Joe continually redefines his vocation with periodic updates that reflect changes in customer demand. That's all part of being a collector. Today, he can trace his demonstrated ability to collect knowledge, market information, and customers back to his years in night school, where he learned to value knowledge and information. Collecting knowledge and information has economic value only if you are focused and have specific business goals. If you don't have a niche, then you may collect nothing or you will collect things that don't matter.

A few days before Christmas I was having lunch at a restaurant close to Joe's flagship store, so after lunch I went hardware shopping. The place was packed with shoppers, but I discovered that's true most of the time, not just at the holidays. In spite of the crowd, I was greeted and offered assistance. Clerks were everywhere helping people. It didn't matter how small the purchase or how unique the problem, the clerks were all attentive. Many of Joe's patrons at this flagship store are millionaire homeowners. Typically, their homes were built before World War II, so they often need something replaced. Whether it's a light switch or a crack that needs filling, both the do-it-yourself millionaire and the one who hires repair talent get their hardware from Mr. Smith's.

A GENERALIZATION ABOUT A SPECIFIC

Allow me to make a point. The students who get the most out of their formal education are those who fully realize the specific value of what they are studying. They are the ones who have the least difficulty earning their degrees and who get the most out of their programs. While I was a graduate student, I noted that people with some teaching or work experience prior to entering our program had a very clear understanding of the value of their course work and research. Many others had problems motivating themselves to perform at a high level in each course.

They asked, "Why should a Ph.D. candidate in marketing have to study mathematical statistics, macroeconomics, and microeconomics?" In the program I completed, we had the equivalent of a master's degree in both statistics and economics by the time we graduated: seven four-hour qualifying exams in statistics, quantitative analysis, microeconomics, and macroeconomics, then an eight-hour exam in one's major.

It was easier to deal with all this if you had a firm grip on your future job description. Along with many of my classmates, I had taught before entering the Ph.D. program. We all realized that having a Ph.D. was like having a union card —

it's nearly impossible to be hired by a major university if you don't have one. If you really enjoy teaching and lecturing and want to enhance and broaden your skills, then you are likely to find some element in each and every course that will help you reach your goal. When I studied, I kept the same picture in my mind. It was a vision of myself, lecturing with the material I was studying to a classroom filled with attentive students. The same technique works even today. When I write books, I envision readers who, hopefully, will increase their economic productivity by reading my material.

You must have a goal if you want to be economically successful. It is so much easier to get through the "basic training" of college if you know what you will be doing for the rest of your working life. That is why so many pre-med students can successfully complete the rigors of difficult undergraduate courses. Conversely, just try to generate straight As in all those science courses for the sake of a mere letter grade. It's much easier if you keep your eye and mind on a goal.

If you are without goals, college may be a nightmare. The earlier in life you determine what you really want to do, really want to become, the easier and more purposeful your training will be. That's why so many students who have work experience eventually do well in life. Just ask the Joe Smiths of this world.

What if you have a goal in mind but you still

generate poor grades? Some of the most successful entrepreneurs today were once C, D, or even F students. Many were working full-time and pursuing a college degree full- or near full-time. Others went the night-school route, but they all had some self-confidence because of their ongoing work experience and focus on a vocational goal.

Many had something else that helped them select the ideal vocation. Their parents, often during mealtime, discussed stories about economically successful people. Newspapers, magazines, books, and even personal experiences were the sources for these stories. It doesn't take much time to share this type of information with children, and the benefits of teaching them to begin conceptualizing their "ideal" vocation early in life can be enormous.

ON BECOMING A COLLECTOR

When did I become a serious collector? It was June 1980, when I was first introduced to Jon Robbin, founder of the premier geocoding firm in this country. We both served on the same task force assembled by a client. Jon had devised a way to segment efficiently the household population by neighborhood. This concept was the key to targeting the marketing, advertising, promoting, and distributing of products and services.

On this project, Jon's input was needed to estimate the size of the millionaire population, and he had a statistical model that estimated the average net worth of each neighborhood in America. My job was to design questionnaires and survey methodology, analyze the survey responses, and prepare a strategic market report.

Jon ranked each neighborhood in this country according to its average net worth, and then I surveyed millionaires in those neighborhoods that contained the highest concentrations of wealthy households. The moment Jon made his first presentation on the distribution of millionaire households, a light went on inside my head. What he told us was that many so-called upscale neighborhoods had few millionaires, while some had a disproportionately large number. Similarly, about one-half of all millionaires do not live in so-called upscale neighborhoods.

I was completely fascinated by this information and its implications. Jon's presentation lit the spark for much of my work since then. I have been a serious collector of information about wealthy people. I wasn't certain how the information would ultimately be presented, and I wasn't even sure what major dimensions would ultimately appear. But I kept collecting concepts, squirreling away all the facts I could find about the topic of millionaires.

AN IMAGINARY DIALOGUE
Q: Dr. Stanley, how do you go about finding all the other millionaires that you profile in detail?

A: Often I read their trade journals.

Q: You mean the *Wall Street Journal* and the like?

A: Not really. I'm referring to publications that target members of well-defined industries.

Q: Could you give me an example?

A: I will give you several, but assume for a moment that you own a small chain of pizza restaurants. What publications would you be interested in reading? You would likely read a trade journal that will give you critical information about trends, competition, tactics, products, markets, strategies, and suppliers.

You would read *Pizza Today*. Or, if you are in the muffler business, you'd read *Exhaust News*. Or if you wish to find some bargain on earth-moving equipment, *Rock and Dirt*. If I want to find and then interview the top veterinarian in America, I refer to the current issues of *Bovine Veterinarian*, *Swine Practitioner*, and *Equine Practice*. Occasionally I even read *Publishers Weekly*. *My* most recent acquisition is *Tugboat Review*.

Q: That's hysterical! Do you really read *Tugboat Review*?

A: Yes, and it's funny that no one else except Tom Stanley ever bothered to interview some of the most economically successful people in America who are featured in trade journals. What's funny is that the national media ask me to find millionaires for them to interview. ABC's *20/20* asked. The *Wall Street Journal* asked. *Money, Success,* and many others asked the same question.

Q: How many trade journals are there in the country?

A: Nearly ten thousand, by my own estimate. I think that readers of *The Millionaire Mind* will be enlightened when they read the profiles of people whom I identify from these trades. Again, a big question answered in this chapter relates to how people discovered the benefits of being in businesses featured in *Pit and Quarry, Trade-a-Plane, Pork, Waste News, Alaska Commercial Fisherman,* and the *Dixie Contractor.*

The answer is simple. Most millionaires don't feel the need to have their story told in the *Wall Street Journal,* in *Money,* or on *20/20.* They prefer to be featured in their industry's "trade." They enjoy their status as *Turkey World*'s cover story or *Exhaust News'* man of the year. Over the years, I've been impressed with many of these trade journals. Not only do they feature America's millionaires, many of the owners of these trades have also become multimillionaires through their vocation.

Q: But don't most of the owners or publishers of trade journals have a lot of experience and capital behind them?

A: Not necessarily. In fact, a lot of the founders of various trade journals had no experience in publishing at all. Most were not even journalism majors in college. Note the comments made to me recently by the founder of *Pizza Today*, one of the top trades in America:

Dear Tom:

I was pleased to hear of your familiarity with our business-to-business title, *Pizza Today*. I assure you, this magazine has been an absolute joy to conceive and execute, just filled with exciting and entertaining moments.

For example, in the early months of startup, an excited advertiser called to ask how we got our letters [business stationery] to smell "just like a pizza shop." I told him that was a trade secret. But in fact, it was both easy and automatic since during the first two years of our existence, the magazine, trade show, and trade association shared space in my small Indiana pizzeria. Storage was at a premium and the pizza spices were kept on a shelf next to the envelopes and letterhead of the magazine, which absorbed the distinctive odors like a sponge.

Enjoy the reacquaintance of our magazine and past Pizza Expo programs. I look forward to talking more at length about your possible participation in our show.

> Sincerely yours,
> Gerry Durnell
> Founding Editor and Publisher

Q: Are you telling me a boy who ran a small pizzeria started a multimillion-dollar publishing firm?

A: Absolutely. Today he is the major force in the entire trade association, including Pizza Today and Pizza Expo, but he was not originally part of any publishing company. Nor did he major in journalism. He was a hands-on pizzeria owner in Santa Claus, Indiana. He wanted to read a trade journal about pizza, but one did not exist fifteen years ago, so he started his own. He knew there was a market need because he was part of it.

LEVERAGING ONE'S COLLECTION

Eventually I realized that the insights about the wealthy I was collecting would make exciting reading for book buyers. After years of collecting data, interviews, research reports, and surveys, it wasn't hard for me to produce a unique work that has fascinated and helped many readers. When people ask how long it took, I refer them to June 1980. It may sound like a lot of work for a long time, but I love my job, and I'm never bored. If you:

- love your work and it excites you every day,
- know that your chosen vocation is one that allows full use of your abilities and aptitudes,
- get high self-esteem from your work,
- are absolutely certain that your vocation will make you financially independent one day,

then you should have no difficulty focusing on your goal and working at a high level of productivity.

All this revolves around your becoming a collector of data and information that have value if they are concentrated. Too many people today lack focus; they are not collectors of anything — not data, not customers, not specific marketable skills. On the other hand, collectors can read one newspaper and find several ideas or pieces of information about their chosen vocation. In twenty years they can generate a collection of treasure. Noncollectors often don't understand what they should be doing given their aptitudes and abilities. They can read thousands of newspapers and not add one item to their collection. Perhaps they never started one or, worse, they hate their jobs. In the long run, it's impossible to work at a high level of productivity if you dislike your work.

The key is to find the job that's well suited to your talents, and then it's easier to fall in love with it. But you should also find one that has the potential to make you rich. If you account for these factors, you'll be amazed at how well disciplined you become. Time and work hours pass quickly when you're having fun.

The ideal vocation is not always easy to find. In fact, most millionaires told me they had several other jobs before they found the ideal one.[1] If they had been content to stay with that first job they accepted right out of college, or if they had stayed in a job they disliked and were not content with, then most would never, ever be millionaires today.

Often it's something in our past, some training or work experience that leads to the idea for that ideal vocation. Look for ways to fill market needs that others have ignored, those with little or no competition. Start thinking about and conceptualizing it today. The very best vocations that I find in my research on millionaires are genuinely unique. Even areas that seem traditional can have some degree of uniqueness. I was trained to be a plain old marketing professor, but I selected a specific, unique topic of research that has enabled my success.

TOM STANLEY'S DISCOVERY FACTORS

I know that past exposure can influence the search for the ideal vocation from my own life experience. When I was a boy, we lived in a small apartment in a blue-collar section of the Bronx. Just a quarter mile away was the wealthiest neighborhood in New York City, a residential

[1]A complete list of the businesses owned or managed by the millionaires surveyed is included in the Appendix.

337

community called Fieldston. The neighborhood had a high concentration of extraordinary single-family homes. To my young eyes, they could have been in Sherlock Holmes movies — they had everything but moats and alligators! I was nine years old. I told my eleven-year-old sister, "Sissy, you know, I'm disgusted with the marginal propensity of the people in our own blue-collar neighborhood to give to trick-or-treaters on Halloween. I think we need to move out of our blue-collar neighborhood on Halloween night and go to Fieldston." She said, "Great, Tommy, let's do it." So Tommy, Barbara, and two of her friends began by cold-calling a home on Waldo Avenue in Fieldston. First home identified. Two acres in New York City. Large gate. Large wall. One hundred and fifty feet from the street. No lights on.

My sister said to me, "It's your idea, you go to the front. We'll stay out here." I knocked on the door for five minutes. Finally, it opened up and there, in front of me, was James Mason, the distinguished British actor. Facing him was Tommy Stanley, the nine-year-old Halloween commando. I said, "Trick or treat." He said, "Young man, I have no candy." I said, "Mr. Mason, sir, there are two parts to this equation. Where do you want to go from here?" That was my first affluent experience. He said to me, and I'll never forget him, ascot and all, "Young man, I'll give you all the silver in the house." Whoa! What did he mean? I was about to find out. He left the door ajar and went back into the house. Then my sister showed up and said, "Tommy, what's going on?" I said, "Barbara, it's either coins, flatware, or some combination of both." That kind man gave us two handfuls of nickels, dimes, quarters, and half-dollars, the equivalent of what we would have received if we had trick-or-treated at three hundred blue-collar households. That's what it means to be wealthy in America.

After we landed Mr. Mason as our first Halloween client, we noticed that the lights were on at the English Tudor–style home across the street, but our forecast changed as we approached the house. There was a sign attached to the front door: "Attention, trick-or-treaters. My husband is ill. Don't ring, don't knock. You'll find coins in the milk box." I said to myself, "Coins in the milk box, indeed. Stiffing young people — these folks just put a few pennies in the box, then went inside and locked the door." I opened the milk box and guess what? Treasure Island! It was loaded with more than twenty business envelopes with lovely black writing on them: "The contents of this envelope are designated for a group of one or two trick-or-treaters." There were envelopes for three, for four, for five, six, and seven. Eight-plus was the big one, and there were three for each category. We removed only one envelope, for the group of four, then we left Fieldston and went home. Twenty years later I began studying the affluent in America.

Dan R.'s story isn't as straightforward as mine. How did he reach millionaire status before he was forty, earning more than $1 million in one year, a status earned by only one in every one thousand households in America? Many factors contributed to Dan's success, and many trials and errors were involved. He was very wise when he eventually selected the ideal:

Vocation vocation vocation.

Dan is like the vast majority of first-generation millionaires, because most will tell you they selected the perfect vocation. For people who are interested in becoming wealthy in one generation, the perfect vocation is the one that allows full use of their abilities and aptitudes.

NINE JOBS

It took Dan R. quite a long time to introduce himself to the other ten members of the focus group. Halfway through his presentation, I almost stopped him because I thought the recruiter had made a mistake. Dan was supposed to be a millionaire who succeeded because of his high-performance skills as a sales professional, but in his introduction all he talked about was a series of sales positions where he either underperformed or was fired. I thought Dan was in the wrong place that night, but I let him continue, and it was a good thing I didn't interrupt. He actually documented nine poor-performance jobs before he described how he eventually succeeded in his tenth time at bat. Consider Dan's path to finding the ideal vocation.

- Position 1. After graduating from a top business school with a degree in marketing, Dan took a job with a corporation selling calculators and electronic watches to large retailers. "I never seemed to get the knack of it . . . didn't sell a lot. After two years I was asked to resign."
- Position 2. Dan then went to work for a major producer of electronic games, but "once again I couldn't get the knack of selling and they asked me to leave about a year and a half later."
- Position 3. Hired by a start-up computer company, Dan resigned after nine months of "never selling one computer."
- Position 4. Dan was hired by a small computer company. He "didn't sell much of their product either" and resigned after a few months on the job.
- Position 5. Dan's fifth position was also with a computer company. He didn't meet his sales quota and again was asked to resign.
- Position 6. In Dan's next job, "I was really doing well because I wasn't in sales . . . [I] was in marketing. . . . But nine months later, the company ran out of money and went out of business."
- Position 7. Dan accepted a sales position with "a start-up computer company and made only

$45,000 annually until the last year I was there . . . I made $200,000! But then the market slowed up and the company went out of business."

- Position 8. Dan accepted another sales job. But "the company had problems with me because of low sales volume."
- Position 9. Dan hired on with a company that produces scanners at cash registers. "They let me go."

I wasn't the only one who thought Dan was in the wrong place. The fellow who sat next to him laughingly blurted out the following comment after Dan's story of position 5: "I don't want to sit next to this guy anymore!"

Finally, at position 10, Dan's search for the ideal vocation paid dividends. Six years ago, he found a unique career that closely fit his abilities and aptitudes. He landed a job that was entitled "sales professional," but it was much more than selling as defined by most of his previous positions. This job not only required Dan to close major deals, it also called for considerable market planning, understanding of each customer's unique needs, preparing detailed proposals, and, most important, focusing on major accounts. It gave Dan a lot of discretion in how he pursued business. In reality, Dan viewed his position as being more of a market consultant than merely a sales caller. Almost immediately after he began working in his tenth position, Dan recognized that he had been ill-suited to his previous jobs. They were purely sales positions, and Dan was consistently outperformed by other sales professionals because he is a thinker, not a sales commando. The most successful sales professionals were those who aggressively called on the largest number of prospective customers — preplanning was relegated to making appointments. But Dan was often kidded by his fellow sales professionals as one with: many plans, few clients.

Dan is more than a strategic planner. He has an extraordinary ability to uncover major market opportunities and generate millions of dollars in revenue from these opportunities. But it took nine experiences with other employment situations before Dan fully conceptualized his definition of the ideal position. During these nine equivalents of the stations of the cross, he often agonized.

I would sit in my car and drive all around . . . I would get so depressed because I had all this drive and was a really hard worker. . . . I was letting myself down and my parents down.

Dan intuitively knew that there was an ideal vocation somewhere — that's why he kept looking for the opportunity that would allow him to fully utilize his aptitude as a highly intelligent and gifted marketer.

. . . If I could just find the right product and the

right opportunities, I could do well.

Dan realized that the computer industry gives major compensation to top-performing marketers, but that was too broad a description. It was like trying to find someone's room in a large hotel. Dan had the correct address for the hotel, but he didn't have the room number. So within the domain of "marketer of computer systems," Dan began his search for the ideal combination of company, compensation package, product, and target market. He never regrets his previous experiences working in sales for nine other employers — they helped him conceptualize his ideal vocation. Six years ago, Dan was convinced that he'd discovered the right opportunity, one that allowed full use of his abilities.

Why did he waste his time working in nine previous positions that were unsuitable, given his aptitude and abilities? According to Dan, it took some experience with situations that were less than ideal for him to appreciate the right vocation. But he knew that he would always be the "marginally productive man in sales" if he remained in any of his previous positions.

I would be still selling watches and calculators if I was marginally good. . . . What was different in my case was I became a good searcher of opportunities, searcher of future or just different niche markets.

A man is repeatedly fired or resigns because he fails to meet sales quotas, and then he turns around and becomes one of America's best-paid, most-productive revenue generators. Dan knows the reason for his success.

For the last seventeen years I have been searching. . . . I'm a good searcher. I've been practicing how to search for opportunities and to look at my business in a certain way. And that's what I'm still doing today. I found this company. My first year I made $200,000 . . . my second another $200,000.

This success encouraged Dan to work even harder at being "really focused." He realized that he'd found his niche — his marketing orientation perfectly matched the needs of his current employer, who manufactures, markets, and distributes custom-designed handheld computers.

. . . This past December . . . after working (planning) for five years and getting no orders from Home Depot . . . I received a $35 million dollar contract from Home Depot . . . selling six thousand handheld computers to them. . . . My W-2 read $1,033,000 commission on the check.

When Dan made this statement, every one of the focus group members clapped and cheered. Every one was a self-made millionaire, and each had a similar story. They had great empathy for

Dan's journey to success.

Contrary to what you might expect, Dan is not constantly "stressed out" by his intense productive efforts. As most millionaires report, stress is a direct result of devoting a lot of effort to a task that's not in line with one's abilities. It's more difficult, more demanding mentally and physically, to work in a vocation that's unsuitable to your aptitude. It's even worse if you know that you are a round peg assigned to working square holes. Add the realization that your vocation has little or no probability of making you wealthy, and you are stressed out big-time.

Dan will tell you that it was more stressful earning $45,000 per year as a marginally productive sales commando than it is closing multi-million-dollar deals in his current environment. Two leading scholars recently studied the relationship between the task environment and intelligence.

> . . . *Intelligent people are more likely to rely on intellectual effort in solving problems than those who have relatively low intelligence.* . . . (Fred E. Fiedler and Thomas G. Link, "Leader Intelligence, Interpersonal Stress, and Task Performance," in R. J. Steinberg and R. K. Wagner, eds., *Mind in Context: Interactionist Perspectives on Human Intelligence* [New York: Cambridge University Press, 1994], p. 163)

One of the reasons Dan currently performs so

well is that his employer appreciates his combination of aptitudes and abilities, while most of his previous employers did not. They preferred sales personnel who "knocked down doors" if necessary to gain immediate sales revenues. But Dan was too creative, too analytical, too deliberate, too intelligent to perform at a high level of productivity in the "don't think, just sell" situation.

The stressful situations require quick and preferably automatic responses; careful deliberation and weighing of alternatives will impede rather than assist with solution of the problem. Thus intelligence will correlate negatively with performance. (Fiedler and Link, p. 163)

THEY SEE, BUT THEY DON'T SEE

Don spent more than an hour mulling over the comments from the other ten members of my focus-group interview. I could tell he was deep in thought as he listened to the other self-made millionaires talk about "choice of vocation and economic opportunity."

I was especially interested in what Don would say. He'd started a successful business more than twenty-five years ago and has had three other highly successful businesses since then. How did Don explain his four-for-four hitting streak?

You must be an opportunist. . . . You must be an

347

opportunist. Every one in this room is an oppor-
tunist!

In your business, Dr. Stanley, how did you get
into the book business? We all have different sto-
ries, but we all had an opportunity.

Does this mean that successful people are merely lucky — did they just happen to walk into the opportunity of a lifetime? Are unsuccessful people those who just never came across a significant economic opportunity? Don asked the same rhetorical questions of the group, and all fully agreed with his answers.

. . . Everybody out there has an opportunity to get
into business. . . . The opportunity to sell some-
body something. . . . Some can't see it. You have
to be able to see it.

Don's discussion about seeing economic opportunity was almost word for word from the biography of Erich Hartmann, the successful fighter pilot (Raymond F. Toliver and Trevor J. Constable, *The Blond Knight of Germany* [Blue Ridge Summit, PA: Aero Books, 1970], pp. 43, 44, 84–85). Major Hartmann often commented about "combat blindness." He wondered why so many pilots had difficulty seeing the enemy target of opportunity, and he had the same problem as a rookie. How is it possible, he asked, that pilots with extraordinary eyesight, measured ophthalmologically, have combat blindness? These same pilots could read every letter on an eye chart at greater distances than normal, but they could not see in real combat conditions. Hartmann said it best:

They see, but they don't see!

This is the same message Don related to the group. Don pointed out that some of the brightest people never see an opportunity staring them in the face. They received all As on tests in college, like the fighter pilots who got all As on eye tests. But unless you are experienced, trained, and really want to see an opportunity, you will always have combat or economic blindness. Although many people think it's a genetic trait that explains the ability to see targets of opportunity, I firmly believe people can be taught to see what others do not see.

Based on scientific measures, eye charts, depth perceptions, and so forth, Hartmann's eyesight didn't change much during his more than fourteen hundred combat missions. But his ability to see targets improved tremendously with the help of his mentors and with more and more experience. Also, he trained himself to focus his receptors in areas of the sky where he anticipated his targets would be concentrated.

He could spot aircraft . . . [at] a phenomenal distance, sometimes minutes before anyone else airborne with him. (Toliver and Constable, p. 170)

THE VISION OF FIRST-GENERATION AMERICANS

Think of the opportunity issue from another perspective. During the 1970s, fewer than fourteen households in one thousand had incomes of $100,000 or more, but certain groups had a greater proportion. For example, according to my analysis of 1970s data provided by the U.S. Census, Korean-Americans were about three times more likely to have six-figure incomes than the typical American household.

The economic success enjoyed by a disproportionately large number of Korean-American households was a direct result of their ability to see economic opportunities that others overlooked. This may seem amazing, given their backgrounds, because most were first-generation to this country and were not college educated. Also, English was a foreign language to them. Few inherited any of their economic wealth — their incomes came from earned sources as opposed to trust accounts. How is it possible that a group of recent arrivals to America saw significant economic opportunities, while at the same time most native-born Americans "see, but they don't see"?

For several years I ran an experiment in my university classes. I asked all my undergraduate, graduate, and executive MBA students this question:

What are the top ten most profitable

small businesses in America?

Time and time again my students were unable to come up with even one correct answer. This ignorance about the economic opportunities in America among some of our brightest students is not for lack of genetic intelligence — I believe there are several reasons. One is that most business majors have no intention of starting their own business. They plan to work for some major corporation, so profitability is someone else's problem.

Another reason is that most students are never taught about the inherent profitability of various types of businesses — perhaps because most textbook writers and professors think that profitability numbers "are not technically challenging to students."

But there is an even more compelling reason why our students cannot see what recent immigrants can see about significant economic opportunity. Hartmann said it best: One's ability to see a target is a function of experience, training, and need. Who needs to know about the variation in profits among countless categories of business: Our sons and daughters, the well-educated, confident, and easily employed, or the first-generation Korean-Americans?

The answer is clear — Korean-Americans came to this country with a strong desire to become financially independent. In their minds, they had one chance to accomplish the goal; owning and operating a business was the only highway open to them.

Many first-generation Korean-Americans correctly chose the businesses that have a high probability of success and high profits. There are numerous Korean trade associations and Korean-American cultural organizations that provide this type of information. Also, there is an informal interpersonal communication network between successful business owners and those who want to start their own enterprise. The information it supplied appears to have been quite accurate.

Among the most profitable categories of business in America during the 1970s was dry cleaning. Note that there are so many Korean-Americans in the dry-cleaning business today that one industry trade journal publisher had no choice but to publish two versions — one in English and the other in Korean!

There are many other categories of businesses that have been prime targets for perceptive Korean-Americans. Just walk down Main Street, USA, and you will get a good view of the economic opportunities that some see and others ignore. Korean-Americans have become a major force within a variety of profitable business categories such as: fruit and vegetable retailing and wholesaling, shoe repair, and convenience markets. They also know that if they provide a good product or service at a competitive price, they can have high expectations of economic success. In turn, economic success translates into financial independence.

SEEING IS NOT ENOUGH

Most first-generation millionaires have told me that recognition of an opportunity does not automatically translate into dollars — there must be something else in the equation. Don, a self-made millionaire, said it concisely:

You have to be able to see it, then you have to believe you can do it.

Belief in one's ability to succeed is a very big foundation stone. It explains much of the variation in performance among people in the vast American economy. In turn, belief in oneself is a direct result of knowing the odds are stacked in one's favor. A more detailed discussion of "belief in oneself" is given in chapter 4, "The Relationship Between Courage and Wealth."

Why do so many businesses fail within a year or two of opening? Certainly one reason is the odds issue: Most people who select a category of business to operate don't have a clue about the real probabilities of success. Remember, it isn't how much you study and how long — it's also what you study and how well it can be leveraged in the business world. Knowing the odds of success can make all the difference. Pick a long shot and your college degree may not be enough to

save you; pick a winner, and the law of economics may not punish you for never spending a
day in college, never fully mastering the English
language, and being born outside the United
States.

Don also spoke of the importance of desire.
One must be highly motivated to succeed in a
particular vocation.

You have to have something inside of you that
wants to kill. . . . You go out . . . and take that
opportunity, that chance. . . . You [are] king of
the mountain.

He explained that the "something inside of
you that wants to kill" is an emotion or instinct
that is vocation specific. In other words, he believes that there is some very specific vocation,
product, or service out there that will excite each
of us, but if we lack this emotion, this killer instinct, it's unlikely that our venture will be productive.

Don feels that most people possess some of
this instinct, but for many it remains dormant
throughout their entire lives because they never
encounter the catalyst of the ideal vocation or
economic opportunity. Thus the enormous
power of this emotion will never be exploited.
Every product, in all of Don's four businesses,
was a labor of love. He loved conceptualizing the
products based on his assessment of market
needs, and he felt strong positive emotions

354

about product development, design, and marketing. Without this enormous emotional energy, Don will tell you, none of his products would be a reality today.

Don's emotional energy made what would be viewed as hard work by others fun for him. The risks and lifestyle sacrifices that he took as a young entrepreneur rarely entered his mind — they were easily suppressed by focusing his mind on the product and business that excited him.

There is a simple lesson that can be learned from Don's experiences: Extraordinary levels of economic productivity can be accomplished by searching for and finding the vocation that evokes and conjures up emotional energy. But Don will also state that it's important for one's vocation to have significant profitability, and this, in turn, can be altered by one's enthusiasm and ability to sell. Unfortunately, this can be overestimated when strong love of a product blinds its creator. That's precisely why everyone needs objective third parties to evaluate ideas. Trusted advisers, often enlightened CPAs or attorneys, are very valuable resources. They have experience in separating emotion from economic reality. One of Don's main advisers is his accountant.

Following Don's discussion about emotional energy, another respondent made a valuable contribution to the interview. He defined other reasons for Don's success:

You have the best description of your product. . . . You did a wonderful job of explaining your company, your technology, and how your products work.

You understand the technology, the fit in the market, and how it's going to benefit somebody else.

Some people fall in love with a particular product idea, and that love can bias our own assessment of market demand. Don's love is not only for product concepts — his emotion is firmly rooted in his accurate estimate of the market's strong need for his product. His motivation is a direct result of envisioning buyers being able to solve problems with his technology, and that is, in essence, why he is a success today. He has great empathy for the needs of the market, and he is literally thrilled when his technology fills these needs.

The market environments in America are very democratic. They reward people like Don who fill a need, and it doesn't matter if Don is tall or short, wide or narrow, male or female, white or black. This is especially true in the entrepreneurial environment, but it also applies in situations where employees are paid on the basis of performance, such as in full-commission sales positions.

The market does not care. So what if a person worked for nine other companies, did not receive all As in college, and never read Amy

Vanderbilt's book on etiquette? As another respondent stated in the same focus group:

I think the irony of it all is that you don't have to look like the [corporate] guys who have to look good.

Don agreed that corporations hire executives who are ambassadors. They are symbols of excellence, so they must be handsome, well grounded, educated, well dressed, politically oriented, personable, and articulate. But according to Don, they aren't required to have his same level of "killer instinct" or his need to develop successful new ideas for the marketplace. At one time, he had a very different view about the corporate environment.

. . . [I] grew up . . . [in a] blue-collar background. Graduated with a degree in applied physics. I went to work for a big company. . . . Always dreamed of going up the corporate ladder and being some high executive.

[Executives] in corporate structures just didn't live up to what I thought they would. . . . I put them on a pedestal. I got really discouraged being around them and the things they did. So . . . I started my own company . . . I was twenty-nine years old.

Don learned how businesses operate from his corporate experiences, but the most important thing he learned was that a vocation in the corporate world would never "light his emotional fire." This knowledge helped him define the vocation where his talents and aptitudes would be best suited. Without his corporate experience, Don might never have decided to go out on his own.

A GENERIC AUTHOR?

A member of my audience recently asked me: "What about your vocation? You emphasize the importance of specialization and that choice of vocation is a critical element in accounting for variations in wealth. But you, yourself, are in a very competitive vocation. Are you guilty of not practicing what you are preaching?" No, I'm innocent, but let me prove my point. I estimate that there are several hundred thousand authors in America. If I had to compete directly with each of them, I'd go out of business in short order.

I am not a generic author. My vocation is not ever listed as "writer." In fact, I am a specialist within the large population of authors and writers. I write about how common people become wealthy in one generation. I write about topics that others overlook. I am the "Mr. Richard" of literature. Even *Webster's* defines *vocation* as "the special function of an individual or group."

It may be easy to say this now, since I've already written a bestseller. Hindsight is always twenty-twenty. But I never doubted that *The Millionaire Next Door* would be a hit. I planned this work for many years. I tested my ideas in hundreds of seminars across America. I knew that two major concepts turned on the attendees. First, I defined who the American millionaire was and was not. Second, I described *how* common people become millionaires in one generation.

For several years within the past seven I received requests to do more than two hundred seminars and speeches on these two topics. Why all this interest? It was because I had information that no one else possessed. Not just information, but survey-based insights into how to become financially independent.

The responses from my audiences and the insights millionaires gave me refined my job description. My work provides answers to questions asked by many people, and when it comes to competitors, I am like Mr. Richard's listing in the telephone book. One of the millionaires featured in *Money* magazine's cover story on *The Millionaire Next Door* said it best. Mr. John Shmilgenko is a real estate investor. He was asked about the source of his wisdom about becoming wealthy.

Playing Monopoly as a kid, I bought . . . properties because they were cheap. . . . I took a similar approach in real life. (Tony Cook, "7 Secrets to Achieve Your Money Dreams," *Money*, June 1997, p. 76)

It was the millionaire respondents who encouraged me to specialize, to monopolize.

I would never have succeeded as a writer of love stories, mysteries, or any other type of generic fiction. Some of my relatives remind me that the Stanley ancestry is filled with writers and poets dating back to ancient Ireland. They think success is a genetic factor, but I don't think that the quality of the writing explains the demand for *The Millionaire Next Door.* Where were all these ancestors' genes when I was getting straight Cs in high school and college English and writing courses?

The big issue is what is said, not how it is said. The market I selected defines what I do. I know from thousands of contact hours with the public what it is they want. I know the questions they want answered. With this knowledge in hand, I always felt confident about the demand for my work.

You don't need to be Shakespeare if you have excellent market research. The basic premise of my vocation is giving the market what it wants and is not currently receiving from other authors. It's that simple.

I do feel just a bit guilty about the success of my best-seller. There must be thousands of A students who never made it onto the *New York Times* best-seller list, let alone stayed there for more than one hundred weeks. On the other hand, most of these writers repeatedly ignore rule number one in marketing: me, me, me, is dull, dull, dull. It's the A student who more often than not writes beautifully and states concepts with great elegance. His works are grammatically sound, but his criteria for selecting a theme is strictly me, me, me. He writes about things that are of interest to him and forgets about the interests of the market. So what if you write beautifully but your main theme is strictly Dullsville? Or what if there are so many competitors in your subject area that you cannot even get a publisher to take a second look at your manuscript?

I have the best of both worlds. I have great interest in my main topic area, and the market demand is strong for my work. But I must admit that my first love was American history. Long ago, however, I realized that the level of competition in this area is extremely high. What if I attempted to publish in the arena of American history? I would be living proof that:

Me, me, me is dull, dull, dull.

Of course, I can offset my guilt about being successful by reminding myself about my investment in time, energy, and money. I have a few million frequent-flier miles! That's the number it takes to visit millionaires who want to tell their success story. That's the requirement for addressing hundreds of audiences and asking for advice and suggestions. So, in many ways, the ideas in *The Millionaire Next Door* and *The Mil-*

lionaire Mind are the product of my personal hands-on market research, the type that few writers ever have a chance to conduct.

Occasionally, I've had the chance to advise other writers about theme selection and other marketing issues. However, most believe that what I'm suggesting is blasphemy! I recently attended a book fair with more than twenty other published authors, some of whom at one time or another taught creative writing, and several were professors of English. I really felt way out of place, but I said to myself:

> *Tom, every one of these people can write, that is, state concepts, better than you. But not one of them ever had a book on the best-seller list.*

Several of the authors who taught creative writing clustered together in a corner. They spoke of style, creativity, and the burden of grading 130 papers this term. One of them told me that he really had little time to contemplate, to give deep thought to the theme of his next work. But he will have to come up with something soon — it's still publish or perish in his business. The best part of his energy resources are given to commuting, faculty meetings, teaching, and grading papers. What energy remains is allocated to his next book. I strongly believe that it's nearly impossible to write effectively if the book is relegated to a third or fourth priority.

Some of these insights originated in the school of hard knocks. Others were gathered from reading about productive people. In fact, for many years I looked for a template of productivity that I could follow. I never found it. Much has been written about the productivity of groups and businesses, but writing is an individual event. It's different from corporate sports. Even many of the biographies of great team leaders and economically productive businesspeople do not apply to my vocation.

6

Choice of Spouse

Can you live forever? Marry the wrong spouse and every day will feel like an eternity. Marry the right spouse and life will be a joyful and perhaps even a rich experience.

A ROCKY ROAD

Several booking agents have told me there are five top-rated conventions held annually in this country, and an invitation to be a main platform presenter at any of them indicates genuine superstar status on the lecture circuit. That made me somewhat nervous when I was invited to speak at one of those conventions, the Million Dollar Round Table, a trade association composed of the world's top-producing life insurance agents.

At the time I was a college professor from Georgia State University, but the head of the speaker selection committee read about me in the *Wall Street Journal* and liked the idea of having an expert on millionaires address his colleagues. I've never thought of myself in the superstar category, but there I was in front of fourteen thousand people, along with distinguished speakers like Eunice Shriver, Marvin

Hamlisch, and Lee Iacocca.

Another speaker on the platform that day was a former football player who'd had an outstanding professional career and had played in four Super Bowls, in spite of being wounded in the Vietnam War. Rocky Bleier was a delightful, down-to-earth man who had made a successful transition from pro football to celebrity speaker status. Every important group wanted to hear him because he was an excellent speaker. He could write his own ticket — demand considerable fees and be very selective in his choice of clients. Few men can play ball at that level and then become a star in a completely different field, so I suspected he was unusually talented and would surely become an economic success for the rest of his adult life.

Surprisingly, I never heard anything about Rocky Bleier again until our local newspaper published a story under the headline, "Bankrupt Bleier Hocks Super Bowl Rings" (*Atlanta Journal-Constitution*, January 4, 1997, p. F3). How could it be that a fellow with considerable talent for earning a high income turns up as the subject of a newspaper story detailing his bankruptcy? There it was in black and white:

> *. . . Bleier, who overcame Vietnam War wounds to play in four Super Bowls, filed for Chapter 7 bankruptcy . . . two days after selling his championship rings . . . to help pay back federal taxes.*

The article went on to say:

His former wife . . . said in a countersuit that Bleier just wants to avoid paying her $837,948 from the sale of their home.

In the bankruptcy petition he filed, Mr. Bleier stated that he had already ". . . paid [his ex-wife] $1.3 million in cash and property." Could it be that Mr. Bleier's economic reversals were related to his divorce?

Divorce generally has a devastating impact on an individual's net worth, and that's true for both millionaires and nonmillionaires. Since 92 percent of the millionaire households in America are composed of a married couple, and these millionaire couples have less than one-third the divorce rate of nonmillionaire couples, we can conclude that here is another factor that distinguishes the millionaire mind — the ability to choose the right mate for life. Being divorced doesn't exclude one from becoming and remaining a millionaire — it just makes it significantly more difficult, as Mr. Bleier may have discovered.

THE ECONOMIC PRODUCTIVITY OF MARRIAGE

Studies have consistently found a significant correlation between length of marriage and wealth accumulation. One study of over twelve thousand respondents is particularly illuminating (Janet Wilmoth and Gregor Koso, "Does Marital History Matter? The Effect of Marital Status on Wealth Outcomes Among Pre-retirement Age Adults," Proceedings of the 1997 North Central Sociological Association). The authors found that "consistent participation in marriage results in significantly higher wealth." Conversely, those people who are not married continuously over time have a propensity to accumulate lower levels of wealth during their adult life cycle.

What is it about marital status that affects one's level of wealth? According to the research conducted by Wilmoth and Koso, legal marriages have certain institutionalized features that are conducive to accumulating wealth, an important one being the division of labor within the marital relationship. Also, certain economies of scale are present in a married-couple household that are not normally associated with a single-person household. The positive correlation between length of marriage and level of wealth is very strong and holds true throughout all education and income groups in America.

MILLIONAIRES AND MARRIAGE

What would happen today if all the millionaire couples in America immediately broke up? Of course, there would be a lot more singles heading up millionaire households. There would also be one-third fewer millionaire households, because their assets have to be divided, domestic overhead would double, and legal fees would take a nice share. But like the rest of the population, millionaires stay married because of reasons other than economics. Millionaires and those who will probably attain this status have a unique ability to select mates with a certain set of qualities. Some of these qualities are significant in explaining their long-term, happy marriages, while other traits are more directly related to wealth accumulation.

People who stay married for the full term ("till death do us part") tend to be unselfish, caring, forgiving, patient, understanding, disciplined, and virtuous. It also helps if the couple has similar interests, activities, and opinions. Like Tina Turner, you may ask "What's Love Got to Do with It?" Underlying any happy marriage are love and deep affection, but affection can cloud one's judgment. If you are deeply in love with a potential spouse who lacks traits like patience and understanding, you may give him or her grades that are too high because of your emotional involvement. Only later, through direct experience prior to your divorce, are you able to recognize your spouse's shortcomings.

The millionaires I have interviewed seem to have early warning systems — they have the uncanny ability to determine if a prospective spouse is unselfish, caring, and virtuous before they become emotionally involved, and that accounts for the high frequency of full-term marriages in this group. Ask the prototypical millionaire who has been married to the same spouse twenty-five, thirty-five, or even fifty years:

What can you tell me about your spouse?

Among the first things they say include:

Down to earth	My emotional
Unselfish	backbone
Has traditional values	Patient
	Understanding

There is an even more revealing question.

What was it that initially attracted you to your spouse?

Respondents will, more often than not, mention some physical attribute, but physical attractiveness is never the only factor. Most suggest that they had some intuition about other qualities, such as those listed above, that their prospective spouse possessed.

Consider the case of Barbara "Bobbie" and Forester, who have been married for more than thirty-five years. They have four grown children and they own and operate three manufacturing companies. They are economically successful.

Bobbie was raised in a small western Kansas town near the Colorado border. Forester grew up on a farm in southern Georgia. How did a girl from western Kansas ever meet a farm boy from southern Georgia at a college mixer in Boston? Both Bobbie and Forester came from modest backgrounds, but both were extremely bright and excelled in high school. Their families sacrificed to put together a college fund for their children, and both received additional support from academic scholarships. Forester attended MIT; Bobbie went to Wellesley.

According to Forester,

The first thing I noticed was that her clothes were handmade. They were well made, but home-made.

From the very beginning, Forester was fascinated with Bobbie. Certainly she was cute and charming, but it was her wardrobe that impressed him most. Her mother had made her clothes. This fact told him a lot about Bobbie's background. It was obvious that she came from a family of modest means, but nevertheless they had sent their daughter to one of the top women's colleges in America. He reasoned that both Bobbie and her parents had their priorities ranked in the proper order. Bobbie was impressed with Forester's presence at MIT, given his modest background as a farm boy.

They both had a sensitivity about their choice of an ideal spouse, and their choice has tested true for over thirty-five years. Bobbie and Forester were suited for each other, and they were also ideally suited to own and operate a family business. Early in their marriage they made trade-offs between buying expensive consumer goods and funding a business — the business was their first priority. It's no wonder they are also financially successful today.

No one ever became wealthy by spending the household's money on expensive consumer artifacts, like clothes and new cars. No one ever became a millionaire by using consumer goods as status symbols while neglecting their investments in private business or publicly traded stocks. Both Bobbie and Forester learned these realities from their frugal parents.

MARRIAGE VOWS AND THE SECRET OF
WASHING CARS: COMMON INTERESTS

Couples who share common interests tend to remain married, and there is a correlation between length of marriage and net worth. But the sharing of common interests and duration of a marriage are nowhere near perfect predications of wealth accumulation. If a couple has a common interest in spending all their income they may shop together and stay married for a long time, but it's unlikely they'll ever become financially independent.

So it's the types of activities and interests that a couple shares that are key. Shared interests that are related to accumulating wealth are important, including preparing a household budget, planning and making investments, setting financial goals, and owning and operating a business. Couples who share these interests are much more likely to attain millionaire status. To them, it seems a lot more sensible to purchase an expensive new car out of gains made from wise investments than from earned income.

I recently bumped into an old acquaintance who told me he had just bought a boat for $23,000. He also made it clear that the purchase was funded from part of the dividends paid on just one of his investments in a public corporation. He and his wife of twelve years both enjoy boating, and they also enjoy working together on the family budget, studying investment opportunities, and planning long-term financial goals. For this couple, boating is especially enjoyable because it's not a substitute to building wealth. In fact, the boat was a reward. They rewarded each other for exceeding their goal of accumulating wealth. They purchased their boat with just a minor portion of the gains they realized from a stock purchased nearly ten years ago. Beside the money they invested, the couple allocated a few hours of time to studying *Value Line*'s assessment of stocks, where they discovered this particular one. They didn't even have to purchase this fine publication — they found it on the shelf in the local library.

Having a common interest in wealth-building activities is a key for couples who wish to become financially independent, and the most common of these activities is owning and operating a family business, like B. and D. Ferguson. Neither Mr. or Mrs. Ferguson ever attended college, but their household's net worth exceeds that of most college graduates. Both were ambitious and hardworking, and had a keen interest in becoming financially independent so they could retire earlier than most couples. They reasoned that business ownership would provide them with the highest probability of achieving their goal. The couple was very careful in determining the ideal type of business — they searched for a category that had a high profit potential, and found one they thought people would never recognize as generating high earnings. In their selected trade area, it had few competitors. Mrs. Ferguson told me:

Thank you for not including the car-wash industry as one of the businesses of self-made millionaires. . . . The less public attention, the better. . . . The reality is that there are many self-made millionaires in this industry.

People often ask me about the size of the investment required to start a business — the common belief is that it's always very costly. People think that it takes millions to make millions. But the Fergusons had a different view. You don't necessarily need to invest millions to become economically independent if you start out with a small, efficient operation. According to Mrs. Ferguson:

At the age of twenty-six and twenty-nine, respectively, my husband and I leased a run-down, full-service car wash with $5,000 we borrowed from my husband's parents.

Five thousand dollars put the couple in the car-wash business. It was a wise investment — thirteen years later, they sold the business for $750,000. Yes, the Fergusons had found a diamond in the rough. Most other married couples wouldn't have purchased a "run-down" car wash, but it never bothered the Fergusons that their business wasn't glamorous and didn't denote high status or wealth. The Fergusons were never concerned that most of their customers viewed them as "strictly blue-collar."

Their beliefs were part of the couple's strength. Any time one of them questioned their career decision to "wash cars," it was countered with arguments like this:

Most car-wash owners (including my husband and me) are probably better off than our college-educated, professional customers. The sacrifices are definitely worth it long-term.

The couple actually turned the potential disadvantage of not attending college into an advantage. They motivated themselves into being frugal and productive by constantly reminding themselves that they had accumulated more wealth than most of their well-educated, well-dressed, upscale customers. Even during hard times, when it rained for several days and they had no customers, they thought of the long term, not minor setbacks.

Long-term we will retire with more!

ONE IN A MILLION:
ATTRACTION AND SUCCESSFUL CHOICES

One issue is very clear. Income and wealth are not the most important factors that account for a millionaire's successful marriage. Nor were either of these the primary factor in the initial interest they discovered for the man or woman they ultimately married.

Why all this interest in what millionaires think makes up a successful marriage? The typical millionaire couple in America has been married for twenty-eight years. One in four have been married for thirty-eight or more years. Considering the divorce rate in contemporary America, millionaires as a group can teach us all something about finding the right mate for life. Also, choice of spouse is a major factor in explaining variations in wealth. There is a highly significant negative correlation between divorce and wealth, and, conversely, there is a highly significant relationship between years of uninterrupted marriage and net worth.

In essence, why are millionaires millionaires? Because they made the right decisions concerning several major issues in their life, and one of these is choice of spouse. So it's not surprising that their spouse's physical attraction wasn't considered to be very important in a millionaire's successful marriage. In my personal and group interviews, "physically attractive" was mentioned by nearly all respondents, and it does make some contribution to successful marriages. However, the importance of this quality by itself is grossly overstated in the current literature. As one of my respondents said about physical attractiveness:

Given the choice, I prefer to be physically attracted to a woman who is intelligent, honest, unselfish, well-adjusted. . . .

In a nutshell, that's what most millionaires tell me about the "physically attractive" quality. They almost never even consider marrying someone merely for "physically attractive" reasons.

Intelligence is important as a choice criterion in the millionaire group, but other very important qualities must also be present. Future millionaires seem to be able to judge potential partners with respect to traits like sincerity, cheerfulness, reliability, and affection. How and where do millionaires acquire this ability to distinguish an ideal spouse from other candidates? You will recall the discussion in chapter 3, "School Days." What was one of the most important aspects of school and college that influenced millionaires in becoming economically productive adults?

Learning how to make accurate judgments about people.

In this regard, 88 percent indicated that their school and college experiences had a significant degree of influence on them. This dimension was second in importance only to "developing a strong work ethic."

Most millionaires said that school- and college-related experiences taught them to be sensitive to variations in the qualities of people. The more interaction they had with a variety of fellow students in many different social environments, the better they were able to make accurate judgments about candidates for the role of life partner. Is this person truly sincere, reliable, and so forth? That's the question that is a critical part of the spouse-selection process.

Parents, have you encouraged your children to be sensitive to variations in sincerity among their boyfriends and girlfriends? The key issue here is how sincere their friends are with all people — not just those they are trying to impress. How do they treat people? Are they sincere because of their nature and upbringing? Or are they able to turn sincere only when it benefits them?

Not all of the intelligent people one meets in college have all the other important qualities. In fact, the quality of high intelligence can often act as camouflage. Some people are so taken with a suitor's high level of intellect that the suitor's deficiencies are concealed or overlooked, just as others are blinded by physical attractiveness. If one places too much emphasis on a quality like intelligence, then he may be insensitive to variations in sincerity, cheerfulness, reliability, and virtue, for example.

IMPORTANT QUALITIES

Why is it that most millionaire couples stay married? Both husbands and wives have strong views about the factors that contribute to a successful marriage. They know what the components of a lasting marriage are, and they have no difficulty describing them. A successful marriage is a direct function of the presence of several qualities — both husbands and wives have almost identical views about these qualities in their spouses.

Nearly all of the males (99 percent) and the large majority of females (94 percent) indicated that being honest is important (see Table 6-1). Both groups are also quite similar in the frequency with which they rate four other qualities as important. Ninety-six percent of the males and 92 percent of the females believe that their mates are "responsible." The same percentage (95 percent) of both husbands and wives view their respective spouses as being "loving." The large majority of both groups also believe that their spouses are "capable" and "supportive."

378

TABLE 6-1

THE TOP FIVE QUALITIES OF A SPOUSE THAT CONTRIBUTED TO MILLIONAIRES' SUCCESSFUL MARRIAGES

PERCENTAGE INDICATING IMPORTANT

Quality of Spouse	All Mil-lionaires	Male (N=625)	Female (N=73)	Significant Difference[1]
Honest	98	99	94	No
Responsible	95	96	92	No
Loving	95	95	95	No
Capable	95	95	96	No
Supportive	94	94	91	No

[1]Probability at less than 0.05 level.

All of these qualities are important components of a long and successful marriage.

These views provide much food for thought. The typical millionaire couple has been together for nearly thirty years, and their bond tends to be permanent as well as economically productive. And no matter if you ask the husband or the wife to explain their household's productivity, the answer is the same. Each gives substantial credit to the other.

For every 100 millionaires who say that having a supportive spouse was not important in explaining their economic

success, there are 1,317 who indicate their spouse was important. Of the 100 who did not give credit to their spouse, 22 were never married and 23 were either divorced or separated. That leaves only 55 in 1,317 who believed that their spouse did not play an important role in their economic success.

Mr. S., an entrepreneur, spoke of his success in a focus-group interview. He made it abundantly clear to the group that his family's business would have never been so productive without the support of his wife of thirty-eight years.

I'll . . . hand it to my wife. . . . If it hadn't been for her . . . we couldn't do what we've done up to this point. We had five children. I never had to go to the doctor with her or with one of the children. She managed all of that. . . . She did it all. . . .

A large majority of millionaires concur with Mr. S.'s views. Each has his or her individual story, but they all have common features. They all state that his or her spouse is very supportive, and that in order for one's mate to be supportive he or she must be honest, responsible, loving, and capable. These are the basic components of successful marriages among millionaires.

Mr. Don D., a self-made multimillionaire entrepreneur, provided me with an excellent profile of a supportive, responsible, and capable spouse. When Don was twenty-nine, he asked his wife about her views on his starting his own business. He explained that certain sacrifices would have to be made. First, he would have to leave his well-paying corporate position. Don asked her opinion about financing the start-up of a business. "What if we have to sell everything?"

My wife said, "What happens if you don't make money?" I said, "Well, I'll get another job." And she said, "Fine."

But two years after Don started the business, the venture didn't make it. His wife, who worked with him, never once complained. Don then returned to corporate life. Five years later he quit his corporate job — with his wife's blessing and encouragement again. Don started another business, which has been a success since its founding in 1976. Since then he has also started three other businesses.

How does Don define "capable and responsible"? His wife not only took responsibility for almost all the domestic tasks, she also did much more. She never had Don's technical expertise in physics, but she took the initiative and learned about the business and its technology. Today, Don says with pride and admiration that two of the four businesses that he started are owned and very efficiently managed by his wife.

TABLE 6-2

THE TOP FIVE QUALITIES THAT INITIALLY INTERESTED MILLIONAIRES IN THEIR SPOUSES

PERCENTAGE INDICATING IMPORTANT

Quality of Spouse	All Millionaires	Male (N=625)	Female (N=73)	Significant Difference[1]
Intelligent	96	95	99	No
Sincere	95	95	95	No
Cheerful	92	93	83	Yes
Reliable	92	92	91	No
Affectionate	91	92	88	No

[1]Probability at less than 0.05 level.

I've been married thirty years . . . my wife hasn't changed. Just the same person today. I could never imagine it without my wife. . . . I'm sort of headstrong; she's a quiet, calming type of person.

Don indicated that he and his wife are the perfect match. Both recognize and admire each other's qualities, and both possess many of the five major qualities essential for a productive and lasting relationship. They are mutually honest, responsible, loving, capable, and supportive.

Beyond physical attractiveness, there are also

five major qualities that account for millionaires' first becoming interested in their spouses. Again, Don is like most millionaires, who will tell you that they were drawn to their mate because he or she was intelligent, sincere, cheerful, reliable, and affectionate. How accurate were these perceptions, developed during the early stages of courtship? Nearly all of the millionaires say that intelligence is an important quality (see Table 6-2). I once asked a group of ten millionaires to describe their wives, and the word *intelligent* was frequently mentioned. But what did these men mean when they referred to their spouses as intelligent?

> *. . . My wife has the ability to learn and adjust to anything. . . . Right now she could run the business better than I can.*

Ninety percent of the husbands and 85 percent of the wives in the millionaire household graduated from college. The wives in particular did well — about 80 percent ranked in the top quarter of the class. Of course, there are other ways to measure intelligence, but no matter how you define it, millionaires feel that their spouses have a lot of it.

What about the other factors? As detailed in Table 6-2, 95 percent of both husbands and wives became interested in their future spouses because they were sincere, and it seems that most were good judges. According to these respondents, sincerity is a precursor to honesty, which is very important in ultimately contributing to a successful marriage.

Most millionaire respondents have had nearly thirty years to judge the accuracy of their early evaluation of their mates. They probably have a firm understanding of their spouses' qualities. Those future spouses who were judged to be reliable early in the courtship proved to be more than just reliable; they were also responsible. Reliability is a precursor of responsibility, another marital success factor.

THE MONEY FACTOR

What role does high-income-earning potential play in attracting a spouse and contributing to a successful marriage? Husbands and wives within the ranks of millionaires have different views about the wealth and income qualities of their mates.

Women are four times more likely than men to indicate that the "high-income-earner" quality of their spouse was important in accounting for a successful marriage. Nearly one-half of the wives (49 percent) indicated that high income was important (see Table 6-3). In sharp contrast, only 12 percent of the husbands indicated that their spouses' earnings were significant in contributing to their successful marriages.

As I have so often stated, income is not wealth. And it is often said that money income can't buy happiness. Although the "wealthy" quality was

TABLE 6-3

MALES VS. FEMALES[1]: IMPORTANT QUALITIES OF SPOUSE THAT CONTRIBUTED TO THEIR SUCCESSFUL MARRIAGE

PERCENTAGE INDICATING IMPORTANT QUALITY

Quality of Spouse	Male (N=625)	Female (N=73)
High Income Earner	12	49
Wealthy	12	37
Virtuous	88	71
Tidy	69	55
Unselfish	86	74
Cheerful	88	80
Physically Attractive	88	80
Well Mannered	91	84
Frugal	46	39
Honest	99	94

[1]All differences are significant, probability at less than 0.05 level except for the frugal quality.

not rated as significant by the majority of millionaire husbands and wives, the wives were three times more likely (37 percent) than husbands (12 percent) to believe that "wealthy" was a key success factor (see Table 6-3).

This doesn't necessarily mean that a majority of America's millionaire couples would remain successfully married if they were broke. What these husbands and wives are telling us about their wealth and marriage is that they could be just as successfully married with much less income and with a fraction of their wealth. Most of these husbands and wives are more sensitive to variations in qualities other than wealth and income.

Millionaires, both men and women, tell me over and over again about their mates: He/she is honest, responsible, loving, capable, and supportive.

These qualities are most important in explaining their successful marriages, and most millionaire husbands and wives have not and will not substitute wealth or income for these five basic elements.

Women are more sensitive to income and wealth qualities of their mates for good reason. Most wives in millionaire households have traditional values and feel that the man of the house should be the main income generator. The men share this view. Few millionaire husbands, about only one in eight (12 percent), feel otherwise.

These survey results are congruent with the views espoused by John Gray, a leading authority on the differences between men and women with regard to motives, habits, and drives. According to Gray, men have a biological need to provide for women (see John Gray, "Mars and Venus: Do Men Buy Love? Are Women Needy?" *Currency*,

April 1998, pp. 56–67). In fact, man's "primary need is to be needed" by a woman.

A large part of this need is in the context of income and wealth. Here again, Gray's views are supported by my survey research on millionaires. Do women actually search for men who have high-income-producing capabilities? Gray believes they do. But the men are different. Not only do they want to provide economically for women, they also are likely to be turned off by women who are generating or have the potential to generate high incomes on their own (Gray, p. 51).

The data illustrated in Table 6-4 documents some of these major differences between men and women in the millionaire household. A significantly greater percentage of wives (59 percent) as opposed to husbands (13 percent) indicated that the "high-income-earning potential" quality was important in initially interesting them in their spouse. What about the other economic factor? The "wealthy" quality was not as critical for the majority of either wives (23 percent) or husbands (9 percent), but women do outpace men in this regard.

Interestingly, the "ambitious" quality was more important to a higher percentage of both women (82 percent) and men (48 percent) than the "wealthy" quality. "Self-disciplined" and "secure" are also more important for women. Men are more likely to become interested in women if they are well-dressed (80 percent vs.

TABLE 6-4

MALES VS. FEMALES[1]: IMPORTANT QUALITIES THAT INITIALLY INTERESTED MILLIONAIRES IN THEIR SPOUSES

PERCENTAGE INDICATING IMPORTANT QUALITY

Quality of Spouse	Male (N=625)	Female (N=73)
High-Income-Earning Potential	13	59
Ambitious	48	82
Well Dressed	80	60
Virtuous	79	61
Wealthy	9	23
Self-Disciplined	71	82
Frugal	34	23
Secure	71	81
Cheerful	93	83
Encouraging	87	80

[1] All differences are significant; probability at less than 0.05 level.

60 percent); virtuous (79 percent vs. 61 percent); cheerful (93 percent vs. 83 percent); and encouraging (87 percent vs. 80 percent).

Women who marry men who become millionaires are attracted to those who have more than the five big "attractive" qualities (intelligent, sincere, cheerful, reliable, and affectionate). They must also be ambitious and have high-income-earning potential. For nearly four in five women, "wealthy before marriage" was not an important quality. Of course, these women married men who eventually became millionaires along with their wives.

Men have the same five big qualities in mind when initially evaluating potential spouses, but many do not want to compete with their spouse in terms of money, income, or wealth. They do want their spouse to be intelligent, but only a minority became interested because of such qualities as "income potential" or "ambitious." More often than not, the wives allow their husbands to take the role of main breadwinner for the family.

THE CRITERIA FOR CHOICE

How did millionaires determine beforehand that a potential spouse would eventually turn out to be the ideal husband or wife? First, the criteria they used to evaluate potential mates are the same ones that produce long-term, successful marriages. Second, they are able to accurately predict whether a potential spouse will rate high on these criteria. The large majority of millionaires made such predictions and corresponding selections long before they became millionaires.

Why is it that so many adults in our population are unable to make the same kind of accurate predictions about a potential spouse? Making accurate predictions is actually a two-step process. First, you must identify the right criteria that are compatible with a long-term marriage. If the criteria are wrong, then it doesn't matter if you can accurately predict them in your prospective mate.

What criteria do most people (nonmillionaires, non-potential millionaires) use when selecting a mate? How are these different from what you have already read about millionaires in this chapter? Dr. Belinda Tucker, of UCLA, recently conducted a major study of 3,407 adults from the general population, ranging in age between eighteen and fifty-five, on the criteria adults use in selecting mates. She presented her findings at the 1997 national conference of the American Psychological Association.

Professor Tucker found that men give more weight to the physical attractiveness dimension than to any other criteria. Men rated the income criterion (salary and earning potential) as second only in importance to attractiveness. Contrast these findings with what has been reported about millionaire men. They say that the factors that contributed to their successful marriages are:

Honest, responsible, loving, capable, and supportive.

So if you marry an attractive, high-income-earning woman who is not honest, responsible, loving, capable, and supportive, your marriage may not succeed.

Dr. Tucker's study also determined the criteria that are most important in mate selection for women. The "salary and earning potential" dimension was rated highest — more important than attractiveness, education, or occupation. Again, this is in sharp contrast to the mate-selection criteria used by women who are millionaires. Most of these women indicated that honesty, intelligence, and ambition are more fundamental to a lasting marriage than the income or earning potential of their mates.

Contrasting millionaires with the general population does shed some light on why the divorce rate is so high among the nonmillionaires. Dr. Tucker stated that:

Satisfaction with your partner's financial contributions is strongly related to how you feel about your relationship and whether you feel you will stay in the relationship.

Dr. Tucker also found that, overall, both men and women would contemplate divorcing a spouse who lost his or her job! This attitude is diametrically opposed to the attitudes of couples who are or are likely to become millionaires. Remember, to build wealth one may likely have to forgo realizing a high income for many years. It's not unusual for wealth-building couples to realize "just enough" to live on, while investing every spare dollar. Nor is it unusual for self-made millionaires to report that:

*Just after I was fired from my job . . . I started our
business. . . . Spent every bit of our savings. . . .
My spouse's income kept us alive for the first few
but long, long years!*

Another woman, with her husband the
cofounder and owner of a family business, stated
that:

*No longer will I feel apologetic for being so
frugal. . . . We are not cheap . . . only true entrepreneurs. We . . . resist the urges to fall into the
traps of our high-consuming neighbors who make
more yearly income than we do. But we will retire
with more wealth.*

Dr. Tucker's data would suggest that in today's world, this woman is unusual. She never
thought of breaking her wedding vows because
of income-related issues, and that's one reason
she and her husband are wealthy today. They
toughed it out in good times and bad and
through many years of having a small income.
They would never have become millionaires if
income had been the main thing that held them
together. They both had the same set of attitudes, beliefs, and values, and both believed that
attaining financial independence was worth
making short-term sacrifices.

Dr. Tucker found that men in general ranked
the physical attractiveness dimension above all
other mate-selection criteria. Whatever hap-

pened to the belief that beauty is only skin deep? To most millionaires and those who are on track to becoming wealthy, attractiveness is only one of many qualities, and not the most highly rated.

Perhaps our high divorce rate is related to the importance many men place on attractiveness. A woman might be attractive at the time of her wedding, but if she doesn't stay that way he may have grounds, in his own mind, for a divorce. This is the reality of too many weak marriages in America. According to Dr. Tucker's findings, there may be an even higher rate of husband-inspired divorces when a woman loses both her attractiveness and her income-producing job at about the same time. In this event, the wife may actually be blessed that she'll be divorced from a loser of a husband — he's not likely to become wealthy or even content, because he has a history, a habit of entering into unstable marriages. Divorces take a great toll on one's net worth and happiness.

A CASE OF STABILITY AND COMPATIBILITY

Victor Ganz and his wife, Sally, were married for fifty years. They were a low-key Manhattan couple who spent much of their spare time studying and investing in art.

... They had a passion and a commitment to collecting art, spending every Saturday touring art galleries. Often they would sacrifice things like a

new winter coat whenever they couldn't resist making a purchase. (Acrol Vogel, "Prized Picasso Leads Collection to Record $206 Million Auction," *New York Times*, November 11, 1997, pp. A1, A18)

The Ganzes' art collection recently sold at a Christie's auction for $206 million. One of the paintings, Picasso's *The Dream*, was originally purchased by Mr. Ganz in 1941 for only $7,000. At the auction it sold for $48.2 million.

The Ganzes not only had a full-term marriage, they also had an economically productive one. It was not based on attractiveness and income but on much more. They shared a common interest in art. They both were willing to forgo the purchase of consumer goods and instead invested in high-quality art. The Ganzes were a "cheap date," spending their Saturdays walking through art galleries. These galleries usually charged no admission fees.

EOC INNOCULATION

A self-made decamillionaire telephoned me about a week after my article was published in *Medical Economics* (Thomas J. Stanley, "Why You're Not as Wealthy as You Should Be," *Medical Economics*, July 1992). He told me he'd read the article three times, and he repeatedly quoted material from it:

Wealth is more often the result of hard

work, perseverance, and most of all self-discipline.

He was especially taken by the fact that most American millionaires are self-made and that they are frugal. During our discussion, I also emphasized that most millionaires receive zero cash gifts or other economic outpatient care (EOC) from their relatives. He was particularly interested to learn that there is an inverse relationship between EOC and the level of wealth of recipients. As soon as I spoke those words, he interrupted me: "I have to have reprints of your articles. Can you send me some?"

He wanted to share my articles with three young men. It seems that this decamillionaire had three daughters — one in law school, one recently graduated from a top undergraduate college, and the youngest in her senior year of college. All three had steady boyfriends, and, in his estimation, these three young men needed to be enlightened.

The decamillionaire felt certain they were all well aware that he was wealthy, and he also believed that these young men might be "wealth oriented" (WO), or inclined to become interested in a prospective spouse because his or her family is wealthy. Further, he felt that these suitors might believe that the road to wealth begins and ends with OPM, other people's money.

This decamillionaire felt compelled to do

something to enhance his daughters' spousal se-lection process, and that's where the reprints of my articles came into the picture. How could he test whether or not his daughters' suitors were interested in his wealth? He gave each of them reprints of several of my articles discussing the importance of hard work, discipline, and a frugal lifestyle, and highlighting the detrimental effects of EOC. This, he made very clear to me, was a nice way of telling them: No EOC!

Yes, it's a nice way of telling three young suitors that they will be receiving zero economic outpatient care. If a suitor suddenly lost interest in his daughter, he could assume that the fellow was just WO.

What are the odds that the three suitors will suddenly lose interest in their respective girl-friends? According to my own data, it's unlikely. Only about nine in one hundred married male millionaires initially became interested in their spouses because their parents were wealthy, and even those nine indicated that other qualities were important. In fact, none of these people became interested in their mates because of the "wealthy" quality alone. At least eight out of ten were attracted because their future spouse was sincere, down-to-earth, intelligent, affectionate, reliable, accepting, wise, cheerful, and secure.

WEALTH-ORIENTED WOMEN
What about women who were attracted to their mates because of the "wealthy" quality?

Wives in the millionaire couple household are more likely than husbands to indicate that the "wealthy" quality in a spouse was important. About 23 in 100 wives, as opposed to 9 out of 100 husbands, stated that they were initially interested in their mates because of "wealthy" — about two and one-half times more women than men.

It's the perceived wealth of a potential mate's parents that is key. Are all those women your son has dated just interested in his mother and father's treasure chest? The data suggests not. Even those women who indicated that "wealthy" was an attraction felt that many more qualities were significant. More than 90 percent were also attracted to a prospective spouse who was sincere, intelligent, affectionate, reliable, accepting, wise, cheerful, secure, and had high income-earning potential. Also, 85 percent of these women were attracted because of the "ambitious" quality.

This is refreshing news. Overall, most men and women who marry and become millionaires don't care how much money their in-laws may have accumulated. They are indeed wise — it's much better to marry based upon qualities and traits that are person specific rather than ancestor or parent specific. The large majority of millionaires have told me that the economic qualities of their in-laws had little to do with their choice of spouse, and it's a good thing, because oftentimes one is better able to predict the qualities of a spouse than the behaviors of in-laws.

There is a simple rule about becoming wealthy in America:

Never consider relying on other people's money to make you rich.

Those who ignore this rule can be in for surprises, as this case study illustrates.

Peggy is from a working-class background. She earned an undergraduate degree from a major university. She was charming and very attractive. Her parents were impressed with people who were rich, and they taught Peggy to feel the same way. However, both Peggy and her blue-collar parents assumed that people who have high occupational status have high levels of wealth. Thus, anyone who is a physician, attorney, accountant, or corporate officer is wealthy. Unfortunately, Peggy violated this rule of wealth-oriented people:

Lesson Number One: **If you are inclined to marry the son or daughter of a wealthy family, first make certain that it is, in fact, wealthy. The appearances of wealth can be deceiving.**

Her selected spouse came from a prominent family and was a direct descendent of important people. His father was a well-known business leader in the community, and both parents were active in a variety of civic and other noble causes. They lived in a large home and drove luxury motor vehicles. They were members of a prestigious country club. His sister was a member of the Junior League.

But as Shakespeare said, "All that glitters is not gold." Unfortunately, Peggy was unable to distinguish gold from iron pyrite, or fool's gold. She became initially interested and ultimately married a young man because of the "wealthy" quality. But none of the facts cited above are perfect predictors of variations in wealth.

It was only after she married that Peggy discovered the truth. Her spouse's family had been in financial difficulty for years, even before the wedding. They had done a lot to keep up the face of a successful and prosperous family. Peggy thought that she and her husband would be given a home, but no EOC in cash or equivalents was ever distributed. Even more unpleasant was the ultimate cold-turkey realization — her husband told her she would have to go to work.

Peggy's marriage didn't last three years. Still, she was determined to meet and ultimately marry a wealthy man, and that's when her past experience and intuition kicked in. Searching for a "convoy," Peggy accepted a position at a large trust company. She met and married an affluent client of this trust company, a man many years her senior. This time she made the right choice. She hit pay dirt — a multimillionaire! At present he works; she does not. She spends, he builds wealth. It's a balancing act. Will his financial balance sheet accommodate Peggy's hyperconsumption lifestyle? We'll see.

Lesson Number Two: **Even if your in-laws are very wealthy, you or your spouse may never receive a dollar's worth of inheritance or even EOC.**

Not all wealthy parents provide their sons' and daughters' households with EOC. Some do not even leave an inheritance to them. In fact, 46 percent of people in such situations never receive an intergenerational transfer of wealth.

About one in three women who married men from wealthy families report that their household received an average of about $400,000 from their spouse's relatives. This translates into about $13,333 per year of marriage. When I first revealed this dollar amount to a group of my associates, one especially insightful character remarked: "She'd be better off financially working thirty years at McDonald's!"

You may not agree with this statement, but it's hard to disagree with the facts. Most people who marry for OPM are surprised. In some cases, the target's family only looked wealthy. In others, the family of the targeted spouse doesn't believe in providing EOC to their sons or daughters, in-laws, and others. Many wealthy parents believe that EOC dampens ambition.

What about men who are WO? They are more productive in their quest for OPM than are the women. But for every 100 WO men, there are about 255 WO women. Only about one in three WO men report that their household received zero dollars of EOC or inheritance. The large majority of WO men report that about $700,000 in intergenerational transfers benefited their households.

Why do WO males often benefit more from EOC than women who are WO? The answer is actually part of Lesson Number Three.

Lesson Number Three: About one-half of the women who marry WO men become housewives. Daughters of wealthy parents who are housewives are among the most likely to receive EOC. Conversely, most WO women marry men who are economically productive. Wealthy parents give the fewest number of dollars of EOC to their most productive offspring.

If a WO person marries a productive mate, the more the productive person earns, the less likely he or she will receive EOC. So the choice is clear. It seems to be true that one can marry wealth *or* income, not wealth *and* income.

Lesson Number Four: Wealthy parents

prefer providing EOC to their grand-children than to WO sons-in-law and daughters-in-law.

If you marry an offspring of a wealthy couple, it's better emotionally and spiritually to assume that none of this wealth will ever come your way. For the large majority of millionaire couples (more than 80 percent), other people's wealth was never an important factor in their choice of spouse. Nor was it ever important in explaining a long-term, successful marriage.

Love vs. Honesty

I once asked Henry, a self-made millionaire, if he ever thought that he and his steady girlfriend, Sally, would be married someday. He answered with a firm yes. But after seven years of dating he broke off the relationship. Oh yes, Henry loved Sally, and she loved him. Everything seemed to be a proper fit. The couple had much in common; they enjoyed the same lifestyle elements; their opinions and interests were in harmony; they liked the same foods and beverages; both enjoyed clothes shopping.

Then several years into the relationship something happened — Henry discovered that the love of his life had deliberately hidden more than $35,000 of outstanding debt. Even more significant, she was in default on more than $20,000 in loans. The balance of the outstanding debt was a combination of credit card balances, auto loans, and store credit accounts. All her outstanding loans were in arrears.

One of Sally's creditors contacted Henry because he was listed as a credit reference on a loan application. He received a letter from the lender, who was apparently having a problem locating Sally. She had changed addresses several times since the loan was made, and she was well aware that she had violated her loan agreement. Sally had never paid back a penny of her student loans, even though she had completed her undergraduate and graduate education years ago.

The lender who contacted Henry was not the only one trying to track down Sally — several others were also in pursuit of what was owed them. Given these facts, Henry was shocked. Sally had never given him any indication that she had credit problems. In fact, she gave signs that she was well off financially. She had a well-paying job, a new automobile, lovely clothes.

Henry confronted Sally with the evidence of her financial crisis. At first, she said that it wasn't a problem. She told him that she was about to make good on her outstanding loans, but when he pressed her for the details, she told him the real story. After a while, she revealed the dollar amount that she owed. Henry asked how she planned to pay off the creditors.

Sally had a simple plan, and it almost worked. She realized that Henry was well off financially. He had confided in her about the money he was able to accumulate from his position as a corporate vice president. Sally felt that Henry's income and net worth were the keys to solving her credit problem. She thought that once Henry married her, she could use OPM to pay off her debts. The "other people" in this case were just Henry!

Sally had never planned on telling Henry about her outstanding credit balances until after they were married. She didn't anticipate that he'd discover her true financial position beforehand. Sally also believed that her credit problems would not be of major concern to Henry once he said "I do."

However, she had misjudged Henry. He felt that she had committed a serious breach of faith, but even independent of her subterfuge, he didn't wish to marry anyone who owed more than $35,000. In reality, this was just a sign of a bigger problem — Sally was totally and completely irresponsible concerning money. And she'd betrayed the trust of a man who prides himself on being fiscally responsible.

Henry broke off the relationship, but all is not lost. He is now wiser, and the next time he contemplates marriage, things will be different. He swears that he will never marry a woman without first running a credit check on her. He says that he'd be quite willing to provide his next prospective spouse with his income statement and balance sheet. If this information reveals problems, the revelations are better coming before marriage than after. Some problems can be solved —

just the willingness of a couple to share information can strengthen a relationship. But it's doubtful that Henry would ever even consider subsidizing the credit obligations of a prospective spouse.

Is the case of Henry and Sally atypical? No. Nearly all millionaires surveyed (95 percent or more) feel that the "honest" and "responsible" qualities of their spouse were significant in explaining their successful marriages. Sally was unwise. She thought that Henry's love for her was so strong that he wouldn't mind paying off her loans. But it was more of an issue than loan payoffs. Henry would have no part of a woman with a hidden agenda.

A Class as a Convoy

What mementos do married couples keep from their courtship experiences? Many treasure their early courtship photographs, or keep movie or football-game ticket stubs from their first date. I have many such artifacts, but I also have something unusual. During twenty years as a professor, I have kept only one of my grade books from just one semester, in the top drawer of my desk. I keep it there because it's an important symbol of my courtship, and it's also a good luck charm. It reminds me that I am a very lucky fellow.

Luck does have a role in explaining successful marriages and success in life overall. I was very lucky to find Janet, my one and only wife for over twenty-five years. I wasn't looking for a bride the day we met. At the time, I was a twenty-four-year-old instructor at the University of Tennessee, assigned to teach Marketing 3110, fall term, Section 33243, 2:20–3:10 P.M., Monday, Wednesday, Friday.

The class contained a high percentage of nice-looking young women, including the one seated in row six, seat number one. I remember noticing some qualities about Janet even during the first period. Not only was she attractive, she was attentive and well-dressed. During the term I had the wonderful opportunity to learn more and more about her. Even from afar she appeared to have many of the attributes of an ideal spouse.

My teaching job at the time didn't pay much, nor did it have many fringe benefits. But teaching that semester provided me with a convoy that contained an ideal spouse and mother for my children. I won the ultimate lifetime benefit. There are many other qualities that are more important than income or wealth, and Janet has all of them. How many other spouses would have been content under the following conditions? Janet spent her first three years of marriage in a small apartment. It was all we could afford while I was in a three-year Ph.D. program with an annual stipend of $3,600. Janet cheerfully accepted a secretarial position at the university for $4,500 per year. It's a good thing that we didn't have much money — given the rigors of the Ph.D. program, there was little time to spend it.

In addition to her daytime job, Janet typed all of my papers and my dissertation twice. Never once did she complain. When I had my first meeting with my dissertation committee, they wanted me to redo much of the proposal, which was over one hundred pages long. That was on a Friday, and the committee wanted the "redo" back as soon as possible. I started the rewrite early that Friday afternoon. When Janet came home from work later, she asked how the committee had responded to my proposal and I relayed their message.

How did Janet respond? She retyped the rewritten proposal that night and for much of Saturday. I never had to ask her for help — Janet thrives on helping others. This applies not only to her family but to school and civic good causes. She is the ultimate in unselfishness.

Given her Scottish background, she is also frugal. She never enters a food store without a complete list and her coupon folder. And before she even considers buying new furniture, she gives lots of thought to refinishing or reupholstering what we already have in the house. We have a house full of "reprocessed" furniture. We've had the same sofa for more than twenty years — the fabric has changed, but the guts are original.

I should have guessed that Janet was frugal. During our first date, she ordered a grilled cheese sandwich and a Coke for lunch. How come someone so well dressed was such a "cheap" date? Later I found out that her father was a salvage merchant, and his specialty was quality women's wear. He traveled all over America to bid on the inventory of stores that were damaged by fires or natural disasters. In fact, her mother once told me that "everything Janet wore to college was in a fire, so I hope you will buy your children clothing that wasn't."

Looking back on our courtship, I now notice some important patterns that weren't so obvious until I began studying people who've had successful marriages. The people in Janet's family were very respectful of one another, and her family members were also unselfish, supportive, and cooperative. I visited Janet at her parents' home several times during the various holidays. The place was filled with aunts and uncles and cousins. They all had one thing in common — they were all trying to do something to help someone clean up tables, serve beverages, take the dog out, clean the dishes, and so on. Listening in was almost like watching a musical play on Broadway. With the "I'll do that, I'll do this, let me give you a hand, I will, I can," it was better than the Boy Scout's creed.

Janet's mother tells me that it's genetic. She and her husband have been married for over fifty years. She believes that both just came from "people who are unselfish and supportive." But there may be another factor — both sets of

Janet's grandparents were farmers. Certainly qualities such as unselfishness and respect were instilled in the farm environment. Everybody works on a farm, including the children.

Janet's mother was one of eleven children. Her mother died when she was just four years old. All the children were taught the value of sharing household chores. For the most part, they were on their own. They cooked, cleaned, shopped, and did every other chore associated with rural living. Perhaps adversity encouraged them to respect and support one another.

But in spite of all her wonderful attributes, Janet is embarrassed when I praise her. She dislikes being in the spotlight under any circumstances. Once *People* magazine sent a photo team to my home to do a set of "family shots." The lead photographer insisted that Janet be in the picture, but she was even more insistent about not being in *People*. The photographer was no match for her. In spite of typing and editing every one of my books, including this one, Janet did not wish to be in the media. Certainly she deserved to be included in all photographs with her best-selling author husband, but more basic things like family and close friends give rewards that are more satisfying to her.

I am really glad she didn't marry that other guy. He sat right behind her in the class I taught until I objected to his talking while I lectured. Rick kept talking to Janet even though she didn't return the conversation. In order to keep harmony in the class as well as to isolate Rick, I moved him to the back of the room!

Because it was improper to date someone in my class, I had to wait until Janet was no longer a student before I could ask her out. But it was proper to reduce my competition in the meantime, so Rick was moved. There was another problem — what if Janet decided to take the other course I was scheduled to teach the following semester? Oh, no — another semester to wait and wait. Something had to be done. What could I do to enhance the probability that Janet would select another class, one not taught by me? I'd often heard that it's better if students take courses from a variety of faculty members, so on several occasions I told my class that they should take their next course in the sequence with a different faculty member.

Janet took my advice, and our first date materialized when I just happened to bump into her on campus. I said hello and then asked her to have lunch with me. She looked a bit surprised, maybe somewhat puzzled, but she said yes. Was it by luck or design? We were engaged within seven months after our first date, and we were married about ten months later. The class certainly was a top-quality convoy for me.

LISA, A.K.A. LISA LIBRARY

Consider the qualities of an ideal spouse mentioned in this chapter, such as ambition, intelligence, discipline, and physical attractiveness.

Where do you find people with these qualities? You can find them on college and university campuses all over this country. It is the convoy of convoys for ideal spouses.

Many millionaires have told me that they met their spouse at college by chance — someone on campus just introduced Joe and Gloria or Bill and Helen. But all of these people were in a target-rich environment. If you are looking for an intelligent spouse, the odds are high that you will find many of them on campus. Quality people are found in quality convoys — pick the right one and you may be amazed at how much luck will come your way. Consider the case of "Lisa Library."

One of a professor's more enjoyable tasks is working with students who have great merit and potential, like my student Lisa. She had straight As in a rather competitive undergraduate program, and her scores on the Graduate Record Exam and the Graduate Management Aptitude Test were very high. She was also charming and attractive and had a wide variety of interests and extracurricular activities to her credit.

Lisa was enrolled in one of my undergraduate courses during the fall semester of her senior year. During the second week, she and three classmates stopped by my office and expressed an interest in learning more about an area of marketing to which I had devoted a considerable amount of time. Lisa was the spokesperson for the group. They proposed that the group conduct research and write a paper based on their survey. Even though what they were proposing did not qualify for credit, Lisa and her classmates wanted to enhance their knowledge in a new area, and in their minds, the project would enhance their records for graduate school admission.

We agreed to meet for an hour or two each Monday morning during the term. They updated me on the project, and I provided them with direction and outside reading materials. All went as planned for nearly the entire term, then something extraordinary happened. On the Monday of the second to last week of the semester, Lisa was absent for the first time.

Just a few weeks before, she had dropped off her requests for recommendations. I was delighted to support her applications for admission to three of America's top MBA programs. Innocently, I asked, "Where's Lisa?"

Didn't you hear? Lisa's getting married. She's not going to graduate school.

I was surprised because Lisa had never mentioned being engaged, so I queried the group and learned that most of them were as unaware as I. Her backup as leader of the group informed us that Lisa wouldn't be completing our independent study program because she didn't need it to bolster her applications to graduate school — now that she was getting married, she no longer had any interest in graduate school.

Lisa had decided to marry a doctor in his last year of medical school, someone she'd just started dating and to whom she'd quickly become engaged. We all expressed surprise that she had abandoned her major goal of graduate school, but our informant told us that, actually, graduate school was her number two goal, just in case she was unable to marry a doctor!

He also let us in on Lisa's secret in achieving goal number one. Every night she studied in the medical school library — a tip passed on by her mother, who'd told her that if she married a doctor, she'd never have to work or be concerned about money. She'd also suggested that the medical school library was the perfect place to meet that doctor.

I didn't show it, but I was shocked by these revelations. Lisa was a young scholar who could easily become a major economic success all by herself. It was incredible to me that she had withdrawn prematurely from the American economy. Why did Lisa's mother strongly encourage her to marry a physician, literally pushing her brilliant young daughter into the perfect convoy, the medical school library?

The more data I collect about wealthy people, the more I understand Lisa's mother's motives.

Today, there are five men for every one woman who achieves a six-figure earned income. Even worse, fewer than 10 percent of those earning seven-figure incomes are women.

Women, even in the top-paying professions, earn only about 55 percent of what their male counterparts earn. As I have often said, the economic deck is stacked against them.

Although the popular press has celebrated the predicted growth in the female affluent population for over twenty years, my survey research does not indicate much change at all. More than 90 percent of the millionaire population in America is composed of married-couple households, and about one-half of the other 10 percent is made up of widows and widowers. Who is the main breadwinner, financial decision maker, and head of domestic investing within the millionaire household? The national surveys that I have conducted over the years document that in more than 80 percent of the married millionaire households, it is the husband.

Given these facts, how good was the advice Lisa received from her mother? I suspect that her mother was, sadly, rather intuitive about the economic odds facing her daughter, but I still maintain that Lisa, with her extraordinary aptitudes, could have overcome them.

THE OTHER BENEFIT OF NIGHT SCHOOL

A student in one of my recent seminars indignantly asked me, "What makes you such an expert about marriage?" I want to make it very clear that I am not a marriage counselor or even a psychologist. My job is much simpler than those. I study productive people who earn high incomes and accumulate substantial wealth. Underlying this productivity are several factors, and one of the very most important relates to choice of spouse. Who you marry and how long you stay married can be major determinants. If you make the correct selection, then the tide will be with you on your journey to becoming a productive household. It doesn't ensure that you will become wealthy one day, but I can tell you from surveying thousands of millionaires about the importance of marriage to their success that about nine in ten believe it was a major factor.

What if you make a bad choice? Why did you initially become interested in the spouse you just divorced? He was very charming. He was able to hide from you the elements of faulty character. He drank a lot even during the early stages of your courtship, but you felt he would grow out of this college craze. Unfortunately, his drinking continued throughout your marriage. As you later found out, he was insincere, selfish, undisciplined, unreliable, and prone to lose his temper. And what happened to his early pronouncements about great ambitions and his self-designated superior intelligence? You fell for his sales presentation.

Where did you first encounter Mr. Perfect? It was on a Friday during happy hour at a singles bar. Perhaps some people are luckier than you and they found their ideal spouse at a similar place, but this is hardly the ideal convoy in which to hunt for a spouse.

Think of the prospective spouses who make up the singles bar convoy. Where do you think they rank on the criteria that most millionaires use to evaluate the spouse they selected? Remember the importance millionaires place on qualities like ambition, intelligence, reliability, self-discipline, unselfishness, honesty, work ethic, and respectfulness. Note that two out of three millionaires indicated that the moderate drinker or abstainer quality of a spouse was also important in contributing to a successful marriage.

If criteria like ambition and intelligence are important qualities in your mind, you can enhance your chances of finding an ambitious and intelligent spouse by hanging out at night where they do. I would suggest that night classes at the local university are a better place to hunt for a spouse. And you can kill two birds with one stone. In addition to finding a mate, you can obtain a degree or even an advanced degree.

Even if you don't want to spend a lot of time and effort pursuing a degree, you can still enhance your chances of surfacing in the middle of an intelligent convoy. Many colleges and universities offer noncredit self-improvement courses. You can learn computer programming or conversational Spanish and, simultaneously, prospect for a spouse.

You can even enhance your chances by selecting a class that has a high concentration of students from the opposite sex. Although some recent changes have taken place, patterns are still present. Most education classes usually contain a disproportionately high number of women, while engineering and accounting classes normally contain more men.

TERRY'S DILEMMA

Terry's problem was not unique. At the time she asked me for advice, she was in her early thirties and already owned a small professional-service firm. Terry was married and had one child. When we spoke, she seemed down in the dumps. She told me that she and her husband had recently decided to divorce, but that was not her major concern. Actually, she looked forward to shedding her current spouse.

Terry was dreading "going back to the dating game." She had done that once in her mid-twenties. She had run the gauntlet before. She had found her current spouse in a singles bar convoy.

What's wrong with searching for a spouse inside the singles bar convoy? According to Terry, it's the frog problem — you have to kiss a lot of frogs before you meet a prince. She felt certain that fewer and fewer princes were to be found in singles bars. Terry believed in marriage and the traditional family concept. Where would she find a quality spouse? In her mind, the process could take years with the singles bar route. She had been out of the market for nearly ten years and felt a bit insecure about her ability to get back into the dating game.

If she were your friend, sister, or daughter, what would you suggest that Terry do? Here is what I recommended. Simply stated, I told her to join a church group. Her community was filled with churches and temples that had well-organized, adult singles groups. I anticipated Terry's reaction. She was not a member of any church and had rarely been in one since her marriage. But church people love to attract those who've been away from the flock, so I told Terry she could go back to the singles bar environment or, as they say, "get religion." Where else can one learn religion and possibly find a suitable mate at the same time?

I believe that one is likely to find better prospects in a church setting than in singles bars. Of course, there are no guarantees, but people with a religious orientation are more prone to respect the principles espoused in the Good Book. Where is the higher concentration of people with traditional values likely to be found? I'll pick the church environment over any singles bar.

It's not just the differing orientations of people in these environments. Churches and their related groups, such as "adult singles," are more stable and they have formal membership systems. Over time, members get to know each other, making it much easier for someone like Terry to inquire about the characteristics of a fellow church member than she could a singles bar patron. Members of singles clubs and groups that are affiliated with churches are looking for a place where they can meet people who have good traditional values. And, in turn, many of these people are looking for long-term relation-ships — not one-night stands.

MISS ANN GEOCODES CHURCHES

Terry was advised to join a church-related sin-gles group, but what church? What group? That decision was easy — one of the largest church-affiliated singles groups was near her home, so she didn't feel a need to search or shop affinity groups. Terry made a hit immediately. But it wasn't the same for Miss Ann.

Miss Ann is an intellectual. Extremely bright and very well educated, she was the senior editor at a major publishing company at the time she sought my advice. She had just divorced her hus-band, and like Terry, she was having a bad case of the post-divorce blues — bad enough for her to consider moving to another city.

Miss Ann was like many recently divorced people when I met her. She questioned her ability to attract members of the opposite sex and told me that the city she lived in "had no eli-gible men to date." In reality, she was wrong, but she'd been out of the dating game for quite some time, and it was easy for her to believe that.

For many months, Miss Ann complained about the lack of prospects. But all the while, local churches were doing a booming business attracting adult singles to their affinity meetings. I strongly suggested that Miss Ann seek a church-related solution to her problem. But her problem was more complicated than Terry's.

It was clear that Miss Ann wouldn't feel comfortable in just any church's singles group. Miss Ann is a unique individual, an intellectual with very traditional values. She needed a group that contained a high concentration of men and women who were on her intellectual plane. They didn't necessarily have to be rich or even earn high incomes, but they did have to have educational and vocational backgrounds similar to Miss Ann's.

How does one go about finding a church affinity group that contains a high concentration of people with a particular set of characteristics among the hundreds of churches within driving or commuting distance from one's home? It would take a lifetime to visit each one and check out their respective singles meetings. I suggested a better way — geocoding. This system is based on the theory that birds of a feather flock together — people who live in a particular neighborhood have similar socioeconomic characteristics, and they tend to patronize nearby churches.

To help Miss Ann find a suitable church singles group, I identified the areas or neighborhoods within her city that had high concentrations of well-educated people. Once this was established, then the legwork began. We had to rule out the churches that didn't have active singles groups, and the religious sections

420

of local and neighborhood newspapers were very helpful in that regard. The newspapers also carried advertisements including the prices for residential real estate that was for sale. It was easy to figure out where the "high-rent" districts were in Miss Ann's community.

Denomination was not important in Miss Ann's selection process — she was more interested in finding a suitable singles convoy than in religious thought. Overall, there was one absolute winner in terms of the mathematics and guesstimates. It contained the mother lode of well-educated attorneys, physicians, accountants, architects, executives, and entrepreneurs, but the church wasn't in Miss Ann's neighborhood, so she drove past all the other interesting churches on her way to the "church of the available high intellectuals."

Finding a spouse is a serious business, and it generally becomes more difficult after one leaves school and grows in age and gray hairs. So I told Miss Ann that she must take affirmative action. Like her, most people can significantly enhance the probability of finding a suitable spouse by identifying one or more affinity groups that contain high concentrations of prospects. Not all church singles groups are equal. Some are more suitable than others, given one's background and needs.

Unfortunately, most singles spend more time shopping for automobiles than for affinity groups. Looking for a spouse is a numbers game in a special way: The greater the concentration, the greater the probability of meeting large numbers of possibilities. Give these prospective spouses an opportunity to meet you. It is mind-boggling to think that there are millions of great prospective mates like Miss Ann who are unattached for yet another year, year after year.

I cannot leave Miss Ann's case without making one more point. Once inside a religious affinity group, what do you do then? The answer, in a word, is volunteer, as I told Miss Ann. Singles groups often ask personalities from around their areas to be guest speakers, and no one wants the job of organizing such programs. Most members are there to meet and mingle. But there are wonderful advantages of being the head of the speakers' recruitment committee.

Miss Ann can select anyone she would like to speak.

I am sure that she and the publishing company she works for would be delighted to find a new source for book manuscripts. What if Miss Ann did a bit of research? She could identify successful single men in her area who might be interested in writing a book about their experiences. In the process of asking someone to speak, Miss Ann could also uncover a prospective spouse who is on her intellectual plane. Many local business periodicals regularly publish lists as well as profiles of the people who are tops in their respective fields and might be suitable speakers. Just to get the ball rolling, I made

Miss Ann an offer. Although I am not single or hoping to be, I volunteered to be a speaker. Perhaps having a best-selling author discuss millionaires would make points for her with the other members.

THE MEAT OF THE PROPOSAL

John waited patiently for his turn. I had just completed a two-hour seminar for nearly one hundred corporate executives, and many members of the seminar class approached me as I prepared to leave the podium. I noticed that John kept allowing people who were behind him in line to move ahead. Finally he was the only person left. It was obvious that he wanted a private audience.

At the time of our discussion, John was the vice president of a major corporation, earning over $300,000 per year. He was also a self-made millionaire. His parents had never been rich, but they gave him more than money. He contends that his ambition, integrity, and work ethic came from his mother and father.

I suspected that John's high degree of common sense also came from his parents. These qualities served him well throughout his career. But even before his career started, John was confronted with a tempting proposal, one that he turned down. He never regretted his decision — John was always and still is his own man.

When John started his senior year at a major

state university, he had a steady girlfriend, Becky, also a senior. According to John, Becky was a delightful person. Not only was she attractive, she also had many of the positive qualities discussed throughout this chapter. John saw her as sincere, down-to-earth, and intelligent. During the fall semester of their senior year, John and Becky developed great affection for each other. So the couple decided the Christmas holidays would be a good time for John to meet Becky's parents.

Becky's father was the founder, owner, and manager of a highly successful meat-processing and -packing company. Her mother was a housewife. According to John, Becky's folks were very pleasant people. They went out of their way to make him feel at home, and they made John feel wanted. That's where the proposal came into play, but it was no ordinary proposal. Apparently, John was a big hit with Becky's parents.

After a long Christmas day, Becky and her mom retired for the evening. Becky's two sisters and their husbands had already left for their nearby homes. That left John and Becky's father sitting and talking in the den. Becky's father was an American success story. He came from economic ground zero in terms of family background and education, but nevertheless he became a multimillionaire with his meat-processing business. In terms of wealth, Becky's dad thought he was the luckiest man in the world —

he was "Mr. Meat" in that part of America.

Becky's dad assumed that every young man in America would want the opportunity to work for "Mr. Meat" and eventually have an equity position in the business. John could one day become "Mr. Meat Jr." Mr. Meat started his presentation with a leading question. "John, you and Becky are serious about getting together, aren't you?" John admitted that he "was serious" about Becky. Then, for nearly two hours, Mr. Meat spoke nonstop.

First, he gave a verbal profile of his trials and tribulations. A big part of this presentation focused on "the opportunity" versus the long odds of anyone making it from ground zero to Mr. Meat status. Mr. Meat kept on pitching. John sat and listened politely to what seemed to be a well-rehearsed sales presentation, apparently the same one that Mr. Meat had made to the two young men who were now married to his other daughters.

Mr. Meat's deal was more involved than just an employment opportunity. It was a proposal for a programmed lifestyle. John paraphrased in detail what Mr. Meat had proposed, playing the part of Mr. Meat for me. It reads like a classified advertisement in the *Wall Street Journal*, but that's the way John described it. What would you have done if you received the same offer?

EMPLOYMENT AND LIFESTYLE OPPOR-
TUNITY:

SON-IN-LAW AND SENIOR EXECUTIVE
WANTED

"Mr. Meat," the owner of a highly successful, privately held meat-processing company, seeks qualified man to marry his daughter Becky. Becky must approve of the applicant who is selected. Becky prefers a man who is ambitious, reliable, intelligent, honest, self-disciplined, and personable. Ideally, applicant should be a recent college graduate or college senior with an excellent academic record. The applicant who is selected by Becky must further qualify in regard to his employment. He must be:

1. Willing to work for his father-in-law, Mr. Meat. The selected applicant will eventually be given the title of vice president. His duties will be assigned after the agreement and wedding take place. Salary will be generous and significantly above what recent college graduates with similar academic records receive.

2. Agreeable to living near Mr. Meat and his family and adjacent to Mr. Meat's other married daughters and their husbands. Applicant and his wife, Becky, will be given a home of their choosing.

3. Excited about the prospects of vacationing each summer with Mr. Meat and his

entire family. The applicant and his family will have free and unlimited use of Mr. Meat's luxury beach house. The applicant will receive a two-week summer vacation. He and his family are expected to spend all this time with Mr. Meat and his family. The applicant's wife and children (when produced) will spend the entire summer cost-free at the beach. The applicant will join his family on weekends. Mr. Meat's other daughters and their families will follow suit.

4. Willing to work closely with Mr. Meat and his two other sons-in-law. The applicant will become a member of the executive committee headed by Mr. Meat. The applicant may be given some equity in the business, with the prospect of taking over when Mr. Meat retires. Details will be negotiated at some later date with Mr. Meat and his executives.

This is a once-in-a-lifetime opportunity as well as a lifestyle and lifetime obligation. Becky's hand will be given only to the applicant who accepts employment from Mr. Meat. Those unwilling need not apply.

John listened to all of it. Then Mr. Meat made the "assumptive close," as it is called in Salesmanship 101: "I know exactly what you are thinking. You are saying to yourself, 'John, you are the luckiest guy in the world.' " Why would he think otherwise? After all, Mr. Meat was two for two.

John was never actually given a real opportunity to respond that night — Mr. Meat thought he had signed up another son-in-law. So John just went to his assigned room and went to sleep. He left for his parents' home the next day. He did speak with Becky a few times by phone before the next semester — she seemed as excited about the "family plan" as her father.

John waited until he and Becky were back at the university to break the news. There would be no engagement and ultimately no marriage with the family plan. Becky was true to Mr. Meat more than to her beau's wishes. In reality, she probably loved John, but she was not interested in marrying someone who would take her outside the lifestyle designed and programmed by her parents.

Why did John turn down what some might call an opportunity of a lifetime? In a nutshell, he has a strong need to be independent. He found it insulting that anyone would propose to dictate his lifestyle. Mr. Meat was in love with the meat business, but John had no affection for it, nor was he even marginally impressed with any part of Mr. Meat's operating style.

John had a great deal of confidence in his own abilities. He was an excellent student at a rather demanding state university, and his sights were set on being recruited by a top public corporation. In his mind, the corporate world had high-quality executive training and great opportunities for bright, ambitious people.

John had other problems with Mr. Meat's proposal. He wondered about the productivity of hiring executives based on who they married. If Mr. Meat's two other sons-in-law were losers, who would pick up the slack? Common sense told John that nepotism was not the best way to select and promote executives. He was particularly incensed by the potential domestic problems that were likely to occur. John and Becky would be given a home by Mr. Meat, but whose name would be on the deed? How would domestic disputes be handled? It would be easy for Becky to say:

John, this is my house. It is the house that my daddy paid for . . . so if you don't like the way I'm doing things, you can leave.

Of course, it would be difficult for a son-in-law of Mr. Meat's to leave. Leaving would mean more than moving out of the home — it would also mean giving up one's career as an executive at Mr. Meat's operation. John realized that under such conditions he would never be the head of his own household. Disputes would probably be handled outside the home, inside the court of Mr. Meat. John also realized that he had misjudged Becky. He'd never thought that she would be willing to live under such conditions. Clearly, she had more affinity for her parents and their domineering lifestyle than for the orientation of her future husband.

Given John's ambition and need to be independent, he clearly made the proper decision. Today he is a successful corporate executive and has reached millionaire status on his own. John realizes that it's the struggle, the self-made journey to success that makes us strong. Subsidies from the Mr. Meats can make one dependent. What if Mr. Meat dies suddenly? What if it turns out that he has no intention of giving his business to his sons-in-law? Worse, what if he is merely looking for dependent stooges to dominate? How many Mr. Meats have dangled the prospect of business ownership in front of the noses of unsuspecting candidates? How many of these candidates were looking for love and marriage but not emasculation?

My survey data are very clear that many people who select a spouse because of the wealth factor are eventually disappointed. Sometimes the parents of the spouse leave little or no wealth. Other times, the parents only act rich but in reality they are "big hat, no cattle" types. It's better to marry for love, respect, and ambition than for a spouse's ancestors and their financial artifacts.

7

The Economically Productive Household

Dr. Stanley . . . you must have interviewed my parents . . . funky millionaires. Mom drives her ten-year-old Caddie to the grocery store with her shoe box of coupons on the seat beside her. Then when Macy's wants $20 for a pair of cuff links, she'll trot off to the thrift store for a bargain. I . . . came to realize that although my husband and I often feel "poor" we really aren't. We are property rich and cash poor, and we live a rather frugal lifestyle (although we really don't have to).

Not only are millionaires productive in terms of accumulating wealth, running a successful business, and generating a high income, they are also inclined to run productive households. Most people are shocked when they learn that many millionaires enhance the productivity of their households with the following practices:

- Having furniture refinished instead of buying new
- Switching long-distance telephone companies
- Never buying from telephone solicitations
- Having shoes resoled or otherwise repaired

- Using discount coupons when shopping
- Buying household supplies in bulk

People in my audiences often ask why a millionaire would clip coupons. It's not just to save fifty cents today — it's how much can be saved and invested over a lifetime. The typical affluent family in America spends over $200 a week for food and household supplies. That's more than $10,000 per year. During an adult lifetime in current dollars, it translates to between $400,000 and $600,000. If you cut off just 5 percent of this amount, between $20,000 and $30,000, and invest it in a top-ranked equity fund, given the rate of return during the past few years the amount earned would be more than $500,000.

Most millionaires look to the future. They are very likely to compute the lifetime costs and benefits of various activities that have some potential in saving money. This type of behavior is a high correlate of accumulating wealth, and it's just one such element in the millionaires' overall frugal game plan.

Here is the point. More than two-thirds of grocery store shoppers in America today are impulse buyers. They show up at a supermarket without a list or with a short one. They wander around the store without a game plan and, therefore, are likely to spend more time just searching. The more time one spends, the more money one spends. This fact has been proven time and time again. And without a list, people often buy things they may not need until later in the week, or at all. Also, you may think that most millionaires have a maid or au pair do the shopping. The large majority do their own food shopping.

So what is the best way to shop in a food store? One of the millionaire couples I interviewed had an ideal system. They made maps of the interiors of the two food stores they patronized and included the names and location of each category of product. Then they made copies of the two maps, which served as weekly shopping lists and planning templates. During the week when they ran out of a grocery item, they circled the item on the map. They also planned their menu purchases this way. And, of course, menu items were often included because of coupons and related offers.

It sounds like this is a lot of work, but it's not, really. In fact, they look at it another way. Assume you are without a list, without a shopping plan. Then ask yourself: How much pleasure do I get spending the extra twenty or thirty minutes or more in my favorite food store each week? That's what happens when you don't plan ahead of time. Thirty minutes a week taken over an adult's lifetime translates to between 62,400 and 78,000 minutes; 1,040 to 1,300 hours; or 65 to 81 waking days.

It isn't very productive spending more than 62,000 minutes of your life in a food store —

wouldn't you be better off allocating some of that time to planning investments, watching your son or daughter play baseball or softball, taking a few extra vacations, thanking the Lord for his wonderful blessings, upgrading your computer skills, exercising, making your business more productive, or writing a book?

COUPONS . . . IF ONLY FOR THE CHILDREN

There is another important reason why so many millionaires prepare detailed grocery shopping lists — it's the same reason they use discount coupons when buying groceries. Their children and grandchildren observe these processes and eventually develop an understanding of what an organized household is.

Envision the typical kitchen table in the home of Mr. and Mrs. American Millionaire — a game is in progress. The young children are searching the newspaper and coupon flyers for coupons that Mom and Dad can use. Their reward for finding the right coupons is more than a smile. They are acting out an important lesson that will help them as adults. Not only does Mom teach her children to search for coupons, she also teaches them basic organization. She has an expanding alphabetized folder where she stores her coupons, and she teaches her young children how to file and sort coupons.

This experience also teaches them to be price sensitive and to play good defense. It is never too early to learn how to protect one's money. It's also useful for the children to help prepare a shopping list, integrating the coupons and certain sale items listed in advertisements. Teaching young children how to organize, plan, and integrate information will serve them well in the future.

Most self-made millionaires will tell you that planning and being well organized are of significant importance in explaining their economic success. And guess what? They will also tell you that their parents, especially their mothers, were planners and organizers. As previously discussed in chapter 4, "The Relationship Between Courage and Wealth," four out of five millionaires believe that being well organized in dealing with big issues and planning are major factors in overcoming fears and worries that appear when major career, business, and financial resources are on the line.

Think of your own young children as they develop your shopping list by integrating your verbalized needs with coupons. They are designing a strategic plan for allocating financial resources properly and selecting suppliers. You can even ask them to prepare maps of supermarket interiors, with details of item placement. They can check off what items are needed, then give you the map and command you to go shopping, like senior executives.

Even if you don't save much money clipping coupons, even if you think that preparing a shopping list is personally counterproductive, the mere fact that you work with your children in the role of "instructor of planning" will benefit them someday. The same applies to keeping a strict calendar of household bills, family activities, and household chores. The Month-At-A-Glance brand is ideal for young and old alike — it has a lot of room in which the kids can write.

As soon as children can ride a bike, they should be sensitized to the benefits of a planning system with a monthly calendar. Children should be instructed and required to keep their own calendar. They can begin by listing their chores, but it should also include the fun things like birthday parties and other social events.

Keep in mind that if you demonstrate being organized and disciplined, your children will imitate your actions. If you are disorganized in your household environment, your children may follow your lead. It's more effective to teach by example than to talk about being disciplined and organized when you are not.

For years I taught a course in strategic market planning that required a planning project. It counted for 50 percent of the students' grades. Each student had to develop a plan for an actual company that operated in our market area. For most students, the most difficult part of this assignment was preparation of a day-to-day schedule for each piece of the plan to unfold. To remedy this, I had each MBA student purchase a Month-At-A-Glance and then had them start filling in processes by date in pencil. Ink would never work, since they were constantly making mistakes in their planning process. They had to place every single act, process, and task on three-by-five-inch cards — about one hundred to two hundred cards, each with an action. Then they were required to integrate the tasks with the calendar.

I always asked my students if they had ever done something like this before. Far too many said no. No matter how analytically intelligent these students were, they had little or no experience being truly organized. Even without organizational skills or being trained to plan, they received their undergraduate degrees by doing exactly what their professors told them to do — when to study, read specific assignments, and take tests. There's not a lot of organizing necessary when someone else designs your plan. Successful people are the ones who do the planning and organizing.

CARL THE MENTOR

A few days before one Christmas, a courier delivered to my home a large box with a gift for my wife and a few bottles of high-quality spirits for yours truly. The gifts were sent by Carl, a retiree who was previously the CEO of two major corporations.

After listening to an audiotape of a talk I gave at the Downtown Atlanta Rotary Club earlier in the year, Carl had telephoned me and asked for a favor. He told me that he was going to make a proposal to his three school-aged grandkids. All three would be required to read *The Millionaire Next Door* and then to write a short review of the material, focusing on the key point that each grandchild learned from the reading assignment. The reviews would be evaluated and each given a letter grade. The grandchild who received the top grade would get a cash prize of $500. The two runners-up would each receive $250 in cash. But if Granddad Carl did the evaluating, he might be criticized for "playing favorites." So Carl asked an impartial third party to grade the three reviews, and yes, I agreed to act as judge.

The reviews were very well done. Frankly, I was amazed that three grade school students could interpret and write so well. Carl's granddaughter received an A on her review. The other two were also very competitive and were graded A-.

Carl is wise. He knew that *The Millionaire Next Door* could teach his young grandchildren many important facts about accumulating wealth and the factors that contribute to financial success. He knew that young people, even in the first few years of grade school, can learn a great deal about the benefits of planning one's financial future.

Parents should train their children how to plan. Many young adults today have no clue about how to prepare for the future, so how can we expect them to become financially independent? We must be mentors like Carl, role models and planning instructors for our children and grandchildren. We also have to make learning a fun, even an immediately rewarding experience. Carl knew this intuitively. I suspect that's why two major corporations once hired him to be their CEO.

PROFESSIONAL VS. AMATEUR PLUMBING

The plumber who just installed your new water heater makes more per hour of professional time than you charge — was it a mistake to hire him instead of doing it yourself? In some states, the law requires that only a licensed plumber can install gas hot-water heaters, and I don't think you want to study plumbing and become licensed. What would the millionaires whom I interviewed suggest?

Millionaires and those who are likely to become wealthy someday are not "first-cost" sensitive; they are life-cycle-cost sensitive. "First cost" refers to the dollar cost savings if you install the water heater instead of using a skilled plumber. You may have saved $150 in the process, but the figure is very deceptive.

You see, the plumber's quote included a high-efficiency water heater. You shopped and found a low-priced (first cost) water heater with the same gallon capacity as the high-efficiency one, but over the projected life of the heaters, the plumber's will save you more than the $150 in terms of operating costs. Also, the plumber's is estimated to last longer and heat water faster.

Over the life of the heater you would install, there is no warranty on the installation. You could easily install it incorrectly and burn out the system. Even worse, if it's not installed correctly, gas could escape and asphyxiate you and your family. These issues all relate to the real cost savings when contrasting first cost versus life-cycle costs. What value is your life and the lives of your family members? These are priceless elements in the equation.

The other issue relates to trade-offs. You cannot install a water heater and at the same time carry out assignments that are part of your work. Of course, the plumber still charges more per hour than you charge for an hour of your time, so you could save by doing it yourself. But you are not thinking of life-cycle differences. You are not thinking like a millionaire. Look at it this way: If you decide to install the water heater yourself, you have to shop for a unit, which takes time and energy. You could be using this time and energy to enhance your professional skills or study investments. It's time you could be using to shop for new clients — acquiring one new client would be worth much more than $150. Then you have to study water-heater installation techniques and acquire the proper tools. Whether you rent tools or buy them, it still takes time and money. Finally, how many other hot-water heaters will you be installing during the remainder of your working life? I bet you'll never want to install another one once you've suffered through the first campaign to save $150. Why study plumbing if you're not going to be a plumber? After all this, ask yourself about the actual dollars you really saved. In terms of a life-cycle cost-benefit analysis, select option number two: Call the plumber!

I have repeatedly told people that millionaires are frugal, but many think the entire do-it-yourself concept defines frugality. Millionaires are frugal when frugality translates into real increases in the economic productivity of a household. *Webster's* defines *frugal* as "characterized by or reflecting economy in the expenditure of resources." The key word here is *resources*, and not just first-cost money or dollar resources. There are full-life-cycle resources associated with making a purchase or other economic decision. The large majority of millionaires are *not* do-it-yourselfers! They reason that it's more productive to earn income from their vocation and use it to hire professional painters, carpenters, and plumbers.

I once asked a high-income-producing cartoonist-painter-illustrator the do-it-yourself question. At the time I was in his home, a large English Tudor house overlooking the Hudson River Valley. As we spoke, I looked out and noticed a group of house painters setting up scaffolding around the house. I asked him about the cost of having such a large home painted. The price seemed so high I felt compelled to ask: "You're a painter. Why not paint your own home?"

He responded quickly and to the point, telling me that he could make more money doing his job than the cost of having a crew of house painters do the work. Perhaps even more importantly he said:

What if I fall off a ladder while painting the house? I could be killed or permanently disabled . . . never to be able to earn a good living.

The cartoonist in this case is like most self-made millionaires — they are not penny wise and pound foolish.

The things millionaires do to enhance their economic productivity by reducing the cost of operating their household are lifecycle-cost sensitive. Dangling on a ladder could jeopardize their ability to earn millions of future dollars in their own vocation. They are much more likely to reinsulate their home and have high efficiency heating and air-conditioning systems installed. Remember that millionaires often live in the same home for twenty years or more. Over the years, these changes will more than pay for their first costs.

TO WRITE OR TO COMMUTE?

I use the analysis of my own resources as a way of motivating myself to write my books. How long did it take me to write *The Millionaire Next Door*? I wrote the entire 477-page manuscript in about 180 days, or 43,200 minutes. I wrote on average for four hours each and every day, about 240 minutes a day for 180 days. This may sound like a whole lot of time and effort, but I don't see it that way. It was more than just 43,200 minutes; it was 1.5 million symbols made by my hand with a No. 1 blue medium-point Papermate pen. I looked at the task the way most productive people view their work. They motivate themselves by selecting from various alternatives for allocating their time.

So when I contemplated writing *The Millionaire Next Door*, I told myself:

Tommy, it will take you less time to write this book than the time you spent sitting in traffic, over a period of thirteen years, commuting to and from the university where you once were employed as a professor.

The mundane task of commuting took many more minutes of my time and units of mental and physical energy than writing a book. You only have a few hours each day to work at your peak mental efficiency. In my case, that's about four hours maximum, so I had to decide if I wanted to spend another 50,000 minutes in my car or writing a book. What royalties are paid for commuting? How much more productive will I become careerwise by mastering stop-and-go driving? Unfortunately, millions of Americans waste their mental and physical energy doing unproductive things.

Thus, it's a good idea to allocate a few minutes each month to enhancing your productivity. Ask yourself some simple questions about your allocation of time:

- How much time will I spend doing each task during my lifetime?
- Is there some way I can reduce this time allocation?
- Are there better uses for my time than doing the tasks I have been doing habitually?
- Is there some task I can undertake that will pay me benefits for the rest of my life?

BUILD, DEVELOP, OR RENT

I recently had a conversation with Mr. D. D. Thompson, a master builder of homes. He and the other members of his family do most of the construction on each home they build. The family business produces a quality product.

Mr. Thompson mentioned that folks like me "have it easy. . . . We hammered or shot 250,000 nails in the process of building that home. You folks just sit at a desk." I enjoyed his comment. Then I told him that "it's always greener on the other side of one's vocation."

It took 1.5 million symbols [letters] made by my hand to complete my book manuscript. Plus it takes a lot of thought about the choice of letters.

Though D.D. got a kick out of my comments,

444

I'm not sure he got the whole point. Nailing takes effort, and so does writing a book, but there is a very big difference. What if the letter placed on a page eventually becomes part of a best-selling book? It's like each letter has some future income stream. Once D.D. puts a nail in a piece of wood, he gets paid once. He has no inventory. He gets paid only once; no royalties are paid on nails.

Even worse, D.D. builds homes for a developer. D.D. gets about 20 percent of the profit; the developer gets the rest. That's like being a ghostwriter who gets a flat fee and no future royalties. D.D. would be much better off building homes as his own developer — perhaps even better, he should build and rent small apartment properties. That's akin to having nails as an annuity. However, D.D. doesn't have the capital to underwrite his own construction, nor does he have the discipline or forethought to develop a savings plan that would enable him to put away enough income to become a developer some day. Perhaps D.D. hasn't yet hammered enough nails. Someday he may grow really tired of spending all his time and energy inserting nails that never pay dividends.

I find that many college graduates are employed in positions that involve inserting nails. For example, take most CPAs in America. They are intelligent, hardworking professionals who prepare many, many tax returns each year. But you cannot inventory tax returns. It's a new task each year, year after year.

A few CPAs went beyond inserting more nails each year. They developed tax-related software programs, sold thousands and thousands of these programs, and will sell even more in the future. The programs are the equivalent of the goose that keeps laying royalties and related payments. The great thing is that these products can be inventoried — they generate revenue without their creators having to hammer one more custom tax return.

The key point is this: You are going to work hard hammering anyway. You can hammer nails that will pay you once or pay you a hundred times — it's up to you. If you go through life like D.D., it will always be one nail, one payout. If D.D. just spent a few more hours each week building his own spec house, perhaps with an investor who put up money for materials for a one-half share, he would be in transition from the treadmill existence of nailing to one of inventorying the cash equivalents of nails, capital.

People often ask my opinion about the high salaries of many professional ballplayers. I believe they are paid what they deserve, and I'm not at all envious of athletes who earn big incomes. Many have very short careers. Some realize that goals, home runs, even touchdowns cannot be inventoried. Even though they receive many more dollars for hammering hits or even blocking for quarterbacks, it's still the same old nail game. The dollars you earn for the nails you inserted today don't matter so much — the real issue is how many future dollars your efforts today will pay.

The press loves to tell us how much some young ballplayer will make with his contract. But once his playing days are over, where is the annuity? Dead as a doornail. The really smart people in professional athletics are the team owners and the agents.

These agents are an especially crafty group. They don't have much specific talent themselves — they don't run, kick, block, or score goals. They don't sing or dance. Yet they last and last. So what if you are one-in-a-million on the football talent scale? You were a high school All-American, a first-team college All-American, and the first running back drafted in the pros this year, but you blew out a knee. Your agent, on the other hand, has a growing stable of your kind. He grows his business like people grow apple trees. Once you are in his orchard, you keep producing for him. When you can no longer produce apples or hammer nails, they remove your dead or dying trunk from the field. A replacement apple tree is inserted like the interchangeable parts of a machine.

THE FRUGAL AND PRODUCTIVE POINTS

The Points are a retired couple who live in a fine four-bedroom home in one of Austin's nicest neighborhoods. They have a net worth in the high seven figures. They are a frugal couple, very careful about how they spend their money. As Mrs. Point says, "My husband and I grew up during the Depression, so we both are careful with our money." Although they currently live in a home worth $800,000, it has paid for itself over the years through appreciation.

To the Balance Sheet Affluent, careful means selecting a home and neighborhood very carefully. It may also mean paying more for a home initially and having higher property taxes. Make the correct selection and you may do even better than having the home pay for itself in real-dollar terms. Mrs. Point expressed her attitude about this:

I believe in living in the best *section of the city . . . location, location, location. . . . I will do without fine cars, but insist on having the* best *home possible.*

Certainly, the Points could have it both ways. They could purchase expensive automobiles and clothing and still remain in the millionaire league, but that's not their style. Mrs. Point graciously outlined the philosophy that she and her husband have always maintained.

They believe that it's very important to be price sensitive with respect to products that lose all or most of their initial value as soon as they are purchased. In terms of dollar value, these items are highly perishable. For example, clothes. If you purchase an expensive suit or dress today, how much is it worth at tomorrow's garage sale? Perhaps 5 or 10 percent or less of the original purchase price. Mrs. Point never wants to spend big dollars on clothes — they depreciate in value too rapidly. They put a hole in one's net worth. But she always wants to look well dressed. Here is her solution:

> *Oh, yes, I wear couture clothes that I buy at the Junior League shop. Most of them have been donated by the —— family [one of the wealthiest families in the U.S.]: Yves Saint Laurent, Armani, Valentino, Oscar de la Renta, Gucci, Dior. I love clothes. In fact, you could say I collect them. I even have Balenciaga.*

If some of these clothing items don't fit perfectly, she and Mr. Point do what about four in ten millionaires do to solve this problem — they have the clothes altered instead of buying new. The money Mrs. Point saves as a result of her thrift-shopping orientation is allocated to items whose prices are "highly durable," that actually appreciate in value.

> *I am mindful of the fact we live in a time of medical miracles. . . . I . . . invest in stocks related to medicine.*

Mrs. Point believes that stock purchases will enhance the couple's net worth, while paying retail for expensive clothing has the opposite effect. It's not that the Points are miserly people; clearly they are not. They just want to always be financially independent. They also have other people in mind when they operate under a philosophy of being highly productive — they plan for their six children to have substantial inheritances.

Let's review Mrs. Point's style. She believes in buying a home that will appreciate in value, but she doesn't believe in paying retail for clothing and other items that retain little of their original price. Better to invest in medical stocks that have longevity.

There is another reason why Mrs. Point invests in medical stocks. Being very health conscious, she reads about health issues and attends many seminars and programs about health and medicine. She is very productive in terms of killing two birds with one stone — she enhances both her physical and her economic well-being by reading about and studying up on health medicines and new drugs and patents.

Most food items are perishable. Does this mean that Mrs. Point skimps on food in order to enhance her economic wealth?

I am a big believer in eating healthy food and exercising. . . . But I am very careful with food purchases. I clip and organize coupons, do my own cooking, etc.

I'm sure that Mrs. Point seems like a confusing mixture to many people. She wears expensive clothing but doesn't spend much for automobiles. She uses discount coupons but lives in an expensive home situated in a top neighborhood. People might think that she and Mr. Point are just hanging on financially, but appearances can be misleading.

We have land . . . [and] mining operations and oil leases. We do not tell our friends about our holdings because many of those we associate with do not have as much as we do.

Mrs. Point is like many millionaires when it comes to purchasing furniture and household accessories. She spends money on furniture that has lasting qualities. Furniture that is "highly perishable," that essentially dissolves when hot coffee is spilled on it, has never entered her home.

We buy quality items and make them last. We buy eighteenth-century antique furniture!

People like Mrs. Point are wealthy because they allocate a disproportionate share of their furniture dollars to categories that have lasting value. Even if you pay $10,000 for an antique table and chairs, this furniture has two functions — you can sit on the chair and eat off the table, and you are maintaining an investment.

This is a major reason why most decamillionaires regularly attend antique fairs. So many of them are self-made — their parents were not rich. Their parents and grandparents were likely to be what I call preservers and collectors, a trait that is nurtured in well-functioning, loving families that extend over several generations. Today's millionaire has a home that contains Grandma's prized chest, Great-Grandma's manual Singer sewing machine, Grandpa's pre-1864 model 70 Winchester rifle, and Uncle Bill's coin collection.

Some people believe hand-me-downs are junk. To them, new is always better — it defines success. Old indicates economic failure and reversals. But not millionaires like Mrs. Point — she is very confident and proud about who she is and how she accumulated considerable wealth. No one from Madison Avenue will ever tell her how to think. She has her own ideas about the value of new versus old or real wood versus wood dust. That's why she and Mr. Point are wealthy.

RECYCLING: TASSELS VS. NIKES

Are the affluent in America the ultimate consumers of goods, buying today and discarding tomorrow? Perhaps the thought of recycling, or specifically resoling, shoes is abhorrent to them. The findings from my national survey of millionaires contradict that hypothesis: Seventy percent of the millionaires surveyed have their shoes resoled. This number is something of an underestimate because about 20 percent are retired millionaires who normally give up wearing their "dress uniform," which includes footwear that tends to be resoled.

These shoes are often referred to as "dress shoes" or "executive footwear," normally worn by men, including the four in five millionaire respondents who are males. These shoes have brand names like Alden, Allen Edmonds, and Johnson-Murphy and are normally sold in men's specialty stores and upscale department stores. These are specialty goods that are not likely to be found in the closets of every household in America.

Shoes of this type are favorites among senior executives of public corporations, owners of top private corporations, and top-producing physicians, attorneys, investment bankers, and stockbrokers. Why do they pay $200, $300, or more for a pair of shoes? It's all a matter of perception and preference. Most people, especially men, make purchase decisions about shoes according to initial price or first cost. When they need "dress" shoes, they buy a pair of black shoes at the lowest possible price. These people are price or first-cost sensitive, and they are one of the major reasons that so many discount shoe stores exist today.

The other segment of the market for "dress" shoes, many of whom are multimillionaires, is relatively first-cost or initial-price insensitive. They are less concerned with variations in the price of shoes than they are about the quality of "dress" shoes. These quality-sensitive people define quality in terms of life-cycle cost. My Alden tassel loafers are more than ten years old, and they've been resoled (full soles replaced) twice. Plus they never go out of style. They are by far the most comfortable shoes I have ever owned. At the end of many twelve-hour work-days, my feet have never given me discomfort when I was wearing my Aldens. They are built to last, support, and give comfort to one's physical foundation, so they are not inexpensive relative to other types of shoes offered on the market. If you are a business executive or a professor of business, you want to wear "the uniform." Cross-trainers don't cut it, nor do cheaply con-structed "dress" shoes. A survey respondent cited his experiences with so-called cheap dress shoes.

Cheap shoes wear you, you don't wear them!

Allow me to expand on the point about life-cycle cost. In the ten years that I have owned my Aldens, I've had them on my feet approximately 1,600 days. I initially paid $100 for the shoes, and they've been resoled twice at about $50 a turn. So my out-of-pocket cost was $200. Add the $20 I put out for a good pair of shoe trees, and the total cost was $220. The shoe trees are critically important in enhancing the life cycle of quality shoes.

Divide 1,600 wearings into $220, and that computes to just under 14 cents per wearing. In sharp contrast, let me advise you how much it costs for my teenaged son's shoes. He goes through — that is, wears out or styles out — about six pairs of Nikes or Adidases per year. Mostly he wears them out from just walking around a very large college campus, but he also does some running and sand-lot touch football in them. Brad's mom estimates that he gets between eighty and one hundred wears per pair of shoes. These shoes cost between $65 and $85 per pair. Even with the best case of one hundred wears, the life-cycle cost of these shoes is 65 cents per wear.

Given these numbers, I have to ask who pays more for the shoes they wear each day. Is it the millionaire executive in his $300 calfskin loafers or the college student in his $85 super-cross-trainers? Appearances can be very deceiving, and so can the first-cost or purchase price. For many products, life-cycle cost is a much more relevant criterion to use when shopping.

YOU CAN REFINISH WOOD
BUT NOT SAWDUST

Look inside the home of a millionaire, and you may be surprised at what you see. You may expect a highly decorated home filled with the latest styles in furniture and accessories. So much for yet another myth about the affluent. The interior-design and furniture-purchasing habits of millionaires are not what you see in movies or on television. They don't change their furniture like Hollywood movie stars change husbands and wives.

Most millionaires live in single-family homes of traditional design. These homes are well-built colonials, including English Tudors. The interiors are filled with traditional furniture, with Early American designs most prevalent. When it comes to modern furniture, millionaires are not major consumers. They prefer high-quality traditional furniture, which never goes out of style. Their furniture has another notable characteristic — it's usually made of wood, not sawdust glued together or thin layers of quality wood on particleboard. Millionaires prefer furniture made of solid wood or, in some cases, quality veneers placed upon high-grade solid hardwoods.

To get a look at the actual style, not necessarily the brands, of the furniture these people own, visit a local furniture store. Look in the Yellow Pages under the heading of "Furniture" and note the stores that sell high-quality eighteenth-century and other traditional furnishings. Look for key words like *Baker Williamsburg*, *Councill Craftsmen*, and *Henkel-Harris*. These aren't the only brands you're likely to see inside the homes of wealthy people, but they give you a good start.

Millionaires not only tend to have traditional or old-style furniture in their homes, they are also significantly more likely than the nonmillionaire population to own furniture that is actually "old," or antiques. Ask the dealers of genuine antiques about the characteristics of their main target market, and they will tell you that the largest portion is composed of affluent people with traditional taste who are more sensitive to the quality of furniture than variations in price.

There are several sources for the traditional furniture owned by millionaires. First, they purchase high-quality reproductions that are made of real wood, most from dealers. Some have the furniture custom-made. Second, millionaires have a propensity to purchase high-grade antique furniture of traditional style. Third, they acquire some of their furniture from intergenerational gifts and hand-me-downs.

Independent of the source, the furniture tends to be of the same caliber. It is traditional in design, well constructed with real wood. In the eyes of the millionaire, this type of furniture is in the high-quality category. The quality doesn't just refer to construction, it has something to do with how long a piece will last. The best furniture, even with minimal care, will last a century or more, and the issue of physical longevity is important. But how long will traditional furniture remain in style and thus in high demand among the affluent population?

No one can be completely certain, but past trends often predict the future. High-quality furniture will probably appreciate in value. How many consumer goods purchased today will appreciate in value tomorrow — that automobile you paid $30,000 for four years ago, that $500 or $800 suit you purchased yesterday? In sharp contrast I have seen ten- and twenty-year-old Henkel-Harris and Baker furniture, just to name two brands, sell for more than twice the original purchase price.

By definition, millionaires tend to be accumulators, a trait they inherited from parents who were collectors. Their parents and grandparents held on to things that had value. So the majority of millionaires have a family legacy of collecting, saving, and preserving. Waste not, want not is a theme acted out by first-generation millionaires today. Their ancestors passed on possessions that had lasting sentimental as well as monetary value. They intuitively knew the value of collecting and preserving things that would appreciate in value. Their prediction about the appreciation of certain objects was not their only motive — even today, their sons and daughters who are millionaires tend to purchase with others in mind. They deliberately purchase furniture today they can pass on to the younger generation tomorrow. This, in essence, is their definition of quality furniture. It will outlive a person's normal adult life span, will never lose its appeal, and will probably appreciate in value.

Think of the selection process for furniture through the eyes and minds of millionaires.

They see the real benefit of furnishing their homes with the furniture I have described. They may pay two or three times more for a quality chest or dresser than for a piece of molded and glued sawdust imitation. If the lower-priced chest is a veneer on sawdust, it may never last for a half generation. Leave a bit of water or coffee on top and the veneer might separate from the sawdust. Then:

You can't saw sawdust; you can't even sand sawdust!

You can refinish high-quality furniture over and over again. Why would wealthy people have their furniture refinished? They don't think of furniture as a consumption item or a nondurable — they don't buy new furniture as soon as the old furniture has a scratch on it. Nearly one-half (48 percent) of the millionaires who responded to my latest national survey report:

Having furniture refinished or reupholstered instead of buying new.

Mrs. Claurice Rector, a multimillionaire, once told me that she refinishes and reupholsters "everything in the house."

Because it's just so much more convenient than searching . . . shopping [for new furniture] hour after hour, looking at high-priced nothings!

Mrs. Rector has developed a list of great refinishers as well as several reupholsterers.

I call. They send me swatches. They pick up. No malls; no hassles.

Her favorite reupholsterers carry a wide variety of fabrics. According to Mrs. Rector, fabric selection is much easier than selecting new furniture. She has had the same family-owned shop reupholster her favorite couch five times in thirty years.

Along these lines a recent news article by James R. Hagerty and Robert Berner asked: "On the couch, ever wonder why furniture shopping can be such a pain?" (*Wall Street Journal*, November 2, 1998, pp. 1A, 18A). The article documents the difficulty people have finding furniture to purchase. Even after countless hours of searching, the buyer may have to wait weeks, even months for delivery. There are so many styles and colors of furniture today that it's very confusing, even to a seasoned buyer. The *Wall Street Journal* mentioned one company that offered 1.7 billion possible combinations of sofas and upholstered chairs. Given the variety of fabrics and styles, is it any wonder that many millionaires refinish and reupholster as opposed to searching through so many combinations of furniture?

There are certain actions that reveal a lot about our households and whether they are economically productive. When I began studying the traits of affluent households, more than two hundred actions and habits were proposed. These were developed, in part, in my focus groups and personal interviews with millionaires. Eventually, thirteen actions were included in the questionnaire used for this national survey of millionaires (see Table 7-1).

Why only thirteen actions? Because response patterns to these actions could predict the responses to others. In turn, four major patterns emerged from the survey data. Take Pattern 1, *extending the life cycle.* About one-half of the millionaires (48 percent) indicated that they reupholstered or refinished furniture to reduce the cost and enhance the productivity of operating a household. These same respondents also tended to respond that they have their "shoes resoled/repaired" and "clothes mended/altered."

Now consider Pattern 2, *reducing the monthly burdens.* Overall, the responses to the three actions under this heading are independent of those items included as *extending the life cycle.* In other words, responses to the "switching long-distance telephone companies" action are not significantly associated with responses to the "having furniture reupholstered" item.

In order to understand the millionaires better, one must analyze several distinct response pat-

TABLE 7-1

ACTIONS TAKEN BY MILLIONAIRES TO REDUCE THE COST/ENHANCE THE PRODUCTIVITY OF OPERATING A HOUSEHOLD

Percentage of
Millionaires (N=733)

1. EXTENDING THE LIFE CYCLE

Having shoes resoled/repaired	70
Having furniture reupholstered/refinished instead of buying new	48
Having clothes mended/altered instead of buying new	36

2. REDUCING THE MONTHLY BURDENS

Raising the thermostat setting on your air conditioner during summer/daytime	57
Switching long distance telephone companies	49
Paying off/paid off home mortgage early	48

3. PLANNING PURCHASES

Never buying via telephone solicitations	74
Developing a shopping list before grocery shopping	71
Using discount coupons when buying groceries	49
Purchasing appliances and/or motor vehicles "top-rated" by Consumer Reports	44
Leaving department stores as soon as a purchase is made	36

4. PATRONIZING DISCOUNT INSTITUTIONS

Buying household supplies in bulk at warehouse stores, i.e., Sam's, Costco	49
Doing more and more business with a discount brokerage firm(s)	25

terns. There are four factors in all — the two mentioned, Pattern 3, *planning purchases* and Pattern 4, *patronizing discount institutions.* I have determined that of all the actions, there are two that best represent the millionaires' approach to reducing the cost and enhancing the productivity of operating a household. The two actions that are key to understanding millionaires are:

• Switching long-distance telephone companies
• Having furniture reupholstered or refinished instead of buying new.

I looked at two samples of millionaires. The first group contained only respondents from economically productive households who switch long-distance telephone companies and have furniture reupholstered or refinished. The other sample contains respondents from nonproductive households who didn't do either of these actions.

How do millionaires in group one, who operate economically productive households (EPMs), differ from the non-economically productive millionaires (NEPMs)? The two groups have very different styles when it comes to accumulating wealth. EPMs are wealthy for several reasons. Of course, they operate productive households (see Table 7-2), but they are also much more deliberate in their approach to purchasing a home, and they spend more time studying and planning their investments.

What about those in the NEPM category —

TABLE 7-2

ECONOMICALLY PRODUCTIVE VS. NONPRODUCTIVE HOUSEHOLDS: ACTIONS TAKEN BY MILLIONAIRES TO REDUCE THE COST/ENHANCE THE PRODUCTIVITY OF OPERATING A HOUSEHOLD

(PERCENT TAKING ACTION)	OPERATES AN ECONOMICALLY PRODUCTIVE HOUSEHOLD	
	Yes (N=182)	No (N=190)
1. EXTENDING THE LIFE CYCLE		
Having shoes resoled/repaired	81	55
Having clothes mended/altered instead of buying new	62	17
2. REDUCING THE MONTHLY BURDENS		
Raising the thermostat setting on your air conditioner during summer/daytime	76	36
Paying off/paid off home mortgage early	57	44
3. PLANNING PURCHASES		
Never buying via telephone solicitations	77	74
Developing a shopping list before grocery shopping	84	57
Using discount coupons when buying groceries	65	33
Purchasing appliances and/or motor vehicles "top-rated" by *Consumer Reports*	58	31
Leaving department stores as soon as a purchase is made	50	26
4. PATRONIZING DISCOUNT INSTITUTIONS		
Buying household supplies in bulk at warehouse stores, i.e., Sam's, Costco	57	41
Doing more and more business with a discount brokerage firm(s)	35	13

how can they be millionaires and not run an efficient household? They earn so much income that it's difficult not to become wealthy. In order to fully appreciate the contrasting styles of these two groups, case studies are in order.

MR. OAKS VS. MR. O'TOOLE
THE PRO FORMAS

Mr. Oaks has a net worth of approximately $7.5 million, but he's not in the EPM group. He and other members of his household never took the two key actions, i.e. switching telephone companies and reupholstering or refinishing furniture. Mr. O'Toole is worth about $5 million, and he indicates taking almost all these actions. It's a matter of strategy and styles. Mr. Oaks has an annual realized income of $829,000. He works very long hours as an attorney. He is focused, and his energy is devoted to his career. As long as he is tops in his field, he feels that wealth will show up accordingly. Mr. Oaks and his wife believe that most if not all of the actions listed in Table 7-2 take time and energy away from a very high paying career. He is of the strong opinion that his single best strategy for becoming wealthy is to focus his superior intellect on the practice of law.

Mr. O'Toole is very different in his orientation. He is an entrepreneur in the recycling/scrap metal business. His annual realized income is $544,000, and his net worth is estimated to be about $5.2 million. He has a lower level of net worth than Mr. Oaks, in large part because of income differences. Mr. O'Toole would have considerably less wealth if he did not have an economically productive household. In fact, since his marriage more than twenty-five years ago, he and his wife have always operated their household productively. They had to do so, or they would not have been able to build their recycling business.

Mr. Oaks and his wife are different kinds of householders. Mr. Oaks graduated from a top college near the top of his class in both undergraduate and law school. He was immediately hired by a top law firm. Before long, he was a partner of the firm. Sixty-, seventy-, even eighty-hour work weeks are not uncommon for Mr. Oaks. He works hard and plays hard. He has the pro forma answer when quizzed about actions that might be taken to reduce his household's operating costs:

Penny wise, pound foolish.

He maintains that household operating costs are in the penny category. The pound category involves focusing all his intellectual energy on helping a client win a $100 million settlement. If his client wins, Mr. Oaks' income will be more than $1 million next year. That's why he has little interest in reading about the variations in value of stoves and washing machines in *Consumer Reports*. The Oaks just buy the most expensive household appliances, theoretically the best.

Here are some other interesting differences between Mr. Oaks, the NEPM, and Mr. O'Toole, the EPM. They were asked about why they are successful, and they share certain common success factors, as do most millionaires. Both claim it has something to do with being well disciplined, working hard, getting along with people, and being competitive. But Mr. Oaks, the high-income-producing attorney, also attributes his success to:

- Having a high IQ/superior intellect
- Attending a top-rated college
- Graduating near/at the top of my class.

Mr. O'Toole has his own set of group-specific explanations for success.

- Investing in my own business
- Having a supportive spouse
- Willing to take financial risk given the right return

And there is one more success factor that is very important to Mr. O'Toole:

Living below my means.

More than one-half (53 percent) of those millionaires in the EPM category rate this factor as either very important or important. Only about one in three of the NEPMs rate this factor in a similar fashion. Mr. O'Toole and his fellow EPMs have a different lifestyle than Mr. Oaks and the NEPMs. The EPMs are significantly more likely to:

- Attend religious services
- Read the Bible
- Shop at Wal-Mart and Kmart
- Eat at McDonald's and/or Burger King
- Be involved in do-it-yourself carpentry projects
- Shop via the Internet
- Mow their own lawns
- Garden
- Attend antique fairs/sales
- Consult with an investment adviser.

Mr. Oaks and the NEPMs are more prone to:

- Attend major league sporting events
- Attend fund-raising balls.

Part of the EPM lifestyle is integrating shopping behavior and investing behavior. EPMs shop aggressively for homes, and they perceive their home as part of their investment portfolio. Many NEPMs don't see it that way. About 81 percent of the EPMs, but only 52 percent of the NEPMs, indicate "taking weeks, even months, to shop around for the very best deal overall" (see Table 7-3).

This is not to suggest that either group made a

bad decision, in financial terms, when buying their current homes. The median year of their home purchase was 1988, and since that time, on average, the value of the homes owned by NEPMs more than doubled. The O'Toole group did even better — their homes nearly tripled in value. EPMs strongly believe that it is economically productive to shop for homes aggressively. Both bought fine homes in high-ranking established neighborhoods, and both were very wise to do so. But Mr. Oaks and the NEPMs took very little time shopping for the very best deal. Essentially, they bought a fine home, but they paid for quality. The O'Toole EPMs shopped and shopped; they exhibited great patience. They bought fine homes, but at discounts generated by aggressive price negotiating and by looking for foreclosures and other real estate that had to be sold in a hurry.

Both the Oaks and the O'Toole types were winners in the residential real estate market. The O'Tooles did better, but they spent much more time and energy in the process. Mr. Oaks, the high-income-producing attorney, hates to shop and he has no time to look for the "buy of the decade."

Under these circumstances, people like Mr. Oaks buy trophy homes in trophy neighborhoods. They generally deal with the cream of the crop of real estate agents. They tell the agent, "Find me a trophy home within a week or month!" In the long run, their home appreciated, and it will continue to do so. Thus, a rule from the Oaks types can be appreciated:

When faced with lack of time, it's better to buy a quality home at a high price than a nonquality home at a reduced price.

Analyze the net worth and income characteristics of the NEPM and EPM types, and you'll see that they are quite similar. The Oaks NEPMs have an average annual realized income of $830,000, versus the O'Toole EPMs with $544,000. The Oaks have an average net worth of $7,550,000, versus the O'Tooles, who have accumulated on average $5,200,000. This translates into dollars of net worth accumulated for each dollar of income realized at $9.56 for the O'Tooles and $9.10 for the Oaks.

Contrast $9.56 and $9.10 as productivity measures. The EPMs at $9.56 are more productive than the NEPMs at $9.10, but not by that much. It's only about a 5 percent difference. In essence, both groups are productive in generating high incomes and corresponding high levels of net worth. Each adopted a wealth-building strategy that suited their respective abilities and interests well.

What if Mr. Oaks, the high-paid attorney, and Mr. O'Toole, the scrap-metal dealer, changed styles? Both would probably have a severe reduction in both their incomes and net worths.

TABLE 7-3

ACTIONS TAKEN IN THE PROCESS OF PURCHASING A HOME: MILLIONAIRES FROM ECONOMICALLY PRODUCTIVE VS. NONPRODUCTIVE HOUSEHOLDS

	EPM %	NEPM %
1. PLANNING AND DELIBERATING		
Never paying the initial asking price for any home	91	80
Being willing to walk away from any deal at any time	84	77
Researching the prices of recent home sales in the neighborhood	89	72
Taking weeks, even months, to shop around for the very best deal overall	81	52
Never trying to purchase a home within a short span of time	64	44
2. SEARCHING		
Seeking a neighborhood that has excellent public schools	80	74
Purchasing a home that is easily affordable	66	53
Searching for a low-maintenance energy-efficient home	42	20
Searching for a "bargain" home that was part of a foreclosure, divorce settlement, or estate sale	45	14
Searching out a neighborhood with reasonable property taxes	39	21

471

TABLE 7-3 (Continued)

ACTIONS TAKEN IN THE PROCESS OF PURCHASING A HOME: MILLIONAIRES FROM ECONOMICALLY PRODUCTIVE VS. NONPRODUCTIVE HOUSEHOLDS

	EPM %	NEPM %
3. NEGOTIATING		
Testing seller's price sensitivity by making a deeply discounted price offer	55	36
Asking realtor to reduce the commission so that the seller can reduce the price	35	27
Purchasing a building lot and then having a contractor build home	27	25
Demanding that the builder/seller price the home at or near cost	21	13

Never try to adopt an economic orientation that is incongruent with your abilities and aptitudes.

About 80 percent of both groups suggested that their current vocation allows full use of their aptitudes and abilities, and so do both of their respective philosophies about enhancing the productivity of their households.

8

The Home

Q: How can you be wealthy? You live in a $1.4 million home. That's a lot of risk.

A: But I only paid about 40 percent of $1.4 million when I bought it. Risk is buying a home in a neighborhood where nothing appreciates.

We've learned something about how millionaires' lifestyles result in economically productive homes. But what about the homes themselves? What are their homes and neighborhoods like, and how do they buy and sell them? This chapter explores the answers to these questions provided by my survey and explodes many more myths about America's affluent. The following section describes the millionaires' homes "in their own words."

WELCOME TO THE NEIGHBORHOOD

I am the prototypical millionaire — call me Brian Abel. I live in one of America's Balance Sheet Affluent (BA) neighborhoods, neighborhoods containing high concentrations of millionaires. Nearly 80 percent of my neighbors are millionaires. In sharp contrast, only about 5 percent of the approximately 100 million house-

473

TABLE 8-1

YEAR OF PURCHASE OF CURRENT HOME
(N=733)

Percentage That Purchased Home This Year or Later

Year of Purchase	Earlier	Later
1968	10	90
1977	25	75
1986	50	50
1993	75	25
1995	90	10
1996	95	5
1998	99	1

holds in America are in the millionaire category. Thus, as residents of such neighborhoods, we are fully sixteen times more likely to be wealthy than the average for the nation.

I purchased my home about twelve years ago, and my family has lived there ever since (see Table 8-1). The approximate purchase price was just under $560,000 (see Table 8-2). According to conservative estimates, it would sell today for just under $1.4 million. I increased my wealth in nominal terms by approximately $850,000, or about $70,000 per year. Most of us have the same old-fashioned orientation — we buy homes and tend to hold on to them for long periods of time. In contrast, about 20 percent of American

TABLE 8-2

THE MILLIONAIRE HOME: ORIGINAL PURCHASE PRICE PAID FOR HOME VS. CURRENT VALUE (N=733)

Price Paid for Current Home	Percentage of Homes Purchased at This Price
Under $300,000	29.7
$300,000–$399,999	7.8
$400,000–$499,999	9.2
$500,000–$999,999	28.1
$1,000,000 and over	25.2

Current Value of Home	Percentage of Homes Currently Valued at This Level
Under $300,000	0.6
$300,000–$399,999	2.0
$400,000–$499,999	4.9
$500,000–$999,999	31.2
$1,000,000 and over	61.3

households move each year. We are different kinds of people. More than one-half of us (53 percent) have not moved even once during the past ten years. About one in four of us (24 percent) moved just once in the past ten years. About 80 percent of these moves were local in origin. As a group, we have a very strong tendency to stay put.

One reason why we seldom move is that many of us are self-employed professionals or owners and managers of our own businesses. Moving away from our clients, patients, customers, or key suppliers would have a significant negative influence on the productivity of our enterprises. Just the process of preparing to move can be extremely disruptive, especially in long-distance moves.

As BAs, Mrs. Abel and I have noticed one change in the mobility patterns of our group. An increasing number are "upgrading," hoping to capitalize on a rising market in their respective geographic areas. They are selling homes they paid $500,000 for ten years ago for $1.4 million today, and then reinvesting "locally" in more expensive homes. They anticipate that these "upgrades" will appreciate even more rapidly than did their previous homes.

Many of the "upgraders" have considerable knowledge of the real estate markets in their areas — some are even upgrading with intra-neighborhood moves. This type of move is more common in the newer cities of the South, Southwest, and West. In most other areas, especially in the Midwest and Northeast, the buy-and-hold orientation is alive and well.

Most BA neighborhoods were established decades ago. On a national basis, the median year of construction of homes owned by millionaires was 1958 (see Table 8-3). In fact, fully two-thirds of us live in homes that were originally

TABLE 8-3

THE MILLIONAIRE HOME: YEAR OF CONSTRUCTION
(N=733)

	% of Homes Constructed Earlier	% of Homes Constructed This Year or Later
1922	10	90
1935	25	75
1958	50	50
1978	75	25
1989	90	10
1993	95	5
1997	99	1

built before 1973. In sharp contrast, only about one in twenty of us live in homes that were constructed in the last five years.

Most of us enjoy living in well-established neighborhoods. There is nothing flashy or even modern about the style of houses in these neighborhoods. Our homes give us away — for the most part they are conservative in style, like our lifestyles.

Our homes range from well-constructed and -designed traditional colonials to English Tudors. Even though most of us are multimillionaires, we typically don't live in large mansions. Only about

TABLE 8-4

THE MILLIONAIRE HOME: NUMBER OF BEDROOMS AND FULL BATHS (N=733)

BEDROOMS

Number	Percentage	Cumulative Percentage
1 or 2	2.1	21
3	14.1	16.2
4	35.9	52. 1
5	30.2	82.3
6	11.8	94.1
7	4.2	98.3
8 or more	1.7	100.0

FULL BATHS

Number	Percentage	Cumulative Percentage
1 or 2	12.7	123
3	33.9	46.6
4	28.2	74.8
5	15.8	90.6
6	5.5	9,5.1
7	1.7	97.7
8 or more	2.3	100.0

two in one hundred (1.7 percent) live in homes with eight or more bedrooms (see Table 8-4). More than one-half (52 percent) of us live in homes that have four or fewer bedrooms.

Typical among us are married couples with two or three children. So who needs eight or more bathrooms? Only 2.3 percent of BAs live in homes that have eight or more bathrooms — nearly one-half of our homes (46.6 percent) have three bathrooms or less.

CHANGES IN THE NEIGHBORHOOD

Mr. and Mrs. Abel, the prototypical BA household, have noticed some changes in their neighborhood recently. The BAs are selling, but they are not always being replaced by others with the same orientation. Allow me to introduce the prototypical Income Statement Affluent (IA) couple, Mr. I. Steve Adams and his wife.

Throughout the BA neighborhoods of America today, the IAs are purchasing homes. "Stever" is a thirty-five-year-old stockbroker who earned over $500,000 last year. He and his wife were euphoric about earning so much money, and they purchased a home for $1.4 million. The original owner paid less than $400,000 for the home fifteen years ago.

Stever paid for his purchase with a jumbo $1.2 million mortgage. Only one in twenty of his neighbors has a mortgage balance of $1 million or more (see Table 8-5). It's common for people in Stever's age and occupational group to be purchasing million-dollar homes with jumbo mortgages. In fact, according to my data, high-income-producing people in their thirties and early forties make up a disproportionate share of

TABLE 8-5

THE MILLIONAIRE HOME: OUTSTANDING MORTGAGE BALANCE
(N=733)

Size of Unpaid Mortgage Outstanding	Millionaires Percentage	Millionaires Cumulative Percentage
No mortgage	39.9	39.9
Under $100,000	10.2	50.1
$100,000–$299,999	15.9	66.0
$300,000–$499,999	13.0	79.0
$500,000–$999,999	16.3	95.3
$1,000,000 or more	4.7	100.0

the jumbo mortgage market.

Stever is not a millionaire — he doesn't even come close to the crude definition of BA, i.e., having a minimum net worth that is ten times one's annual realized income. Stever will find that, even today, most of his neighbors are BAs who are not dependent on sales commissions or even a booming stock market to sustain them.

Never borrow long-term with the prospects of short-term income.

Stever can only hope that his sales commission income and client base will not turn away from him. If the stock market declines or if his income is cut in half, Stever will be bankrupt. And who will buy his home at a large discount? Probably a BA couple. They will be the only ones with a pile of dollars set aside who love to look for "nests that fall from trees." These people don't allow the euphoria of upswings in income to intoxicate them into making unwise and ill-financed purchases.

It isn't only stockbrokers who are leveraging today's sales commissions. The generic category called high-performance sales professionals, in their thirties and early forties, are getting into BA neighborhoods — late in the upswing of home prices. The homes they are buying have already doubled, even tripled in value in the past ten or twelve years. They are also late because they had to wait until the economy was already in an upswing. They get paid commissions only after they make a sale, and sales volume increases as the economy expands. But real estate prices are directly attached to changes in the economy. When the economy and corresponding stock market is booming, so are the prices of homes in BA neighborhoods.

Sales professionals are rarely in a financial position to do it at any other time. In good times they are high in income, but even then they are low in wealth because they spend, spend, spend and borrow, borrow, borrow.

Most BAs are very different. They buy homes only after they have accumulated wealth, and only after they have a well-established, predictable cash flow. Assume, for a moment, that you're a longtime resident of a BA neighborhood. Recall the last time when the economy was going nowhere and the stock market was at Dullsville. Who bought houses in your neighborhood then?

- Owner/operator of funeral homes
- Scrap-metal dealer
- Owner/operator of parking lots
- Heart surgeon
- Senior partner with major law firm
- Owner/operator of waste-management business
- Senior partner of accounting firm

These BAs bought a home when they felt they were fully qualified to do so, one that will likely be affordable for them.

FINDING A "LOVELY HOME"

Have you ever spent time shopping around for a home? Many of the respondents to my interviews have told me that shopping for a "new" home can be frustrating. It's as if all the homes on the market at any one time have significant drawbacks. Many have been on the market for months. Where are all the resales that are truly "lovely" homes?

Homes that are "lovely" sell very quickly in most instances. I use the term "lovely" to define those that are in excellent condition, nicely decorated, well situated on a quality lot, and located in a fine neighborhood with good public schools. These homes often sell within days of first being listed with a real estate broker, and some are sold even before the listing is public. In some instances, "lovely" homes are sold without the help of the third party, a professional real estate broker.

When the wisest potential buyers seek help from top-rated real estate agents, they advise the agent:

1. We are not in a hurry to buy. We can wait, but we are serious buyers.
2. When a "lovely" home is listed, we want to be told as soon as possible. But remember our parameters — it must be in top-notch condition and in the right location.

Most millionaires are in this category. The majority surveyed indicated that they:

Never even tried to purchase a home in a short period of time.

It's not that they procrastinate when the opportunity to purchase an ideal home arises; they are just satisfied to wait for the right "lovely" home to appear. The millionaires never place themselves in a position where they are forced to accept a substandard home. This is in sharp contrast to many employees who must relocate to a new town and have two days or less to find a home, or who accept "new" jobs that require re-location. Is it any wonder that frequent geographic mobility is a negative factor in accumulating wealth? Again, more than one-half of the millionaires in America have not moved in ten or more years. More than one in five are living in the same home they purchased at least twenty-five years ago.

Let's say you are looking for a new home and your search turns up two choices. One is twenty-five years old, occupied by the original owner. The other home for sale in the same area has been occupied by eight different owners. Odds are that, like most millionaires, you would pick the first home as your first choice. Eight owners leave eight different traces of their existence on and in the home. Wise buyers prefer the "one owner, 'low mileage' model."

How does one go about finding the "low mileage" home? One method is to hire a top real estate agent. But there are many situations where ownership of a "lovely" home is trans-ferred with literally no advertising, no real estate agent, and no parade of prospective buyers walking all over the home.

For example, when my father died, we knew my mother would have to sell our family home eventually. Everything about the house fit the definition of "lovely" — well built, well de-signed, well maintained in a good location, with only two owners in forty-five years. Mom waited until six or seven months of her designated moving day, and then let several neighbors know the house was for sale. She said no to the real estate agent who called and asked for the listing at 7 percent commission. As word spread, my mother made it clear to neighbors she wasn't in a hurry to sell. She exuded confidence that the home would go in an instant, further enhancing the image of the house. Ultimately, there were several hungry buyers, and she wound up selling with less than $1,000 in miscellaneous costs.

The lesson is that, like many wealthy sellers, you can use the local grapevine to find buyers without having to pay an agent's commission.

My friend Billy Gilmore has found another successful technique. When he was searching for a "lovely" home, he approached a local developer with many condominium units to sell. He reasoned that the developer might have an inventory of potential buyers who were unwilling to sign up without first selling their current homes. The developer was able to refer Billy to a number of those, and one suited his family's needs perfectly. So everybody won in that situation.

I have encountered situations where very aggressive prospective buyers have canvassed neighborhoods. They merely knocked on the doors of homes they were interested in purchasing. These homes had no visible For Sale signs or other indications — buyers just targeted them because they are appealing. Yes, even these cold calls can work. But I estimate that normally it would take a long time to find that "lovely" home owned by a longtime resident who is just beginning to feel the need to sell.

PROACTIVE SEARCHING

It seems logical to the man on the street that people who have accumulated less wealth would be more careful, more deliberate when purchasing a home, and those with considerable wealth would not have to be as concerned. If they make a bad home-related decision, it's not going to bankrupt them. In fact, millionaires are much more deliberate in their home-buying process than nonmillionaires. Even among the ranks of millionaires, however, there is an interesting correlation.

Who is more likely to search for a "bargain" home that was part of a foreclosure, divorce settlement, or estate sale — those with net worths in the $1 million to $2 million group or decamillionaires?

More than one in three (36 percent) of the decamillionaires indicate "bargain shopping" for a home that was part of a foreclosure, divorce settlement, or estate sales. Fewer than one in five (18 percent) of millionaires in the $1 million to $2 million net worth category indicate bargain shopping for a home in this way.

Note that these millionaires and decamillionaires were responding to questions about searching for homes that they themselves would own and occupy, not just "fixer-upper homes" they intended to use as rental property. You may also be surprised to find that some wealthy prospective home buyers search the obituaries for early evidence that an estate sale may be forthcoming. One enterprising millionaire wife couldn't wait for owners of trophy homes to pass away. She placed the following notice in the mail boxes of residences in a lovely neighborhood.

NOTICE
I would like to purchase a home in your neighborhood. If you have *any interest* in possibly selling your home in the next year, contact me immediately at the phone number below.

She had a number of interesting responses within days.

GUIDELINES FROM MILLIONAIRE BUYERS
What do millionaires tell me about how they purchase homes? This set of guidelines is based on survey responses from 733 millionaires, as well as focus-group and personal interviews. For most millionaires, at least part of their financial success can be attributed to careful selection of residential real estate. They report significant appreciation in the value of homes they have

purchased. You don't have to be a millionaire to capitalize on their recommendations. The large majority of these millionaires are self-made affluent, and they started at economic ground zero. Their home-buying processes are generally part of an overall investment plan. Planning and studying investments and investment opportunities is a regular task for about nine in ten millionaires.

1. Be willing to walk away from any deal on any home at any time. For every 100 millionaires who report that at least once in the process of buying a home they were unwilling to walk, there are 456 who never, ever entered into a home-negotiating process without being willing to walk away. In other words, 82 percent (see Table 8-6) of these millionaires felt they just could say no to a seller. This percentage is also correlated with net worth. Decamillionaires are the largest percentage of all millionaire groups who believe in the importance of one's "willingness to walk."

A self-made decamillionaire once gave me sound advice. He told me I should never even start negotiating to buy anything that I would have difficulty "walking away from." That's how he conducts his own purchasing lifestyle. He went on to say that it's a bad idea to let emotions dictate purchasing. According to this decamillionaire, one should never fall in love with things, and that includes houses.

TABLE 8-6

ACTIONS TAKEN: THE PROCESS OF PURCHASING A HOME
(N=733)

	Percentage of Millionaires
PLANNING AND DELIBERATING	
Being willing to walk away from any deal at any time	82
Never paying the initial asking price for any home	86
Researching the prices of recent home sales in the neighborhood	79
Never trying to purchase a home within a short span of time	54
Taking weeks, even months, to shop around for the very best deal overall	65
SEARCHING	
Seeking a neighborhood that has excellent public schools	79
Purchasing a home that is easily affordable	58
Searching for a low-maintenance energy-efficient home	25
Searching out a neighborhood with reasonable property taxes	26
Searching for a "bargain" home that was part of a foreclosure, divorce settlement, or estate sale	25
NEGOTIATING	
Testing seller's price sensitivity by making a deeply discounted price offer	46
Asking realtor to reduce the commission so that the seller can reduce the price	32
Having a contractor build a home	27
Demanding that the builder/seller price the home at or near cost	18

2. Don't pay the initial asking price for any home. Have you ever paid the asking price for a home? If so, it's unlikely that you are a millionaire. For every 100 millionaires who've paid the asking price, there are about 614 who never, ever paid the initial asking price. Eighty-six percent of these millionaires ask for a discount, and even the other 14 percent didn't just roll over and blindly pay "full retail." They spent considerable time studying prices, and when a true bargain presented itself, they paid the asking price.

Holly and her husband, Bill, were in their mid-forties and fit the perfect picture of the "live below your means" millionaire household, but they always knew the value of owning a trophy home in a trophy neighborhood. Homes of this type were constantly in short supply in their market area, and often sold the first day they were listed in the newspaper. Some were never listed at all because they were sold the day the seller called a real estate agent. Agents often have a waiting list of prospective buyers for trophy homes.

Holly played bridge with several homeowners who lived in the trophy neighborhood, and during a bridge party, one of the players mentioned that her next-door neighbor was moving. The home would go on sale in a week or two.

Two hours after learning of the availability of this trophy property, Holly was knocking on the seller's door. She immediately recognized the bargain price the seller was asking, so she and

Bill put down a cash deposit on the home the next morning.

The case of Holly and Bill is not pro forma for most millionaires. When they purchase homes, they generally play the game of competition. They usually select at least two homes that satisfy their needs, and then the price negotiations begin. The key is knowing the market and the value of homes and being resolved not to pay "full retail." This requires some time and researching the prices of recent home sales in selected neighborhoods.

Nearly five in ten millionaires (46 percent) report that they actually test for price sensitivity among various sellers of homes by making deeply discounted price offers. Then these prospective buyers gauge the responses from sellers. Many of the "testers" go a step beyond — they ask the listing agent to lower the commission rate. They hope this will, in turn, increase the probability that the seller might lower the asking price even more.

Who would you expect to aggressively negotiate the price of a home this way? It isn't what you would expect — people who have a difficult time "making ends meet." There is a highly significant positive correlation between net worth and "aggressive commission/price"–related negotiating. Fully 42 percent of all decamillionaires are "aggressive commission/price negotiators." Only 29 percent of millionaires in the $1 million to $2 million net worth category negotiate this way.

3. Never try to purchase a home within a short span of time. Does haste make waste? In most cases the answer is yes. Yet we can all learn from our mistakes. Fool me once, shame on you; fool me twice, shame on me. Even millionaires admit to having made less than optimal home-buying decisions some time in their past, and more often than not these decisions were made in haste.

If you find yourself in a situation where you must purchase a home in a short span of time, make sure you find the best real estate agent possible. A highly skilled, top-producing agent is a walking, talking information database. He or she should be able to forecast what homes sold today will be worth next year, in five years, and in ten. Ask for references. Contact people who bought homes from the agent years ago, and ask how well the agent predicted home values.

These people have a history of finding homes that are winners, and they can sell homes quickly even in down markets. But remember two numbers: 10 and 65. I have found in my long experience studying the affluent and the sales professionals who represent them that about 10 percent of the sales professionals account for more than 65 percent of the business generated by millionaire households. I consistently find that economically successful people patronize the most productive CPAs, attorneys, physicians, and real estate agents. Millionaires have a knack for finding great talent, and they have developed a keen sense of evaluating various suppliers.

How does one go about finding a top gun of a realtor? Your corporate employer may have a database and experience with such talent. Go out and buy the Sunday edition of the newspaper, or check out the Internet for real estate companies. Then call the managers of these firms and ask for the names of their top guns, and call them that. Ask about the accuracy of their forecasts about home values. Ask for and check the previous clients. Ask previous clients how well the real estate agent predicted the future.

Another technique used by economically successful people involves their legal help. They patronize law firms that have multiple offices, generally well-known, large- to medium-sized firms. So if they are moving from New York to Atlanta or Chicago to Denver, they can ask their attorney to refer them to an associate who lives in that city, and then ask the associate for referrals to real estate agents.

You don't have to be a millionaire to patronize a large- or medium-sized law firm. At the very least, you can have them construct a will for you and your spouse. Often you will not only get great professional core services, you will also have access to their information network. These law firms often have partners and associates who are real estate specialists and can point you to highly productive agents. And you should use your attorney to help you consummate the closing and advise you about pros and cons of the purchase contract. But that isn't all — there is yet another potential benefit from working closely with quality law firms.

4. Consider searching for a home that was part of a foreclosure, divorce settlement, or estate sale. Have you ever bought a home from a bank? I did — I'd like to tell you that I was hunting for a real bargain home, but I wasn't. I just saw a For Sale sign on the lawn, and later found out that this brand-new home was a foreclosure. Yet some millionaires I have surveyed are more proactive than yours truly.

> **One in four millionaires report searching for a "bargain" home that was part of a foreclosure, divorce settlement, or estate sale.**

In the thirty-six months that followed the stock market crash of 1987, fully 37 percent of those who purchased homes were in the "searching for a foreclosure" group. Many of these people are just waiting for the next market plunge.

Some millionaires discovered such opportunities through their affiliation with a quality law firm. Why not ask your attorney some creative questions:

• Does anyone in your firm specialize in foreclosures, divorce settlements, or estate sales?

494

- If so, would it be possible that I, as your client, be referred to any possible "bargain"-priced homes that need to be sold?

According to my surveys, attorneys are more likely than any other occupational group to indicate that they have searched for bargain homes in the distressed categories. Not all distressed homes are physically distressed, nor are they necessarily lower priced. Builders and buyers involved with luxury homes are not immune to the laws of economics and bankruptcy. There are plenty of those cowboys of speculation currently living in million-dollar homes whose short-term income will not always be enough to cover long-term mortgage debt. There are many credit-related sales of expensive homes even in good economic times.

Consider a recent advertisement ("Trophy Property Auction — Atlanta's Three Finest Mansions," *Wall Street Journal*, February 26, 1999, p. W13). It seems that America's trophy property auctioneers have a different definition of trophy property than I do. To me it means those "lovely three-, four-, and five-bedroom homes" that are located in fine, older neighborhoods. They aren't mansions, but their owners are quite wealthy. However, the three mansions listed may have once been owned by people who are not currently wealthy — what else can one conclude from the statement "Bank orders these properties sold"? Could it be that someone spent more than they earned? Why else would they part with:

- "Buckhead's most palatial mansion"?
- An "opulent French Renaissance palace with grand salon"?
- "24K gold fixtures"?
- An "opulent 22-room mansion"?
- A "lagoon pool with waterfalls and spa"?

5. Observe the millionaires' guideline about building a custom home. Only a minority (27 percent) of millionaires has ever had a home custom built for them. Most buy previously owned homes, although some have purchased new homes built speculatively by a builder or developer at or near completion. In fact, at least once in their lifetime, about one in five millionaires purchased a so-called spec house. There are various reasons why millionaires are averse to the custom route, and these are detailed later in this chapter.

If you are insistent on having a home built for you, I tell people who ask for advice about construction ventures that building a home is like going into a business about which you know little or nothing. Not only are you going into business, often you are also going to work with a stranger. A stranger, the building contractor, will be your partner, but he is usually a limited partner. Since you are underwriting this venture, much of the economic risk will be on your shoulders.

First, I advise you to exploit your patronage relationship with your accountant and your attorney. Both of these professionals and their respective colleagues have considerable knowledge about various home-building contractors. They have experience with the good ones, the bad ones, and even some great ones.

You want seasoned, astute professionals on your side if you're going into a venture with a builder. You want them to help you put together a long list of potential partners, and then prune the list. Once you have a short list of two or three builders who qualify, then it's time to deal. But don't you be the senior negotiator. Specify certain requirements about budget, time constraints, and construction plans, and then leave it in the hands of your CPA and lawyer.

These professionals have an extraordinary ability to satisfy a very wide variety of needs. Consider, for example, the role an enlightened accountant recently played in helping a wealthy client who expressed interest in having a custom home constructed. Keep in mind that the accountant, Mr. Art Gifford, is a skilled and experienced negotiator. He often negotiates the purchase of everything from businesses to automobiles.

In the process of speaking with a client, a neurosurgeon, I discovered that he was about to be taken advantage of. He was about to cut a deal with a building contractor . . . but he had no ex-

perience in dealing with contractors.

Many . . . many problems. The builder wanted to charge my client cost plus 15 percent for his fee. It's a bit stiff when you're talking about a $1.1 million home.

There were some other problems, too. The builder also wanted my client to pay a 5 percent sales commission on the $300,000 lot where the home was to be built.

The builder wanted to be the agent. . . . He also owned the lot. Nice deal. He proposed to my client that he pay a $15,000 sales commission on the lot. Plus 15 percent of the $1.1 million for his fee. That $15,000, plus $165,000 for the builder fee, a profit of $180,000 not including the more than $100,000 profit on the lot alone.

I told him [the builder] that the client gave me full authority to negotiate. Also, reflected upon what other . . . ah, competing builders were currently charging in this economy. And added that several of my clients were home builders. They would be pleased, very pleased, to build a home of this value for 10 percent.

I told him that there should be no sales commission on the lot. Also, I thought that a 10 percent fee on the home would be more reasonable.

My client [the neurosurgeon] hates to hassle . . . doesn't have the time . . . and a lot of people, especially doctors, find it a bit degrading to have to quibble over price. So I offered to negotiate on his behalf.

I enjoy the negotiating process . . . especially

when I'm representing a client. I do it all the time.

The first thing I did when I spoke to the builder was cut out the 5 percent sales commission on the lot. So I saved my client $15,000 with just a few moments of effort. After several conversations, the builder agreed to a fee of 10 percent instead of 15 percent. . . . Saved my client about $70,000.

Mr. Gifford did not charge his client, the neurosurgeon, a fee for his negotiating efforts. This is what he told me.

He is a client. He pays for our accounting and tax planning. Everything else is free. It's just part of our service. But I tell them, send me some business . . . tell your friends about us . . . referrals. That is how we do business.

This is one of the reasons for the growth of Mr. Gifford's accounting practice, but there is more. Eventually, the builder in this case became a Gifford client because Mr. Gifford referred several of his other wealthy clients to the builder. He did an excellent job constructing homes for both the neurosurgeon and several of Mr. Gifford's clients. In essence, Mr. Gifford knows how to win friends and clients and make them all happy, but he never will try to gouge a supplier, or cut a builder's profit, to the bone.

But you never want to cut a deal so one-sided that the supplier, a builder or whoever, resents you.

499

They want a fair deal. And remember, if you cut them to the bone, they will likely ignore your request to come back and repair things after the home is completed.

It's just the same . . . about auto dealers. Sure, I can cut deals so that they sell cars at cost . . . even below. But they will hate me and my clients. Just try and go back under these circumstances and see what kind of warranty work they will do. Or ask for a free loaner car. You cut them to the bone, and you can just about forget service after the sale. On the other hand, you can't sit by and let your own clients get ripped off. Nobody should have to pay 15 percent to build a home or [the] list price of any automobile. Be fair and be balanced, and everyone will win in the long run.

If I were contemplating the construction of an expensive home, I would have my attorney cut the deal with my builder. I am far too inexperienced to go up against a builder who has negotiated more than a hundred construction deals. I would also add my accountant to the team. I would ask him to iron out the mathematical details of the contract with the builder.

Why bring in all these third parties? Because in the long run you can save many dollars. Even if your CPA and attorney charge you several hundred dollars per hour for their input, and you have to pay $5,000 or even $10,000, skilled professionals can save you five, ten, even twenty times their fees by cutting a reasonable deal for their clients.

There is something else involved in this equation. Builders and other suppliers tend to perform better when they realize that a customer is well represented by enlightened professionals. Some of these suppliers have a name for such a customer:

He's a businessman!

People in business tend to have more respect for businessmen and businesswomen than for Mr. and Mrs. "R. Likely Naive" consumer, so be businesslike when contemplating major expenditures like home construction.

6. Always understand the meaning of an easily affordable home. Have you ever once in your life purchased a home that was easy to afford? If your answer is yes, you may be wealthy or on your way to becoming wealthy. But often millionaires have, at some time in their lives, purchased homes that were not easy to afford. In fact, about four in ten millionaires (42 percent) have done so.

How is it possible that someone can buy a home on which it's difficult to make mortgage payments, yet they become wealthy? The key is not only the purchase price of an expensive home — a major factor is whether or not the home will appreciate in value. Another consideration is whether or not the purchaser's income

501

will significantly rise in real-dollar terms.

Keep some things in mind when you consider purchasing a home that may be a bit out of your league. Would the proposed mortgage payments be difficult to make? What about tomorrow — will your income rise or fall? Will the value of the proposed home increase substantially in the near future? Answer these and related questions honestly and you are less likely to make a major financial mistake.

What if you are not candid even with yourself, and you convince yourself there is nothing wrong with buying a $1.2 million home with just 10 percent of your own money as a down payment? But after you make your mortgage payments each month and cover household operating costs, you will have zero dollars left over. The "luxury-home-buying cowboys" convince themselves this is only a temporary problem. They tell me:

- My income will continue to rise each year.
- The value of the home will explode over the next few years.
- I'm a seasoned investor. That's why I'm not risking much of my own money — just 10 percent. It's a leverage deal.
- With just $120,000 of my own money, I control nearly $1.1 million of the bank's.
- The value of that home will double in five years — I can just feel it. So for an investment of only $120,000, I will soon own a $2.4 million home.

After I pay back the mortgage, I'll walk away with over $1 million profit.

My response to such logic is to give these cowboys the names and addresses of the top bankruptcy lawyers in the country. In sharp contrast to cowboys, most millionaires were already wealthy before they purchased their current homes in their mid-forties to early fifties.

When people ask me about the meaning of affordable, I have a simple answer. Before you purchase your next dream home, assume that within a year of your purchase, your total annual realized income is cut in half. How long would you be able to make mortgage and related payments given your reduced income? Go the next step and assume that your investments also decline in value by 50 percent. Could you still make ends meet for at least five years? If the answer is no, then the home you wish to purchase is *not easily affordable!*

It's difficult to tell a pro forma cowboy that bad times follow good times. Most of them have never had to earn an income during bad times. They think that because the economy is booming it will go on indefinitely. It will not. But try telling that to a young stockbroker who earned $300,000 in commissions last year. These sales professionals are the very ones who overpay for homes and overextend themselves in good times. They judge their ability to pay for expensive homes and lead an opulent lifestyle on their single best income year.

It's no wonder that many seasoned and productive sales professionals actually have mixed feelings about so-called good economic times. They enjoy participating in a prosperous economy, but they can produce even in bad times. They like bad times because the cowboys, especially the young ones, get eliminated, and seasoned veterans have fewer competitors.

The same applies to home buyers. The smart ones realize that low interest rates and the rapid growth of high-income households translate into significant increases in the purchase price of homes. The price of expensive homes today is a direct function of the number of high-income-producing cowboys. The greatest number of cowboys were born in 1957. So today these early forty-something home buyers seem to be everywhere that million-dollar homes and mortgages exist in high concentrations. Watch what happens to many cowboys during the next downturn — there will be many trophy homes available.

GREEN OR BLUE?

Why does Mr. Green have a significantly higher net worth than others in his income bracket? He will tell you that he is an extremely productive investor. He's wealthy today because he has a fully integrated process of allocating his investment dollars, and he doesn't limit his investments to the stock market. Mr. Green recognizes that there are many other great opportunities. He does indicate that investing in the equities of public corporations has helped him become rich, but there are other factors that are significant in his investing habits. He has a hunter's nose. He can look around at his environment and hunt out or recognize good investment opportunities. Or as Mr. Green responded on the questionnaire he completed:

Seeing business opportunities others did not see.

Mr. Green has considerable knowledge of the real estate market trends in his area. He wrote to me:

The Millionaire Next Door is a significant publication. My wife and I loved it, discussed it with friends and family and still compare ourselves to the norms.

Where we differ is in making real estate a major investment opportunity. We are not wed to our house, but enjoy it. We'll sell it in the next year or two and expect a profit of $2.1 million or 125% before taxes. We'll build another, smaller house, pay off our relatively small (11%) mortgage, pay the taxes and still be up a million dollars. Welcome to Greenwich, Connecticut, in the '90s!!

The Greens built their current home six years ago at a cost of $1.7 million, including the land.

What is it worth five years later? According to Mr. Green, "$3.8 million is [the] actual value." According to my own research, this figure is a very conservative estimate — the property could bring more than $4 million. The Greens are charter members of the Balance Sheet Affluent group.

If you follow Mr. Green's actions regarding the purchase of real estate, your balance sheet may be enhanced. The Greens have bought and sold homes four times in ten years, and they learned something each time. Today, they buy something they feel will be relatively easy to sell at a good profit someday. They know that the more homework and negotiating they do as buyers, the better they will do one day as the seller of the same property. Contrast their methods with the Blues, charter members of the Income Statement Affluent Club. They have a net worth about twice their annual realized income, and could have a difficult time living on it for more than a few years. The Blues are on a consumption treadmill. They earn to spend, spend to earn. They purchased their $2.5 million dream home with a multimillion-dollar mortgage.

Mr. Green and Mr. Blue reported the actions they have taken in the process of purchasing a home (in Table 8-7). During their adult lifetimes, both have purchased existing homes, but most recently both decided to have homes built for them. Whether you purchase an existing home or have one built, these contrasting styles and processes may be useful to you. Note that Mr. Green has taken thirteen of the fourteen actions in attempting to get the best possible deal when acquiring a home. Mr. Blue indicated taking only four of the actions listed.

Mr. Blue purchases homes he cannot easily afford, and he avoids testing a seller's price sensitivity; like most members of the IA group, he is impatient. He believes in the "buy now, pay later" philosophy. Today, IAs feel euphoric because of sudden upswings in their income. So why wait until they become wealthy in terms of balance sheet pro formas? They spend in anticipation of becoming rich tomorrow, and in their minds they are already economic successes based on their income statements. Mr. Blue was assured that he could pay for his $2.5 million home — after all, his private banker approved his jumbo mortgage.

Mr. Blue counted the income dollars he expects to earn over the next ten years and forecasted the contributions that each of his clients will make in fees and commissions to his mortgage fund. This top-producing, extraordinary salesman has it all figured into his purchase equation.

Mr. Blue looks at credit as a weapon to enhance his balance sheet, so he believes in using other people's money through mortgage loans. He assumes that his $2.5 million home will significantly appreciate even in the short run. Like

TABLE 8-7

ACTIONS TAKEN IN THE PROCESS OF PURCHASING A HOME: MR. GREEN VS. MR. BLUE

	AFFLUENT TYPE	
	Balance Sheet: Mr. Green	Income Statement: Mr. Blue
PLANNING AND DELIBERATING		
Never paying the initial asking price for any home	Yes	Yes
Being willing to walk away from any deal at any time	Yes	Yes
Researching the prices of recent home sales in the neighborhood	Yes	Yes
Taking weeks, even months, to shop around for the very best deal overall	Yes	No
Never trying to purchase a home within a short span of time	Yes	No
SEARCHING		
Seeking a neighborhood that has excellent public schools	Yes	No
Purchasing a home that is easily affordable	Yes	No
Searching for a low-maintenance energy-efficient home	Yes	No
Searching for a "bargain" home that was part of a foreclosure, divorce settlement, or estate sale	Yes	No

508

TABLE 8-7 (Continued)

ACTIONS TAKEN IN THE PROCESS OF PURCHASING A HOME: MR. GREEN VS. MR. BLUE

	AFFLUENT TYPE	
	Balance Sheet: Mr. Green	Income Statement: Mr. Blue
Searching out a neighborhood with reasonable property taxes	No	No
NEGOTIATING		
Testing seller's price sensitivity by making a deeply discounted price offer	Yes	No
Asking realtor to reduce the commission so that the seller can reduce the price	Yes	No
Having a contractor build home	Yes	Yes
Demanding that the builder/ seller price the home at or near cost	Yes	No

most IA types, he firmly believes that "he got a real deal" on his home. But Mr. Blue is in for a surprise.

Who really gets most of the "real deals" in residential real estate? It's not the Blues, the IAs; it's the Greens, the BAs.

Once he decided to build a home, Mr. Blue wanted to "cut" the deal immediately. The experienced building contractor sensed that Mr. Blue is "a dog in heat," and that "the dog" has to have the home right away. By definition, he is insensitive to price and costs but very sensitive to the size, facade, style, jacuzzi, and other expensive features.

Mr. Green would never pay $2.5 million for the home that Mr. Blue currently occupies. He is far too experienced to pay full retail, and he is extremely patient. Builders can also sense this trait. Mr. Green demanded and convinced a builder to work near cost. He did his homework, made some reasonably good estimates, and boldly asked the builder for the actual cost data from homes he recently built. Mr. Blue is in a rush, and he has no idea what it actually cost to build his home!

There is another element present. Mr. Blue wants to express himself. He feels a compulsion to reflect his inner being with a totally unique home and home-building experience. His need for self-expression can be satisfied, but at a high cost. Mr. Blue's dream home is so unique that not one builder could even come up with a recent cost analogy. This being the case, how can a builder be expected to give a firm cost figure? With no firm cost figures, you cannot negotiate to or near a builder's cost. Some builders work only under the conditions of cost plus. It is Mr. Blue's builder's cost, the a priori great unknown, plus, say, a 20 percent add-on as his fee. What happens when you force a builder to construct a home that is so unique, so custom oriented, so architecturally self-actualizing that every day is a new learning experience for him? And every day his meter is running. You are paying big dollars to move him along the learning curve.

If your home eventually costs considerably more to build than a traditional one, prospective buyers don't care when you have to sell it. They aren't interested that you were self-actualizing during the design and building phases. They are insensitive to your builder's problem with starting at ground zero on the learning curve.

Mr. Green has consistently been able to "cut" a much better deal, in part because he has much more experience with builders and residential real estate in his area. He insisted that the real estate agent reduce her commission so the seller of the property could reduce the price even more. As an astute negotiator, he believes in the power of competition among all the actors in this play. He is much more patient than Mr. Blue; he is not "the dog in heat." The builder, the real estate agent, and the seller of the property figured this out because he actually made it easy for them to understand his motives and home-buying needs:

- I never, ever try to purchase a home or lot within a short span of time. I'm always looking for a great opportunity. I can inventory a building lot for years before I decide to build a home on it.
- I take weeks, months, even a year or more to

shop around for the very best deal overall. I'm never in a hurry.

- I'm always searching for a "bargain" home or lot that may be part of a foreclosure, divorce settlement, or estate sale.
- Mr. Builder, if you're willing to work with me on a price, I'll work around your schedule. When you have some slack time, perhaps you might be interested in building for me.
- I'm an unusual customer. I buy residential real estate not only as a place to live but as an investment. I always buy with the idea of having to sell some day. Reduce your commission on the sale, and I'm sure the seller of the property would also offer an additional discount.
- People look to me as an opinion leader. They often ask me about real estate agents I would recommend.
- I know a lot of people in this community. They are constantly asking me about helping them select a builder.

There are several other factors that account for Mr. Green's success in his home-buying experiences. He is life-cycle, not first-cost, sensitive. First cost is the price he pays for lots, homes, and construction. Life-cycle cost refers to the direct and indirect costs associated with a particular home over time.

What about Mr. Blue? He is relatively more first-cost sensitive than he is life-cycle-cost sensitive, but overall he is less sensitive on both di-

512

mensions than is Mr. Green. The IAs often delude themselves when making home-buying decisions — they paint a rosy picture of both first and life-cycle costs.

It's the variation in life-cycle costs that shows the most contrast between BA and IA groups. For example, take the various costs associated with selecting a neighborhood that has excellent public schools. Mr. Green always picks one of those, but not Mr. Blue. Before he moved into his new neighborhood, he didn't research the school situation. When he realized the public schools were subpar at best, private-school-tuition shock set in. Mr. Blue discovered that his children wouldn't be able to gain admission to quality colleges given the preparation they were receiving in the public schools. Add private school tuition of $33,000 per year onto the other life-cycle costs associated with "getting a real deal" on a building lot.

It isn't true that all millionaires are oriented toward private school and are averse to public school education for their children. Not really. The majority indicate that the quality of public schools was a significant factor in making a "neighborhood" decision. Nearly eight in ten (79 percent) stated that an important decision criteria underlying their home selection process was:

Seeking a neighborhood that has excellent public schools.

It isn't difficult to appreciate the relationship between wealth, home values, and the quality of public schools. Just consider for a moment how much it costs to send three children to a private school. The typical millionaire has three children — why would he want to live in a school district that necessitated the patronage of private schools? He doesn't. He even prefers paying high first-cost prices for homes located in neighborhoods that have quality public schools.

The additional evidence is that only 26 percent of the millionaires surveyed:

Searched for neighborhoods with reasonable property taxes.

Most of the BAs, like Mr. Green, realize the trade-offs between paying higher property taxes and having quality public schools. Not once in his life did Mr. Green even consider moving into a neighborhood because it had so-called reasonable school-tax rates. In his mind, low tax rates equate with low-quality public schools.

Most people in America would never pay $1.7 million for a five-bedroom home. Even if they could pay for it, most would build elsewhere. It's clear that Mr. Green could have purchased a five-bedroom home of similar design and space for much less money "if only" he and his wife were willing to live in some other town in the tristate area. But they were wise to stay in Greenwich. They could have purchased a five-bedroom home for less than one-half of $1.7 million, but it wouldn't have been in the same or similar quality neighborhood.

Mr. Green refused to compromise. He never viewed his decision to invest $1.7 million in a home as a risk. To him, a risk would be buying a home for $700,000 in a neighborhood with less potential than the one he chose. Mr. Green's investment of $1.7 million has more than doubled in just under six years, because he owns a trophy home in a trophy neighborhood. The area and the home are very desirable to an increasing number of affluent home buyers.

Risk has another face as far as Mr. Green is concerned. Finding and purchasing a home in a nontrophy neighborhood is relatively easy, but the real risk is in the difficulty of selling it, especially in situations where the public schools are subpar. So if Mr. Green had paid only one-half of the $1.7 million, five years later that investment might have appreciated only in a nominal sense. Public schools have a lot to do with the real return on investment.

Why are people like Mr. Green better able to make wise decisions about homes than the Mr. Blues of America? Mr. Blue has narrow vision, and he is an investment sales zealot. He sells investments in the stock market, and that's how he earns a high income. He is totally engrossed in this form of telephone dogfighting, and as a result he neglects other opportunities to generate both realized and unrealized income.

Mr. Blue is not alone. One of the factors underlying the behavior of IAs is that they tend to be workaholics. Work consumes them. One might assume that these high-income-producing types adopt the "work hard, play hard" lifestyle, but in general, they are involved in significantly fewer social, religious, civic, and recreational activities than the BAs. They tend to work more and play less, and they are least likely of all the high-income groups to indicate that they "love their jobs."

Note that many BAs work long hours and work hard, but they are not workaholics who don't enjoy their work. There is nothing so exhausting as working on a job you don't like.

The IAs earn big and spend big, and they are unlikely to take defensive actions to reduce the cost of operating their households, because in their minds, such actions are not worth the effort. Reducing operating costs and shopping for homes the way Mr. Green does is also viewed as work — work that in their view pays much less overall than does their main vocation.

In some situations they have a valid argument. You may never get rich using discount coupons to buy groceries, but such activities taken together have a significant influence on one's balance sheet. The IAs don't have a valid argument when it comes to purchasing homes — it's very clear from this national survey of BAs that a home can be more than a man's castle. For them, it can be and is a good investment.

If a buyer doesn't plan, and doesn't study the opportunities that are available, a home can be a poor investment. Many IA couples have discovered that when it comes to the home-buying process, haste does make waste. That's even more apparent when they try to sell the home they hastily purchased years ago.

THE HUNTER'S NOSE

Early in the 1980s, interest rates were at an all-time high. Even money-market funds were paying at or near 20 percent. People were out of the stock market because they were receiving guaranteed returns on cash and equivalents that were unparalleled. What about the residential real estate market? With mortgage rates near or at, in some areas, 20 percent, people were not in the mood for buying, which had a dampening effect on real estate prices. Sellers were begging to unload their homes, but they often sat unsold and unoccupied for months, even years.

At this same time, the Stanleys wanted to buy a home closer to downtown. My commute was nearly thirty miles one way, and the worst part was the bottleneck at a two-lane bridge. It seemed that all my neighbors and I sat bumper to bumper each workday at the same ridiculous bridge approach. While sitting there, I thought, "If I could live on the other side of this river, I'd save an hour each day." But I always countered with, "It's stupid even to consider selling a home and buying another when interest rates are so high." This give-and-take went on for months and months.

But the argument ended after I interviewed ten multimillionaires. The results from this focus group made a major impression on me about real estate. As part of my introduction, I mentioned that I lived in Atlanta, Georgia. In turn, they introduced themselves — all lived and worked in the New York metropolitan area, and all were business owners and first-generation affluent.

Oddly, I noticed that one respondent referred to Atlanta as the land of opportunity. Others repeated out loud: "Atlanta, Atlanta." During the half-time break and following the conclusion of the interviews, several respondents approached me with Georgia on their minds. They asked if I was currently buying real estate in Atlanta. They also commented about the great prospects for real estate there.

This made no sense to me at all. First, none of these multimillionaire respondents were real estate professionals. On their bio cards they mentioned other industries: printing, office supplies, appraising, manufacturing, and so on. Second, I was confused about their enthusiasm for investing in real estate. It seemed foolhardy, given the current interest rates. Why were these people interested in the real estate market, and why in Atlanta?

I told them that I wasn't interested in buying real estate because of the high interest rates and general doldrums in the market. Yes, even wonderful Atlanta was suffering from high interest rates. One of the respondents said something that made a major, lasting impression upon me.

MR. BROWN: Tom, this is the best time to buy!

DR. STANLEY: But the interest rates are so high. Who is buying?

MR. BROWN: Smart people — they don't always need to borrow. Have you considered buying?

DR. STANLEY: Yes, many times. Actually, we are thinking of building a home. But it's the old interest-rate problem.

MR. BROWN: Do you have enough cash to buy a building lot in a quality area?

DR. STANLEY: Yes.

MR. BROWN: Then do it. Do it now. Never follow the crowd. I'll wager there's plenty of property for sale. Look in the classifieds. . . . Call a few banks that have foreclosures.

The day after this lesson, I started searching for a lot. Mr. Brown was right — there were quite a few lots for sale in the classifieds. In short order I purchased one, but I did consider a variety of offerings and I had a chance to visit several sellers. The lot I selected was one acre, on what was once a plantation. The price for this prime lot was $29,500. Just two years before, a lot of this type had sold for double this price. During the next upswing in real estate, some comparable lots sold for $100,000.

Who was selling at the time I was buying? Several builders were suffering under the bad economic conditions but still had bills and debts to pay. Some of them had homes, lovely homes, just sitting and sitting. Many owned lots as well. Yet there were few buyers, in spite of the fact that these homes and lots were priced well below builders' cost.

There was another interesting group of sellers who fit the definition of Income Statement Affluent. Each had purchased lots not as investments but as places to build their dream homes during periods when economic-driven euphoria had infected Atlanta. They'd paid premium prices in a seller's market. The economy was producing an abnormally large number of high-income or high-commission-generating stockbrokers, life insurance sales professionals, new-business-development officers in engineering and contracting, and health-care professionals. Most of these people made such purchases via credit while simultaneously expanding their inventory of consumer goods and loans. They bought and borrowed as if happy times were going to exist forever. They were buying in a seller's market.

What about the Balance Sheet Affluent? At the same time, they were selling their lots. When the market turned the other way, the Balance Sheet Affluent were buying once again. Some held on to their building lots for years, through several ups and downs in the economy. Then, just at the peak of real estate prices, they placed their homes for sale. Many built homes on the lots purchased at bargain prices. Some bartered their lots and purchased homes held by builders. Others found "best buys" in the residential areas that they routinely monitored. Some deliberately waited for the bottom of the market to have builders construct homes — at a time when builders were more than delighted to build at or near cost just for the work.

That's why New York City–based millionaires in the focus group were interested in real estate and, particularly, real estate in Atlanta. Several in the group indicated having children or grandchildren who attended Emory University or Georgia Institute of Technology. Visits with these students gave them a chance to look over the Atlanta market. Another hallmark of the affluent is productivity. In essence, they "killed two birds with one stone," proving again that another hallmark of the millionaire mind is productivity.

REAL ESTATE AS PART OF ONE'S PORTFOLIO

There is something else about the Balance Sheet Affluent — they do not place all their investment eggs in one single, vulnerable basket. It's a major myth about the affluent that they "have all their money in their own businesses." Not by a long shot. Nor do most millionaires completely rely on the stock market, the real estate market, the fruit and vegetable markets, or the appliance market. Most are well diversified, and most have some type of investment real estate. Even many of those millionaires who have a strong affinity for common stocks hold some real estate holdings.

There is a strong correlation between net worth and the proportion of one's wealth that is invested in real estate.

I learned this early in my career. I was hired by a large investment organization to conduct a study of the investment habits of multimillionaires. When I asked the focus group about investment habits, most had a chunk of their wealth in conventional financial investment categories, but they had much, much more than stocks and bonds. Most were astute private investors. The business owners owned some industrial real estate; others owned their own office complex, factory, medical science complex, rental property, vacation rental property, shopping centers, and so on.

Several of the respondents occasionally invested in single-family homes, and one of these respondents, Alvin, had a hunter's nose. He was a high school dropout who owned a distribution business worth over $30 million. He lived in a fine neighborhood just outside New York City. He made it very clear that his home was purchased after he became a multimillionaire, during a buyer's market. The home had appreciated almost threefold in about fifteen years.

Alvin took more credit for some of his other home-related investments. He noticed that in his own fine neighborhood, pockets of economic opportunity often existed. His first target was a home near his own that had been unoccupied for almost a year because of a divorce. During this time, the home had been neglected. Finally, it was put up for sale, but the real estate market was weak for prospective sellers.

Alvin eventually purchased the home at a bargain. He then had it cleaned, painted, and generally improved. He rented it for several years to a relative, then the tide turned in the market. Buyers began to outnumber sellers, so he put the home up for sale at 20 percent over the appraisal price.

Alvin is Balance Sheet Affluent, and BAs sell to earn a profit, not because they are in dire need. He didn't need the money, and he knew the market was rising, so he priced his property with that in mind. In the rising market, the value of the home increased each day — all that he needed was one buyer who wanted to pay top dollar for a home in "Trophyville."

Alvin sold the property for near his asking price, and grossed over 50 percent on his investment. He made more than he would have at the time if he'd invested in the stock market.

Doing what Alvin did is not for most people. Remember that he owned his own company and had a large maintenance and clerical staff that he paid to "moonlight" on his real estate venture. And Alvin was not starting at ground zero on the learning curve. He told me that if he was at or near ground zero he would never have contemplated buying "investment" homes. If you are not in a similar position, you may wish to think twice about following Alvin's lead, but even those without his staff and experience find it productive to buy homes for their personal use in a neighborhood with which they are familiar.

A growing number of millionaires in the BA category are doing what Alvin has done — pricing their own homes in Trophyville and waiting to get the price they name. They sell in seller's markets, buy in buyer's markets. They often buy bargains in their own or adjacent neighborhoods. Some take residence in these bargain-priced trophies; others use them purely as investment vehicles.

HOME GAME/AWAY GAME

A growing number of BAs are becoming area-specific experts. When they see an opportunity to enhance their net worth in a certain neighborhood they know well, they take it. Today, it's not unusual to find an affluent household that has traded up or traded down to another home several times. More and more it's within the same or adjacent residential community. When these BAs discover a bargain-priced home in their "area of expertise," they pounce on it.

Many times a home soon to be on the market was discovered not in the classifieds but during a conversation at a bridge party or a chance discussion at a PTA meeting. I call this the *home game,* as in home team. The home team has the advantage of playing on its own field with the home crowd; Alvin's case relates well to this concept. He has the home-field advantage over many prospective buyers who don't know nearly as much about the neighborhood. And they may be on a quick two-day house-shopping visit related to an employment change. Think twice about ever considering the purchase of an expensive home "over the weekend." If you have no alternative, at the very least hire the top real estate agent in the area to assist you. Often it's these types, including a few other non-self-employed workers, who are placed in *away game* situations.

WINNING THE AWAY GAMES

You don't need the home-field advantage if you play the game the way Mr. Dye does. Mr. Dye is an employee who has worked for two major corporations during his much-traveled career. During each of his last six long-distance residential moves, he and his wife have made a considerable profit each and every time. No matter that he was in Chicago for several years, then in Houston for several more, and then was transferred to Orlando — Mr. and Mrs. Dye always made money each time they moved. They bought low and sold high. How did a member of the *away team* bat six for six while playing away games?

Each time, Mr. and Mrs. Dye transformed themselves into members of the home team, as they did again in their most recent home purchase and sale. Mr. Dye told me that he never puts himself in the position of having to buy or sell homes in a panic. Like most BAs, he and his wife are very patient. They have a plan and a set of goals to follow.

When Mr. Dye was told by his Fortune Fifty corporate employer of yet another reassignment, another relocation, he and his wife were well prepared. They didn't allow the euphoria of a new assignment and a move to an exciting town translate into a bad decision.

In this most recent venture, the couple took six months to sell their old home and make a purchase decision. Mr. Dye's employer was very fair, even generous. He reported that his corporate employers had offered to buy each of the six homes he needed to sell — each time at a good, fair market price. But Mr. Dye turned down each offer, and he was wise to do so. Each time the couple sold their homes, they made at least 15 percent more than the fair market value. Fair market value is often computed by analogy —

appraisers rely on the prices that homes in a particular area have recently sold for, given certain size and style parameters.

Mr. and Mrs. Dye were able to outsmart the experts, the seasoned appraisers, and generate top dollars for each home they sold. They strongly believe that:

Cleanliness is next to godliness!

Their homes were always spotless inside and out. The Dyes don't just spruce up their home today in anticipation of selling it tomorrow — it's always in turnkey condition. And they are extremely demanding about the homes they purchase — they only buy those that are in excellent condition. Then they go a step or two beyond excellence. Interior and exterior color and decor are always up to date. They only buy homes they feel they can sell later at a profit.

Who would be most likely to purchase a home in above-excellent condition but at a minimum premium of 20 percent above market? What buyer would place a premium on being able to move into a turnkey home immediately? In the most recent case, Mr. and Mrs. Dye sold their home to a two-career couple employed in the computer industry. The couple moved frequently. Both were in their late thirties, and both had very demanding, high-paying jobs that involved a great deal of travel. Neither had any interest in restoring or even redecorating a home, nor were they interested in purchasing a new home out of a builder's existing inventory or building a home on a custom basis. They correctly assumed that new homes need new lawns, new decorating, new drapes, and other materials. This couple was all about work, aggressively pursuing a career and earning big incomes. To them, time and effort spent outside their vocations translated into big negatives.

They wanted a home they could immediately occupy, and they were very sensitive to variations in the conditions of homes they considered. But they were significantly less sensitive to the variations in price among homes that competed for their dollars. Also, the couple allocated one weekend to find a suitable home, and they knew nothing of the real estate market in the city where they were reassigned. In essence, they were yet another IA couple playing yet another away game. This couple paid the largest percent premium over market value in the history of the subdivision — nearly 33 percent. Seventeen months later the same couple sold the same home for only 85 percent of what they'd paid. But at that time, the home was not in above-excellent condition, and the couple was in a hurry to sell. Their employers subsidized part of their loss.

Always have a plan in place before you or your employer decide that it's time to change addresses.

Part of this plan is to keep your home in excellent condition, but you should also keep in touch with top real estate agents in your area. Contact them every six months or so. Periodically note the names of the superstars in residential real estate, and rely on this list completely. Ask business associates for referrals, and canvas real estate firms for the names of the top guns. When you interview them, ask about market conditions and don't be shy about asking about recent productivity. In particular, ask how many of their recent sales have come from clients moving into the area. Ask about the average amount of time these clients allocated to searching before actually purchasing a home.

Often the very best agents have close working relationships with top firms in major industries in your area. If you are in San Francisco, for example, you may wish to consider an agent who services corporations in the computer and high-technology industries. When a major company is hiring an important employee from out of state, the firm wants the transition to go smoothly. Part of the process is to ask a top-notch real estate agent to assist, so your plan should include familiarizing yourself with agents who have excellent track records in making these companies and their inbound executives happy. Give strong consideration to hiring one of them to list your home. I have found that many of these top-producing agents work especially hard to sell homes that they also list. I take no pleasure in saying that it's often a bad mistake to hire a neighbor, friend, or even a relative as a real estate agent. Business is business, and today more than ever before, you can ill afford to be represented by someone other than a highly productive and completely professional real estate expert.

In my mind there is a very clear distinction between three types of real estate agents. First, there are what I refer to as "listers," then there are "sellers," and finally there are those extraordinary sales and marketing commandos who are great at both acquiring listings and selling what they and other agents list. Ask yourself which type you want.

There are some exceptional listers and sellers. Some very aggressive listers have built up tremendous goodwill with other brokers so that other brokers take special note when their name is on a For Sale sign. But most agents are not sales and marketing commandos by any stretch of the imagination. From their perspective it's much easier to encourage a neighbor, friend, or relative to list with me, me, me. It's much more difficult to sell, because most sales are made to strangers. But in my mind the very, very best real estate agents both list and sell.

I WILL ALWAYS RECOMMEND
CONNIE GLENN

Not everyone can sell real estate. Only a small number of real estate sales professionals achieve ESP [what I call extraordinary sales professional] status and maintain that status during downturns in the real estate market. Connie Glenn is one of them.

I was once in the unenviable position of having to sell a house when the mortgage rate was near 20 percent. What there was of a real estate market in Atlanta at that time was a buyer's market. Like millions of other home-owners, I made the mistake of asking the first person who came to mind — a friend, neighbor, and part-time real estate agent — to sell the property. This was the easy thing to do. After more than two months, the only results were no offers, no nibbles, and very little traffic.

It became apparent that a change had to be made. I called the manager of the largest real estate agency in Atlanta. "I want the name of your very, very best agent. . . . No, not the best in Dunwoody or Roswell. I want the best horse in your stable."

Connie and her assistant appeared at my home soon after I called her. She agreed to accept my case. Traffic increased overnight. Within a month, the house sold for 95 percent of the asking price. I was amazed at her success. Not only was the market difficult, but the home was cedar. Cedar is not my first choice for siding in Georgia. It discolors and mildews. Periodic cleaning is necessary. Who would pay 95 percent of the asking price?

Connie found an executive from the lumber industry who loved cedar! "After all, Tom, what would you expect a lumber expert to live in — a brick colonial? It would be bad for his reputation and the image of the lumber company."

My experience with Connie taught me something about marketing. If you want to avoid losing money on your real estate dealings, call an ESP. (Thomas J. Stanley, *Marketing to the Affluent*, Homewood, IL: Dow-Jones Irwin, 1988, pp. 40–41)

Note that Ms. Glenn both listed and sold our property. Her manager told me that Connie established her reputation as a top gun by "aggressively seeking listings of homes that others were unable to sell." In her mind every home had a potential buyer — the key was to find that buyer. Connie always had the ability to do so. What Connie Glenn does to establish herself as an ESP is so simple that most people can't see it. Brilliance in sales and marketing is often indicated in the simplest, most practical ways, and ultimately in the results. Connie recognized that every real estate market has a particular set of characteristics. These characteristics have significant bearing on home-purchasing behavior.

Georgia is a top-five state in the production of lumber. It's a state with vast tracts of forests. Many firms involved in lumber directly or indirectly have a presence in Georgia. These range in size from the Georgia Pacific Corporation to the smallest forest farm. It's wood and wood people, no matter what else you call it.

Knowing that Georgia is a "wood state" tells you that many inbound movers are employed or will be employed by wood companies. Connie understood this, and she developed contacts and a great reputation in wood and several other key industries. She has the so-called hunter's nose, and she has the determination of a bulldog.

If you move several times during your career, and if you hire a Connie Glenn type each time, you will likely net much more money from her expertise at selling. It's not unusual that after five or six moves, you will net more than the full purchase price of your first home. The Connie types can and do account for hundreds of thousands of dollars in your pocket — in some cases, even millions over a millionaire's life cycle.

PLAN OR PANIC?

As part of your plan to sell or buy a home, decide your time parameters. Don't panic when you find that you'll be moving to a different geographical area. Anticipate that if you are an employee, your employer could ask you to move someday. So decide beforehand how long you'll be willing to search for a home. The Dyes were quite willing to wait up to six months to find a home and, of course, to sell the home they currently owned, but that's not for everyone. Mr. Dye's employer was generous and paid all of the

Dyes' moving expenses, including the rent incurred while the couple searched for a home. If your employer is not so liberal, you may still find it worthwhile to rent so you have the time to transform yourself from a member of the visiting team to one of the home team. A few months' rent is not a lot to pay to acquire a home that will appreciate and eventually be easy to resell.

NO SUCH THING AS A PERFECT PREDICTION

It's amazing to me that some people spend more time shopping for automobiles than for the homes they purchase. As the saying goes, a fool and his money soon are parted. Before you even give consideration to purchasing a home, take time to study the clues. Ask why the owner is selling. He may not tell you that it's because his neighbor's home is becoming an eyesore. It is very easy to overlook the condition of the homes that surround the one you are interested in. Often people speed past these other homes. Slow down, walk the neighborhood, and closely examine the other homes. What percentage need exterior work? How many need new gutters? How well are the lawns and shrubs kept? Who are your prospective neighbors? What do they do for a living?

Ask your real estate agent about the trends in the neighborhood. Are the values of the homes on the rise, or are they flat or even in decline? Ask such questions, and you will benefit. Your agent will be impressed with your sensitivity and may be more candid with answers.

As you walk the neighborhood, knock on doors. Talk to people who may be your neighbors, and look them over carefully. Ask about the schools in the area. Ask what they enjoy or dislike about the neighborhood.

These questions can help you make an educated purchase decision. What if the values of homes in a neighborhood are not keeping pace with those in nearby neighborhoods? What if one in five homes need exterior paint? What if the homeowner next door has recently lost his job as a corporate middle manager? What if his home needs exterior work? Give serious consideration to buying elsewhere.

Many neighborhoods decline in real-dollar-value terms — that happens even in affluent areas. Often it is impossible to predict whether a particular neighborhood will decline or appreciate in value, and this is especially true in brand-new or near-new subdivisions. In this regard, I have a simple rule. Look carefully at the homes in a well-established neighborhood. If more than one in five clearly needs painting or landscaping, you may wish to avoid the risk of buying there.

BUILD OR BUY

On the day I began writing this chapter, my friend John stopped by to ask my advice about whether to buy or build a home for his family. I told John he was lucky — the numbers were fresh in my mind. What do millionaires do regarding the "build versus buy" issue?

- Only about one in four (27 percent) millionaires ever had a home built for them. This includes all categories — primary homes, second homes, summer homes, winter homes, and so on.
- The proportion of millionaires who build instead of buying increases with the level of net worth. However, only 35 percent of the decamillionaires ever had a home built for them.

John seemed a bit shocked by these revelations, but I had anticipated his response. It seems that John wants to build because he thinks he can save money that way, and he thought most millionaires built as opposed to buying existing homes. After I gave him my data, he came up with a brand-new thesis.

Now I got it. Millionaires don't need to save money building. But I'm not [rich]. That's why I want to build.

THE "I'LL SAVE MONEY" MYTH
Why is it that the large majority of millionaires never build homes? They believe that there are some benefits of building versus buying, but they also feel that those benefits don't offset the marginal costs of their time, energy, and other

important resources.

This fact differs from conventional opinions. It's a popular belief that wealthy people have the need for custom products. Don't millionaires have such enormous egos they want things designed specifically for them? Make no mistake about it, there are some who express themselves this way. To these people, there is no substitute for a custom-designed and -built home. Their home is not just a home — it's an extension of who they are and what they wish to tell people about themselves. A resale, no matter how nice, just will not satisfy their needs. This is a small segment of the millionaire population — fewer than one in ten fall into this category.

A very small segment, fewer than fifteen in one hundred millionaires, decide to build their primary residence because they believe they can save money this way. In reality, these millionaires are very sensitive to variations in the cost differences of building a home versus buying one. Some act as if they put a lower premium on the value of their time. They believe that it's financially beneficial to spend more time on the process of building than working at their primary vocation. This group includes the most price-sensitive bargain shoppers of all the millionaires. They build because they think they are going to save a lot of money doing so. They may look at an existing home priced at $400,000 and say to themselves: "I could have it built for $300,000, including the lot."

What if you are a young attorney in a position that has great prospects for advancement. If you make partner, your income will jump from $78,000 per year to over $300,000. Should you take time to have a home built for you? Are you up for taking hundreds of phone calls from your builder, suppliers, and subcontractors at your office during a six- to ten-month period? Do you think it valuable to visit your construction site every few days to make sure it's done right?

Just envision that two young attorneys are competing for one opening as partner. Who would you bet on — Mr. Build or Mr. Buy? Even if Mr. Build saved $100,000 off a comparable home, he spent so much time and energy on the project that it took the edge off his performance as an attorney. He did not make partner.

GOOD LEGAL ADVICE

There is a very wide variation among occupational groups in regard to building versus buying a home. Millionaires in some occupational categories are significantly more likely to build as opposed to buying an existing home. As a rule, wealthy attorneys are averse to building.

- Nearly nine in ten attorneys (88 percent) have never had any type of home built for them.

- Millionaires in the senior corporate executive occupational category (32 percent) and those who are business owners or entrepreneurs (31 percent) are somewhat more likely to build homes than the average (27 percent) for all millionaires.

- There is a relationship between one's level of wealth and the propensity to build a home. About one in four (24 percent) of the millionaires in the $1 million to $2 million net worth category indicate having built homes. Conversely, about 35 percent of decamillionaires have built homes.

Wealthy attorneys are unlikely to have homes built specifically for them for two reasons. First, they are extremely productive. Fully 80 percent earn incomes in excess of $200,000 annually, and about one-half earn incomes of more than $400,000. Consider the time and effort it takes to generate such incomes in the light of one fact: Legal services can not be inventoried; they have to be rendered constantly. Many respondents from the legal profession said that they and their colleagues have no time to get involved with home construction. Attorneys are good judges of the value of their time, and having a home built is a time-consuming event.

The second reason is that attorneys understand the legal and corresponding economic risks involved in hiring a home builder. You can hire the best, most honest builder in your state and still have problems. If he is disabled or passes away just after your home is framed or just after you paid him a small fortune to get the project started, who will now build your home? What is the disposition of the money you advanced your builder?

Here are some other "problems" that millionaires have shared with me about their recent building experiences.

- My builder hired a "sub" to install the wallpaper in our eighteen-foot foyer. Afterward, the "sub" called and asked my wife if she was pleased with the wallpapering. She reported that everything was fine except one detail — the wallpaper was installed upside down! As a result, our builder never paid the "sub," but he put a lien on our home. This, in turn, prevented us from having our permanent mortgage approved. We had to hire a lawyer and purchase a bond. It all took more time than money. All the wallpaper had to be removed and new paper installed. Our builder was not a lot of help.
- . . . Built on a steep hill . . . great view . . . contractor poured the basement slab just following torrential rains. The whole thing [slab of wet concrete] broke loose. . . . Concrete [all] rushed down the hill. . . . Contractor said it was my fault for insisting on having a full basement. My lawyer persuaded him to see it our way!
- Our builder assured us that there were no rocks underground [on lot]. The first day of groundbreaking he called . . . [and] asked, "Could ya go with a slab? No basement? . . . We hit granite just below the surface." After more than 200

sticks of explosives and more than a week of blasting and removing we were in the financial hole. . . . So much for cost-plus pricing. . . . Cost more than $10,000 just to truck the rock away!

- Worker knocked a hole in our foundation for pipes. Then filled in around pipes with the wrong type of mortar. . . . Cracked our nine-foot foundation . . . top to bottom. . . . It's still cracked. . . . it still leaks when it rains. . . . [I've] called my attorney.
- . . . Subcontractor [framer] overbilled our builder. He passed the problem [the bills] on to us. When we questioned him . . . [he] just got angry.
- He [the builder] said that the framing would be Wednesday. We thought he meant Wednesday of next week, not two months from now.
- [The builder] told us that our fireplace would be finished as soon as his rock mason came back to work. . . . Our builder was his own rock mason!
- Carpet installers stapled through the floor sensors for our alarm system. Got to know a lot of police people just after moving into our new home.
- . . . Contractor hired a rookie with a bulldozer to complete the grading. Leveled every single tree in our 100' X 200' backyard. . . . It was once filled with a variety of hardwoods.
- At completion we had receipts from 360 suppliers. We probably spoke to at least half of them during the project.

- I have a stack of complaints from my clients about their builders. These are very expensive homes . . . and very angry people.

So if you are interested in having your dream home built for you, consider what I've learned from millionaires. Consult your attorney, and, if possible, ask him to help you find a builder. If your attorney is a partner in a large firm, you have some advantage. Out of fifty or a hundred lawyers, you are likely to find at least five or ten who had homes built for them and a few may have been completely satisfied with their builders — or at least they may have clients who hired "high-grade" builders.

Allow your attorney to relate to you all the legal issues involved in building your own home. Never even consider signing a construction contract without the input of your attorney. Even better, ask him to write the contract, then let him work out the details with your builder.

Don't go out of control regarding your need to express yourself in the home you build. If you insist that every single element in your dream home be unique and custom designed, prepare yourself for delays, disappointments, and cost overruns. In terms of time and money, it's more productive to avoid the fully customized dwelling.

MORE THAN THE PURCHASE PRICE

He telephoned my office one morning — a parent with an unusual question. Mr. Adam, as I refer to him, had a net worth of about $20 million. He seemed puzzled by my response. He thought I would just say, "What a great idea!"

> MR. ADAM: Should I buy my thirty-year-old son Nate a $425,000 home?
>> I told Mr. Adam that I would first have to ask him a few questions, then I'd give him some data. With the data, I assumed he would make up his own mind.
> DR. STANLEY: Do you think that your son can afford it?
> MR. ADAM: Perhaps I am not making myself clear. I'm going to buy the home for my son . . . outright.
> DR. STANLEY: I understand that. I'm not talking about the purchase price. I'm talking about the costs associated with operating a $425,000 home and the lifestyle associated with such a home.

I explained to Mr. Adam that $425,000 was like the initiation fee at a country club. The monthly fees are another issue. Mr. Adam didn't seem to get the point that I was making. He believed that Nate, his son, would have few financial burdens. After all, Nate would have no mortgage payments and he'd have the title to a home valued at $425,000 — what could be simpler?

I began to think that Mr. Adam had already made up his mind. He seemed inclined to purchase the home for Nate — after all, $425,000 was only about 2 percent of Mr. Adam's net worth. But there is a problem with his logic. In many ways, it's irrelevant how much or how little of his wealth is involved, for it's Nate and his family who will be living in the home.

> DR. STANLEY: How much does your son earn annually?
> MR. ADAM: . . . About $30,000.
> DR. STANLEY: What does he do for a living?
> MR. ADAM: He recently started a new career in the insurance and investment business.
> DR. STANLEY: What about his wife? Does she work?
> MR. ADAM: She is a part-time hair stylist, but she wants to quit and be a housewife full-time.
> DR. STANLEY: So are you saying that the couple has a combined earned income of a bit over $40,000? That is pretty close to the average for all households in America.

Nate and his wife may be just average in terms of their combined earned income, but they would be extraordinary if they lived in a neighborhood filled with $425,000 homes. I was well aware of the demographic characteristics of the neighborhoods where Nate and his wife had been home shopping. The typical household there had an annual earned income of more than three times the couple's.

DR. STANLEY: Do you think your son and his
wife will fit in living at Legacy Estates? I
have to tell you that many of the households in that area are in the six digits of
annual earned income. Most of the
earners there are executives, professionals, or successful business owners.

MR. ADAM: She [the daughter-in-law] insti-
gated this. She likes the area [Legacy Es-
tates] in the north county. It has a tennis
and golf club as part of the development.
She wants to be a full-time housewife and
play tennis.

THE HARSH REALITY

Even after this exchange, I was not getting my
point across. Mr. Adam still thought that with
one single $425,000 purchase his related financial
responsibilities for housing Nate would be zero. I
realized it was time for deployment of heavy reality
weapons. Mr. Adam was not yet aware of the
strong possibility that his son and daughter-in-law
would probably need large and continuous doses
of economic outpatient care (EOC). Mr. Adam
couldn't appreciate the fact that it costs a great
deal to sustain a household in a $425,000 neigh-
borhood environment. It requires lots of money
independent of mortgage payments.

DR. STANLEY: Do you have an idea about
what the property taxes will be on a
$425,000 home?

MR. ADAM: Don't know.

DR. STANLEY: Well, it is somewhere between $7,600, and $8,000. But taxes there keep going up. The household takes home [net after income taxes, social security, and such] probably less than $35,000 of the $40,000 gross. So let's see, that is a minimum of $7,600 over $35,000, or about 22 percent of their income.

With this revelation, I started making progress. I followed with a series of questions about other household expenses.

I also illustrated several multiples to Mr. Adam. A $425,000 home is more than three times the current value of the average for a single-family home in America. On a national basis, people who purchase homes valued at $425,000 have incomes that are more than three times the average.

How much are the homes of the wealthy people in America worth? This is not an easy question to answer with my survey data because most of it is geo-specific. I deliberately oversampled those neighborhoods with high concentrations of millionaires. Conversely, more than one-half of the neighborhoods in America are not surveyed. They contain no or low concentrations of millionaires, but there may be one millionaire in every one hundred households. This is in sharp contrast with the geo-specific sample upon which most of this book is based. On average, more than seventy in one hundred households surveyed were in the millionaire category. It's not surprising that these very affluent neighborhoods contain many expensive homes, but the same is not true on a national basis.

Who has the most complete data on millionaires? Not yours truly — the answer is our own Internal Revenue Service. The IRS recently provided data that can be used to estimate the value of homes by various wealth groups. The beauty of this information is easy to appreciate. It includes all millionaires, not just those who live in exclusive residential areas, and contains all of them — from multimillionaire farmers in rural America to wealthy scrap-metal dealers from blue-collar neighborhoods to very wealthy executives residing in exclusive neighborhoods filled with multimillion-dollar homes.

My analysis of this data can be used as a great defensive weapon. What if your son and his wife are putting pressure on you to buy them an expensive home? They tell you, "Everyone lives in homes valued at this amount!" They also tell you that "it's only a small portion of your wealth." Mr. Adam and others should answer with a simple fact, the same one I gave Mr. Adam. Most millionaires, nationwide, live in homes valued at much less than $425,000, and if the typical millionaire is comfortable living in a home like that, millionaires' less affluent sons

TABLE 8-8

THE HOMES OF MILLIONAIRES IN AMERICA: AVERAGE VALUE BY NET WORTH[1]

Net Worth	Average Net Worth	Personal Residence/ Homes: Average Value
$1,000,000 to under $2,500,000	$1,470,553	$220,796
$2,500,000 to under $5,000,000	$3,392,416	$354,043
$5,000,000 to under $10,000,000	$6,809,409	$545,499
$10,000,000 to under $20,000,000	$14,045,501	$779,444
$20,000,000 or more	$58,229,024	$1,073,980
All $1,000,000 or more	$2,938,515	$277,640

[1]MRI database 1999 and IRS estimates 1996.

---

and daughters-in-law should be too.

Note the data given in Table 8-8. According to the IRS database, which encompasses all millionaire households nationwide and thus includes certain geodemographic categories not surveyed in my study, such as farmers and others, the average value of the American millionaire's home is estimated to be $277,640.

Millionaires in the $2.5 to under $5 million net worth category live in homes worth $354,043, on average. Nate is proposing to live in a home that's more expensive than those owned by most millionaires!

THE DEFENSIVE MEMO

There are hundreds of thousands of affluent parents in America today who have or will experience problems similar to Mr. Adam's. What defense do they have against the pressure for EOC in the form of subsidized housing? Now they have a counterargument. It could be given in oral or written form.

MEMORANDUM
TO: Nates and Natettes
FROM: Affluent Parents
RE: Your Request for Subsidized
    Housing, i.e., a gift of a $425,000 home

Please reconsider your request that we buy you a $425,000 home. Along these lines, note the following:

• On average, the American millionaire has a net worth of just under $3 million. Yet he or she lives in a home that is valued at only $277,640. You are not a millionaire. So why is it necessary for you to live in a $425,000 home? Contrast $277,640 with $425,000 and you may see the light. You are proposing to live in a home that is

153.1 percent more valuable than the home of the typical millionaire.

- Note that, on average, the typical millionaire who lives in his or her $277,640 home has a total realized annual income of about $145,000. Your household's current annual income is about $40,000. That is about 27.6 percent of what millionaires earn on average. Perhaps you could use these numbers to determine the value of a home that would be more suitable, given your current income. Why not consider a home valued at 27.6 percent (your income as a percent of a millionaire's) of the typical millionaire's ($277,640)? This translates into roughly $77,000.

- There are some small "starter" homes within twenty or thirty miles of here that are in that price range. A home valued at this level is a good fit for someone in the $40,000 income bracket. If you insist on living in a more expensive home, we will only subsidize your purchase up to $77,000. You will have to pay the additional cost. Thus, you may wish to postpone your purchase until you have acquired more capital.

Mr. Adam's case is not unusual. He is a dedicated father to Nate, and he is still in the denial stage. He still believes that once he hands over the $425,000 home, Nate will somehow be self-sufficient. But even with an income of twice what Nate and his wife currently earn, they would have difficulty supporting themselves.

TABLE 8-9

SELECTED AVERAGE ANNUAL EXPENDITURES AND CHARACTERISTICS: HOUSEHOLDS WITH INCOMES OF $90,000 AND OVER AND THOSE WITH LESS THAN $90,000[1]

Items	Less Than $90,000: The Nate Types	$90,000 and Over: Nate's Prospective Neighbors
Number of households (000s)	79,704	5,022
Income before taxes	$30,220	$136,898
Age of reference person	47.9	47.1
Average number in household:		
Persons	2.5	3.1
Children under 18	0.7	0.8
Persons 65 and over	0.3	0.1
Earners	1.2	2.1
Vehicles	1.8	2.7
Percent homeowner:	61	91
With mortgage (percent of total)	36	75
With mortgage (percent of homeowners)	59	82
Renter	39	9
Black	11	4
White and other	89	96
College	46	82
Total expenditures	$30,167	$80,645
Food	4,331	9,010
Food at home	2,721	4,451
Food away from home	1,608	4,559

TABLE 8-9 (Continued)

SELECTED AVERAGE ANNUAL EXPENDITURES AND CHARACTERISTICS: HOUSEHOLDS WITH INCOMES OF $90,000 AND OVER AND THOSE WITH LESS THAN $90,000[1]

Items	Less Than $90,000: The Nate Types	$90,000 and Over: Nate's Prospective Neighbors
Housing	9,448	25,121
Shelter	5,251	14,532
Owned dwellings	3,080	11,887
Rented dwellings	1,864	940
Utilities, fuels, and public services	2,091	3,491
Household operations	423	1,876
Housekeeping supplies	412	967
Household furnish., equip.	1,272	4,255
Apparel and services	1,540	4,732
Transportation	5,690	12,521
Vehicle purchases	2,547	4,964
Gasoline, oil, other	2,831	6,101
Public transportation	312	1,455
Health care	1,696	2,747
Entertainment	1476	4,467
Education	389	1,816
Cash contributions	863	4,019
Personal insurance, pensions	2,870	12,614

[1]Source: U.S. Department of Labor Bureau of Labor Statistics, for Period 1994–1995. As reported in Summary 98-10, November 1998.

What will probably happen when Nate takes possession of his $425,000 home? He and his wife will require constant doses of EOC from Mr. Adam. Such subsidies can have a dampening effect on ambition and the development of a strong self-image. Yes, Mr. Adam still feels that his son will be more ambitious, more self-confident if only. If only what? If only Nate could live in a neighborhood filled with ambitious high-income achievers. But ambition and confidence are not contracted like a disease. Living near and around ambitious, high-income earners will not automatically transform Nate into a productive person. I have enclosed some statistics about the expenditures of households with Nate's annual income (see Table 8-9). It also includes data about the income and expenditures of Nate's prospective neighbors, those with incomes over $90,000. Note that the total expenditures for these households is $80,645, or more than twice Nate's and his wife's current income.

THE FULL COST OF ACCEPTING EOC

There are often strings attached to the EOC one accepts. A married couple in their mid-forties wanted to build a $570,000 home, but they were a bit short in terms of capital. So the husband asked his wealthy retired parents for a subsidy. They had lived in Ohio for most of their lives and had some interest in moving closer to their son and his family. Atlanta appealed to them, but they had never taken the step of shopping for a home in the area.

Their prospects for moving to Atlanta brightened the day their son called and asked for a home subsidy. Without it he could never afford to build his dream home. If you were his parents, how would you respond to his request? Sure, you may be worth several million dollars, but you are now retired. Your big income-earning years are behind you. You deserve to enjoy your remaining, golden years without providing your adult, college-educated children with a few hundred thousand dollars.

How can you say no without hurting your son's feelings? Should you dare mention that you subsidized his last home purchase? The couple considered various responses, then hit on a sure winner. They told their son that they would provide the subsidy, but there was one condition — his architect would have to make some changes to the home plans.

The parents suggested that the entire basement area be made into an apartment with two bedrooms, full kitchen, one and one-half baths, a den, wall-to-wall carpet, and full appliances. When they finally decided to move out of Ohio, they could just move in with their son and his family, rent free. The move could even be sooner if one died or became disabled. What a great offer! The son would not only receive several hundred thousand dollars; he would also get Mom and Dad. It's hard to believe that he turned down the deal.

9

The Lifestyles of Millionaires: Real vs. Imagined

Thoughts from a "Connecticut Yankee" millionaire:

A joke that struck home. . . . Two friends were walking down a sidewalk when one looked up . . . saw Mr. Crane coming in the opposite direction. Quickly he crossed the street. Then his friend asked: "Why are you avoiding Crane?" "Because he's a man who's living off his capital!"

Although few of us Yankees would shun friends for squandering capital, we certainly wouldn't be caught dead doing it ourselves!

— W.H.H., Ph.D.

Contrast the philosophy of the "Connecticut Yankee" with Mr. RRP's. Mr. RRP (Regional Radio Personality) is the "ultimate consumer." He called me one day and asked if I would be interviewed, and I agreed. He was very persuasive and had a great telephone voice — his show was rated number two or three in the broadcast area.

I wondered why he asked me to show up an hour before airtime, but I found out soon enough when I arrived. He said hello and then got down to his problem. His contract was up for renewal, and he had spent considerable time negotiating with the station's senior executive. He strongly believed that he'd save many dollars if he didn't hire an agent, so he was his own manager. Unfortunately, he wasn't represented by a skilled negotiator. Within ten minutes, Mr. RRP told me his financial problems. At the time, he had more than $30,000 in credit card debt, which translates into over $7,000 in annual interest payments.

This $30,000 balance wasn't unusual for him, either. He'd had this kind of balance outstanding for many years, and often it was more than $30,000. But this was just the first stop on the "tell me your story" trip. Mr. RRP earns more than $100,000 annually, placing him in the top 7 percent of all income-producing individuals in America. What about his level of net worth? Would you suspect that this fellow in his late thirties would be worth several hundred thousand dollars? Actually, Mr. RRP has a negative net worth. How is this possible? Does he have a large family to support? Is he paying medical expenses for an elderly relative? Did he and his wife purchase an expensive home? Is Mr. RRP paying off all of his education loans?

The answer to all of these and related questions is *no!* He is single. He rents his home, and he leases his automobiles. But that's not where all his money goes, and Mr. RRP is not alone. There are many others with the same lifestyle, and they all have one thing in common: They believe that one must spend a lot of money to enjoy life. Mr. RRP is a hyperspender. It's in his mind and in his habits. He believes that buying certain products and services has a direct influence on one's happiness.

Mr. RRP and his group all want to be happy and enjoy life, but there's a problem. He can only do this if his income increases. How should Mr. RRP approach the issue of compensation needs with the senior executive? You probably have an answer that is very different from the strategy he employed. Mr. RRP told his boss what I just outlined, that he was in debt and was unable to make ends meet. But he told him a lot more. Mr. RRP was becoming progressively more worried about the prospect of not being happy, and the only way to be happy is to spend your way into "Enjoyment World."

If you were Mr. RRP's boss, how would you respond to this theme? Your employee needs more money because he's broke. Perhaps, as his boss, you'd be more responsive to a theme based on increases in his productivity, but that wasn't part of Mr. RRP's negotiating theme. Should Mr. RRP's boss give him a raise? It all goes back to basic needs — Mr. RRP needs a job, and he has less than zero wealth. He is at the mercy of his employer, not the other way around. It makes no difference that Mr. RRP owns a dozen watches, two expensive automobiles, has bar tabs at the top singles bars in town, dines at fine restaurants, and has every conceivable type of recreational equipment. He has no wealth. He is at the economic razor's edge. He cannot live for more than a month or two without a paycheck.

This is all bad enough by itself, but Mr. RRP went one step beyond in telling his boss about his economic situation. You probably wouldn't give this guy a raise. Even worse, you might start looking to replace Mr. RRP because you may believe that any key employee who is possessed by possessions and consumption cannot be productive. Having a negative net worth can be very distracting and often has a dampening effect on job performance.

This is an unfortunate situation for Mr. RRP — he forgot something about life. One does not have to buy products and services in order to get a lot out of it. Mr. RRP's lifestyle is one of shopping and consuming. To him, it's impossible to enjoy the summer without having a Jet Ski or two (perhaps on credit). How can he have fun without spending a few hours downing "premier label" scotch at $7 a hit at a trendy bar? Mr. RRP is overspent, overfed, overdressed, overliquored, overtraveled, overentertained, and overindulgent in general. It seems that everything he does outside of working and sleeping costs a lot of money. His focus is Mr. RRP and Mr. RRP's problems, and he believes he can spend his way into the "Club of Happiness."

Mr. RRP's lifestyle is very different from the activities and interests of most millionaires. He thinks millionaires are even more indulgent than he is, but he's completely wrong. Moderation in consumption and a healthy, disciplined lifestyle are the hallmarks of the affluent in America. Are your lifestyle habits congruent with becoming more and more productive? For most people with the millionaire mind the answer is yes. For Mr. RRP the answer is no! Keep Mr. RRP and his lifestyle in mind as you review the activities and interests of millionaires discussed in this chapter.

REAL VS. IMAGINED

Let's review the lifestyle activities that 733 millionaires engaged in during the past month. Before you absorb this information, picture in your mind the typical millionaire. Do you think he is very different in his lifestyle from most people? Remember that the millionaires described in this book are among the most productive business owners, senior corporate executives, physicians, and attorneys in America. They also live in many of the better-quality neighborhoods. Their homes, on average, are worth $1.4 million. They are well educated — about 90 percent are college graduates. They have an average annual realized income of over $600,000 and a net worth in the high seven figures.

Outside of working, what do these people do with their time? If you think that all millionaires are workaholics, you're wrong. Most have a well-balanced style of life, and their activities and interests are not as flashy as Hollywood movie producers and writers in the popular press would have us believe.

Would you expect that attending religious services is too common an activity for self-made millionaires? Surely these people only believe in themselves and their ability to generate high levels of income and wealth. Wrong. Maybe you expect that these millionaires would be more likely found shopping at Brooks Brothers or Saks than eating at Burger King or McDonald's. Try again.

Keep one thing in mind. Millionaires are extraordinarily successful at producing high incomes and accumulating wealth. Activities that directly relate to these goals, like planning investments and consulting with advisers, normally make up a large part of their activity lists. In many other aspects of their lifestyle activities, millionaires are anything but extraordinary. They have a few habits that set them apart from most of us. The proof is in the data. When people ask me about the lifestyles of millionaires, I have a short answer. The typical millionaire is, in three words:

A cheap date!

In Table 9-1, twenty-seven lifestyle activities are listed, along with the percentages of millionaires who engaged in each during the past month. These activities are ranked from 1 to 27 according to the percentage of millionaires who indicated participating in each activity. Table

9-2 groups various activities in larger categories. What activity ranks first, number one?

Socializing with your children and/or grandchildren.

FRIENDS VS. THINGS

Family interaction is ranked first. Second on the activity scale is:

Entertaining close friends.

Remember how much fun you had as a child with your close friends. It didn't cost much to play in the dirt or on the swings with your friends. Millionaires don't spend much to entertain close friends either. How much does it cost to play bridge or have a few friends over for dinner? Not a great deal — it's the interaction with people you care about that's most important.

Too many young people feel that real fun has a dollar cost built into the equation. Fun has become a marketing tool for many consumer goods and services. Do you really need to buy a $50,000 boat so you can hang out with your best friend? Can you live for just one more day without a Jet Ski? If you don't have one, who'd want to be your friend? Is fun only experienced by spending a small fortune at Disney World? Will you fail to make new friends and keep old ones if you don't own a mountain ski lodge?

TABLE 9-1

LIFESTYLE ACTIVITIES OF MILLIONAIRES: A THIRTY-DAY DIARY
(N=733)

ENGAGED IN ACTIVITY DURING THE PAST MONTH/30 DAYS

Activities/Lifestyle Orientation	Percentage	Rank
Socializing with your children/ grandchildren	93	1
Entertaining close friends	88	2
Planning investments	86	3
Studying investment opportunities	78	4
Taking photographs	67	5
Watching your children/grandchildren play sports	61	6
Consulting with an investment adviser	59	7
Studying art/investments	53	8
Attending religious services	52	9
Jogging/running	47	10[1]
Praying	47	10[1]
Eating at McDonald's and/or Burger King	46	12
Playing golf	45	13
Attending lectures	43	14
Attending religious events	37	15
Caring for elderly relatives	35	16
Shopping at Wal-Mart and/or Kmart	31	17[1]
Do-it-yourself carpentry	31	17[1]
Playing the lottery	27	19
Shopping at Saks Fifth Avenue	26	20
Studying/collecting fine wines	25	21
Playing tennis	23	22

TABLE 9-1 (Continued)

LIFESTYLE ACTIVITIES OF MILLIONAIRES: A THIRTY-DAY DIARY (N=733)

ENGAGED IN ACTIVITY DURING THE PAST MONTH/30 DAYS

Activities/Lifestyle Orientation	Percentage	Rank
Shopping via the Internet	22	23[1]
Bible/devotional reading	22	23[1]
Shopping at Brooks Brothers	19	25
Shopping at Sears and/or J. C. Penney	17	26
Off-roading via 4x4	5	27

[1]Tied for this position with another lifestyle activity.

Good friends like you and want to be with you for reasons other than the consumer goods you own.

It's important for America's youth to discover that millionaires, even most decamillionaires, don't depend on consumer goods to enjoy life. Their pleasures and self-satisfaction have more to do with their families, friends, religion, financial independence, physical fitness, and perhaps a bit of golf. Look at it the other way: There is nothing more pitiful than a person who has no close friends, no loving family, yet owns millions of dollars of consumer goods. People like that are a very small segment of the millionaire population. In fact, there is a strong positive correlation between the number of people-related

TABLE 9-2

CATEGORIES OF LIFESTYLE ACTIVITIES OF MILLIONAIRES: A THIRTY-DAY DIARY (N=733)

ENGAGED IN ACTIVITY DURING THE PAST MONTH/30 DAYS

Activities/Lifestyle Orientation	Percentage	Rank
RELIGIOUS		
Attending religious events	37	15
Attending religious services	52	9
Praying	47	10[1]
Bible/devotional reading	22	23[1]
Attending lectures	43	14
INVESTING		
Studying investment opportunities	78	4
Planning investments	86	3
Studying art/investments	53	8
Consulting with an investment adviser	59	7
LOW-BROW/DOWN HOME		
Shopping at Wal-Mart and/or Kmart	31	17[1]
Shopping at Sears and/or J. C. Penney	17	26
Do-it-yourself carpentry	31	17[1]
Eating at McDonald's and/or Burger King	46	12
FAMILY		
Socializing with your children/ grandchildren	93	1
Watching your children/grandchildren play sports	61	6
Caring for elderly relatives	35	16

TABLE 9-2 (Continued)

CATEGORIES OF LIFESTYLE ACTIVITIES OF MILLIONAIRES: A THIRTY-DAY DIARY (N=733)

ENGAGED IN ACTIVITY DURING THE PAST MONTH/30 DAYS

Activities/Lifestyle Orientation	Percentage	Rank
UPSCALE SHOPPING/RECREATION		
Shopping at Brooks Brothers	19	25
Shopping at Saks Fifth Avenue	26	20
Playing golf	45	13
GRAPES IN WOODS		
Off-roading via 4X4	5	27
Studying/collecting fine wines	25	21
FRIENDS AND PHOTOS		
Taking photographs	67	5
Entertaining close friends	88	2
FITNESS		
Jogging/running	47	10[1]
Playing tennis	23	22
INDIVIDUAL EVENTS		
Playing the lottery	27	19
Shopping via the Internet	22	23[1]

[1]Tied for this position with another lifestyle activity.

lifestyle activities one engages in and the level of one's net worth. It's just as a multimillionaire once told me. He coached his daughter's softball team for several years, and although it was not premeditated, he met many successful parents who were business owners. Some of these people ultimately became his clients. It doesn't matter if you're marketing commercial real estate or legal services — it helps to be active, to interact with other successful people.

MORE THAN JUST WATCHING

Many jokes have been written about the high propensity of successful people to play golf and hang out at the country club playing tennis. Many wealthy people do play golf and tennis. As a side note, there is a rather strong positive correlation between one's level of wealth and playing golf.

Decamillionaires are nearly twice as likely to play golf than high-income-producing nonmillionaires.

Golf is important to many millionaires. How does its importance stack up against watching their children play sports? Golf comes in second. Even during the prime golf season, only 45 percent of the millionaires indicated that they played golf in the past month. Golf ranks thirteenth overall. Contrast this with another sports-related event — fully 61 percent of the millionaires indicated:

Watching your children or grandchildren play sports.

A larger percentage of millionaires watched their children play sports (61 percent) than played golf (45 percent) or tennis (23 percent). The significance of watching children play sports is more than their love for the children. About one-half the millionaires surveyed played competitive sports at some time in their lives, even if it was only JV football or freshman softball in high school. Most of the participants believe they benefited from playing competitive sports. A certain competitive nature may have been enhanced as a result. They learned about the importance of teamwork through these experiences. There is an additional benefit — the data indicate that people who played sports in school exercise more often during their adult years. The health and psychological benefits of regular exercise are well documented.

Most affluent parents encourage their children to participate in sports. They believe that it's part of becoming a well-rounded individual. And they spend time watching them play. This doesn't mean that millionaire parents are superior to others or that they love their kids more. It's a matter of the discretion people have over their time, and about priorities.

There is a strong positive correlation between one's level of net worth and the

frequency with which they watch their children play sports.

How can it be possible? The hallmark of being wealthy is having control over how you allocate your time. Data from my national surveys indicates this relationship is a strong one indeed. Therefore, it's not surprising that the turnout of parents at after-school athletic events is greater in affluent areas as opposed to blue-collar districts, because the affluent have more discretion over their time than the nonaffluent. Since most millionaires are self-employed business owners or professionals, they make their own schedules. Even senior executives employed by public corporations have much discretion over their time. They are given a task, and how they complete it is up to them. For blue-collar workers on an assembly line or driving a truck during game time, work takes priority. The major difference between millionaires and those of average wealth is how they are compensated. Millionaires are usually paid according to performance and results, while most others are paid by the hour, pieces produced, or some other specific constraints on their time and motion. In sharp contrast, economic success is a direct function of being able to define one's own allocation of time and motion.

CHEAP DATE
Since you can't be in two places at one time, if

you're watching your kids play ball you can't be shopping at Brooks Brothers or Saks. If you're socializing with your children, even just playing catch in the backyard, you can't be putting money in a slot machine at a casino. This all is part of the "cheap date" concept.

Just look at the numbers in Table 9-3. Contrast the percentages of millionaires who reported engaging in various activities. The "cheap date" activities outpace the ones that cost dollars. It's actually more than an issue of costs — many "cheap date" activities actually enhance one's productivity. Note also in Table 9-3 that nearly one-half of the millionaires (47 percent) engaged in prayer. It doesn't cost much to consult with God, and for a significant percentage of millionaires, their religious faith is a major force in their lives. It's also an important factor that actually underlies their economic and spiritual success, as detailed in chapter 4, "The Relationship Between Courage and Wealth."

There are several other dimensions to the "cheap date" concept. Most millionaires are not the do-it-yourself types, especially when a task takes more than a few hours to complete. They know that time is money. The typical millionaire earns more than $320 per hour from his or her main vocation. If they need a shelf installed, it may take an hour just to saw, sand, and finish, not to mention the additional time to shop for wood. Then it takes more time to install it. If it ultimately requires three or four hours to install

TABLE 9-3

"CHEAP DATE" VS. COSTLY ACTIVITIES: LIFESTYLES OF THE MILLIONAIRE'S
(N=733)

"Cheap Date" Activity	Percentage	vs. Costly Activity	Percentage
Watching your children/grand-children play sports	61	Shopping at Brooks Brothers	19
Planning investments	86	Shopping at Saks Fifth Avenue	26
Praying	47	Shopping at Brooks Brothers	19
Entertaining close friends	88	Shopping via the Internet	22
Studying investment opportunities	78	Studying/collecting fine wines	25
Attending religious services	52	Playing the lottery	27
Socializing with your children/grand-children	93	Shopping at Brooks Brothers	19
Taking photographs	67	Off-roading via 4X4	5

THE REALITIES OF THE MONTHLY DIARY

Absolute Difference (Percentage)	Ratio: Higher Percentage to Lower Percentage	Activity with Higher Percentage
42	3.2	"Cheap Date"
60	3.3	"Cheap Date"
28	2.5	"Cheap Date"
66	4.0	"Cheap Date"
53	3.1	"Cheap Date"
25	1.9	"Cheap Date"
74	4.9	"Cheap Date"
62	13.4	"Cheap Date"

a $10 piece of wood on a wall, that shelf actually costs between $1,050 and $1,400 in lost opportunity.

It's not only economics that dictates the millionaire's aversion to do-it-yourself tasks. What's the number one substitute for do-it-yourself activities? For millionaires, it's playing golf. There is a very strong negative correlation between the time spent playing golf and do-it-yourself activities. Golf can be expensive, considering the cost of club membership, greens fees, equipment, and clothing. But millionaires justify the expenses and opportunity costs associated with playing golf.

It's not golf. The real game on the fairway is cultivating new customers and keeping current ones happy.

Golf ranks thirteenth on the activity scale, well below planning investments, at number 3. Planning investments is an individual sport, and no special equipment is needed. Just ask all the millionaires I bump into at the library. I'm there doing research for my books, and they're there waiting in line to review the latest *Value Line* and *Standard & Poor* reports. It doesn't cost a penny to get into the library, and you don't even need a library card to gain access to many of the finest investment-research vehicles.

There is some benefit to studying lifestyle activities in terms of a twelve-month period because then we can include annual activities like vacations and preparing personal income tax returns. Table 9-4 lists thirty lifestyle activities, along with percentages and corresponding ranks of millionaires who engaged in each activity at least once during the past twelve months. Table 9-5 groups these activities into categories of similar pursuits.

Most of these lifestyle activities are very different from the lavish lifestyles that people imagine — those are more common among nonmillionaires with high incomes than among first-generation millionaires. This same pseudo-affluent lifestyle among the nonmillionaires in America explains why most high-living people never become wealthy.

When the term *millionaire* is mentioned, most Americans have visions of a highbrow, high-consumption lifestyle. Ask the general population about the activities and interests of millionaires on an annual basis — which of the following do you think would rank high?

- Skiing in the Rockies?
- Skiing in the Alps?
- Sailing on a yacht?
- Gambling at casinos?
- Taking an ocean cruise around the world?
- Vacationing in Palm Springs?

- Attending a Grand Slam tennis tournament?
- Vacationing in Paris?

If you guessed any of these activities, you'd be wrong. They all rank in the bottom half on the frequency scale.

The number one activity is consulting with a tax expert.

Is this your vision of millionaires and multi-millionaires in America? Why do so many millionaires participate in this activity? It may have something to do with the fact that the typical millionaire in this study paid more than $300,000 in taxes on last year's income. Nearly one in five paid more than $1 million. The rich pay a lot more than their fair share of taxes in this country. Those with annual realized incomes of $1 million or more make up less than one-tenth of one percent of the households in America, but they account for about 14.7 percent of all the income tax collected. Obviously, most millionaires see the benefit of consulting with tax experts. Even a 5 percent or 10 percent reduction in taxes is the equivalent of paying for all or a big part of their child's college tuition.

Note something else related to income tax: Only 30 percent of the millionaires surveyed prepare their own taxes, and one-third of these are CPAs or tax attorneys. There's a pattern here that's interesting. There is a very strong, statisti-

TABLE 9-4

LIFESTYLE ACTIVITIES OF MILLIONAIRES: A TWELVE-MONTH DIARY
(N=733)

ENGAGED IN ACTIVITY DURING THE PAST YEAR/12 MONTHS

Activities/Lifestyle Orientation	Percentage	Rank
Consulting with a tax expert	85	1
Going to museums	81	2
Community/civic activities	68	3
Gardening	67	4
Raising funds for charity	64	5
Attending a major league sporting event	62	6
Trade/professional association activities	61	7
Attending a Broadway play	60	8
Attending fund-raising balls	57	9[1]
Vacationing overseas	57	9[1]
Attending antique fairs/sales	49	11
Shopping for original art	42	12
Playing the lottery	33	13
Preparing your own taxes	30	14[1]
Fishing	30	14[1]
Do-it-yourself plumbing	27	16
Camping/hiking	25	17[1]
Gambling at a casino	25	17[1]
Skiing in the Rockies	22	19
Vacationing in Paris	20	20[1]
Sailing on a yacht	20	20[1]
Mowing your own lawn	19	22
Attending a rock concert	17	23[1]

TABLE 9-4 (Continued)

Activities/Lifestyle Orientation	Percentage	Rank
Vacationing in Palm Springs	17	23[1]
Painting your home's exterior	13	25
Attending a Grand Slam tennis tournament	11	26[1]
Hunting/shooting	11	26[1]
"White-water" activities	9	28
Skiing in the Alps	4	29
Taking an ocean cruise around the world	3	30

[1]Tied for this position with another lifestyle activity.

cally significant, negative correlation between the do-it-yourself activities listed and wealth. In rank order according to the degree of significance these include:

1. Mowing your own lawn
2. Do-it-yourself plumbing
3. Preparing your own taxes
4. Painting your home's exterior

Those with lower levels of accumulated wealth have a higher tendency to do all or most of these activities. In sharp contrast, there is a strong correlation between one's level of wealth and hiring a professional to do one's taxes.

Perhaps multimillionaires once did many do-it-yourself tasks prior to becoming decamillionaires. As a rule, this is not the case, nor does age account for much of the variation in do-it-

TABLE 9-5

LIFESTYLE ACTIVITIES OF MILLIONAIRES: A TWELVE-MONTH DIARY GROUPED BY DOMAINS (N=733)

ENGAGED IN ACTIVITY DURING THE PAST YEAR/ 12 MONTHS

Activities/Lifestyle Orientation	Percentage	Rank
CIVIC RESPONSIBILITIES		
Raising funds for charity	64	5
Community/civic activities	68	3
Attending fund-raising balls	57	9[1]
ART, ENTERTAINMENT, AND/OR TRAVEL		
Shopping for original art	42	12
Attending antique fairs/sales	49	11
Going to museums	81	2
Attending a Broadway play	60	8
Vacationing overseas	57	9[1]
Vacationing in Paris	20	20[1]
DO-IT-YOURSELFERS		
Gardening	67	4
Mowing your own lawn	19	22
Do-it-yourself plumbing	27	16
Painting your home's exterior	13	25
Preparing your own taxes	30	14[1]
SPORTS		
Skiing in the Rockies	22	19
Skiing in the Alps	4	29
Attending a Grand Slam tennis tournament	11	26[1]
Attending a major league sporting event	62	6

OUTDOOR ADVENTURES		
Camping/hiking	25	17[1]
"White-water" activities	9	28
Attending a rock concert	17	23[1]
SPORTSMAN		
Fishing	30	14[1]
Sailing on a yacht	20	20[1]
Hunting/shooting	11	26[1]
GAMES OF CHANCE		
Gambling at a casino	25	17[1]
Playing the lottery	33	13
Trade/professional association activities	61	7
UPSCALE TRAVELER		
Vacationing in Palm Springs	17	23[1]
Taking an ocean cruise around the world	3	30
TAX SENSITIVE		
Consulting with a tax expert	85	1

[1]Tied for this position with another factor.

---

yourself activity among the high-income or high-net-worth groups. In fact, there is strong evidence that do-it-yourself activities are substitutes to building wealth.

Actually, you are not the first to hear these results. I told my wife about this relationship just moments after examining the computer output. She was not moved by the empirical data.

MRS. STANLEY: Millionaires . . . not doing things around the home! What do they do with their spare time?

DR. STANLEY: They are involved in activities that enhance their wealth.

MRS. STANLEY: Enlighten me after you take out the beagle.

THE
MOST SIGNIFICANT SUBSTITUTE

Of the thirty lifestyle activities listed in the twelve-month diary, one stands out as having the most significant inverse relationship with net worth.

PLAYING THE LOTTERY

The higher a person's net worth the less likely he is to ever play the lottery.

OUTSIDE THE OFFICE

What high-income-producing young person today will probably become tomorrow's millionaire? One who works hard and selects an ideal vocation. But if this person plans to enhance his net worth in the future, he must become involved in certain outside activities. First, work closely with tax advisers and tax-advantaged investment consultants. Then become active in your community. There is no more noble lifestyle activity than:

Raising funds for charity.

Note that nearly two-thirds of the millionaires (64 percent) engaged in this activity in the past twelve months, and there was a very strong positive correlation between this activity and net worth.

Some may contend that fund-raising is an activity for those who are already very rich, the "seniors" of the affluent population. Or they suggest that raising funds for charity is an activity dominated by people who inherited their wealth. In fact, volunteering time to raise funds for charity is not significantly related to age or inherited wealth, and it's not dominated by older multimillionaires. Nor is it purely the domain of those who are already wealthy. Most of today's millionaires were raising funds for good causes before they became financially independent, and most did it because of noble intent.

Good deeds do get rewarded even here on earth. Financially successful people and the next generation of economically productive people volunteer. When they cluster in various fund-raising situations, they get to know and appreciate each other. People are always seen at their best when involved in noble causes, and their reputation and integrity are, in turn, enhanced.

Over the years of studying successful people, I have discovered a simple rule.

If you wish to become affluent, associate with economically productive people.

Outside of fund-raising, are there other life-style activities related to one's level of wealth? The more wealth one accumulates, the more likely one is to engage in art, entertainment, and travel activities. Fifty-seven percent of the millionaires took overseas vacations during the past year, but decamillionaires are even more prone to international travel — seven out of ten engaged in this activity.

Does this disprove the theory that millionaires only spend money in ways that enhance their wealth? It's logical to assume that vacations are for pleasure, not for business, investment purposes, or tax-advantage expenditures. But for many millionaires a vacation, especially overseas, can and often does enhance their net worth.

Consider the physician who is self-employed. Last year, he had a net income of nearly $1 million. Dr. Edwards is an outstanding physician in part because he constantly keeps up with changes and innovations in medicine. He also writes and publishes articles related to his own work, and he is often asked to present research papers at regional, national, and international medical conventions.

There are many conventions and opportunities for Dr. Edwards to lecture — he usually has several letters on his desk from different associations that want him to make a presentation at their meetings. Some even offer a modest stipend of $1,000 and pay for his lodging. He has many frequent-flier miles built up from all those trips taken in the past — enough to fly his whole family for free anywhere in the world.

Given the choice of Chicago in February or Paris in May, it's no wonder that Dr. Edwards takes frequent overseas vacations. He can kill two birds with one stone. He can give his presentation, in part a cost of doing business, and he and his wife can do what about one-half of the other overseas-bound millionaires do — go to Europe to purchase or "invest" in original art and attend antique auctions.

Dr. Edwards' case is typical among multimillionaires. Only a minority of multimillionaires travel overseas for the sole purpose of vacationing. For most, there is some other issue at hand, usually a mix of business, investing, and pleasure, but not necessarily in that order. There are certain tax advantages of blending business with pleasure, but before you plan your travel overseas with tax and business benefits in mind, consult a CPA or tax attorney. There are many gray areas about blending business, pleasure, and investments in art and antiques.

In general, productive people have more opportunities to accomplish this blending, and they often have their vacations subsidized.

IN SEARCH OF THE MILLIONAIRES

Imagine you are a young, inexperienced market researcher who had been assigned to interview millionaires. You had a large expense account that enabled you to travel all over the world, and you found some millionaires in the places you looked. Your boss was not completely satisfied with your work.

You reported that you found millionaires vacationing in Paris, but your boss referred you to Table 9-6, showing that only 20 percent were vacationing in Paris last year. Then he asked if you'd visited any of the tax consultants that millionaires patronize. You didn't think of this angle, because, like most people, you envision wealthy people at play, on expensive vacations. You never thought of them sitting in an adviser's office working on their tax situations, but they are more than four times as likely to be found there than vacationing in Paris.

So your boss was not at all pleased with your efforts to find millionaires who were skiing in the Alps. Only four in one hundred did that last year. There were a lot of millionaires on that ocean cruise you took last year, but they were not a representative sample. Only three millionaires in one hundred were aboard such cruises. Your boss suggested strongly that you find another line of work. In fact, you're in the process of being replaced. Your boss just hired a young woman who is very active in raising funds for charities. Ellen persuaded your boss to hire her because she claims that most millionaires are active in raising funds for noble causes, and she already works with many of them. As the num-

TABLE 9-6

"A DATE" WITH A TAX EXPERT AND FUND-ACTIVITIES: THE REALITIES OF THE (N=733)

The "Tonier" Activities	Percentage
Vacationing in Paris	20
Skiing in the Rockies	22
Skiing in the Alps	4
Attending a Grand Slam tennis tournament	11
Sailing on a yacht	20
Vacationing in Palm Springs	17
Taking an ocean cruise around the world	3

bers in Table 9-6 indicate, Ellen is correct in her assertion that extravagant consumption is out and fund-raising is in among millionaires. Fund-raising outpaces:

- Vacationing in Paris   3 to 1
- Skiing in the Alps   16 to 1
- Attending a Grand Slam tennis tournament   6 to 1
- Sailing on a yacht   3 to 1
- Taking an ocean cruise around the world   21 to 1

RAISING VS. THE "TONIER" MILLIONAIRE'S TWELVE-MONTH DIARY

Consulting with a Tax Expert Percentage (Ratio to Tonier Activities)	Raising Funds for Charity Percentage (Ratio to Tonier Activities)
85(4.3)	64(3.2)
85(3.9)	64(2.9)
85(21.3)	64(16.0)
85(7.7)	64(5.8)
85(4.3)	64(3.2)
85(5.0)	64(3.8)
85(28.3)	64(21.3)

A WAKE-UP CALL

Is it true that the early bird catches the worm? Perhaps. But people are not robins. If becoming a millionaire was a direct function of getting up earlier than others, many school-bus drivers and milkmen would be rich. Most are not millionaires. It would be too easy. Look at it another way. There are no sure things about becoming wealthy. Certain significant factors can explain variations in wealth, and probability statements can be made. But it's not possible to say with 100 percent certainty that John Smith or Jane

Doe will become millionaires if they wake up early in the morning.

At one time I did believe what my folks taught me — that waking up earlier than others would enhance my income and ultimately my net worth. Way back when, I spent many weekend hours caddying. During my first year, the caddy master had a problem. Several senior caddies complained that the caddy master was "playing favorites." They told some important people at the club about the political nature of allocating caddy assignments.

I'm not sure that there was a political agenda, but the caddy master was on the hot spot. Frankly, I was not much concerned. I was the youngest and least experienced twelve-year-old in the caddy stable, so I was always given the bags of two guys who never tipped. I always ended up with "Bob and Andy Ancient" or some of their relatives. They were typically in their late eighties or nineties. Not only did I have to carry their bags, I also had to carry their folding seats. As a rule, it took the "Ancient" brothers six to eight hours to play eighteen holes of golf, including their ninety-minute lunch. Even with many "mulligans," these so-called golfers never broke 110!

But the "Ancient" brothers' act never really bothered me. I was the lowest caddy on the experience scale, and they were multimillionaires, household names in American industry. So I suspect they thought I was overpaid. But some of the older caddies hated to work for these guys.

Some felt the caddy master gave the really good tippers to his relatives and to friends of his sons.

To solve this problem, the club agreed to an objective method of assigning work — the "first in, first out" method. The caddy who arrived first each morning would be assigned to the first twosome or foursome. How simple. How very democratic. Yet how unproductive.

The system didn't last very long. The better, more competitive golfers were the first to protest. In the past they always got the best, most experienced caddies to work for them. They insisted on it. And they often employed the same caddies each time they played golf. More often than not, they were very generous in allocating tips according to the performance of the fellows who carried their bags. But there is more to being a caddy than carrying a bag.

A good caddy is an instructor, consultant, coach, and motivator all in one. When the best players were hooked up with caddies who lacked these qualities they got angry. They hated the "first in, first out" system.

In a way this is analogous to building wealth in America. The more productive people, whether they be caddies or attorneys, earn more than less productive ones. Just because an attorney shows up earlier than others at a court proceeding does not ensure that he'll win the case.

At any rate, the caddy system based on arrival time failed big-time. On the first Saturday it was introduced I arrived at the caddy station at 7:00

A.M. The place was already filled with caddies. So the following Saturday I woke up at 4:00 A.M. and pedaled my bike through beautiful Westchester County to the club, arriving before 5:30 A.M. But I still wasn't first in line — there were five or six fellows already standing in front of the caddy house. The really early arrivals were sleeping on the men's room floor. They'd been there since about 11:00 P.M. the night before.

How could anyone win this contest? Was this the most productive use of anyone's time and energy? It's the same answer in regard to accumulating wealth. People who are self-made millionaires had to figure out a way to become financially independent. They selected a vocation that rewarded them for being productive during the hours that they work. In essence, it's not what time people start their workday or get up in the morning that makes them financially successful — it's how productive they are during the working hours that counts.

Are the best-prepared, most knowledgeable, most productive teachers and professors paid more than the less productive ones? Not usually. Only in the most competitive colleges and universities are the most productive faculty members rewarded for their superior performances. In other schools, it's just a matter of how many hours, days, years a professor has been a member of the faculty. A "first in" mentality is not tolerated by ambitious and productive people. Seniority should only be relevant when objective performance measures are given most of the weight in allocating economic resources. Without such incentives the productive people will move on or become less productive. Those who remain are the people who watch clocks and calendars. So what if they were hired first yet produce little?

What does this have to do with becoming wealthy in America? If you work in an environment that rewards performance, you will probably be motivated through economic opportunities to perform at a high level.

Getting up earlier than others isn't difficult. It does not take a great deal of intelligence. But being first is important in another regard. If you are the first to come up with an innovative product, you'll probably beat out all those who get up earlier than you because they place greater importance on arriving early than on developing a creative product. So let all those who want to offer "me too" products and services wake up before dawn. Working twelve-hour days may be a requirement to just getting by in a cutthroat industry.

Keep one thing in mind about the "first in" mentality, the system that is so pervasive in the civil service sector of our economy. Very few millionaires are civil servants, and they have a completely different orientation. They want to be compensated on the basis of performance. They do not want it any other way. They would never be able to motivate themselves if they worked in an environment where the first to arrive or the first to be hired was automatically given the lion's share of the economic resources.

In terms of millionaires and high-income-producing nonmillionaires:

There is no statistically significant correlation between the time one wakes up in the morning and one's wealth.

The typical millionaire wakes up each workday about 6:40 A.M. The median figure is approximately 6:25 A.M. Only about one in five rises before 5:40 A.M.

I used to wake up much earlier. I also used to write for eight or ten hours a day when I wasn't teaching. But I discovered that my books and papers were completed faster when I wrote for just three or four hours per day. Ultimately, it's the quality of the writing, not ten-hour days, that produces a best-selling book. If a writer's brain, the idea generator, shuts down after three or four hours of writing, the result of six-hour writing days may be pure junkola.

How often have you heard about the hard-charging entrepreneurs who awaken at 3:00 A.M. each day? So much for common knowledge. There is no statistically significant difference among millionaires in various occupational groups in regard to the time that they wake up each workday. Senior corporate executives wake up a bit earlier, on average, than others, but this is not a significant difference.

One of my mentors was Dr. Bill Darden, a leading authority on lifestyle research. His office was directly across from mine while I was in graduate school. At that time, Bill was an associate professor. I noticed that he arrived each day in the mid- or late-morning hours. His door was always open while he was there — Bill was very kind to graduate students who sought his advice. He gave a lot of his time to those who asked for it. When then did Bill do all his research and writing? I found out early one morning.

I entered the computer center at about 2:00 A.M. one day to run some very large programs that required a lot of computer time and thus were relegated to the late-night shift. Not too many people were there, but Bill was running his programs. He told me that most early mornings he was working, writing programs and "crunching numbers." He had no graduate assistant who could do these things for him.

My fellow graduate students thought that Dr. Bill Darden started his day at 10:00 or 11:00 A.M., but they were at least half wrong. Bill actually had two workday mornings. The first began around 1:00 A.M. and lasted until his programs ran; he went to bed at 3:00 A.M. Then he was up at 9:00 A.M. and arrived at the office between 10:00 and 11:00 A.M. At most top universities and colleges, faculty members work long and hard, but you may not see many of them in their offices at 8:00 each morning. They work when they want to work and make their own hours. So it is with many affluent and productive people. If you could control your workday and make your own schedule, perhaps you would decide that the 8:00 to 5:00 mandate doesn't fit your style. As long as you are productive, it matters little that you are crunching numbers at 2:30 A.M. or at 10:00 A.M. But don't try this if your employer stipulates that you must be at your desk from 8:00 to 5:00.

Why do the Dr. Bill Dardens of the world sometimes work better at 2:30 A.M. than at 9:00 A.M.? He discovered that the computer center was always too crowded, too distracting during normal office hours. He became a distinguished professor, in part, because his ideas were published in top academic journals. The people who judged his work never asked if the author worked from 8:00 to 5:00 or from 2:00 to 9:00; they looked at the finished product. Not everybody is at their mental and physical best from 8:00 to 5:00. Bill told me that his best, most productive work and ideas usually showed up before dawn. That's when most other people were asleep. When are you most productive? Does this time coincide with your scheduled work time? If not, consider changing your schedule, and it's much easier to do that when you are your own scheduler!

10

A Final Note About the Millionaire Mind

What do most millionaires tell me they learned in their salad years? They learned to:

Think differently from the crowd.

Much of this book has been designed around a central theme: It pays to be different. I have never been interested in studying what one of my respondents calls the "beautiful people." He described them as people who seem destined to succeed in life. They supposedly have extremely high IQs; received all As in grades pre-K through law school, medical school, graduate school, or other school; have graduated with top honors from the best schools and colleges in America; possess great looks; are tall with blue eyes; were Division I All-Americans in four varsity sports; trace their ancestors and trust accounts back to the Battle of Hastings in 1066; never break a sweat yet earn millions of dollars each year; play par golf; are on every board of every noble cause; have no cavities or physical ailments whatsoever; have had five adoring wives or husbands, all of whom were supermodels; and so on, and so on.

Why do I have no interest in beautiful people? I have never met one millionaire who had all these qualities. Yet most nonmillionaires think that these so-called beautiful people make up the bulk of the millionaire population in America. But I am still searching. I am most interested, however, in people like Paule Rossmann, the fighter pilot ace with an injured arm. You will recall from chapter 1 that he compensated for his deficiency. He adjusted to his problem. Actually, his lack of one normally key attribute was the catalyst for his change in strategy. He was an ace because he tapped his creative sense. He found a better way to defeat competitors who were, in the context of fighter pilots, beautiful people. They were physical perfection.

Physical perfection may be important in dogfights, but Rossmann avoided such contests. He won because he selected the target, the time, the place, the altitude, the angle of attack. He was proactive. I have to wonder how many of the beautiful people whom he shot down realized that their opponent had only one good arm. Rossmann was also the mentor to the Ace of Aces, the holder of the world's record for in air victories, Erich Hartmann.

Whom do you want for a mentor? I want someone who is not a beautiful person. I want to learn about how to become economically productive from those who had one or more imperfections. They are the ones who figured out how to win. Most of these aces of economic productivity have few of the characteristics of beautiful people. Interestingly, many of my respondents have told me that if they were beautiful, partly beautiful, or totally beautiful, they would have never become so productive. Why not? Because they would never have had the need to be so very careful in selecting the ideal vocation vocation vocation.

Consider the following case example. You decide if Donald and Winifred Sonner are beautiful people. Or perhaps they have a bit of Paule Rossmann in them.

A PROFILE OF DONALD AND WINIFRED SONNER, SOUTHERN BLOOMER MANUFACTURING COMPANY

The way Donald Sonner tells it, he has never really had a job in his life — at least not working for anyone else. The sixty-four-year-old head of Southern Bloomer Manufacturing Company in Bristol, Tennessee, says he has been up and down the ladder many times since he became a millionaire for the first time when he was twenty-four. What led him to work for himself? And how did he come up with the idea of manufacturing underwear for prisons and patches for guns — all out of scrap cloth? "As a very young man on a farm, we worked awful hard," he remembers.

In those days we had to get our mail from a post office, that was in a country store, and I would go to the store for the mail.

While I was in the store, many times, these peddlers would come through selling gloves, pipes, socks — that type of thing. Whenever the man who ran the store would pay them, they'd stick it on a big roll in their pocket. They always had a big roll of money, and coming from a farm, we'd never seen money. These guys had more money than God.

When I was fifteen — I had an old pickup truck — I went to North Carolina to buy socks. I had sold two heifer calves and I was looking for [the socks] cheap. When I came back, I realized I'd bought seconds and couldn't sell them to the stores. So I went to sawmill camps and sold my socks. Finally, I sold them all and made a pretty good profit. Next time I went and bought more, but I knew more what I was looking for.

Since that experience, Mr. Sonner has made (and sometimes lost) his fortune by divining perhaps unusual markets for his less-than-top-quality goods.

I'm in the junk business. I'm the guy that buys the seconds, the odd-lot cloth, out of textile mills. I'm their dumpster man. And I've developed a business that will consume those goods.

What makes a business like mine function is the fact that we have the capital to take [the cloth] whether we're moving it or not, like a used-auto-parts place with car parts. We try to sell off

596

everything we can and the last resort is we turn them into rags and sell them to industries.

For example, the Sonners have almost cornered the market for gun-cleaning patches, which he makes from the scrap gathered from the cutting-room and even the sewing-room floor after he's made his garments (also, of course, made from imperfect cloth). He says of the gun-patch business:

At first I was laughed at. People said, "He can't last long." But this was money from heaven: I had an endless supply. And it has grown into a substantial business for us.

Sawmills for second-quality socks, the military for gun patches — in between these markets he built Southern Bloomer on another market most folks wouldn't have thought of: prisons and mental institutions for his second-quality garments.

He began making underpants for prisoners after he had lost all his fortune. His choice of market meant he didn't have to have uniform, first-quality goods, so he could start with a smaller operation.

There was a mental institution up the road and I said, "They got women there." They needed an item that would go through their big heavy steam laundry. By buying this odd-lot cloth, I could give them a lot for their money. And with this little operation, I could put a lot of sewing into it.

When you have something to sell, you've got to learn where there's a market.

In today's apparel market, where the big chains have erased the old market of thousands of smaller stores, a smaller business must be more creative, he says, and develop ideas that do not require much capital.

Mr. Sonner's wife, Winifred, runs the business with him, and he says she is a great partner, spearheading marketing and allowing him to handle manufacturing. "She's a gorgeous woman, but she's gorgeous in the inside too," Mr. Sonner says, "and willing to fight to win."

In business you have to sacrifice a lot. My first wife was a little country girl from the mountains. As a young man I made an awful lot of money selling women's apparel. As we made money, it became very important to her, to the point where she was rotten with it. Money affects some people differently.

Winifred and I are comfortable with each other regardless of where we are. We make a tremendous team. I don't know who's the boss, but there's a kind of a magic between us.

So what is important in business and life — loving your job, the money, having a good education? Mr. Sonner says:

You have to like what you're doing — like a rabbit dog. You chase this rabbit and forget about everything else but catching the rabbit. You have to live it, but you get enjoyment out of some success in it.

I do not have a great education: just a year of high school. You develop a feel for ideas that don't take much money. I don't think educational background in most cases is as important as the will to win.

Making money while watching his costs was a hard-learned lesson for Mr. Sonner, and one he would recommend to young people who want to go into business for themselves.

A lot of people I don't have anything in common with, they talk about their payments. I wouldn't have anything I had a payment on for anything in this world. Borrowed money has been my downfall. Today I wouldn't borrow a dime.

A self-made person is not a person generally who's trying to impress someone. I could drive any car I want. But I drive an '88 model minivan. It's in good shape. I bought it used in '90 for $5,000. I drive an '82 Volvo. It's clean. It's a nice car. I think I paid $3,000 for it.

You've got to do one of two things. Either have a master's degree in a good field or work like hell and use your mind to start something small.

Borrowing too much money ranks high on his list of bad business ideas.

[Borrowing] a lot of money for a new business is the worst thing in the world. If you don't have any money, you learn how to do things without. If you have money, you make mistakes. The more money, the bigger the mistakes.

You're paying interest twenty-four hours a day, seven days a week. If you don't have any banks breathing down your throat maybe you don't do as much — but it doesn't take so much to feed them.

Another common downfall of start-up ventures is too much inventory, he says.

Inventory is the death of a lot of small businesses. I always thought the produce business was good, because you either sell it or you smell it, so you learn to make it move.

And you have to sacrifice. You learn to do with less and, in turn, you grow the business. That's the reason second- and third-generation kids can't keep their parents' business growing. Their parents watched out for the pitfalls, and the kids don't have that experience.

THE EIGHT PARTS

The case of Donald and Winifred Sonner is a true-to-life pro forma of economic success. It details the importance of hard work, focus, courage, not following the crowd with "me too" product offerings, and choice of spouse. The American economy rewards those who are of the millionaire mind. So keep in mind the eight important elements of the economic success equation:

1. Understand the key success factors our economy continues and will continue to reward: hard work, integrity, and focus.
2. Never allow a lackluster academic record to stand in the way of becoming economically productive.
3. Have the courage to take some financial risk. And learn how to overcome defeat.
4. Select a vocation that is not only unique and profitable; pick one you love.
5. Be careful in selecting a spouse. Those who are economically productive married husbands or wives who had the characteristics that are compatible with success.
6. Operate an economically productive household. Many millionaires prefer to repair or refinish rather than buy new.
7. Follow the lead of millionaires when selecting a home. Study, search, and negotiate aggressively.
8. Adopt a balanced lifestyle. Many millionaires are "cheap dates." It does not take a lot of money to enjoy the company of your family and friends.

Appendix 1

In Search of the
Balance Sheet Affluent

<u>TARGETING BY NEIGHBORHOOD</u>

For each of the 226,399 Census Block Groups/
neighborhoods in the United States, an estimate
of the incidence of millionaire households was
made. Millionaire households were defined in
terms of net worth. The proportion of millionaire
households in each neighborhood was determined by using the proprietary methodology developed by Jon Robbin.

This methodology entails adjusting unearned
income for underreporting, capitalizing it with a
rational rate of real return, and estimating net
worth through a nonlinear fit to a Lorenz curve
expressing the proportion of net worth attributable to the sources measured by the Census as a
function of the size of unearned income (dividends, interest, and rent royalty). The empirical
basis for the model is derived from the Survey of
Consumer Finance (Federal Reserve) and its
wealth oversample. Internal Revenue Service
Statistics of Income series and studies provide
the basis for estimating the real rate of return.

Using this methodology, Jon produced a rank
ordering of all 226,399 neighborhoods in de-

scending sequence of the incidence of million-aires. This step permitted a specific selection of the highest incidence areas for identifying a sample of household within them as prospective survey respondents with a high likelihood of being millionaires as defined above.

Potential respondents were selected randomly from neighborhoods with over 30 percent inci-dence of millionaires within each stratum of mil-lionaire incidence. This stratified sample was designed so that there would be an increasingly higher proportion of millionaires selected for those neighborhoods that contained the highest incidence of millionaire household, i.e., 50 per-cent, 60 percent, 90 percent, and so forth. The 2,487 neighborhoods selected were estimated to contain the highest concentrations of house-holds that were in the millionaire category.

Commercial list organizations were able to supply head-of-household names and addresses for approximately 95 percent of the number of Census-tabulated homes in these 2,487 neigh-borhoods. Addresses with more than three lines and with more than one name at the same phone number were purged because of the high proba-bility that they were commercial organizations. More than 5,000 households were selected at random for use in surveys from the enumerated households in the 2,487 neighborhoods.

The national geodemographically based survey was conducted from May 20, 1998, to August 24, 1998. Each head of 5,063 households received a nine-page questionnaire, a form letter asking for his participation, and a one dollar bill as a response incentive. Also included was a business reply envelope in which to return the completed questionnaire. A total of 1,001 surveys were completed in time to be included in the analysis. Overall, the response rate was 19.8 percent. Out of the 1,001 respondents, 733 or 73.2 percent of the total had a household net worth of $1 million or more.

A PRETEST SAMPLE

I supplemented this survey with an alternative survey. Ad hoc surveys of this type are useful because even the most sophisticated geocoding methods typically ignore millionaires who reside in areas that contain lower concentrations of high-net-worth households. This survey was also used as a pretest for the questionnaire design and the overall research methodology. All 638 millionaires who responded had the income statement and balance sheet credentials that would qualify them for jumbo mortgages.

Appendix 2

BUSINESSES OWNED AND MANAGED BY MILLIONAIRES

(NATIONAL GEODEMOGRAPHICALLY BASED SAMPLE)

The Net Worth of This Respondent Was —— Times the Expected Value[1]	Business Type Designated by Respondent
17[2]	Steel Manufacturing
14	Commercial Banking
13	Construction Contracting
12	Oil Production
9	Computer Software
7	Retail Clothing
7	Outdoor Advertising
7	Fasteners Manufacturing
6	Lumber Distribution
6	Real Estate Investment Companies
6	Landscaping
5	General Contracting
5	Computer Manufacturing
5	Real Estate Investment Companies
5	Beauty Salons
5	Discount Retailing
5	Textile Manufacturing
5	Real Estate Investment Companies

The Net Worth of This Respondent Was —— Times the Expected Value[1]	Business Type Designated by Respondent
5	High-Technology Manufacturing
5	Service
5	Venture Capital
4	Industrial Design
4	Funeral Services
4	Export Services
4	Marketing Services
4	Investment Banking
4	Health Care
4	Distribution
4	Management Consulting
4	Soil Testing/Engineering
4	Management Consulting
4	Marketing Communications
4	Accounting
4	Apparel Manufacturing Design
4	Automobile Dealerships
4	Talent Agent/Music
4	Automotive OEM Products Manufacturing
4	Printing/Graphic Arts
3	Food Processing
3	Manufacturing
3	Safety Equipment Manufacturing

[1]Expected net worth = age X .112 X income. Income refers to the respondent's household total annual realized income.
[2]For example, the net worth of this respondent, the owner and manager of a steel manufacturing company, exceeded the expected value by 17 times.

The Net Worth of This Respondent Was —— Times the Expected Value[1]	Business Type Designated by Respondent
3	Real Estate Development
3	Industrial Engineering
3	Automobile Dealerships
3	Garment Manufacturing
3	Automobile Dealerships
3	Wood Products Manufacturing
3	Shipping/Distribution
3	Construction Contracting
3	Petroleum Distribution
3	Venture Capital
3	Manufacturing
3	Executive Recruitment
3	Real Estate Development
3	Aerospace/Electronics Manufacturing
3	Mortgage Banking
3	Luggage Manufacturing
3	Plastics Manufacturing
3	Petroleum Geology/Exploration
3	Logistics/Trading
3	Aerospace Manufacturing and Sales
3	Building Contractor
3	Construction Contracting
3	Investment Management
3	Manufacturing
3	Restaurant
3	Truck Parts
3	Arts/Crafts Manufacturing

The Net Worth of This Respondent Was —— Times the Expected Value[1]	Business Type Designated by Respondent
3	Aluminum and Magnesium Smelter
3	Real Estate Development
3	Insurance
3	Electronics/Industrial
3	Retail Furniture/Appliance Distribution
3	Auto Parts Manufacturing
2	Marketing/Advertising High-Tech Products
2	Finance/Lending Companies
2	Insurance Agency
2	Packaging Manufacturing
2	Commercial Real Estate
2	Real Estate Brokerage
2	Restaurant
2	Real Estate Development and Construction Contracting
2	Manufacturing
2	Energy
2	Financial Services Company
2	Marketing Research
2	Medical Supply Distribution
2	Pension/Insurance

[1]Expected net worth = age X .112 X income. Income refers to the respondent's household total annual realized income.
[2]For example, the net worth of this respondent, the owner and manager of a steel manufacturing company, exceeded the expected value by 17 times.

The Net Worth of This Respondent Was —— Times the Expected Value[1]	Business Type Designated by Respondent
2	Management Consulting
2	Printing
2	Automobile Dealerships
1	Automobile Dealerships
2	Automobile Dealerships
2	Mortgage Banking
2	Automobile Dealerships
2	Textile Manufacturing
2	Commercial Real Estate and Construction Contracting
2	CPG
2	Manufacturing
2	Manufacturing
2	Promotional Products Distribution
2	Commodity Trading
2	Electrical Engineering
2	Travel
2	Real Estate Investing
2	Printing
2	Facsimile Communications
2	Retail Distribution
2	Health-Care Consultant
2	Credit/Collections
2	Equipment and Instrumentation for Process Industries — Petroleum, Pharmaceutical, Chemical, Power
2	Construction Contracting

The Net Worth of This Respondent Was —— Times the Expected Value[1]	Business Type Designated by Respondent
2	Real Estate Brokerage
2	Garment Manufacturing
2	Advertising Agency
2	Textiles Manufacturing
2	Furniture Manufacturing
2	Chemicals Manufacturing
2	Printing
2	Construction Contracting/Real Estate Development
2	Welding
2	Public Relations
1	Sculpture Supply
1	Building/Developing
1	Management Consulting
1	Construction Contracting
1	International Bulk Commodity Trading
1	Real Estate Management/Investment
1	Steel Processing
1	Automobile Dealerships
1	Textile
1	Computer Design
1	Import/Export
1	Motion Picture Theaters
1	Factoring of Accounts Receivable
1	Oil and Gas Exploration
1	Commercial Real Estate
1	Manufacturing

The Net Worth of This Respondent Was —— Times the Expected Value[1]	Business Type Designated by Respondent
1	Manufacturing
1	Aviation
1	Commercial Real Estate
1	Manufacturing
1	Retail Footwear
1	Construction
1	Printing/Publishing
1	Developer/Builder
1	Fast-Food Franchisee
1	Manufacturing
1	Fluid Control Products Manufacturing
1	Service Industry
1	Life Insurance
1	Construction Contractor Development
1	Wine Distribution
1	Home Furnishings Retailing
1	Computers/Software
1	Rare Coin Business
1	Real Estate Brokerage
1	Construction Contracting
1	Maritime Transportation
1	Insurance
1	Jewelry Distribution
1	Planning/Consulting-Engineering
1	Ladies Evening Apparel Manufacturing

The Net Worth of This Respondent Was —— Times the Expected Value[1]	Business Type Designated by Respondent
1	Real Estate Investing
1	Automobile Dealerships
1	Consulting/Engineering
1	Health-Care Services
1	Military Export Sales
1	Broadcasting
1	Cosmetic Science/Design
1	Landscape Construction
1	Distribution
1	Lamp and Lighting Manufacturing/Distribution
1	Construction Contracting
1	Management Consulting
1	Food Service
<1	Real Estate Investing
<1	Electronics Manufacturing
<1	Health-Care Services
<1	Publishing
<1	Construction Contracting
<1	Advertising Agency
<1	Software Design
<1	Textile Manufacturing
<1	Retailing
<1	Hotel/Lodging
<1	Electronics Manufacturing
<1	Construction, Architecture, and Development of Commercial Real Estate
<1	Food-Industry Services

The Net Worth of This Respondent Was —— Times the Expected Value[1]	Business Type Designated by Respondent
<1	Insurance
<1	Income-Producing Real Estate
<1	Oil-Well-Drilling Contractor
<1	Manufacturing/Ladies Sportswear
<1	Water Purification Systems
<1	Cosmetics Distribution

Appendix 3

BUSINESSES OWNED AND MANAGED BY MILLIONAIRES

(AD HOC SAMPLE)

11^2	Equipment Rental
11	Clothing Retail Store/Real Estate
8	Automotive
8	Construction/ Electrical Contracting
8	Leasing/Financing
7	Tool Manufacturing–Plastics
6	Commercial Banking
6	Furniture and Appliances Retailing
6	Printing
6	Health Care
6	Dredging Company
6	Real Estate Developing/ Construction Contracting
6	Investment Company
5	Real Estate Development
5	Farming
5	Investment Banking
5	Pest Control Company
5	Mushroom Grower
5	Restaurant-Pastries-Candies
5	Nursing Homes
5	Construction Contractor
5	Automobile Dealer
5	Distribution

The Net Worth of This Respondent Was —— Times the Expected Value[1]	Business Type Designated by Respondent
5	Manufacturing
5	Office Furniture
4	Health Care
4	Engineering/Construction
4	Manufacturing
4	Advertising Agency
4	Insurance Agency
4	Small Package Delivery
4	Hotel/Apartment Developer
4	Printing
4	Investment Advisory Services
4	Steel Construction Company
4	Lumber
4	Banking
4	Insurance Agency
4	Financial Service Company
3	Employee Staffing
3	Economic Research
3	Food Equipment Manufacturing
3	Hotels
3	Market Information
3	Urban Development
3	Computer Information Management

[1]Expected net worth = age X .112 X income. Income refers to the respondent's household total annual realized income.
[2]For example, the net worth of this respondent, the owner and manager of an equipment rental corporation, exceeded the expected value by 11 times.

The Net Worth of This Respondent Was —— Times the Expected Value[1]	Business Type Designated by Respondent
3	Public Relations
3	Manufacturing
3	Agriculture
3	Manufacturer's Representative
3	Venture Capital/Private Equity
3	Grocery Business
3	Lamb
3	Transportation
3	Real Estate Investment Company
2	Real Estate Investment Company
2	Industrial Gas/Chemicals
2	Air Conditioning Contractor
2	Wine Importer
2	Pharmacy
2	Ocean Transportation Company
2	Construction Contractor
2	Chemical Manufacturing
2	Real Estate
2	Construction Contracting
2	Health and Fitness
2	Services
2	Investment Real Estate
2	Insurance
2	Insurance Agency
2	Real Estate Brokerage
2	Car and Van Rental
2	Retail Building Materials
2	High Technology
2	Investment Banking

The Net Worth of This Respondent Was —— Times the Expected Value[1]	Business Type Designated by Respondent
2	Real Estate Development/Law
2	Chemical Company
2	Petroleum Company
2	Pharmaceutical Manufacturing
2	Gaming
2	Real Estate Investment Company
2	Real Estate Sales Company
2	Commercial Banking
2	Investment Management
2	Graphic Arts
2	Mortgage Banking
2	Tire Distributor
2	Catering
2	Real Estate Brokerage
2	Investment Banking
2	Investment Banking
2	Lodging
2	Traffic Engineering
2	Advertising Agency
2	Insurance Agency
2	Automobile Dealer
2	Commercial Furniture
2	Timber
1	Specialty Financing
1	Ceramics Manufacturing
1	Management Consulting
1	Real Estate Investment Company
1	Agriculture

The Net Worth of This Respondent Was —— Times the Expected Value[1]	Business Type Designated by Respondent
1	Management Consulting
1	Durable Goods Manufacturing
1	Real Estate Company
1	Surgical Equipment Distributor
1	Art Dealer
1	Finance/Transportation/Real Estate
1	Real Estate
1	Drug Stores
1	Oil and Gas Exploration and Production
1	Contracting
1	Real Estate
1	Collection and Credit
1	Information Technology
1	Sporting Goods
1	Computer Business
1	Sporting Goods
1	Television
1	Low Technology
1	Electronics
1	Manufacturing and Construction
1	Oil and Gas
1	Health Care
1	Electrical Contractor
1	Retailing
1	Medical Supplies
1	Advertising Agency
1	Management Consulting

The Net Worth of This Respondent Was —— Times the Expected Value[1]	Business Type Designated by Respondent
1	Health-Care Management
1	Executive Search
1	Medical Equipment Manufacturing
1	Building Materials–Retail
1	Insurance
1	Broadcasting
1	Commercial Real Estate
1	Retail Wine and Spirits
1	Oil and Gas
1	Venture Capital
1	High Technology
1	Retail Sporting Goods/Law
1	Computers
1	Real Estate Brokerage
1	Software
1	Real Estate Agency Franchising
1	Software
	Packaging/Printing Company
1	Political Strategy/Public Relations
1	Automotive
1	Business Management Consulting
1	Consumer Products Manufacturing
1	Glass
1	Executive Search Company
1	Manufacturing

The Net Worth of This Respondent Was —— Times the Expected Value[1]	Business Type Designated by Respondent
1	Air/Space Research
1	Health Care/HMO
1	High Technology
1	Oil and Gas
1	Publishing
1	Wholesaling Company
1	Semiconductors
1	Computer Consulting
1	Industrial Psychology
1	Computers
1	Naval (Marine) Shipyard
1	Plastics Processing
>1	Apparel Manufacturing
>1	Wholesale Distribution
>1	Steel Manufacturing
>1	Packaging Distributor
>1	Entertainment
>1	Telecommunications
>1	Consulting
>1	Consulting
>1	Automobile Parts Distributor
>1	Finance Company
>1	Specialty Chemical Sales and Manufacturing
>1	Personal Care Products
>1	Aerospace
>1	Advertising
>1	Entertainment
>1	Entertainment

The Net Worth of This Respondent Was —— Times the Expected Value[1]	Business Type Designated by Respondent
>1	Investment Banking
>1	Paper
>1	Stocks and Options Trader
>1	Radio Communications
>1	Marketing Consulting
>1	Telecommunications
>1	Television Production
>1	Plastics
>1	Insurance Agency
>1	Grocery
>1	Securities Company

Author's Note

In the course of my research I have met and interviewed many fascinating men and women who personify "The Millionaire Next Door" and define "The Millionaire Mind." Some of their stories are told in my books and journal articles. Hopefully, they enlighten and inspire readers who wish to increase their economic productivity and achieve millionaire status. If you have a story to tell or advice to share, perhaps for inclusion in one of my future books, please write to me in care of my publisher at the address below.

Dr. Thomas J. Stanley
c/o Andrews McMeel Publishing
4520 Main Street
Kansas City, MO 64111

The employees of G.K. Hall hope you have enjoyed this Large Print book. All our Large Print titles are designed for easy reading, and all our books are made to last. Other G.K. Hall books are available at your library, through selected bookstores, or directly from us.

For information about titles, please call:

(800) 223-1244
   or
(800) 223-6121

To share your comments, please write:

Publisher
G.K. Hall & Co.
P.O. Box 159
Thorndike, ME 04986